Ezra Nehemiah and Esther

Peter A. Steveson

BOB JONES UNIVERSITY PRESS
Greenville, South Carolina

Library of Congress Cataloging-in-Publication Data
Steveson, Peter A. (Peter Allan), 1934-
Ezra, Nehemiah, and Esther / Peter A. Steveson.
p. cm.
Includes bibliographical references and index.
Summary: "This book is a commentary on the books of Ezra, Nehemiah, and Esther"—Provided by publisher.
ISBN 978-1-60682-052-0 (pbk. : alk. paper)
1. Bible. O.T. Ezra—Commentaries. 2. Bible. O.T. Nehemiah—Commentaries. 3. Bible. O.T. Esther—Commentaries. I. Title.
BS1355.53.S75 2010
222'.07—dc22

2009053572

Cover photo credits: Dreamstime.com/Janathonjackson

All Scripture is quoted from the King James Version unless otherwise noted. Credits for other versions cited on p. xi.

Ezra, Nehemiah, and Esther
Peter A. Steveson, PhD

Design: Nathan Hutcheon
Page layout: Mike Boone

Greenville, South Carolina 29614
Bob Jones University Press is a division of BJU Press

Printed in the United States of America

ISBN 978-1-60682-052-0

15 14 13 12 11 10 9 8 7 6 5 4 3 2 1

In memory of
Nokle and Evelyn Steveson,
my parents,
with gratitude for their godly influence
on my life.

TABLE OF CONTENTS

ESTHER

PREFACE

The commentary on Nehemiah was the first commentary that I began. I was beginning my first position of leadership—principal of a Christian school—and the role of this biblical leader drew my attention. I realized, however, that I lacked the training and the credentials to continue the work, and I set it aside. Now, some forty-plus years later, I've completed my studies. I have added the books of Ezra and Esther since they naturally fall into the same time period of Persian influence on Israel.

I'm often asked the question "Who are you writing for?" My standard answer is that I'm writing for pastors and godly men and women who want help in understanding God's Word. At the same time, let me point out that I am not writing for scholars or for those with a liberal philosophy of biblical interpretation. It is for this reason that I have not gone extensively into the reasons why I have dated the books as I have or for assigning the authorship of the books. I have not spent much time in defending the historicity and accuracy of the books. While these topics receive some mention in the introductions to the individual books, much more could be said. Most of this would be of little value to my target audience.

As with any book, I owe a great deal to others. The library staffs at Bob Jones University and Furman University have helped in my research. I have consulted numerous books and, where possible, have given credit to the authors. I appreciate the work of those who have gone before me in my work. Even when I disagree philosophically, many authors have forced me to think through my conclusions. In many cases they have saved me from myself by forcing me to see mistakes in my thinking or in the expression of my thoughts.

The editors and staff at Bob Jones University Press have made many corrections and observations. My thanks go to Todd Jones, Dr. Dan Olinger, Suzette Jordan, and Dennis Cone.

PREFACE

CHIEF ABBREVIATIONS

ANET	*Ancient Near Eastern Texts*, ed. James B. Pritchard (Princeton, NJ: Princeton University Press, 1969)
Antiquities	*The Antiquities of the Jews*, Josephus
BASOR	*Bulletin of the American Schools of Oriental Research*
BDB	Francis Brown, S. R. Driver, and Charles A. Briggs, eds., *Hebrew and English Lexicon of the Old Testament* (1974 repr.)
BibSac	*Bibliotheca Sacra*
BR	*Bible Review*
BV	*Biblical Viewpoint*
CBQ	*Catholic Biblical Quarterly*
DOTT	*Documents from Old Testament Times*, D. Winton Thomas, ed. (New York: Harper & Row Publishers, 1958)
HUCA	*Hebrew Union College Annual*
IEJ	*Israel Exploration Journal*
JBQ	*Jewish Bible Quarterly*
JNWSL	*Journal of Northwest Semitic Literature*
JTS	*Journal of Theological Studies*
KB	*The Hebrew and Aramaic Lexicon of the Old Testament,* rev. Walter Baumgartner and Johann Jakob Stamm, trans. and ed. M. E. J. Richardson (New York: E. J. Brill, 1995)
ISBE	*International Standard Bible Encyclopedia*, ed. James Orr (Grand Rapids: Wm. B. Eerdmans Publishing Co., 1952)
JBL	*Journal of Biblical Literature*
LXX	Septuagint
MT	Masoretic text
NT	New Testament

OT	Old Testament
PEQ	*Palestine Exploration Quarterly*
TWOT	R. Laird, Harris, ed., *Theological Wordbook of the Old Testament*, 2 vols. (Chicago: Moody Press, 1980)
VT	*Vetus Testamentum*
WTJ	*Westminster Theological Journal*
ZAW	*Zeitschrift für die Alttestamentliche Wissenschaft*

BIBLES

CB	*The Complete Bible: An American Translation.* Translated by J. M. Powis Smith and Edgar J. Goodspeed et al. (Chicago: The University of Chicago Press, 1939).
CEV	Scripture quotations marked (CEV) are from the Contemporary English Version Copyright © 1991, 1992, 1995 by American Bible Society, Used by Permission.
ESV	Scripture quotations marked ESV are from The Holy Bible, English Standard Version®, copyright © 2001 by Crossway Bibles, a publishing ministry of Good News Publishers. Used by permission. All rights reserved.
GNB	Scriptures and additional materials marked GNB are from the *Good News Bible* © 1994 published by the Bible Societies/HarperCollins Publishers Ltd UK, *Good News Bible* © American Bible Society 1966, 1971, 1976, 1992. Used with permission.
GW	GOD'S WORD is a copyrighted work of God's Word to the Nations. Quotations are used by permission. Copyright 1995 by God's Word to the Nations. All rights reserved.
NAB	Scripture texts in this work marked NAB are taken from the *New American Bible with Revised New Testament* © 1986, 1970 Confraternity of Christian Doctrine, Washington, D.C. and are used by permission of the copyright owner. All rights reserved. No part of the *New American Bible* may be reproduced in any form without permission in writing from the copyright owner.
NASB	Scripture marked NASB taken from the NEW AMERICAN STANDARD BIBLE®, copyright © 1960, 1962, 1963, 1968, 1971, 1972, 1973, 1975, 1977, 1995 by The Lockman Foundation. Used by permission.

NCV	Scriptures marked NCV quoted from *The Holy Bible, New Century Version*®, copyright 2005 © by Thomas Nelson, Inc. Used by permission.
NET	Scripture quoted by permission. Quotations designated (NET) are from the NET Bible® copyright © 1996–2006 by Biblical Studies Press, L.L.C. www.bible.org/. All rights reserved. This material is available in its entirety as a free download or online web use at http://www.nextbible.org/.
NIV	Scripture taken from the HOLY BIBLE, NEW INTERNATIONAL VERSION®. Copyright © 1973, 1978, 1984 by International Bible Society. Used by permission of Zondervan Publishing House. All rights reserved.
NJB	Scripture taken from The New Jerusalem Bible, Reader's Edition. Biblical text © 1985 by Darton, Longman & Todd, Ltd, and Doubleday, a division of Bantam Doubleday Dell Publishing Group, Inc.
NKJV	Scripture taken from the New King James Version. Copyright © 1982 by Thomas Nelson, Inc. Used by permission. All rights reserved.
NLT	Scripture quotations are taken from the Holy Bible, New Living Translation, copyright 1996, 2004. Used by permission of Tyndale House Publishers, Inc., Wheaton, Illinois 60189. All rights reserved.
NRSV	The scripture quotations contained herein are from the New Revised Standard Version of the Bible, copyright 1989, by the Division of Christian Education of the National Council of Churches. Used by permission. All rights reserved.
REB	Scripture taken from the Revised English Bible with the Apocrypha, copyright © 1989 by Oxford University Press and Cambridge University Press.

INTRODUCTION TO EZRA

The book of Ezra is the work of the priest Ezra. Although Ezra is the author, he does not appear until chapter seven. We see the background of Ezra from the genealogy given in that chapter. He was a descendant of the high priestly family, specifically in the line of Hilkiah, the high priest during the reign of Josiah (Ezra 7:1; cf. 2 Kings 23:24). Ezra 7:6 describes him as "a ready scribe in the law of Moses," i.e., a student of God's Word. This description is repeated in similar words in vv. 11, 12, and 21, with v. 10 emphasizing Ezra's preparation to seek God's Word, to obey it, and to teach it to others. At that time, a "scribe" was one who interpreted the Scriptures. Only later did the legalistic interpretations of the NT times begin. More than anything else, Ezra's devotion to God's Word explains his effectiveness as Israel's leader during this critical time in the nation's history.[1]

The name *Ezra* means "help." The name is a shortened form of *Azariah*, "the Lord has helped." As with so many OT names, the meaning of the name reflects the godly heritage received by Ezra from his family. His forefather Seraiah was Israel's high priest at the time of Zedekiah, when the nation fell to Nebuchadnezzar (2 Kings 25:18; Jer. 52:24). After the fall of Jerusalem, the Babylonians executed Seraiah and several other leaders of the nation (2 Kings 25:18–21; Jer. 52:24–27).

Josephus, *Antiquities* 11.5.1, says that Ezra was the "principal priest of the people" in Babylon, cf. Ezra 7:6.[2] Whether due to this position of leadership among the Jews or for some other reason, the Persian king Artaxerxes agreed to let Ezra lead a return of the Jews to Palestine. Artaxerxes I is also called Longimanus because

---

[1]The Talmud, in *Megillah* 16*b*, identifies Ezra as a student of Baruch, the son of Neriah and the scribe of Jeremiah (Jer. 36:4, 17–18, 26–27, 32; 45:1). While this is an interesting tradition, Jeremiah's date of activity and Ezra's time of leadership are too far apart for it to be true. Jeremiah's period of activity begins in 626 BC and continues for an unknown length of time past Zedekiah's reign (586 BC, Jer. 1:2–3 cf. 43:7–46:28). Ezra's activity is a century and a half later, ending ca. 424 BC.

[2]*Antiquities of the Jews*, in *The Works of Josephus*, trans. William Whiston (Peabody, MA: Hendrickson Publishers, 1987).

his right hand was longer than his left hand.[3] He succeeded his father Xerxes as the king ca. 465 BC. The *first* return of the Jews to Palestine had taken place during the rule of Cyrus the Great in 536 BC (1:2–3). In the seventh year of his rule, Artaxerxes issued a decree allowing a *second* group of Jews to return to Jerusalem under the leadership of Ezra, ca. 458 BC. They could begin there to worship in the temple. Ezra 7:11–26 describes the decree.[4] Thirteen years later, 445 BC, Artaxerxes authorized Nehemiah to lead a *third* return of the Jews from their captivity (Neh. 2:1, 7–8). Artaxerxes died of unknown causes ca. 425 BC.

We can only speculate on Ezra's life apart from the biblical record. The events recorded in c. 7–10 cover about twelve months. This time includes a little less than four months for the journey from Babylon (7:8–9) and eight months for Ezra's work in Jerusalem (7:9 cf. 10:17). There is no further mention of him for thirteen years until he appears as the spiritual leader of the people under Nehemiah (Neh. 8:13 cf. 2:1). Since the priesthood and general population fell into spiritual decline during Nehemiah's later absence from Jerusalem (Neh. 13:6 cf. 13:4–5, 7–13), it is likely that Ezra had either died or returned to Babylon with Nehemiah.

Jewish tradition (2 Esdras 14:23–48) gives credit to Ezra for writing the canon of the Old Testament. According to this apocryphal passage, Ezra, assisted by five scribes and given understanding and wisdom by a special drink, collected and rewrote ninety-four books in forty days. He was then given permission to publish the first twenty-four of these books, the books now included in the OT. The Jews also make Ezra responsible for the building of synagogues in the different towns, allowing them to worship at times other than when they made their treks to the temple in Jerusalem.

---

[3]*Plutarch's Lives*, trans. Bernadotte Perrin (Cambridge, MA: Harvard University Press, 1975), 11.1.

[4]Jacob M. Myers, *Ezra, Nehemiah*, in *The Anchor Bible*, ed. William Foxwell Albright and David Noel Freedman (Garden City, NY: Doubleday & Company, Inc., 1965), p. xxxvii, suggests that "Ezra came after Nehemiah." That view requires that a number must have dropped from both Ezra 7:7 and 7:8, e.g., "*thirty*-seventh year," a textual change without support.

Unreliable tradition relates that Ezra died at the age of 120 years while in Babylon and was buried on the banks of the Tigris River, near Basra, a modern port city located at the confluence of the Tigris and Euphrates Rivers. Another tradition says that he lived to an old age and died while on a trip to the court of Artaxerxes in Persia. Supposedly, he is buried at Samarah, on the lower Tigris River. Still another tradition, recorded by Josephus (*Antiquities* 11.5.5), states that he died shortly after the events recorded in the OT and was buried at Jerusalem.

Several things contributed to Ezra's spiritual success. He was a man of the Word (7:6, 11–12, 21). Ezra 7:10 clearly shows his devotion to God's Word. We see as well Ezra's sensitivity to sin (9:1–3, 6–7; 10:6, 10), which caused him to lead the Jews to confess and turn from their wicked actions (10:1–44). Ezra's reliance on the Lord led him to go to Him in his prayers (8:21–23; 9:5–10:1). Over and over we see him recognizing the work of God in his life ("according to the hand of the Lord [his] God upon [him]"; see 7:6, 9, 27–28; 8:18, 22, 31).

The book of Ezra is historical in nature although several spiritual lessons are illustrated through the related events. Along with Nehemiah, Esther, part of Daniel, and some of the later psalms, the book gives the record of the Jews during the Persian period of dominance. Within the first part of the book, the first two chapters deal with Israel's first return to Palestine from their Babylonian exile. This is important historical information since it tells of the wholesale movement of several thousand people from captivity to freedom. It explains the transition from Babylon to Palestine. After arriving in Palestine, the people began to build the temple. Opposition to the building project by the people at Jerusalem prevailed for a time before the Jews took up the building again. Chapters 3 through 6 record the completion of the building of the temple. Chapter 6 closes with the completion of the temple in 516 BC (6:15). The celebration of the Passover in the first month of the following year came shortly afterward (6:19–22). Chapter 7 opens with an account of the second return, which was led by Ezra in 458 BC (7:9).

Initially the Jews bound the books of Ezra and Nehemiah together as a single book in the Hebrew writings. It was called "The Book of Ezra." In listing the OT books, *Baba Bathra* 15*a* (cf.

also 14*b*; *Sanhedrin* 93*b*), in the Talmud, refers to "Ezra" alone. Many others accepted Ezra-Nehemiah as a single book. Jerome lists twenty-two books with a note explaining that some count Ruth and Lamentations separately. While not separating Nehemiah from Ezra, Jerome refers to the second part of 2 Esdras by the name of Nehemiah. Eusebius, the late third- and early fourth-century church historian, refers to the OT canon in his *Ecclesiastical History* 4.26.14. He quotes Melito, the second-century bishop of Sardis, in his list of the OT Scriptures as including Ezra by itself. Later, Eusebius quotes Origen (third century), the earliest church leader to refer to two books, although Eusebius notes that they occur as one in the Hebrew (6.25.2).[5]

There is early extrabiblical evidence for the joining of the books. Writing late in the first century AD, Josephus refers to the "twenty-two books" of the OT.[6] These included the book of Ezra-Nehemiah, considered as a single book within the *k^etîb*, the "writings."[7]

The Jews divided their Bible into the Law, the Prophets, and the Writings. Ezra and Nehemiah appear as a single book in this last section. In addition to the poetical books (Psalms, Proverbs, Job, Song of Solomon, Ruth, Lamentations, Ecclesiastes), the Writings also included the historical books written after the captivity: Chronicles, Ezra-Nehemiah, Esther, and Daniel. In some editions of the Hebrew Old Testament, a break occurs between Ezra 10:44 and Nehemiah 1:1 so that Nehemiah begins on a new line. The Masoretic notes discussing the number of words, and so forth, come only after Nehemiah, not after both Ezra and Nehemiah.

---

[5]Eusebius, *Ecclesiastical History*, trans. Kirsopp Lake (Cambridge, MA: Harvard University Press, 1953).

[6]Josephus, *Against Apion* 1.8.

[7]I have used a simplified transliteration system to indicate most of the Hebrew vowels. The *a* indicates both the *qameṣ* and the *pataḥ*, the *e* indicates both the *segol* and the *ṣere*, the *o* indicates both the *ḥolem* and the *qameṣ ḥatup*, and the *u* indicates the *qibbuṣ*. The raised *a*, *o*, or *e* indicates a *šewa*. I have used *î* to represent the *ḥireq yod*, *ê* for the *ṣere yod*, and *â* for the *qameṣ he*. The *ô* indicates the *ḥolem waw* and the *û* the *šureq*.

Beginning in the sixteenth century, printed editions of the Bible generally separated the two books.[8] A rabbinic Bible printed at Venice in 1517–18 separates them. The second edition of the Hebrew Bible printed by Daniel Bomberg, ca. 1525, also printed at Venice, does the same. The translation of Myles Coverdale (1535) called Ezra "The first boke of Esdras" and Nehemiah "The seconde boke of Esdras, otherwyse called the boke of Nehemias." In the 1537 edition of Matthew's Bible, they are called "The fyrst boke of Esdras the Prophete" and "The seconde boke of Esdras, otherwyse called the boke of Nehemiah." In the 1551 edition, the title of Nehemiah was changed to "The boke of Nehemias, otherwyse called the second booke of Esdras." The Bishop's Bible was similar. The 1568 edition titled Nehemiah as "The seconde booke of Esdras other wise called the booke of Nehemia." The 1595 edition changed this to "The booke of Nehemias, or seconde booke of Esdras." The Geneva Bible (1560) gives them the titles of Ezra and Nehemiah. The 1609 edition of the Douay Bible refers to "The First Booke of Esdras" and "The Booke of Nehemias which is also called The Second of Esdras."

The MT continues to keep the two works as a single book with the total number of verses, given at the end of Nehemiah, as 685. The midpoint of the book is marked at Nehemiah 3:12. The LXX keeps Ezra and Nehemiah as one book with the title of Esdras B or 2 Esdras. Although 1 Esdras includes biblical material—extracts from 2 Chronicles, most of Ezra, a small part of Nehemiah, and some new material—it is considered an apocryphal writing since a significant part of it (3:1–5:6) is nonbiblical. Certain of the early church fathers (Origen, Council of Laodicea, Can. 60 of Cyril, Jerome, etc.) referred to Ezra as 1 Esdras and to Nehemiah as 2 Esdras. Other apocryphal writings relating to Ezra became 3 Esdras and 4 Esdras.

The Vulgate includes Ezra as 1 Esdras and Nehemiah as 2 Esdras. Modern Roman Catholic versions of the Bible separate the books, but some versions refer to them as 1 and 2 Esdras. Since

[8]Much of the following information comes from Herbert Edward Ryle, *The Books of Ezra and Nehemiah* in *The Cambridge Bible for Schools and Colleges*, ed. A. F. Kirkpatrick (London: Cambridge University Press, 1923), pp. xiv–xv.

Ezra and Nehemiah carried out at least part of their ministry together, this joining of the books is logical. The division into two books, however, is also logical since the two men had distinct responsibilities and the two books likely have different authors.

Early use of the books separated them. Ecclesiasticus 49:13 refers to Nehemiah but says nothing about Ezra. Second Maccabees likewise recounts some of the work of Nehemiah (1:18–36; 2:13) but omits any reference to Ezra. Josephus refers to the death and burial of Ezra (*Antiquities* 11.120.120–158) and then moves to the activities of Nehemiah (*Antiquities* 11.120.159–183).

In addition, the nature of the books argues for separating them. The repetition of material suggests that these are distinct writings. A common author would not have included the list of returnees in Ezra 2 again in Nehemiah 7. Also, Ezra uses Aramaic in quoting official documents and in describing subsequent actions (4:7–6:18; 7:12–26), but Nehemiah uses only Hebrew.

The following chart summarizes the manner in which the early translations, including the Apocrypha, presented the material in Ezra, Nehemiah, and the similar noncanonical material.

<table>
<tr><th>English</th><th>Hebrew</th><th>LXX</th><th>Vulgate</th></tr>
<tr><td>Ezra</td><td rowspan="2">Ezra (a single book containing both Ezra and Nehemiah)</td><td rowspan="2">Esdras B (or Esdras 2)</td><td>1 Esdras</td></tr>
<tr><td>Nehemiah</td><td>2 Esdras</td></tr>
<tr><td>1 Esdras</td><td rowspan="2"></td><td rowspan="2">Esdras A (or Esdras 1)</td><td>3 Esdras</td></tr>
<tr><td>2 Esdras</td><td>4 Esdras</td></tr>
</table>

As with the book of Daniel, Ezra is written in two languages. The majority of the book is in Hebrew, but there are two large sections (4:7–6:18; 7:12–26) written in Aramaic. The book itself does not explain the difference. There is, however, a reasonable explanation. Both of the Aramaic sections deal with correspondence to the Persian court, where this language was used. The first section (4:7–6:18) includes the letter written by the enemies of the Jews to Artaxerxes (4:7–16); the king's answer stopping the

Jews from continuing to build (4:17–22); a brief narrative relating the events from the stopping of the work to its restarting (4:23–5:4); a previous letter notifying Darius of the building activity of the Jews (5:5–17); a brief narrative (6:1–2) followed by the letter from the king authorizing the building (6:3–12); and a final narrative section describing the completion of the temple (6:13–18). The second Aramaic section includes the decree of Artaxerxes (7:12–26). It is logical that both these portions of the book should use the Aramaic language.[9]

Although some dispute Ezra's writing of the book, conservatives generally recognize him as its author. Many also consider him the author of Nehemiah and part of Chronicles, a view first stated in the Talmud, *Baba Bathra* 15*a*.[10] Elsewhere the Talmud, *Sanhedrin* 93*b*, attributes the authorship of Ezra to Nehemiah. Rashi (an acronym for Rabbi Solomon ben Isaac), a late eleventh- and early twelfth-century French rabbi, explained this by noting that the OT grouped both into a single book, called Ezra.

---

[9]Batten, Loring W., The *Books of Ezra and Nehemiah*, in *The International Critical Commentary* (1913; repr., New York: Charles Scribner's Sons, 1972) pp. 18–19, sees the Aramaic sections of the book as evidence for an "Aramaic history of this period" that the "Chronicler" drew from in assembling the book. Since the Aramaic decrees concerned the Jews, it is equally possible that records of them were available to Ezra as he wrote this record.

[10]The authorship question of Chronicles and Ezra is not settled. Menahim Haran, "Explaining the Identical Lines at the End of Chronicles and the Beginning of Ezra," *BR* 2, no. 3 (Fall 1986): 18, asserts that "the catch-lines that connect Chronicles with Ezra are decisive evidence of the compositional connection between the two works. It is generally recognized among scholars that the two books of Chronicles (originally, one uninterrupted book) and the Book of Ezra are the work of a single author, who is often referred to as the Chronicler." After an extended discussion of the books, Hugh G. M. Williamson, "Did the Author of Chronicles Also Write the Books of Ezra and Nehemiah?" *BR* 3, no. 1 (Spring 1987): 57, concludes that "many other technical considerations about the literary history of Ezra and Nehemiah fully support the conclusion . . . that the authors of Chronicles, on the one hand, and Ezra/Nehemiah, on the other, are not the same." Joseph Blenkinsopp, *Ezra-Nehemiah: A Commentary* (Philadelphia: Westminster Press, 1988), pp. 41–54, likewise gives an extended discussion of the authorship. He concludes, "It would be difficult to find a clearer indication of unity of conception which binds together the two works into one history with its own distinctive point of view and purpose." Fortunately, interpreting and applying the book of Ezra does not depend on our knowing for certain the author (or authors) of Chronicles and Ezra.

The Talmud referred to this book, the major part of which was the account of Nehemiah.[11] More probably Ezra's authorship should be limited to the book bearing his name. The introduction to the commentary on Nehemiah (see pp. 95–96) discusses its authorship.

Liberal authors (and some conservative authors) refer to the writer as the *Chronicler*, a term used to designate the one who compiled and edited various historical sources in the book.[12] In the part of the book in which Ezra appears, he sometimes speaks of himself in the first person (e.g., 7:28; 8:15) and sometimes in the third person (7:6, 8, 9; 10:1, 6), depending on the nature of the narrative. The use of the third person is not unusual in ancient historical writings. In his *History of the Peloponnesian War*, the Greek general Thucydides writes of himself in the third person. The Greek general Xenophon, in service to the Persian satrap Cyrus the younger, and later the author of several works including *Memorabilia and Oeconomicus*, does the same.[13]

We must place the writing of the book after the close of 2 Chronicles, which ends with the account of the decree of Cyrus the Great. This same decree begins the book of Ezra, which then continues with history that takes place after that recorded in 2 Chronicles. Since Ezra's ministry took place during the reign of Artaxerxes (465–425 BC), we must date the book during the last part of this period or shortly after.

---

[11]Yosef Rabinowitz, *Ezra* (Brooklyn: Mesorah Publications, 1984), p. 59.

[12]Ryle, p. xviii, understands the book as the work of a "compiler" who brought together various works, together with his own comments, into the books of Ezra and Nehemiah. He sees the use of the third person as evidence for this. This view ignores the similar use of the third person in other ancient writings. R. J. Coggins, *The Books of Ezra and Nehemiah*, in *The Cambridge Bible Commentary*, ed. P. R. Ackroyd, A. R. C. Leaney, and J. W. Packer (New York: Cambridge University Press, 1976), p. 2, and Matthew Levering, *Ezra & Nehemiah* (Grand Rapids: Brazos Press, 2007), p. 39, are among those who refer to the "Chronicler."

[13]Thucydides, *History of the Peloponnesian War*, trans. Charles Forster Smith (Cambridge, MA: Harvard University Press, 1962), e.g., 1.1 & 4.14; Xenophon, *Anabasis*, trans. Carleton L. Brownson (Cambridge, MA: Harvard University Press, 1968) e.g., 8.15; 2.4.15; 2.5.37, 41; and *Memorabilia and Oeconomicus*, trans. E. C. Marchant (Cambridge, MA: Harvard University Press, 1988), 1.3.10, 12, and 13.

Conservative authors differ on the date, although they are generally close to one another. Larson and Dahlen date the book between 440 and 400 BC.[14] Rawlinson dates the book in 444 BC at the latest since this is "the year of Nehemiah's arrival." He argues that Ezra would have mentioned this if he had written later.[15] Mervin Breneman places its writing at "the traditional dating of 458 B.C."[16] Slotki dates it "at about 450 B.C.E."[17]

Liberal authors generally date the book ca. 398 BC or later. Ryle dates the book ca. 320 BC based on Nehemiah 12:26, where he sees the phrase "in the days of Nehemiah . . . and of Ezra the priest" as making the time "as one that is already long past." He further cites 12:10–11 as recording the names of the high priests. Identifying Eliashib as the high priest during the time of Nehemiah (13:4), he sees at least two generations as having passed.[18] Eliashib, however, would likely have been older at the time he held the high priest's office. Nothing here requires a period of two generations. Ryle assumes that Ezra and Nehemiah have long passed off the scene. This is interpretive and speculative. Ryle further concludes that the Jaddua mentioned in 12:11, 22 is the Jaddua mentioned by Josephus as the high priest in the time of Alexander the Great. Once again, this is interpretive, with nothing to prevent the Jaddua mentioned by Josephus from being a descendant or even another priest with the same name.

Batten understands Ezra, Nehemiah, and Chronicles as a composite work, incorporating a variety of other writings. He places this as no earlier than 300 BC but gives no evidence for this date. Holmgren also accepts the date of 300 BC without

[14]Knute Larson and Dathy Dahlen, *Ezra, Nehemiah, Esther*, in *Holman Old Testament Commentary*, ed. Max Anders (Nashville: Broadman & Holman Publishers, 2005), p. 1.

[15]George Rawlinson, *Ezra*, in *The Pulpit Commentary*, ed. H. D. M. Spence and Joseph S. Exell (1887; repr., Peabody, MA: Hendrickson Publishers, 1985), p. ii.

[16]Mervin Breneman, *Ezra, Nehemiah, Esther*, in *The New American Commentary*, ed. E. Ray Clendenen and Kenneth A. Matthews (Nashville: Broadman & Holman Publishers, 1993), p. 46.

[17]Judah J. Slotki, *Daniel·Ezra·Nehemiah* (London: The Soncino Press, 1970), p. 107.

[18]Ryle, pp. xxiii–xxiv. The identification of Eliashib as high priest is debatable. See the discussion at Nehemiah 13:4.

giving any arguments for the date.[19] Bowman argues that Ezra was written after Nehemiah and develops the view extensively by listing the following fifteen arguments.[20]

(1) *It is unlikely that Artaxerxes would send two men to Palestine with official support and authority at the same time.* Ezra, however, was sent to rebuild the temple and to teach the laws of God to the people (Ezra 7:12–26), while Nehemiah was sent thirteen years later to build Jerusalem's wall (Neh. 2:5–8). There is nothing unusual about sending different men to carry out different responsibilities.

(2) *Ezra and Nehemiah ignored each other, surprising if they were contemporaries.* The lack of any mention of Ezra by Nehemiah until c. 8 suggests that he may have been absent. Further, there is no reason to mention him until a spiritual event occurs.

(3) *Nehemiah would not have referred to the people of Jerusalem as those who had escaped the exile if Ezra had led a return shortly before (Neh. 1:2).* Bowman misunderstands Nehemiah's question. Two groups had gone back to Palestine, one under Zerubbabel's leadership about 536 BC and a second under Ezra in 458 BC. Nehemiah is asking about these people.

(4) *In preparing for his census, Nehemiah used the list of those who returned with Zerubbabel (Neh. 7:1–73) but ignored the record of those who returned with Ezra (Ezra 8:1–14).* Nehemiah worked with the list he found (Neh. 7:5). We do not know if he had access to Ezra's list or not.

(5) *Nehemiah found Jerusalem almost uninhabited, while Ezra was in a busy city (Neh. 7:4; 11:1–2 cf. Ezra 9:4; 10:1).* Neither of the references in Ezra indicates that the city was "busy." While 10:1 refers to a "very great congregation," the fact that they assembled in front of the temple argues that it was great for that area but not necessarily numerically great.

[19]Loring W. Batten, *The Books of Ezra and Nehemiah*, in *The International Critical Commentary* (1913; repr., New York: Charles Scribner's Sons, 1972), pp. 2–3; Fredrick Carlson Holmgren, *Israel Alive Again: A Commentary on the Books of Ezra and Nehemiah* (Grand Rapids: Wm. B. Eerdmans, 1987), p. xiii.

[20]Raymond A. Bowman, *The Book of Ezra and the Book of Nehemiah*, vol. 3 in *The Interpreter's Bible*, ed. George Arthur Buttrick (Nashville: Abingdon Press, 1954), pp. 561–63.

(6) *Ezra 8:29 and 10:5 indicate that the priests and Levites lived in Jerusalem, but Nehemiah 11–13 says that Nehemiah sent them to the capital city.* It is reasonable that the priests and Levites had left Jerusalem since first arriving there. With such a small population, the offerings would not have supported them. They likely had gone to areas where they could grow their own crops.

(7) *Nehemiah found the defenses at Jerusalem destroyed, while Ezra thanked God for the city's wall (Ezra 9:9).* Ezra, however, used the word *wall* metaphorically to speak of the protection God had given the people in letting them return.

(8) *No members of the families that returned with Ezra (8:1–20) can be identified with certainty in the list of wall builders (Neh. 3).* Bowman dismisses the names of Hashabiah (Neh. 3:17; Ezra 8:19, 24) and Meshullam (Neh. 3:4, 6, 30; Ezra 8:16) as being "too common to identify." While the names may be common, they do occur in both lists. In addition to these, the names of Meremoth, the son of Urijah (Neh. 3:4, 21; Ezra 8:33) and Binnui (Neh. 3:24; Ezra 8:33) occur. Both lists mention the Nethinim (Neh. 3:26, 31; Ezra 8:17, 20). Since the list in Nehemiah 3 is clearly incomplete, listing only the primary workers in each group, Bowman's objection has no merit.

(9) *Nehemiah was a contemporary of the high priest Eliashib (Neh. 3:1, 20–21; 13:4, 7, 28), but Ezra lived at the time of Jehohanan, the grandson of Eliashib (Ezra 10:6; cf. Neh. 12:10–11, 22).* There are at least two possible answers to this objection.

(a) Jehohanan (also called Johanan) may indeed have been a grandson of Eliashib, who, in anticipation of his grandson's later ascension to the priesthood, named a chamber after him while he was still a child.

(b) The Eliashib named by Ezra may only have been a priest, perhaps the head of one of the twenty-four orders (1 Chron. 24:12), but not the high priest. The name occurs widely at this time, referring to at least five individuals besides the high priest.

(10) *A papyrus mentioning the high priest Jehohanan also indicates that the sons of Sanballat, then an old man, held the power of Samaria.* This objection relies on the previous objection being true. If Jehohanan was a child at the time of Ezra, or if the Eliashib in Ezra was not the high priest, this objection has no force.

(11) *Nehemiah appointed a commission of temple treasurers (Neh. 11:16; 13:13), but when Ezra arrived, he found such a commission (Ezra 8:33).* The text does not mention a formal commission. Several men accounted for the gold, silver, and temple vessels brought by Ezra, a natural precaution when valuables are involved.

(12) *Meremoth, the son of Uriah, belonged to the family of Koz. This family could not prove their priestly status at Zerubbabel's return (Ezra 2:61–62). He served "without priestly title" in repairing the wall at the time of Nehemiah (Neh. 3:4, 21).* It is clear, however, the family must have regained its priestly status under Nehemiah since, in the time of Ezra, he was one of the priests receiving the treasure from Ezra (Ezra 8:33). Since Zerubbabel's return was more than seventy-five years before Nehemiah's work, there was ample time for Meremoth's family to have regained priestly status. The fact that Nehemiah 3 does not call him a priest is not significant. None of the men named in the chapter are called priests, with the sole exception of Eliashib, the high priest.

(13) *Nehemiah's reforms would not have been necessary if Ezra had brought about the acceptance of the law.* Apostasy, however, does not require a long period of years to develop. We see this by comparing Nehemiah 8–10, where the people accepted the law and entered into a covenant to keep it, and Nehemiah 13, where several failures of the people had to be dealt with.

(14) *In correcting the failure to give their tithes (Neh. 13), Nehemiah corrected "a situation of long neglect and abuse."* This is Bowman's interpretation. As already stated, it does not take long for apostasy to take place. The failure to bring tithes in for a year or two would have driven the Levites back to their farms.

(15) *The matter of mixed marriages was clearly a long-standing problem since the children spoke the languages of their mothers (Neh. 13:23–24). This would hardly have happened if Ezra's reforms had taken place shortly before.* Nehemiah 13:6 indicates that Nehemiah had been absent for an unknown length of time. This could have been five to ten years, enough time for the problem of mixed marriages to occur.

In addition to these rebuttals of Bowman's arguments, there is also the clear statement of the text. Ezra 7:1–8 states that Ezra's return took place in "the seventh year" of Artaxerxes. Nehemiah 2:1 places Nehemiah's return "in the twentieth year of Artaxerxes the king." Since Bowman has Ezra following Nehemiah, he identifies the Artaxerxes of Ezra as Artaxerxes II and places the return at 398 BC. This raises the problem of explaining Nehemiah 8:9 and 12:31–36, where Ezra and Nehemiah minister jointly. Bowman considers this an addition of Nehemiah's name by an editor in 8:9 and following the LXX rendering ("they appointed") of 12:31, effectively eliminating Nehemiah. Nehemiah 12:26 and 12:47, both of which mention Nehemiah, become the work of the Chronicler. If we accept the MT, Bowman's view cannot stand.

Outline of Ezra

The following outline of Ezra gives a broad overview. Details are introduced in the discussions of the various parts of the book.

- I. Leadership by Zerubbabel 1:1–6:22
  - A. First Return from Babylon 1:1–2:70
    1. Decree by Cyrus 1:1–4
    2. Gifts to the Captives 1:5–11
    3. Register of the People 2:1–70
       - a. List of the Families and Towns 2:1–35
       - b. List of Temple Servants 2:36–63
       - c. Summary of the Return 2:64–70
  - B. Restoration of the Worship 3:1–13
    1. Practice of the Ritual 3:1–6
    2. Building of the Temple 3:7–13
  - C. Opposition to the Work 4:1–5:17
    1. Attempt at Cooperation 4:1–3
    2. Hindrances to the Work 4:4–24
       - a. Under Cyrus 4:4–5
       - b. Under Xerxes and Artaxerxes 4:6–23
       - c. Under Darius 4:24
    3. Resumption of the Work 5:1–5
    4. Inquiry to Darius 5:6–17
  - D. Continuance of the Work 6:1–22
    1. Search by Darius 6:1–5
    2. Decree by Darius 6:6–12
    3. Completion of the Temple 6:13–18
    4. Celebration of the Passover 6:19–22

- II. Ministry of Ezra 7:1–10:44
  - A. Second Return from Babylon 7:1–8:36
    1. Background of Ezra 7:1–10
    2. Decree of Artaxerxes 7:11–28
    3. List of the Families 8:1–14
       - a. Priestly Families
       - b. David's Family
       - c. Other Families
    4. Recruitment of Temple Workers 8:15–20
    5. Intercession with God 8:21–23
    6. Offering for the Temple 8:24–30
    7. Summary of the Trip 8:31–32
    8. Delivering the Offering 8:33–36
  - B. Reforms of the People 9:1–10:44
    1. Sin of the People 9:1–2
    2. Prayer of Ezra 9:3–15
    3. Covenant of the People 10:1–9
    4. Agreement of the People 10:10–19
    5. List of the Guilty 10:18–44
       - a. Priests and Levites 10:18–24
       - b. Laymen 10:25–44

The Theology of Ezra

Although the book of Ezra is primarily historical, with no direct speeches from God, the recorded events illustrate many important theological truths. The opening verses (1:1–4) demonstrate God's providential care of His people. He shows His faithfulness by leading Cyrus (1:1) to fulfill the prophecies of Jeremiah 25:11–12 and 29:10 that the Jews would return to Palestine after a prolonged period of captivity. Later, He moves the leaders of Israel to rebuild the temple at Jerusalem (1:5). The return under Zerubbabel (1:1–2:70) demonstrates God's knowledge of the future, the return coming after the prophesied seventy years of captivity. It shows the importance of Palestine as being God's promised home for His people (Gen. 12:7; 13:14–17). Over and over, the book credits "the hand of God" or "the hand of the Lord" with working on behalf of the people (e.g., 7:6, 9, 28; 8:18, 22, 31).

The book also illustrates the worship of God by His people. The return from Babylon was motivated by the desire to rebuild the temple at Jerusalem (1:5). After arrival, the people set up the altar and began to offer sacrifices to God (3:3–6). They kept the Feast of Tabernacles (3:4), the Passover and the Feast of Unleavened Bread (6:19–22), and other "set feasts" (3:5), as well as making the daily burnt offering and freewill sacrifices (3:5–6). The people praised the Lord (3:10–11) and dedicated the rebuilt temple (6:16–17). Ezra confessed the sin of the people and appealed to God through his prayer (9:5–10:1). God's Word once more guided the nation (e.g., 3:2; 7:6; 10:3).

Ezra led a second return of the Jews from Babylon, again showing God's providential care of His people (7:1–8:36). In this record we see Ezra's concern that Israel properly carry out the worship of God. He waited until an adequate number of Levites and Nethinim joined the return (8:15–20). We also see Ezra's dependence on God as he fasted and prayed for divine blessing and guidance in the return (8:21–23).

Over and over, the book displays the faithfulness of God. Indeed, this theme should be taken as the dominant theological teaching of Ezra.[21] The return of the nation allowed, after a prolonged interruption, the rebuilding of the temple and the reinstating of the worship of the Jews (3:1–6:22). God then raised up the godly Ezra to lead a return of the Jews to their homeland (8:31–32). Through the king's large initial offering (7:15–20), the right to draw resources from Persian tributaries (7:21–22), the freedom from taxes (7:24), and the power to appoint judges

[21]C. F. Keil, *Ezra*, in *Biblical Commentary on the Old Testament*, trans. Sophia Taylor (1875; repr., Grand Rapids: Wm. B. Eerdmans, 1978), p. 5, sees the historical nature of the book as its main purpose. The restoration of the temple and its associated worship and the separation of the nation from the heathen were necessary so that God could fulfill His promises made to earlier generations. Levering, p. 31, is similar in seeing the main theme as "the struggle to build the temple." Matthew Henry, *Ezra*, vol. 2 in *Commentary on the Whole Bible* (1708; repr., New York: Fleming H. Revell Company, 1935), p. 1028, accepts the historical purpose of the book but sees also "a type of the accomplishment of the prophecies of the Apocalypse concerning the deliverance of the gospel church out of the New-Testament Babylon." H. G. M. Williamson, *Ezra and Nehemiah* (Sheffield, England: JSOT Press, 1987), p. 90, sees "the status and interpretation of the book of the law" as "the single most influential theological topic treated in the books of Ezra and Nehemiah."

(7:25), God provided Ezra with governmental authority and the means with which to accomplish his goals. Most importantly, the Lord allowed the reestablishment of worship (7:25*b*–26). Although not emphasized in the book, these actions show God's use of the heathen to accomplish His purposes. When the events recorded in Nehemiah are joined with those mentioned in Ezra, there is clear evidence of God's faithfulness to His people.

The twin themes of the opposition of the wicked and the perseverance of the godly are set among these incidents showing the faithfulness of God. The people rebuilt the temple altar and began to worship the Lord once more (3:1–13). The Samaritans opposed this work and, for a time, prevailed in stopping its progress (4:1–24). Haggai and Zechariah stirred up the people to renewed faithfulness (5:1–2). Once more, the Samaritans opposed their progress (5:3–17), but this time they were unsuccessful. The Persian king found the original decree authorizing the work. He not only cited this decree but added his own decree giving the Jews the right to proceed in building their temple (6:1–12). The people willingly set to work again and completed the temple (6:13–22).

There are also vivid demonstrations of the need for religious and moral purity. In the initial return, those who could not prove their priestly descent were not permitted to serve as priests (2:61–63). Zerubbabel and the other leaders of the nation refused to compromise by accepting the Samaritan offer to help in building the temple, an offer that would have led to joint worship with those who rejected the teachings of God's Word (5:1–3). Later, when the people fell into the sin of intermarriage with the heathen (9:1–2), the Lord answered Ezra's prayer (9:5–15) and brought a spirit of repentance to the people (10:1–4). They cooperated with Ezra in turning from their wickedness (10:5–44).

The need for purity and the worship of the people assumes the authority of God's Word. The people set up the altar and made offerings according to the Mosaic law (3:2). Ezra was recognized as a scribe of God's law (7:6, 10, 12, 21). The king commissioned Ezra to carry out the law of his God (7:14, 26). The people separated from their heathen wives (10:3–5). In addition, the return to Palestine shows the accuracy of OT prophecy as it fulfilled Jeremiah's prediction of Israel's seventy-year captivity (1:1, cf. Jer. 25:11–12; 29:10).

EZRA 1

I. Leadership by Zerubbabel 1:1–6:22

This first section of the book tells about the first return from captivity, led by Zerubbabel; the establishment of worship once again in Israel; and the overcoming of opposition in building the temple. The record given in this part of the book spans a period of a little over twenty years, from "the first year of Cyrus king of Persia" (1:1, 539 BC) to shortly after the completion of the temple in "the sixth year of the reign of Darius the king" (6:15, 516 BC), but also includes a couple of nonchronological sections (4:7–16;17–23).

A. First Return from Babylon 1:1–2:70

1. Decree by Cyrus 1:1–4

Ezra gives the background to the first return from the Babylonian captivity. Cyrus became king in Elam ca. 559 BC. Twenty years later, ca. 538 BC, he completed his conquest of Babylon.[22] At the height of his rule, the Persian Empire extended from the Indus River in India on the east to the Mediterranean Sea, Egypt, and Libya on the west. The empire included territory in the north from parts of Macedonia on the west, to territory between the Black and Caspian Seas, and further north to the Aral Sea. The natural barriers of the Arabian Sea, the Persian Gulf, and the Arabian Desert generally fixed the southern boundary.

The phrase "first year" here refers to the first year of Cyrus's rule over Babylon, 538 BC. At this time the Lord moved Cyrus to fulfill the Jeremiah's prophecy that Judah would remain in captivity seventy years (cf. Jer. 25:11–12; 29:10).[23] Cyrus made a proclamation giving the Jews the freedom to return. Isaiah 44:28 and 45:1 make it clear that the Lord raised up Cyrus for this purpose. Although the record here mentions the Jews only,

---

[22]Henry, p. 1029, relies on outdated information in making Cyrus subject to Darius the Mede (Dan. 5:31), who "being old, left the kingdom to Cyrus." We know now that Cyrus appointed Darius to govern Babylon.

[23]Batten, p. 56, sees the reference to Jeremiah as "incorrect." He refers the prophecy to Isaiah 44:28; 45:1, since Isaiah mentions Cyrus by name. The objection is trivial. While Jeremiah does not mention the name of Cyrus, he clearly predicts the return to Palestine following the seventy-year captivity.

we know from archaeology that Cyrus allowed captives from many nations to return to their homelands. With minor variations, 2 Chronicles 36:22–23 repeats vv. 1–3. The later discovery of the decree at Achmetha (6:2), another name for Ecbatana, the summer palace of the Persian kings, suggests that Cyrus issued his edict in the summer of 538 BC.

This return to Palestine from Babylon fulfilled Jeremiah's seventy-year prophecy. The first deportation, not mentioned in the historical section of the OT but documented in Daniel 1:1–2, took place ca. 605 BC. Assuming some delay to prepare for the return following the decree by Cyrus and assuming a period of several months for the return journey, the Jews reached Palestine in 536 BC, seventy years after the first captivity. The reference to the word of the Lord "by the mouth of Jeremiah" undoubtedly refers to his prophecy regarding the length of time that Judah would spend in captivity. Jeremiah 25:11–12 and 29:10 both refer to a seventy-year period of captivity. The edict by Cyrus ended this.

Cyrus refers to himself as the ruler of "all the kingdoms of the earth." This is typical ancient Near Eastern exaggeration (cf. Dan. 4:1; 6:25). On the Cyrus cylinder, discovered by the Assyrian archaeologist Hormuzd Rassam in 1879 at Babylon, Cyrus refers to himself as "king of the world, great king, mighty king of the four quarters."[24] Hammurabi, king of the Amorites in ancient Babylon, pictured himself as "the powerful king, the sun of Babylon, who causes light to go forth over the lands of Sumer and Akkad; the king who has made the four quarters of the world subservient."[25] Thutmose III of Egypt described his kingdom: "His southern frontier is to the horns of the earth, to the southern limit *of this land*; (his) northern to the marshes of Asia, to the supporting pillars of heaven."[26]

Cyrus recognized the call of Israel's God to free His people. In referring to Him as the "Lord God of heaven," Cyrus adopted the

---

[24]Trans. T. Fish, in *DOTT*, p. 93.

[25]Prologue to *The Code of Hammurabi*, trans. Theophile J. Meek, in *ANET*, p. 165.

[26]*The Asiatic Campaigns of Thutmose III*, trans. John A. Wilson, taken from *The Temples of Armant: A Preliminary Survey* (London, 1940), in *ANET*, p. 240.

Jewish view of God. As a Persian, Cyrus would have considered Israel's God as simply a localized deity, in control over Palestine but subject to his Persian gods. He used this title, however, since his decree concerned the return of the Jews to their homeland.

Both Isaiah 44:28 and 45:1 state that God raised up Cyrus for the purpose of returning the Jews to Palestine. Josephus (*Antiquities* 11.1.2) records that the prophecy was shown to Cyrus. "When Cyrus read this, and admired the divine power, an earnest desire and ambition seized upon him to fulfill what was so written; so he called for the most eminent Jews that were in Babylon, and said to them, that he gave them leave to go back to their own country, and to rebuild their city Jerusalem, and the temple of God."[27] Isaiah prophesied about two hundred years before the decree from Cyrus.

The hope of a long life apparently moved Cyrus to free the Jews. The Cylinder of Cyrus illuminates the nature of the "writing" referred to here. This Persian record says in part, "To the cities of Ashur and Susa, Agade, Eshnunna, the cities of Zamban, Meturnu, Der, as far as the region of the land of Gutium, the holy cities beyond the Tigris whose sanctuaries had been in ruins over a long period, the gods whose abode is in the midst of them, I returned to their places and housed them in lasting abodes. I gathered together all their inhabitants and restored (to them) their dwellings. . . . May all the gods whom I have placed within their sanctuaries address a daily prayer in my favour before Bel and Nabu, that my days be long."[28]

Cyrus gave the Jews permission to return to rebuild the temple. His statement "his God be with him, and let him go up to Jerusalem" reflects again the Persian belief in localized gods. The parenthetical statement "He is the God" better connects to the last phrase: "He is the god which is in Jerusalem."[29] This

---

[27]William Whiston, trans., *The Works of Josephus* (Peabody, MA: Hendrickson Publishers, Inc., 1987), p. 286.

[28]T. Fish, "The Cyrus Cylinder," in *DOTT*, pp. 93–94.

[29]Without evidence, W. B. Pope, *The Book of the Prophet Ezra,* in *The Layman's Handy Commentary Series*, ed. Charles John Ellicott (Grand Rapids: Zondervan Publishing House, 1961), p. 15, assumes that the decree in Aramaic referred to the Persian god Ormuzd and that the Hebrew replaced this name with the name of Jehovah. Cyrus, however, was polytheistic and would have

again shows the belief that Israel's God is a local god, limited to power in Palestine. From Cyrus's viewpoint, the building of a "house," i.e., a temple, in that location would no doubt please this god, v. 3. Cyrus also charged those Jews who "remaineth" (*šaʾar*)[30] in Babylon to help with silver, gold, goods, and animals for the return as well as with a freewill offering for the rebuilding of the temple. First Esdras 2:7, 9 makes the word *beasts* specific as "horses and cattle," both here and in v. 6. Logically, the beasts would also have included some animals for sacrifice.

The decree given in vv. 2–4 differs from the decree recorded in 6:3–5. Ezra focuses here on the permission given to the Jews to return to Palestine and the material provision provided by the gifts of the people. It is also a translation from the Aramaic original. In c. 6, Ezra records the details of the building, a more natural emphasis in view of the objections to building made by the Samaritans. The two records each likely summarize the original decree. Taken together, they give all that we know about Cyrus's edict, v. 4.

It is important to note that God used an unsaved man to accomplish His will. The Lord has always worked through the resources of this world to bring about His will for His people. He used pagan Egypt to provide a shelter for the people of Israel as they developed into a nation. He used wicked Assyria and Babylon to judge the sins of His people. He continues today to use the surrounding Muslim nations to judge unbelieving Israel. So here, He used Cyrus to restore His people to their land. God is in control. "The king's heart is in the hand of the Lord, as the

---

no particular inclination to single out one god. Since the decree was to the Jews, it was natural that he would mention the Jewish God, from whom he hoped to gain a blessing.

[30]F. Charles Fensham, *The Books of Ezra and Nehemiah* (Grand Rapids: Wm. B. Eerdmans, 1982), p. 44, argues that *šaʾar* should be translated "survivors," referring to "those who have escaped the sword of the Babylonians." The verb *šaʾar* in the *nipʿal* theme occurs ninety-three times in the OT. While the translation *survivor* is possible in several places, in no place is it required. Translations with variations of *remain* are always possible. While Fensham refers to "the Jewish exiles in general" as those escaping the Babylonian sword, there were many others left in Palestine, not exiled, who also had escaped the sword.

rivers of water: he turneth it whithsoever he will" (Prov. 21:1). God uses the resources of the world to accomplish His will.

It is also important to note that God's Word will not fail. Although two centuries passed before the fulfillment of Isaiah's prophecy, it happened as he said it would. The details that a king by the name of Cyrus would conquer nations, open the gates of Babylon, and decree the rebuilding of Jerusalem and the temple all came to pass. The Holy Spirit has inspired the accuracy of God's Word. It is the Christian's privilege and responsibility to trust it today.

2. Gifts to the Captives 1:5–11

The "chief of the fathers," the heads of the families listed in 2:3–19, set about to prepare for the return. The terms *Judah* and *Benjamin* refer to the dominant tribes within the group that later returned to Palestine. These two tribes, formerly the Southern Kingdom that was conquered and taken to Babylon by Nebuchadnezzar, would have made up the majority of the Jews in the captivity. The group included "all . . . whose spirit God had raised." Just as He had moved Cyrus to give permission to return, so He now led specific individuals to bring their families back to Palestine. We will see later that the returned group settled in and around Jerusalem. The towns mentioned in 2:20–29, 33–35—Gibeon (Gibbar), Bethlehem, Netophah, Anathoth, Kirjath-jearim, Ramah, Bethel, Ai, Jericho, and other lesser-known towns—were located in the region of Judah and Benjamin. In view of the make-up of the returning group, this is natural.

There were also some in the other tribes, however, that worshiped the true God (cf. 2 Chron. 11:16; 30:11). First Chronicles 9:3 indicates that tribes other than Judah and Benjamin also took part in the return from Babylon to Palestine. Although some take 1 Chronicles 9:3 as referring to tribes living in Palestine before the captivity, a comparison of 9:2 with Nehemiah 11:3 shows that the same classification of "priests, Levites, and the Nethinims" occurs. This argues for the same period of time. In addition, the rest of 1 Chronicles 9 refers to the worship of the people at Jerusalem (e.g., vv. 19, 21, 23), clearly after the return from Babylon. These joined together with priests, Levites, and others whose hearts had been touched by God to prepare for the return to build the temple in Jerusalem.

These groups banded together to "go up" to Jerusalem. The mention of going "up" is appropriate since Jerusalem is located on a mountain. While not excessively high, about 2,550 feet above sea level, this is still high compared to the elevation of Babylon, which lies about thirty feet above sea level, v. 5.

The phrase "all they that were about them" refers to the neighbors of those who returned. This would have involved Jews who for various reasons did not return. They "strengthened their hands," helping the returnees prepare for the trip by giving them valuable gifts and offerings. The vessels, gold, goods, animals, and "precious things" (*migdanot*) were no doubt intended for use at Jerusalem. From the use of *migdanot* elsewhere (Gen. 24:53; 2 Chron. 21:3; 32:23), it is clear that it refers to valuable gifts. A related word, *meged* (Deut. 33:13, 14; 15, 16 [all trans. "precious"]; Song of Sol. 4:13, 16; 7:13 [all trans. "pleasant"]), supports this idea. It is possible that the animals packed supplies on the trip. The gold and silver may also have served for purchasing needed supplies along the way.

The willing spirit in which these things were given shows the right attitude of those who helped. Many Jews stayed behind in Babylon for good reasons: children too young for such a strenuous trip, old age, or poor health. Others had become settled in their present life. Some may not have wanted to go to a land they had never seen. Yet the Jews in Babylon gave what help they were able to give. This has always been the spirit of true Christianity. As the apostle Paul said, "Every man according as he purposeth in his heart, so let him give; not grudgingly, or of necessity: for God loveth a cheerful giver" (2 Cor. 9:7).

The emperor Cyrus also helped the Jews by returning the vessels that had been taken from the temple. There is a minor problem created by 2 Kings 24:13, which states that Nebuchadnezzar "cut in pieces all the vessels [*k^elî*] of gold which Solomon king of Israel had made in the temple of the Lord." If Nebuchadnezzar had cut up the vessels into pieces, they could not have been returned to the Jews in Ezra. The word *k^elî*, however, may also be translated in other ways beside "vessels." The CEV and NLT translate *k^elî* in 2 Kings 24:13 as "objects," the GNB "utensils,"

GW "furnishings," and the NKJV and NIV "articles." These translations avoid the conflict between 2 Kings 24:13 and Ezra 1:7. Second Chronicles 36:18 notes that Nebuchadnezzar brought "all the vessels" of the temple to Babylon.

Nebuchadnezzar had placed the vessels in "the house of his gods [better 'god']," probably the Temple of Esagila, devoted to the worship of Bel, also known as Marduk (cf. Dan. 1:2). Now Cyrus returned the vessels, hoping to gain favor with Israel's God in this way, v. 7. Mithredath, the treasurer under Cyrus, assisted in this. The name *Mithredath* is a Persian name meaning "gift of Mithra." Mithra, one of the gods that presided over the judgment of the dead, supposedly traveled across the sky in the sun.

Mithredath inventoried the vessels before giving them to Sheshbazzar, whose name means "Sun god, guard the son." This Babylonian name is apparently the name given to Zerubbabel, the leader of the return.[31] Ezra 5:16 credits Sheshbazzar with laying the foundation of the temple. Ezra 3:8, 5:2, and Zechariah 4:9 relate this same event to Zerubbabel. He is called "the prince of Israel." First Chronicles 3:16–19 shows that Zerubbabel descended from the final kings of Judah and thus would have been heir to the throne in normal times, v. 8.

The vessels included "thirty chargers [*ᵓᵃgarṭal*]." The word *ᵓᵃgarṭal* occurs only in this verse. It is thought to refer to some sort of basket or basket-shaped dish, here made of gold. Other suggestions have also been made for *ᵓᵃgarṭal*. The NKJV

---

[31]Others see Sheshbazzar as a princely leader who was later replaced by Zerubbabel, e.g., Philip A. Noss and Kenneth J. Thomas, *A Handbook on Ezra and Nehemiah*, in *UBS Handbook Series*, ed. Donald Slager (New York: United Bible Societies, 2005), p. 12. Similarly, Myers, p. 9, and Batten, p. 70, identify Sheshbazzar with Shenazar (1 Chron. 3:18), a view that lacks support. The name *šenᵓaṣṣar* is significantly different from the name *šešbaṣṣar*. J. Carl Laney, *Ezra/Nehemiah* (Chicago: Moody Press, 1982), p. 24, argues on the basis of 1 Esdras 6:18, which mentions Zerubbabel and Sheshbazzar as separate individuals, that Sheshbazzar was appointed by Cyrus to lead the Jews but that he died soon after the return. Zerubbabel, Sheshbazzar's nephew, completed the task of building the temple. Both men thus participated in laying the foundation of the temple. Laney's view also requires identifying Sheshbazzar with Shenazer. The reference in 1 Esdras likely reflects the attempt of that book to reconcile the references to both men in laying the temple's foundation. However, the biblical references cited in this paragraph support identifying Sheshbazzar with Zerubbabel.

translates it as "platters," the ESV as "basins," and the CEV, NASB, and NIV as "dishes." The Vulgate translates it as *fialae*, a censer, small flask, vial, or shallow bowl. The LXX translates it as ψυκτῆρές, something to preserve cold, thus "wine-cooler." Rabinowitz mentions the view that these were bowls for the blood of the temple sacrifices, the gold bowls being used for the blood of lambs and the silver ones for the blood of bulls.[32]

There were "a thousand chargers [also *ʾagarṭal*]," similarly a dish made of silver, and also twenty-nine "knives" (*maḥalapîm*), an unknown item but probably some kind of dish. This is the only time the word *maḥalapîm* occurs in the OT. The root *ḥlp* means "to pass on, away, or through." This suggests a knife, but other suggestions have also been made, e.g., "dishes" (CEV), "censers" (ESV), "duplicates" (NASB), "silver pans" (NIV), "silver incense burners" (NLT). The LXX translates it as παρηλλαγμένα, "changes," likely referring to clothing of some kind. The Vulgate translates it as *cultri*, "knives," v. 9.

There were "thirty basons" (*kepor*) of gold and 410 "basons of a second *sort,*" silver bowls of inferior quality. The noun *kepor* is from the root *kpr*, "to cover," which occurs widely for "atonement," in which a sacrifice provides a covering for sin. The word here refers to some kind of covered dish, a "bowl" (NASB, NIV) or "basin" (NKJV). The CEV interprets it as "silver bowls," a view also held by the ESV and GNB. GW translates it as "other utensils." Keil uses "covered goblets," which agrees with the Vulgate *scyphi,* "goblet." Blenkinsopp, Fensham, and Rabinowitz translate it as "bowls."

There were a thousand other vessels, v. 10. All together, fifty-four hundred golden and silver vessels were returned to Jerusalem. The numbers given here total only 2,499. This is probably the number of the most valuable vessels since 2 Chronicles 36:18 refers to "great and small" temple vessels. It may well be that the "small" vessels were not of sufficient worth to calculate and are therefore not included here, v. 11.[33]

---

[32]Rabinowitz, p. 72.

[33]It is common to assume that some of the items have dropped out of the MT or that some of the numbers have been wrongly transcribed, e.g., Albert Barnes, *1 Samuel to Esther*, ed. F. C. Cook (1834; repr., Grand Rapids: Baker

EZRA 2

3. Register of the People 2:1–70

a. List of the Families and Towns 2:1–35

Ezra lists "the children of the province," i.e., the Persian province of Judea,[34] who returned from "the captivity" to Palestine. While he refers to the captivity of those carried to Babylon by Nebuchadnezzar, this is a general statement that would have included other Jews taken later. Second Kings 24:14, 25:11, and Daniel 1:3–5 refer to groups taken to Babylon from Judah at different times.

Shumate notes that the listing of those who returned to Palestine illustrates God's faithfulness in five ways: (1) He provided legitimate leadership, (2) preserved Israel as a covenant people, (3) returned Israel to its inheritance, (4) entered into fellowship with His people (through the rebuilt temple), and (5) gave them the necessary resources to return.[35] We can add that the return itself shows God's faithfulness to His Word (Jer. 25:11–12; 29:10).

Book House, 1977), p. 438; Ryle, p. 15; Fensham, pp. 46–47. Keil, p. 29, suggests that the difference comes from an error in the numbers. Instead of fifty-four hundred, he suggests reading twenty-five hundred, a round number used instead of 2,499. While the suggestion is possible, no manuscript evidence supports it. Myers, p. 5, suggests the figures cannot be reconciled because not all of the contributed items were individually recorded. Ezra's list gives only the vessels from the temple, while the summary number fifty-four hundred includes other vessels. This suggestion faces the problem that v. 10 mentions "other vessels." Rabinowitz, p. 73, gives the view of Rashi that the list records only the most valuable vessels. Other less valuable vessels were left uncounted. Rabinowitz also refers to Ibn Ezra, who held that the smaller number referred to larger vessels while the total number included both small and large vessels. Breneman, p. 73, offers the possibility that the author copied only part of the inventory but included the total number. Slotki, p. 115, asserts that only the larger vessels are enumerated while the total includes both small and large vessels.

[34]The GNB translates this as though the "province" is that of Babylon. Most translations and commentators recognize it as referring to Judah, which at this time was an administrative region under the Persian authorities.

[35]David R. Shumate, "The Theological and Practical Value of the Name Lists in Ezra 2 and 8," *BV* 38 (November 2003): 22.

Ezra's list of returnees is similar but not identical to the list in Nehemiah 7:6–73.[36] There is also a similar record in the apocryphal book of 1 Esdras. The people returned to "Jerusalem and Judah," naturally settling in their homeland and around the capital city. They also went "every one unto his city," neighboring towns. In all likelihood, many returned to the areas their families had originally come from. While the captivity in Babylon lasted seventy years, it is not necessary to assume that only those who had been in Babylon the full time could return. The list of returning Jews undoubtedly included some who had gone into captivity later, after Zedekiah's defeat fifty years before in 586 BC (Jer. 1:3), as well as many who were born in Babylon during the captivity.

The lists in vv. 21–29, 33–35 mention Bethlehem, Netophah, Anathoth, Kirjath-jearim, Ramah, Bethel, Ai, Jericho, and several lesser-known towns. Nehemiah 3:2–18 mentions the towns of Jericho, Tekoa, Gibeon, Mizpah, Zanoah, and Keilah. Nehemiah 7:26–33 mentions several additional places. We cannot locate all of these towns with certainty. Those whose locations we do know all are in the tribal areas of Judah and Benjamin, natural in view of those who returned. Nehemiah 11:1–2 indicates that not enough people settled in Jerusalem. Steps had to be taken to bring additional settlers into the capital city, v. 1.

Zerubbabel led the return.[37] He was the grandson of Jeconiah (1 Chron. 3:17–19) and therefore in the royal line of Judah. It is undoubtedly for this reason that he was chosen to lead the

[36] G. Coleman Luck, *Ezra and Nehemiah: A Commentary* (Chicago: Moody Press, 1961), p. 111, adopts the view that Ezra's list, prepared in Babylon, named "those who expected to return" while Nehemiah's list, prepared in Jerusalem, identified "those who actually did return." This view is contrary to the statement in Ezra 2:1 that refers to "the children of the province that went up out of the captivity." H. G. M. Williamson, "The Composition of Ezra I-VI," *JTS* 34 (April 1983): 2, is typical of many who explain the differences "on the basis of later, textual corruption." This explanation is subjective, without textual evidence to support it.

[37] Fensham, p. 47, understands Zerubbabel and Sheshbazzar (1:8, 11) as two separate individuals. (See the discussion of this question earlier, at 1:8.) This leads him to see two separate returns with the return under Zerubbabel "possibly at the same time as the return of Sheshbazzar in 538 B.C." The view is weak, for reasons discussed earlier.

return to Palestine from Babylon. The NT also mentions Zerubbabel as being an ancestor of the Lord (Matt. 1:12; Luke 3:27). There is a minor problem associated with Zerubbabel's heritage. The OT identifies him as the son of Pedaiah (1 Chron. 3:19) and Shealtiel (Ezra 3:2, 8; Neh. 12:1). This often is thought to reflect the custom of levirate marriage (Gen. 38:8; Deut. 25:5–10)[38] since Pedaiah and Shealtiel were brothers (1 Chron. 3:17–18). When Shealtiel died childless, Pedaiah became the natural father of Zerubbabel, but Shealtiel was still his legal father.

In addition to the eleven men listed in v. 2, Nehemiah 7:7 gives a twelfth name, Nahamani. It is possible that these men represented the twelve tribes.[39] Although only Judah and Benjamin were from the south of Palestine, there were also those from the other tribes that participated in the return. Jeshua, also called Joshua (e.g., Hag. 1:1, 12; 2:2, 4; Zech. 6:11), was the high priest at the time of the return (Zech. 3:1). Except for Zerubbabel and Jeshua, the nation's political and spiritual leaders, we know little about the men mentioned here.[40]

---

[38]Breneman, p. 75, note 33, and C. F. Keil, *The Books of the Chronicles*, in *Biblical Commentary on the Old Testament*, trans. Andrew Harper (1866; repr., Grand Rapids: Wm. B. Eerdmans, 1978), pp. 81–82. Earl Radmacher and Ron Allen, eds., *Compact Bible Commentary* (Nashville: Thomas Nelson Publishers, 2004), p. 250, suggest that Zerubbabel was a son of Shealtiel but that his father died young, leaving Zerubbabel to be reared by his uncle Pedaiah. Later, p. 303, they suggest a levirate marriage. Henry, p. 844, makes Zerubbabel the grandson of Shealtiel. Since 1 Chron. 3:17–18 makes Shealtiel and Pedaiah brothers, Henry's view is not possible. In addition, he is called the "son of Shealtiel" nine times in four OT books and twice more in two NT books, strongly supporting his position as Shealtiel's son.

[39]Batten, pp. 74–75, suggests "these men were the leaders of the various caravans of returning exiles which kept coming to Judah throughout the Persian period." Aside from the lack of any mention of regular caravans coming to Palestine, the OT speaks of only three returns to Palestine from Babylon. Zerubbabel led the first (Ezra 2:2; Neh. 7:7), Ezra the second (Ezra 7:6–9), and Nehemiah the third (Neh. 2:4–11). While the naming of twelve men may be coincidental, it may also suggest representatives of the twelve tribes.

[40]Rabinowitz, p. 77, identifies Mordecai (v. 2) as the Mordecai of Esther. The events of Esther, however, take place after 480 BC, while the events in Ezra 1–6 occur ca. 535–516 BC. Since this Mordecai is a leader of the people in Ezra 2:2 and thus already an older adult, it is unlikely that he would still be active in the time of Esther.

The Talmud, *Sanhedrin* 38*a*, identifies Zerubbabel as Nehemiah. Nehemiah appears in Nehemiah 12:47, however, as separate from Zerubbabel. In addition, Nehemiah 2:1 places his return to Palestine in the twentieth year of Artaxerxes. Ezra 5:2 (cf. 6:15) makes it clear that the temple building project was finished in the sixth year of Darius. It is unlikely that Zerubbabel returned to Babylon after completing the temple building, became the king's cupbearer, and then returned to Palestine fourteen years later under the name of Nehemiah.

The father of Jeshua was Jozadak (3:2, 8; Neh. 12:26), a name that is contracted from *Jehozadak*, "the Lord is righteous." From 1 Chronicles 6:14–15, a listing of Israel's high priests, we learn Jehozadak's father was Seraiah, the high priest who was killed by Nebuchadnezzar before the captivity (2 Kings 25:18–21). Ezra 7:1 says that Ezra was also a descendant of Seraiah. Since the genealogies skip some generations (see the discussion in c. 7), we cannot fix Ezra's exact relationship to Jeshua, but he was likely Jeshua's uncle or great-uncle, v. 2.

The first part of the list includes the members of individual families (vv. 1–19, 30–32), along with groups from various towns in Judah (vv. 20–29, 33–35). For the most part, the names and numbers agree with the lists given in Nehemiah and 1 Esdras in the Apocrypha. There are differences, however. We can attribute these to any of several causes. The lists may have been compiled at different times. Married women may have been counted with one group in one list and another in the other list. People may have been counted with a family in one list and with a town in another list. Children under a certain age may have been counted in one list but not in the other. Some could have died during the time that elapsed between the two censuses. It is possible that some of the men were known by different names. Nehemiah 7:5 states that Nehemiah "found" his genealogy, indicating that it was not original. We can only speculate as to the reasons for the differences.[41]

---

[41]It is common to explain the differences as errors of transcription, as do Blenkinsopp, Keil, and Rawlinson, for example. Such an explanation is speculative since it lacks the support of manuscript evidence. It is difficult to see how so many differences could have developed through transcription errors.

The following chart gives the three lists side by side. The asterisks indicate where Nehemiah and 1 Esdras differ from Ezra's tabulation in either the name or the number.

Names of Families 2:2*b*–19	Ezra	Nehemiah	1 Esdras
Parosh, v. 3 (cf. Neh. 7:8; 1 Esd. 5:9)	2172	2172	2172
Shephatiah, v. 4 (cf. Neh. 7:9; 1 Esd. 5:9)	372	372	472*
Arah, v. 5 (cf. Neh. 7:10; 1 Esd. 5:10)	775	652*	756*
Pahath-moab, v. 6 (cf. Neh. 7:11; 1 Esd. 5:11)	2812	2818*	2812
Elam, v. 7 (cf. Neh. 7:12; 1 Esd. 5:12)	1254	1254	1254
Zattu, v. 8 (cf. Neh. 7:13; 1 Esd. 5:12)	945	845*	945
Zaccai, v. 9 (cf. Neh. 7:14; 1 Esd. 5:12, Chorbe*)	760	760	705*
Bani, v. 10 (cf. Binnui,* Neh 7:15; 1 Esd. 5:12)	642	648*	648*
Bebai, v. 11 (cf. Neh. 7:16; 1 Esd. 5:13)	623	628*	623
Azgad, v. 12 (cf. Neh. 7:17; 1 Esd. 5:13)	1222	2322*	3222*
Adonikam, v. 13 (cf. Neh. 7:18; 1 Esd. 5:14)	666	667*	667*
Bigvai, v. 14 (cf. Neh. 7:19; 1 Esd. 5:14)	2056	2067*	2066*
Adin, v. 15 (cf. Neh. 7:20; 1 Esd. 5:14)	454	655*	454
Ater, through Hezekiah, v. 16 (cf. Neh. 7:21; 1 Esd. 5:15)	98	98	92*
Kilan and Azetas (1 Esd. 5:15)			67*
Azuru (1 Esd. 5:15)			432*

Names of Families 2:2*b*–19	**Ezra**	**Nehemiah**	**1 Esdras**
Annias (1 Esd. 5:16)			101*
Arom (1 Esd. 5:16)			32*
Bezai, v. 17 (cf. Neh. 7:23; 1 Esd. 5:16)	323	324*	323
Jorah, v. 18 (Hariph, Neh. 7:24; 1 Esd. 5:16)	112	112	102*
Bethlomon (1 Esd. 5:16)			123*
Baiterus (1 Esd. 5:17)			3005*
Hashum, v. 19 (cf. Neh. 7:22)	223	328*	

Names of Towns 2:20–29	**Ezra**	**Nehemiah**	**1 Esdras**
Gibbar, v. 20 (Gibeon, Neh. 7:25)	95	95	
Bethlehem, v. 21 (cf. Neh. 7:26; 1 Esd. 5:17)	123		123
Netophah, v. 22 (cf. Neh. 7:26; 1 Esd. 5:18)	56	188*	55*
Anathoth, v. 23 (cf. Neh. 7:27; 1 Esd. 5:18)	128	128	158*
Azmaveth, v. 24 (Beth-Azmaveth, Neh. 7:28; 1 Esd. 5:18)	42	42	42
Kirjath-jearim (1 Esd. 5:19)			25*
Chephirah and Beeroth, v. 25 (cf. Neh. 7:29)	743	743	743
Chadiasans and Ammidians (1 Esd. 5;20)			422*
Ramah and Gaba, v. 26 (cf. Neh. 7:30; 1 Esd. 5:20)	621	621	621
Michmas, v. 27 (cf. Neh. 7:31; 1 Esd. 5:21)	122	122	122

Names of Towns 2:20–29	Ezra	Nehemiah	1 Esdras
Bethel and Ai, v. 28 (cf. Neh. 7:32; Bethel-Ai, 1 Esd. 5:21)	223	123*	52*
Nebo (the other Nebo), v. 29 (cf. Neh. 7:33)	52	52	
Additional Families 2:30–32			
Magbish, v. 30 (1 Esd. 5:21)	156		156
Elam, v. 31 (cf. Neh. 7:34; Elam and Ono, 1 Esd. 5:22)	1254	1254	725*
Harim, v. 32 (cf. Neh. 7:35)	320	320	
Additional Towns 2:33–35			
Lod, Hadid, and Ono, v. 33 (cf. Neh. 7:37)	725	721*	
Jericho, v. 34 (cf. Neh. 7:36; 1 Esd. 5:22)	345	345	245*
Senaah,[a] v. 35 (cf. Neh. 7:38; 1 Esd. 5:23)	3630	3930*	3330*

[a]Although Senaah is normally identified as a town, R. Zadok, "A Note on sn'h," *VT* 38, no. 4 (October 1988): 483, suggests the possible view that "the children of Senaah" refers to a clan. The fact that Ezra does not record all the families together in the list (2:2–19; 30–32; 37–42) supports the possibility that Senaah is a family name rather than a place name. In addition, the large number of people involved (3,630 men) agrees with the fact that everywhere else the list mentions a number greater than one thousand people (vv. 3, 6–7, 12, 14, 31, 37–39, it refers to families.

b. Lists of Temple Personnel 2:36–63

The lists of the priestly names and numbers in Ezra and Nehemiah are identical. Three of the names (Jedaiah, Immer, Harim) belong to men who were heads of the priestly courses (1 Chron. 24:7, 8, 14). We know nothing of the background of Pashur. Jedaiah was another descendant of Jeshua. Although Ezra does not specifically mention Jeshua as the current high priest at the time of the first return, both Haggai (1:1, 12, 14; 2:2, 4) and Zechariah (3:1, 8; 6:11) do record that he held that office, vv. 36–39.

Names of Priests 2:36–39	Ezra	Nehemiah	1 Esdras
Jedaiah, v. 36 (cf. Neh. 7:39; 1 Esd. 5:24)	973	973	972*
Immer, v. 37 (cf. Neh. 7:40; 1 Esd. 5:24)	1052	1052	1052
Pashur, v. 38 (cf. Neh. 7:41; 1 Esd. 5:25)	1247	1247	1247
Harim, v. 39 (cf. Neh. 7:42; 1 Esd. 5:25)	1017	1017	1017

Verses 40–42 name the Levitical groups. These include the singers in Asaph's family, the temple musicians, v. 41, and the porters, charged with keeping the temple gates, the treasury, and items used in the ministry (1 Chron. 9:26–29). v. 42. Three of these—Shallum, Talmon, and Akkub—probably descended from earlier families of porters (cf. 1 Chron. 9:17).

Names of Levites 2:40–42	Ezra	Nehemiah	1 Esdras
Jeshua and Kadmiel (who is one of the sons of Hodaviah[b]), v. 40 (cf. Neh. 7:43; Jeshua and Kadmiel and Bannas and Sudias, 1 Esd. 5:26)	74	74	74
Singers: Asaph, v. 41 (cf. Neh. 7:44; 1 Esd. 5:27)	128	148*	128
Porters: Shallum, Ater, Talmon, Akkub, Hatita, Shobai, v. 42 (cf. Neh. 7:45; 1 Esd. 5:28)	139	138*	138*

[b]First Esdras 5:26 transliterates the phrase "of the children of Hodaviah," giving the proper names "Bannas and Sudias." Noss and Thomas, p. 57, follow this to a degree. The MT, however, introduces the phrase "children of" with a *lamed* preposition, which most likely connects Kadmiel and Hodaviah.

Summary of Various Groups

Verses 43–54 lists the "Nethinims" (better "Nethinim" since the *-im* ending in Hebrew makes it plural and eliminates the need for the *-s* ending). These are thought to have been people who carried out menial work in the temple. The group may have descended from the Gibeonites, who were assigned to cut wood and draw water as a penalty for deceiving Israel (Josh. 9:21, 27). The name *Nethinim* means "given." This probably reflects the fact that they were "given" in service to the temple. The Talmud (*Kiddushin* 3:12; 4:1; *Yebamoth* 2:4) assigns them a low position, below that of illegitimate children. Josephus, *Antiquities* 11.5.1, refers to them as "sacred servants." The names in vv. 43–54 include some non-Israelite names, e.g., Mehunim, Nephusim. This suggests that the group included some prisoners of war that were given to the service of working in the temple. It is equally possible that some Israelites had volunteered for this service as a way of serving their God. Since the New Testament does not mention them, they were likely assimilated into the Levites during the intertestamental period.

Verses 55–58 list the "servants of Solomon." According to 1 Kings 9:20–21, Solomon made servants of the surviving Canaanites in the land. Many of these no doubt worshiped Israel's God. They went into captivity with the Jews and now joined in the return with the intention of taking up their position of service once more. Nehemiah 11:3 also mentions them.

Other Personnel 2:43–58	**Ezra**	**Nehemiah**	**1 Esdras**
Nethinims, vv. 43–54 (cf. Neh. 7:46–56; temple slaves, 1 Esd. 5:29–32) and the servants of Solomon, vv. 55–58 (cf. Neh. 7:57–60; 1 Esd. 5:34)[c]	392	392	372*

[c]The phrase "Pochereth of Zebaim" (Ezra 2:57; Neh. 7:59) is better understood as a hyphenated name, "Pokereth-Hazzebaim" (1 Esd. 5:34; ESV, NLT, NASB), or a two-word name "Pokereth Hazzebaim" (CEV, NIV, NKJV). This foreign name means "hunter of gazelles."

The next category was those who could not prove their descent from the priestly line and therefore were excluded from serving in the temple (Num. 3:10, 38; 18:7). We see elsewhere that genealogies of the families were kept (e.g., 1 Chron. 5:7, 17; 2 Chron. 31:16, 17), but these men did not have a genealogy to prove their family connection.

The group includes the children of Delaiah, Tobiah, and Nekoda, vv. 59–60 (cf. Nehemiah 7:61–62; 1 Esdras 5:36–37). These traveled from Tel-melah, Tel-harsa, Cherub, Addan, and

Immer, unknown locations in Babylon. First Esdras 5:36 gives Cherub, Addan, and Immer as the leaders of the three families descending from Delaiah, Tobiah, and Nekoda.

Excluded Families 2:59–60	**Ezra**	**Nehemiah**	**1 Esdras**
Those who could not prove descent from Israel	652	642*	652

In addition to these of doubtful origin, there were several men who could not prove descent from the priestly line: Habaiah, Koz, and Barzillai, vv. 61–63 (cf. Neh. 7:63–65; 1 Esd. 5:38–40).[42] They could not receive their food from the sacrifices until there should be a priest "with Urim and Thummim." These were part of the high priest's breastplate (Exod. 28:30; Lev. 8:8). In some unknown way, the Lord communicated His will through Urim and Thummin (Num. 27:21; 1 Sam. 28:6). *Tirshatha*, a title meaning "feared" or "revered," is Zerubbabel's Persian title as governor. He defers a final decision on these until Jeshua, the priest who would have had the Urim and Thummim, could consult with the Lord about them, probably after beginning the temple worship in Jerusalem. The OT never explains the Urim and Thummim. It has been suggested that they were some form of sacred lot that guided the high priest in decisions.[43]

While given only minor emphasis in the text, this incident shows Zerubbabel's concern with keeping the purity of the priesthood. Rather than accepting the word of these who claimed the right of priestly service, he insisted on proof. So today, only those who have a divine call to the ministry and can

[42]This is the only time in the OT when a man adopted the name of his in-laws. The first Barzillai provided assistance to David at the time of Absalom's rebellion; cf. 2 Sam. 17:27–29. Keil, p. 42, speculates that the daughter here was an heiress, and that the priest took her name for the sake of possessing the inheritance. However, since priests did not receive an inheritance of land (Num. 18:20; Deut. 10:8–9; 12:12), this is not possible.

[43]Noss and Thomas, p. 63, understand the Urim and Thummim as something thrown "like dice to determine a positive or negative answer" to some question. Larson and Dahlen, p. 23, are similar, seeing the Urim and Thummin as lots drawn to determine God's will. While these are possible views, the OT does not clearly explain the nature of the Urim and Thummim.

carry out their service in accord with God's Word should serve. Those with no evidence of a relationship with the Lord and a call from Him to serve have no right to enter the ministry.

c. Summary of the Return 2:64–70

All three lists in Ezra, Nehemiah, and 1 Esdras report a total of 42,360 people returning from the captivity to Palestine. The numbers in the Ezra's list add up to 29,818. The sum of Nehemiah's numbers is 31,089, and the total in 1 Esdras 5 is 30,143. Clearly, the lists are not exhaustive. They mention only the major groups. An older Jewish view explains the difference by saying that the names in the lists were of those from Judah and Benjamin while those from other tribes were not listed.[44] There is, however, no proof of this.

First Esdras 5:41 explains that the lists include only those over twelve years of age.[45] It would, however, be unusual for the number of adults to exceed the number of children by more than 12,500, v. 64. In addition to the names given in the lists, the group included 7,337 men and women servants. Two hundred men and women singers also returned. The singers were not those involved in temple worship (cf. v. 41) but rather those associated with the court, providing entertainment and festivity at governmental occasions (cf. 2 Sam. 19:35; 2 Chron. 35:25; Eccles. 2:8), v. 65.

Kidner notes that about one out of every six persons was a slave.[46] This suggests a wealthy group, a view supported by v. 69. Yet less than twenty years later, Haggai refers to the poverty of the people (Hag. 1:6, 9–11; 2:17). The carelessness of the people

---

[44]Slotki, p. 124.

[45]Rademacher and Allen, p. 304, suggest "the larger total includes women, who are not named in the lists." The inclusion of "singing women" in v. 65 argues against this. In addition, this would require a relatively small number of returning women. Davidson, p. 381, agrees with the older Jewish view that the list includes only those belonging to Judah or Benjamin with the members from other tribes not being named, but the references to the other tribes (Ezra 6:17; 8:35; Neh. 7:7) argue against this. Brenemen, p. 88, sees this as "a composite list" with some families omitted while "the overall total remains correct." We can only speculate as to the reason for the difference in the numbers.

[46]Derek Kidner, *Ezra and Nehemiah: An Introduction and Commentary*, in *The Tyndale Old Testament Commentaries*, ed. D. J. Wiseman (Madison, WI: InterVarsity Press, 1979), p. 44.

toward spiritual things (Hag. 1:3–4) had brought God's judgment on them. This shows the fallacy of trusting in wealth rather than in the Lord.

The returnees brought with them 736 horses (normally ridden in war or by the wealthy, Exod. 14:9, 23; 1 Kings 4:26; 2 Kings 5:9), 245 mules (also used by the wealthy, 2 Sam. 13:29; 18:9; 2 Kings 5:17), v. 66; 435 Arabian camels (with a single hump), and 6,720 asses (the most common animal used for carrying loads; mentioned more than ninety times in the OT). The numbers in Nehemiah 7:68–69 are identical, v. 67.

After arriving at Jerusalem, some of the "chief of the fathers," heads of the families, made freewill offerings to enable worship at the temple to begin, v. 68. They offered 61,000 "drams of gold," 5,000 "pound of silver," and about 100 "garments" or linen tunics to be worn by the priests. The "dram" is the earliest coined money used by the Jews. It is thought to be the "daric" (*darkᵉmônîm*) of the Persians, a coin named after king Darius. The word *darkᵉmônîm* occurs only here and in Nehemiah 7:70–72. A related word, *ʾᵃdarkonîm*, written with a prosthetic *ʾalep*, occurs in 1 Chronicles 29:7 and Ezra 8:27. This is variously translated "darics" (AB, CB, ESV) or "drachmas" (NASB, NIV, NKJV). I prefer "darics" since this was a Persian coin. The drachma came into use during the time of the Greek empire. The Jews would have used darics during their captivity in Babylon. A daric contained about 128 grains of gold. The "pound[s]" (better *minas*) equaled about sixty shekels each, with a shekel being equal to 220 grains of silver.

The 61,000 darics of gold occurs in Nehemiah 7:70–72 as 1,000 + 20,000 + 20,000, a total of 41,000 darics. The 5,000 pounds of silver mentioned by Ezra is more accurately reported by Nehemiah as 2,200 + 2000 pounds. Similarly, the figure of 100 priestly garments in Ezra 6:69 is 530 garments in Nehemiah 7:70, taking into account Nehemiah's contribution. Ezra seems to have used rounded numbers as the total. The gifts may also have arrived at differing times so that Ezra and Nehemiah recorded different numbers, v. 69. The group included priests and Levites, ordinary people, singers, porters, and the Nethinim.

After the return, the people settled into various cities in the land. It is likely that this dispersion throughout the land allowed the families to return to areas with which they had some connection. It is highly unlikely that all of the returnees were elderly Jews who had lived in Babylon through most of the captivity. Some of the returnees may have been taken captive as children at the time of the final deportation of the Jews. Others had been born in Babylon but had been told about their family's home. Many of the returnees would have had relatives who had stayed in the land after its fall to Babylon. Returning to these areas would have been natural, v. 70.

While this historical record only summarizes the return from Babylon to Palestine, it gives enough information to let us see the dedication of those who returned. This was a journey of about a thousand miles, and most of the people made the trek on foot. The return would have required them to leave many possessions behind in Babylon. Some of the parents would have had to carry babies or small children, changing off with others as they became tired. The people spent several months traveling from Babylon to Jerusalem. They faced tiredness, the rigors of the trail, the impact of the weather, sickness, and many other burdens along the way. Yet they voluntarily chose to go so that they could worship God in the place and n the manner that He had commanded. God still calls His children to endure hardship in service for Him. He promises to go with us through the trials. Even in difficult times, however, "we may boldly say, The Lord is [our] helper" (Heb. 13:6).

EZRA 3

B. Restoration of the Worship 3:1–13
1. Practice of the Ritual 3:1–6

The seventh month of the Jewish year, Ethanim (later called Tishri), covers the period from mid-September to mid-October. This was Israel's great month of feasts. In addition to the new moon feast (Num. 28:11–15), specially observed as the Feast of Trumpets on the first day of this month (Lev. 23:23–25; Num.

29:1–6), Israel celebrated the Day of Atonement (Num. 29:7–11) and the Feast of Tabernacles (Num. 29:12–38) during this month. Although the year is not stated, v. 8 suggests that it is the first year of the return to Palestine. It was appropriate to worship the Lord at this time of the year. The people were now settled "in their cities" and traveled from these places to gather at Jerusalem, v. 1.

Although the temple had not yet been rebuilt, the altar was set up for worship. Jeshua (the high priest) and his "brethren" (the other priests) along with Zerubbabel and "his brethren" built the altar. The "brethren" of Zerubbabel probably included other members of the royal family who had returned, but they are not named in the book. It is also possible that the group included the family leaders, mentioned earlier in 2:68.

The name *Jeshua* illustrates a problem in the books of Ezra and Nehemiah. It occurs twenty-eight times in these two books but refers to several different people. It is not always possible to identify which Jeshua is in view. This same difficulty occurs with many other people mentioned in these books, e.g., Maaseiah (occurs 12x), Mattaniah (10x), and Meshullam (16x).

The two groups—the priests and the civil leaders—worked together to build the altar first. They built the altar quickly (cf. v. 6), likely following the Mosaic law in heaping up stones on which to offer their sacrifices (Exod. 20:25; Deut. 27:5–6). This allowed the priests to offer the daily burnt offerings prescribed in "the law of Moses the man of God" (e.g., Lev. 17:2–6; Deut. 12:5–11). The reference to Moses as "the man of God" recognizes his God-appointed leadership of the nation at the time when God gave the law to the nation, v. 2. Verse 3 gives some details of building the altar. It was placed "upon his bases [foundation]" in the same place where it had previously been located. Josephus, *Antiquities* 11.4.1, notes that the Jews "built the altar on the same place it had been formerly built [in Solomon's temple], that they might offer the appointed sacrifices upon it to God." The motivation was the fear the Israelites felt because of the idolatrous people around them.[47] Beginning the formal wor-

[47]Levering, p. 55, sees the primary cause of this fear as the concern "that the returning Israelites will lapse from the Torah's precepts for true worship." Nothing in the book supports this view. Very soon after their return, the

ship of God would bring divine protection. As prescribed by the law given earlier to Moses (Exod. 29:38–39; Num. 28:3–4), the priests offered the morning and evening sacrifices. These offerings involved the burnt offering of a lamb, together with a tenth of an ephah (a little under a quart) of flour mixed with one-fourth of a hin (about one and one-half pints) of oil. One-fourth of a hin of wine was poured out as a drink offering to the Lord (Exod. 29:40–41; Num. 28:5–7).

That Moses is described as "the man of God" shows his continuing reputation among the Jews. This expression always refers either to a theophany (Judg. 13:6, 8) or to a spiritual leader of Israel, e.g., Moses (Deut. 33:1), Samuel (1 Sam. 9:6–10), the prophet Shemaiah (1 Kings 12:22), the unnamed prophet who cried out against the altar in Bethel (1 Kings 13:1–31), Elijah (1 Kings 17:18, 24), Elisha (2 Kings 4:7, 21–27; 5:8–20), and David (2 Chron. 8:14). While he was not perfect, it is clear that Moses sought to live for God.

In v. 6 we see that the people began their worship on the "first day of the seventh month." This was the day on which the new moon sacrifices were made (Num. 28:11–15) and the Feast of Trumpets (Num. 29:1–6) was observed. Since the text does not mention these observances here, it is likely that the day was given over to setting up the altar and preparing for future worship in the temple. After that was completed, the people could observe all of the feasts, v. 3.

Ezra summarizes the sacrifices offered on the altar. The people kept the Feast of Tabernacles, also called the "Feast of Booths" in some translations (e.g., ESV, GW, NASB) or the "Festival of Shelters" in others (e.g., CEV, GNB, NLT). Both variations reflect the custom of living in a hut made from branches (Lev. 23:40–42; Neh. 8:14–17) during the feast. This was

---

people turned aside from building the temple to furthering their own prosperity (Hag. 1:2–4). Later, Ezra deals with the problem of intermarriage with the heathen (c. 9–10). Another possible view of the fear sees the clause as concessive. They built the altar *even though* they were afraid rather than *because* they were afraid. The CEV, GW, and NKJV translate the subordinating conjunction as *though*. The ESV, NASB, and NRSV translate it as *because*. Since the *kᵉ* that introduces the clause is more commonly causal, the fear was most likely related to the threat posed by the surrounding nations to a weak Judah.

a reminder to the nation of God's care for them during the forty years of wandering in the wilderness. The feast was kept "as it is written" (Lev. 23:33–38), offering each day the proper sacrifices "by number," i.e., offering the correct number of sacrifices each day (Num. 29:12–38), v. 4.

Following the Feast of Tabernacles, the people offered "the continual burnt-offering" each day. The phrase "both of" is translated better "and of." The people not only offered the daily "burnt offerings" but also the new moon sacrifices and the "set feasts," i.e., the annual feasts commanded in the law. In addition, those who so desired brought their "freewill offering," v. 5. The people saw the importance of beginning their formal worship. Although "the foundation of the temple of the Lord was not yet laid" (better "the temple had not been founded"), they began making their burnt offerings on the first day of the seventh month, v. 6.

2. Building of the Temple 3:7–13

The priests hired masons and carpenters to rebuild the temple. They paid them with "money" (better "silver," *kesep*). This noun, which occurs twenty-four times in Ezra, Nehemiah, and Esther, regularly refers to silver. In Ezra, it is translated with the word *money* only here (cf. Neh. 5:4, 10–11; and Esther 4:7). These workmen had no doubt learned their skills while in captivity. Zerubbabel also made an agreement with the Phoenicians. He gave them "meat" (or food), "drink" (most likely wine), and "[olive] oil" in exchange for cedar trees. Because of the small size of Phoenicia, there was not enough land to grow the necessary crops. It would have been very natural to trade various foods for cedar.

While several varieties of cedar grow in the region, the most common OT reference is to the cedar trees growing in Lebanon. Commonly found in the Lebanon and Anti-Lebanon Mountains north of Palestine, this tree grows more than one hundred feet tall with a trunk as large as fourteen feet in diameter. Individual trees may live for centuries. Because of the resistance of the wood to decay, it was often used for building homes of the wealthy (2 Sam. 5:11; 7:2), royal buildings (1 Kings 7:2–3), and ships (Ezek. 27:5). Solomon used this type of cedar in building the temple (1 Kings 6:9), and the heathen constructed idols of it as well (Isa. 44:14).

The trees would have been cut in the Lebanon Mountains and then carried to the Mediterranean Sea. From there, large floats of trees, held together with ropes, were towed to "the sea of Joppa," i.e., the Mediterranean Sea in the region of Joppa on the coast of Israel. Finally, men carried them about forty miles to Jerusalem. Cyrus had sanctioned this in his "grant" (*rišyôn*) to the Jews (cf. 1:2–4). This is the only time that *rišyôn* occurs in the OT. The related Akkadian word *rašû*, "to have, acquire, obtain," suggests something like "permission." From the context it is clear that this relates to the decree from Cyrus permitting the Jews to draw on others for aid in building their temple. While this decree does not directly mention the cutting of trees, the act of building presumes this, v. 7.

In the second month of the second year after arriving in Jerusalem, i.e., in the month of Iyyar (called Zif in earlier times, 1 Kings 6:1, 37), which corresponds to mid-April to mid-May, seven months after beginning the sacrifices, the Jews began work on the temple.[48] Zerubbabel and Jeshua led the work with the help of the priests, the Levites, and the rest of the people that had returned from the captivity. The Levites "from twenty years old and upward" had the responsibility of overseeing the construction. In the early years of the nation, the normal age for a Levite to enter his ministry was twenty-five or thirty (Num. 8:24; 4:3). Later, after the temple was established at Jerusalem, they began their work at the age of twenty (1 Chron. 23:24–32). These Levites "set forward" (better "supervised") the work of building, v. 8. Jeshua has already been mentioned as the head of a Levitical family (2:40). The phrase "sons of Judah" apparently refers to the "children of Hodaviah" (2:40; Neh. 7:43), a family of which Kadmiel seems to be the leader. The "sons of Henadad" are a third Levitical family that "set forward" (again, "supervised") the work. While the emphasis here is on the supervisory role of the priests, they also participated in the work (cf. Neh. 3:18, 24), v. 9.

[48]Luck, pp. 27–28, and Pope, p. 24, suggest that the second month was chosen because it was the month when Solomon earlier had laid the first temple foundation, 1 Kings 6:1, 37. While this is possible, it is also likely that the previous seven months were occupied in gathering the materials for building. In particular, the assembling of cedar trees and milling the wood would have required time.

At the actual laying of the foundation, a great celebration took place. The priests put on "their apparel," as required by the law (Exod. 28:40–43). The people had recently provided this (2:69). The priests played their trumpets (*ḥ^{a}ṣoṣ^{e}rôt*, a trumpet made from silver, Num. 10:2) and the Levites their cymbals (*m^{e}ṣiltayim*, flattened disks that were slightly concave, normally made of bronze or occasionally of copper or silver). Together, these instruments sounded a note of praise to the Lord, as David had earlier commanded (1 Chron. 15:16), v. 10. They "sang together," lit., "answered," i.e., engaged in antiphonal singing as they praised God and gave Him thanks for His goodness and mercy.[49] The antiphonal singing suggests that the priests formed two distinct groups, with one responding to the other. The people joined in by shouting their praise to the Lord as they saw the foundation laid for the temple where they would worship. The phrase "for his mercy [loyal love, *ḥesed*] endureth for ever" is a familiar refrain that occurs thirty-four times elsewhere (one time each in 1 Chron. 16:34; 2 Chron. 5:13; 7:3; 20:21; Jer. 33:11; Pss. 106:1; 107:1; 118:29; and twenty-six times in Ps. 136). The word *ḥesed* occurs three times in Ezra and five times in Nehemiah. The term expresses a strong component of loyalty, and it is often appropriate to translate it with this sense, v. 11.

Many older priests, Levites, and leaders of the people ("chief of the fathers") who had seen Solomon's temple (the "first house") wept when the foundation was laid.[50] Recalling the splendor of that first temple and God's presence in it, they cried when they realized the new building was, in comparison, "as nothing" (Hag. 2:3). From the dimensions given in 6:3 (see discussion there), this temple was actually larger than Solomon's (1 Kings 6:2–3), but Solomon's temple was lavish in its use of gold (1 Kings 6:20–22), something not mentioned here. In addition, *Yoma* 21*b* says this

[49]Keil, p. 55, rejects the notion of antiphonal singing. The use of *ʿanâ*, however, translated "answer" over 240x elsewhere, together with the addition of the phrase "by course," suggests that the singing was structured with the second group repeating or responding to the singing of the first group.

[50]Noss and Thomas, p. 84, tentatively suggest that the weeping came because the people did not think they would live to see the completion of this temple. While this is remotely possible, it is doubtful that it would involve "many" within the leadership of the people.

temple lacked five things: the Ark of the Covenant,[51] the fire, the Shekinah glory indicating the presence of God, the Holy Spirit of prophecy, and the Urim and Thummim. Others in the crowd that day shouted for joy at seeing progress in building the temple. The noise of the weeping overcame the sounds of joy. The cacophony was heard a long distance away, vv. 12–13.

The weeping may have been caused by their remembering God's judgment on the nation. It may also have been due to the comparison between the magnificent temple of Solomon and the less luxurious temple now before the people.[52] In my judgment, Haggai 2:3 supports the second view as correct.

EZRA 4

The laying of the foundation of the temple as described in c. 3 took place in "the second year of their coming" to Jerusalem (3:8), ca. 537 BC, but the Jews did not complete the building until "the sixth year of the reign of Darius the king" (6:15), 516 BC. Chapter 4 describes how the Jews faced opposition that was partially responsible for this twenty-one-year delay.

C. Opposition to the Work 4:1–5:17

1. Attempt at Cooperation 4:1–3

After the Assyrians had deported the Israelites, they settled the land with foreigners from many nations. The Assyrian kings Sargon (2 Kings 17:24), Esarhaddon (Ezra 4:2), and Asnapper (better "Osnapper," another name for Ashur-banipal, Ezra 4:10) brought in heathen people as settlers in the land. Sargon also sent a priest to teach these people how to worship the god of the

---

[51]Specifically, *Yoma* 21*b* says "in the ark, the ark-cover, [and] the Cherubim" were missing. A box with no cover and no contents is hardly the Ark of the Covenant.

[52]Pope and Ryle emphasize the judgment of the past. Keil, Rademacher and Allen, and Rawlinson stress the grandeur of the first temple compared to the second.

land (2 Kings 17:27–28). The priest, who was from Samaria, was not one of the true priests of the temple in Judah. The result had been a perverted religion. The people had simply added Israel's God to their other gods (2 Kings 17:29–34).

Over time, these new settlers intermarried with the Israelites who had remained in the land. Their descendants became the group we call the Samaritans (2 Kings 17:29), named after the capital city of Samaria.[53] The religion of these people rested to some degree on their version of the law, the Samaritan Pentateuch. Jewish tradition (Josephus, *Antiquities* 11.8.2, 4) credits this document to Manasseh, a renegade priest who was the son-in-law of Sanballat (Neh. 2:10, 19). Among other things, references to Mount Sinai in the OT were changed to Mount Gerizim. The Samaritans later, ca. 330 BC, built a temple for their worship on Mount Gerizim in Samaria, two miles south of Shechem.

This was the group that heard about the plans of the Jews to rebuild the temple at Jerusalem. To call them "adversaries" may be too charitable in view of their later opposition to the Jews. They were actual enemies, satanically set against the work of God's people. As in 1:5, the Jews are identified in 4:1 as "Judah and Benjamin," the primary tribes in the return from Babylon, v. 1. Initially, the Samaritans wanted to cooperate with the Jews. They claimed to be seeking God and to sacrifice "unto him [*loʾ*]" in the same way as did the Jews. In the MT the phrase "we do sacrifice unto him" literally reads "we have not been sacrificing." This could refer to the turning away of the people from idol worship. The Masoretes, however, considered the negative *lo* as one of fifteen places in the OT where the *qᵉrê*, "to him" should be read. The KJV and most modern translations (e.g., ESV, GNB, GW, NASB, NIV) follow the *qᵉrê* here.

[53]Coggins, p. 27, calls the Samaritans "a conservative group within Judaism" and considers "the story that they were descended from foreign settlers . . . a piece of later Jewish polemic, based on 2 Kings 17:24–41." He rejects the identification of the group opposing the Jews as Samaritans. His view is difficult to defend. By no stretch of the imagination can the Samaritans be considered "a conservative group within Judaism." They rejected or rewrote parts of the OT to support their practices. Josephus (*Antiquities* 11.5.9) identifies the opposition here as Samaritans. In addition, these are "adversaries" of the Jews. Finally, they themselves mention that they had been brought to Palestine (Ezra 4:2), thereby suggesting a foreign origin.

The Samaritans claimed to have followed this practice since the time of Esar-haddon (681–669 BC), the Assyrian king who had resettled them in Palestine. The Bible does not mention this resettlement elsewhere. From archaeology, however, we know that Esar-haddon campaigned and conquered in Palestine, so such a resettlement is possible. The Samaritans may have offered sacrifices to God, but they did not worship as did the Jews, v. 2.

Zerubbabel and Jeshua, speaking for the Jews, rightly turned down the offer of cooperation. Such cooperation with the heathen in a religious endeavor would have violated clear scriptural principles given elsewhere (e.g., Rom. 16:17; 2 Cor. 6:14). The Jews stated their intention to build the temple themselves as Cyrus had commanded them (1:2–4), v. 3.

2. Hindrances to the Work 4:4–23

a. Under Cyrus 4:4–5

As a result of that decision, the Samaritans opposed the efforts of the Jews to build. The phrases "weakened the hands" and "troubled them" are general overviews of the differing forms the opposition took. Both phrases refer to the efforts of the Samaritans to hinder the progress of the Jews in their work of building, v. 4.

The first opposition was legal in nature. The Samaritans hired "counsellors" at the Persian court to oppose the building.[54] This opposition continued through the remaining five years of Cyrus's reign (ca. 534–529 BC), through the reigns of his successors, and into the reign of Darius (522–486 BC). The result was that the temple construction temporarily came to a stop, v. 5.

b. Under Xerxes and Artaxerxes 4:6–23

To illustrate the kind of ongoing opposition the returnees experienced, Ezra cites two examples from his own lifetime. The references to Xerxes (v. 6, 486–465 BC) and Artaxerxes (v. 7, 465–425 BC) involve events that happened many years after the

[54]Among others, Blenkinsopp, p. 108, and Slotki, p. 131, interpret the first verb in 4:5 as meaning they bribed government officials to undermine the standing of the Jews in Palestine with the imperial government. Despite the acceptance of this view by many modern versions (e.g., CEV, ESV, NLT), the verb *sakar* (and *śakar* in Neh. 6:12–13, and 13:2) normally means "to hire." The meaning of "bribe" does not occur anywhere in the OT. The NASB, NIV, and NKJV translate it as "hired."

events recorded in 5:1–6:22. The emphasis here is topical, not a sequential history because the bulk of c. 4 (vv. 6–23) is a parenthesis that does not fit into the chronological flow of events Ezra is recounting. In this way, Ezra shows the continuing nature of the conflict between the Samaritans and the Jews.[55]

At the beginning of the reign of "Ahasuerus," the Hebrew form of the Persian *Khshayarsha* and the Greek *Xerxes*, who ruled Persia 486–465 BC, the Samaritans once again tried to disrupt the Jews' efforts to rebuild the city. They filed a formal written complaint, v. 6.[56]

Since nothing came of the earlier accusation, the Samaritans tried again when Artaxerxes (465–425 BC) ascended to the throne.[57] Bishlam, Mithredath, and Tabeel, joined by unnamed

---

[55]A. Philip Brown II, *Hope Amidst Ruin: A Literary and Theological Analysis of Ezra* (Greenville, SC: Bob Jones University Press, 2009), pp. 52–57, argues "that Ezra purposefully deviates from a strictly chronological presentation to develop a theme crucial to his message." He sees this as retrospective, prospective, narrative, and theological. (1) Retrospectively, it shows the relentless opposition of the people to Israel. (2) Prospectively, it puts the reader in sympathy with Israel, mitigating the negative response to the forced divorces of c. 10. It also gives background information to support the severe measures later taken by Ezra. (3) As narrative, compressing eighty years of opposition into c. 4 intensifies the darkness of the picture. By ordering the narrative so that the later incidents are juxtaposed with the encouraging reversal that he was about to recount in c. 5, he shows God overturning opposition and magnifies His control over history. This gives hope that the most recent opposition, though seemingly successful, will also prove futile. (4) Theologically, the record shows God's blessing on those who obey Him and His wrath on those who oppose Him.

[56]Debra Reid, *Esther: An Introduction and Commentary*, in *Tyndale Old Testament Commentaries*, vol. 13, ed. David G. Firth and Tremper Longman III (Downers Grove, IL: InterVarsity Press, 2008) and Robert Gordis, *Megillat Esther* (New York: The Rabbinical Assembly, 1974), p. 5, are typical of those who identify Ahasuerus as Xerxes. An older view identified him with Cambyses, the son of Cyrus. Linguistically, the name *Ahasuerus* relates better to *Xerxes*.

[57]Henry, p. 1041, and D. L. Emery, "Ezra 4—Is Josephus Right After All?" *JNWSL* 13 (1987): 33–44, identify both Ahasuerus (4:6) and Artaxerxes (4:7) as Cambyses. It is unlikely that both names refer to the same person. The view often held by older sources, e.g., *Unger's Bible Dictionary* (Chicago: Moody Press, 1967), p. 94, and Luck, p. 33. Pope, p. 26, identifies Artaxerxes with Pseudo-Smerdis, the usurper of the Persian throne. There is, however, no supporting evidence calling this king by the name *Artaxerxes*.

cohorts, accused the Jews of rebelling against him.[58] We know nothing more about these accusers. Their letter was written in "the Syrian tongue," i.e., in Aramaic, and "interpreted" in that language, probably meaning it was read aloud at the Persian court (cf. v. 18).[59] Beginning here (4:7) and continuing through 6:18, Ezra writes in Aramaic, which had become the trade language in that area of the world.

The anachronistic narrative in vv. 6–23 focuses on the building of Jerusalem's walls by the Jews. While nothing is said about this work elsewhere in Ezra, it is entirely possible during the fifty-eight years between the completion of the temple and the second return that the Jews attempted to improve their security by repairing the walls. Interference by the Samaritans prevented this until Nehemiah's work later.

Rehum the "chancellor" (or "lord"), apparently the second-in-command of the province, and Shimshai the "scribe," his secretary, wrote the letter to Artaxerxes, v. 8. A group of others joined Rehum and Shimshai in the letters. The names seem to reflect their national or city backgrounds before coming to Palestine. The Dinaites may have been an Armenian people from Dayan, near Cilicia in Asia Minor.[60] The Apharsathchites (also called Apharsachites, 5:6; 6:6) are unknown as are the Tarpelites and Apharsites.[61] The Archevites came from Erech, a city about 120 miles southeast of Babylon and also on the Euphrates River.

---

[58]Blenkinsopp, p. 111, and Kidner, p. 31, follow the translation of the LXX, which understands *Bishlam* as "in peace," a possible translation that has little support. The letter is not written "in peace" but as the opening salvo of a war against the Jews. The Vulgate treated *Bishlam* as a name. Many modern versions have likewise translated it as a name (NASB, NIV, ESV, GW).

[59]Myers, p. 32, understands the word *interpreted* (*tirgem*) as "translated," and relates it to the explanation given "for the benefit of the exiles who had returned." This is a possible view, but why would exiles who have lived their whole lives in an Aramaic environment need a translation? Since this is the only time *tirgem* occurs, it is not possible to be certain of the shade of meaning that we should give it. It is related to the Akkadian *targamannu*, "interpreter."

[60]Bowman, p. 600, identifies the Dinaites as "judges." This is a possible view although the name in this context seems related more to a location than a vocation.

[61]Keil, p. 66, understands the initial *alep* of *Apharsites* as prosthetic. The name therefore refers to the Persians. While this is possible, we cannot be dogmatic in the interpretation. The word occurs only here.

The Babylonians came from the nation of Babylon, not particularly the city. The Susanchites came from the region of Susiana, likely from its capital Susa (biblical Shushan), adjoining Babylon on its eastern border. The Dehavites are thought to be a Persian nomadic tribal people also known as Dal or Dahi. The Elamites came from the region of Elam, located east of the Tigris River on the Persian Gulf, v. 9.

The letter refers to the background of these people as being settled in the land by the "great and noble Asnapper" (better, "Osnapper") the Aramaic form of the name of the Assyrian king Ashur-banipal (669–626 BC).[62] They are "on this side the river" (better "across the river"), referring to the Euphrates River, which they crossed on their way to Palestine. The phrase "and at such a time" simply introduces what follows. Most modern translations omit it in the translation both here and in v. 11 (e.g., CEV, ESV, GNB, GW, NIV), v. 10.

Ezra now gives the content of the accusation. The Samaritans began by describing themselves as "servants" of the king. They were in the region "on this side the river" (again, "across the river"), v. 11. They described Jerusalem as "the rebellious and the bad city," saying the Jews had "set up the walls" of the city and had "joined the foundations" (better "repaired the foundations"). From the account given in Nehemiah, we know that the Jews did not build the walls until ca. 445 BC. There may have been enough work done by this time, however, to justify the accusation. The statement may also have been an exaggeration to support the claim that the Jews intended to rebel against the king, v. 12. The Samaritans warned the king that the Jews would stop paying "toll [*middâ*], tribute [*b^{e}lô*], and custom [*h^{a}lak*]" when they finished their work. The word *toll* (*middâ*) is related to the Akkadian *maddattu*, referring to taxes, tribute, or a fee." *Tribute* (*b^{e}lô*) is related to the Akkadian *biltu*, which was a load, burden or onus, and thus sometimes a tax or tribute. This is here likely a portion of the harvest, paid in kind to the Persian king. *Custom* (*h^{a}lak*) comes from the Aramaic verb *h^{a}lak*, "to go, walk." The noun refers to charges made for using

[62]Rawlinson, p. 53, identifies Asnapper as "an officer employed by Esarhaddon on this service." This is an older view that is not generally held today.

Persian roads. The lack of payment would "endamage the revenue of the kings," i.e., cut down the amount of money brought in to the Persian treasury, v. 13.

The phrase "we have maintenance" (*m^e^laḥ*) is better translated "we eat salt." This comes from "*the king's* palace [*hêkal*]." The expression is an idiom showing their reliance on and subsequent loyalty to the king.[63] They claimed that it was their concern about the king's honor that had led them to write, v. 14. They asked that the king have the "book of the records" searched to see the rebellious nature of the Jews. Their rebellion had caused Nebuchadnezzar to destroy the city, v. 15. If the king allowed the Jews to complete their building, he would "have no portion on this side the river" (again, "across the River"). The statement was an exaggeration. It did, however, heighten the sense of urgency in dealing with the Jews, v. 16.

Since Artaxerxes wanted to avoid rebellion in the empire, he accepted the accusation as true. He addressed Rehum, Shimshai, and their cohorts (cf. vv. 8–9) who were "beyond [or 'across'] the river." The phrase "Peace, and at such a time" is better simply "Peace." The phrase "and at such a time" may be omitted as simply introducing the next phrase, v. 17. One of the king's staff read the document to him, v. 18. In response, he commanded a search to be made as the Samaritans had asked. As expected, he found that in times past the Jews had rebelled against the Assyrian and Babylonian kings, v. 19. He found that powerful Jewish kings who had ruled Judah had forced other nations "beyond [or 'across'] the river" to pay "toll, tribute, and custom" to them (cf. v. 13), v. 20. He ordered that the Jews stop their building until such time as he gave them permission. Since the Persians could not alter past laws (Esther

---

[63]Rabinowitz, p. 124, follows the translation of Rashi, "we are desirous of ruining the Temple." This understands *m^e^laḥ*, "salt," as idiomatic of "ruin" from the sense of "sowing with salt" (Judg. 9:45). The word *hêkal* can mean either "palace" or "temple." This interpretation is possible. It is doubtful, however, that the Samaritans would take such a step on their own authority. They had earlier "hired counsellors" (v. 5) and written two letters accusing the Jews (vv. 6–7). In addition, they knew that the Jews had carried out a decree from the Persian king (v. 3). Why would they suddenly take a step that would go far beyond what they had earlier done?

1:19; Dan. 6:8–17), he phrased his decree in a way that would let him change his mind should this become desirable, v. 21. He urged the Samaritans to carry out his decree so that no damage would occur to him, v. 22.

As soon as the Samaritan leaders received the answer to their letter, they went to Jerusalem and forced the Jews to stop building the walls. With the force of law on their side, they now had the power to block the work of the Jews, v. 23.

c. Under Darius 4:24

The nonchronological positioning of v. 24 can cause confusion. Returning to the sequential account that was interrupted by the examples in vv. 6–23, Ezra now indicates that the opposition mentioned at the beginning of the chapter continued until the second year of Darius (520 BC), which was about seventeen years after the Samaritans had first "troubled them in building" and caused the work on the temple to stop (4:4–5).

The original decree of Cyrus had been in 538 BC; cf. 1:1–4. The returned remnant of the Jews had laid the foundation for the temple (cf. 3:1–3, 8–10), but no more. While there was opposition from the Samaritans, this was not a sufficient excuse for the failure to complete the building. Haggai 1:2–4 gives the real reason for the delay. The people had been more interested in building their own houses than in building the dwelling-place of God.

EZRA 5

With the passage of about seventeen years since the ending of work on the temple, the situation in Persia had changed. Cyrus the king and Cambyses his son had died. The usurper Pseudo-Smerdis was dead, perhaps by suicide. Darius, formerly the general of the Persian army, now ruled the empire. At that point God took action to make it possible for the nation once more to worship Him according to the Mosaic law.

5. Resumption of the Work 5:1–5

At that time (cf. Hag. 1:1; 2:1; Zech. 1:1), ca. 520 BC, God raised up Haggai and Zechariah to stir up the people to work on the temple once again. Haggai was known as a "prophet," one used by the Lord to declare His Word to the people. Zechariah was the "son of Iddo," with *son* used in the sense of descendant. His father was Berechiah, who in turn was the son of Iddo (Zech. 1:1). We know nothing of Berechiah. Iddo is called a "prophet" (Zech. 1:1), but we know nothing of his prophetic ministry. He is likely mentioned here because of his position. He is possibly the Iddo that returned from Babylon with Nehemiah (Neh. 12:4, 16). Both Haggai and Zechariah prophesied in the "name" of God, i.e., on behalf of God, and therefore spoke with His authority. The final phrase, "*even* unto them," is better translated "who was over them" (ESV, NASB, NIV, NLT). The phrase refers to Israel's relationship with God and to their responsibility to obey Him.

The book of Haggai gives some idea of the content of his preaching. He rebukes the people for their self-centeredness (Hag. 1:3–7). He urges them to gather wood for building the temple (1:8). He warns them of God's punishment (1:9–11). He encourages them with the knowledge that God is with them (2:3–5). He prophesies to them of future glory (2:6–9). He reminds them of God's past chastening (2:11–17) and promises future blessing (2:18–19). He prophesies the overthrow of the heathen and the future rule of Messiah, typified by Zerubbabel (2:21–23). Zechariah also mentions the building of the temple in his writing (Zech. 1:16; 4:9; 8:9). His writings, however, generally focus on themes that differ from his preaching, v. 1.

The preaching of Haggai and Zechariah roused Zerubbabel and Jeshua (Joshua) to lead the people again to continue their work of building the temple. From 4:24, we see that this took place in "the second year" of Darius, ca. 520 BC, sixteen or seventeen years after the original decree by Cyrus. The "prophets of God," an unknown group also engaged in a prophetic ministry, joined Haggai and Zechariah in stirring up the people to renewed work.

Haggai began his ministry on the first day of the sixth month (Hag. 1:1), the month Elul (mid-August to mid-September). Zechariah's ministry began two months after the first prophecy of Haggai (Zech. 1:1), in Bul (mid-October to mid-November).

From Haggai 1:12–15, we see that the renewed work on the temple began twenty-three days after Haggai's first prophecy. Some of this time, of course, would have been taken up with planning and securing supplies, v. 2.

The leaders in the nearby region were now "Tatnai" (better Tattenai), the governor "on this side the river" (cf. 4:10, "across the river"), and Shetharboznai. An early-sixth-century Akkadian document mentions a Tatennai who served as governor "across the river."[64] We know little of Tattenai and Shetharboznai except that they held leadership positions under the Persian king. They were Persian, not Samaritan, leaders. Initially, they and their "companions," representatives from other nations allied with the Samaritans (see 4:7, 9), asked who had authorized building the "house," the temple, and the "wall" (*ʾuššarnaʾ*). The word *ʾuššarnaʾ* is unclear. It may refer to the walls of the temple, the beams, paneling, or some other wooden portion of the building, v. 3.[65]

In the next phrase, the LXX translates the verb as though it were *ʾamarû*, "they said," rather than with the MT, *ʾamarnaʾ*, "we said," which makes little sense at this point. From the context, *ʾamarû* must be the right reading. They asked for the names of the men involved in the building project. The question implies that Tattenai and his associates planned to confine these people with a view toward stopping the work, v. 4. The "eye of their God," however, was watching over "the elders of the Jews," their leaders, so that the work continued. Unable to stop the work, Tattenai and his associates contacted Darius by letter while the Jews kept on building, v. 5.

---

[64]A. T. Olmstead, "Tattenai, Governor of 'Across the River,'" *Journal of Near Eastern Studies* 44 (January 1944): 46.

[65]Myers, pp. 42–43, translates the term as "wooden structure," which he thinks may include the woodwork, wooden beams, and planks. Batten, p. 131, tentatively suggests "foundation." Bowman, p. 608, suggests it refers either to supplies for building or equipment or furnishings for the completed temple. Ryle, p.69, draws on 1 Esd. 6:4 and translates it as "roof." Rabinowitz, p. 132, follows Rashi in translating it as "walls." The Vulgate also uses *muros*, "walls." The Akkadian *ašru* is "shrine, sanctuary" but this merely repeats the thought of "place" or "house." Contemporary versions differ. The ESV, NASB, and NIV uses "structure," the GNB "equip," GW and NKJV "walls." We can only guess at the meaning.

6. Inquiry to Darius 5:6–17

The letter was written by Tattenai, Shetharboznai, and their "companions." The "companions" are identified here as "Apharsachites . . . on this side [or, 'beyond'] the River." As in 4:9, all we can say is that this name reflects officials of some kind, possibly governors over various areas within the province.[66] Since this letter was from Persian leaders, they moderated it substantially from the prior accusation by the Samaritans. It was more objective and contained the information given by the Jews regarding the original decree from Cyrus. It seems to have been a genuine attempt to find out the truth behind the building, v. 6.

After the customary salutation wishing peace to Darius (cf. 4:17; 7:12), v. 7, the Persian leaders related the nature of the building. It was a large temple for "the great God," a title showing respect to Israel's God but not acknowledging Him as the God of gods. This temple was made with "great stones" (*ʾeben gᵉlal*) and "timber," probably wooden beams set in the stone to support the upper part of the building. The phrase *ʾeben gᵉlal* is lit. "stones of rolling." These were stones too large to be carried readily. They therefore required rollers to move them into position.[67] Since the stones were so large, it is likely that the three courses of stone (cf. 6:4) served as a foundation for further building with wood. The project was going "fast on" (*ʾosparnaʾ*, better "diligently"), v. 8. Some versions translate *ʾosparnaʾ* with a sense of speed, e.g., CEV, GNB. The idea of diligence is more appropriate here than speed. They asked who had authorized the building of the house and "walls" (*ʾušarnaʾ*, see v. 3), v. 9, and for the names of the leaders so that Darius would know. The fact that they gave no names here suggests that the Jewish leaders had not cooperated, v. 10.

The letter reported the response of the Jews (that they served the "God of heaven and earth"). They were building a place for worship to replace the one built by Solomon, "a great king of Israel," v. 11. The sin of the people had caused their God to give

[66]Luck, p. 40, suggests that the Apharsachites were Tattenai's bodyguard. This is a possible but speculative view.

[67]Rabinowitz, p. 134, notes a rabbinical view that "the stones were small and could have been rolled with relative ease." Such stones, however, would not serve well as the foundation for the temple. It is more likely that the Jews used some of the large original stones for the foundation.

them into the "hand," i.e., power, of Nebuchadnezzar. He had destroyed the earlier temple and carried the people captive into Babylon, v. 12. When Cyrus had become king over Babylon, he issued a decree that the Jews should build their temple again.

This reference to a decree by Cyrus caused Tattenai to act carefully. Rather than opposing the Jews outright, he proceeded cautiously lest he directly defy a decree of the Persian king, v. 13. Nebuchadnezzar had taken gold and silver vessels from Israel's temple and had placed them in "the temple of Babylon," likely the Temple of Esagila. Cyrus had returned these vessels to the Jews. He had given them to "Sheshbazzar," Zerubbabel, appointed the governor over Palestine (cf. Zech. 4:9) by Cyrus, v. 14. Cyrus had authorized Zerubbabel to take the vessels to Jerusalem and to rebuild the temple "in his place," the place it formerly had occupied, v. 15.

The summary of the building is apparently Tattenai's. He was not aware of the delay and so gave his version of the work. Sheshbazzar, i.e., Zerubbabel, had laid the foundation before. The work had continued since that time but the building was "not finished," v. 16. The name "treasure house" (from the root *gnz*) is another name for the "house of the rolls," 6:1. Although "treasure house" is an appropriate translation, it was more accurately a repository for valuables, including important documents. (The word also occurs in 6:1 and 7:20, with related words appearing in 1 Chron. 28:11; Esther 3:9; 4:7; and Ezek. 27:24.) Tattenai also asked Darius to give them direction as to how they should handle the matter, v. 17.

EZRA 6

D. Continuance of the Work 6:1–22

1. Search by Darius 6:1–5

Darius ordered a search for the decree of Cyrus. This was done in "the house of the rolls [lit. "books"]," the place where "treasures" (*gnz*, see 5:17), here referring to important government documents, were "laid up" (or "deposited," *n^{a}ḥat*).[68] The search was made in "Babylon," used generally here for the full scope of the empire.[69] The search was probably conducted in all places where official documents were stored. Archaeologists have found similar collections of governmental documents preserved on baked clay tablets at Nineveh and Babylon, v. 1. The "roll" (or "scroll") containing the decree was found at "Achmetha" (*ʾaḥ-m^{e}taʾ*), also known as Ecbatana, almost two hundred miles north of Shushan, in the region belonging to Media.[70] This was one of the places from which the Persian kings governed. They ruled from Babylon for the seven coldest months, and then moved to Shushan for three months in the spring and to Ecbatana for two months in the summer.[71] Darius moved his court to both Shushan and Babylon but kept Ecbatana as a summer "palace." The "province of the Medes" refers to the area previously ruled by the Median kings. It included the area south of the Caspian Sea down to the Persian Gulf and to the east of Babylon, v. 2.

Darius recounted the details of the decree to give Tattenai the guidance he needed. The decree came "in the first year of Cyrus the king," i.e., in his first year after conquering Babylon (cf.

---

[68]Rawlinson, p. 79, speculates that the books were kept in an underground chamber since the verb *n^{a}ḥat* means "to descend." While the root *nḥt* does have this meaning, in the *haphel* theme the sense is better "to deposit, store," coming from the idea of laying something down. This is consistently the case in the OT (e.g., Ezra 5:15; 6:1, 5). In Dan. 4:13, 23 (*peal*) and in Dan. 5:20 (*hophal*), we see the root sense.

[69]Fensham, p. 86, suggests that the search began at Babylon, then moved to Ecbatana, where the decree was found. This is also a possible view. The Aramaic is *babel*. Strictly speaking, this refers to the city. Since the city is the location of the king, however, it may as well represent the entire province. Since the Persian search turned up the records at Ecbatana, it is clear that the search was not limited to the city. The translations vary. GNB, GW, NASB, and NIV translate *babel* as "Babylon," while CEV, ESV, NLT, and RSV use "Babylonia."

[70]Rabinowitz, p. 138, cites the view of Ralbag and Ibn Ezra that *ʾaḥmetaʾ* should be translated "pouch," referring to "a container used for storing, books, documents and letters." This derives the word from *ḥemet*, a Hebrew word meaning "skin" or "waterskin." It occurs only in Gen. 21:14, 15, 19, and Hab. 2:15, all translated "bottle." It is unlikely that we should relate the Aramaic word here to its Hebrew cognate. Since we know that Achmetha was a Persian capital, it is reasonable that a search of the records there would find the previous decree.

[71]Xenophon, *Cyropaedia* 8.6.22.

1:1–4). Cyrus decreed that the temple where the Jews sacrificed to their God should be built with strong foundations. The height and width should be sixty cubits. This was twice the height of Solomon's temple and three times its width (cf. 1 Kings 6:2). He did not mention the length, apparently assuming that it would remain the same as its former length. Josephus, *Antiquities* 11.4.6, gives this temple's dimensions as sixty cubits high by sixty cubits wide. Other biblical dimensions also vary (e.g., 2 Chron. 3:4), but we are not always certain as to what is being measured. The dimensions in 1 Kings may be the internal dimensions while other references may be external. Some dimensions may be of the temple itself while others include attached outbuildings (1 Kings 6:5) or upper chambers (2 Chron. 3:8), v. 3.

There were to be three courses of "great stones" (*ʾeben gᵉlal*, see 5:8), then a "row" of wood. We are not sure what this pattern means. It may mean to repeat the pattern throughout the height of the building.[72] This view faces the difficulty of placing large stones over a layer of wood. One rabbinical interpretation sees three rows of stone, side by side, with the interior covered with wood paneling. First Esdras 6:25 suggests that it refers to three layers of stone with a layer of wood on top.[73] Josephus, *Antiquities* 11.4.6, described the rebuilt temple as having "three edifices of polished stone, and one edifice of stone of their own country." The most likely view understands three courses of stone, with the "row" of timber referring to the entire upper part of the building. The description is similar to that of 1 Kings 6:36, where "three rows of hewed stone, and a row of cedar beams" describes the construction of the wall surrounding the inner court of the temple. That wall is possibly in view here also.[74] The expense of the building was to come from the king's treasury, referring to money collected by various taxes in the region, v. 4. Cyrus also decreed

[72]Several translations adopt this view, e.g., CEV, GNB, and NLT. The CB, ESV, GW, NASB, and NIV translate it similarly to the KJV.

[73]Fensham, p. 88, and Rabinowitz, p. 140, adopt the idea that the Jews paneled the interior wall.

[74]Bowman, p. 616; Ryle, p. 77.

that the vessels taken by Nebuchadnezzar from the first temple should be returned to the Jews for use in this temple, v. 5.[75]

2. Decree by Darius 6:6–12

Having found the original decree, Darius issued his own decree to authorize the work. His motivation may have come from either or both of two sources. He may have been following the Persian custom that the king's decree could not be changed (cf. Dan. 6:8; Esther 1:19; 8:8). He may also have been seeking the personal blessing of Israel's gods on himself and his family (cf. v. 10). Whatever his motive, he addressed Tattenai, Shethar-boznai, and their "companions" (cf. 4:7, 9; 5:3). Of these associates, he mentions specifically only the "Apharsachites," who apparently governed various areas on the other side of the Euphrates River. He tells them to "be . . . far from thence," i.e., to avoid contacting the Jews with the intention of causing trouble, v. 6. They should "let the work . . . alone." The Jewish leaders were to be allowed to build their house for worship, v. 7.

The Persian leaders were to pay whatever expenses the Jews incurred in building their temple. They could draw on the annual "tribute" (*middâ*, see 4:13) paid to the Persian ruler "on this side [better 'from across'] the river." Ezra 7:20 indicates that this was kept in a "treasure house." They were to pay this tribute "forthwith" (*ᵓosparnaᵓ*, better "diligently," see 5:8). This would let the work go on without hindrance, v. 8. This included furnishing the daily sacrifices to the Jewish priests. The Jews offered "bullocks" (or "oxen"), rams, and lambs in sin offerings, trespass offerings, burnt offerings, and peace offerings. They offered wheat, salt, and "oil" (or "olive oil") in the meat (better "meal") offerings. The drink offerings of wine often accompanied other offerings (e.g., Exod. 29:38–40; Lev. 23:16–18). These were to be given "according to the appointment [better 'word'] of the

[75]Maxwell, p. 24, notes that Cyrus's decree in 1:2–4 makes no mention of the financial aid given to the people. He concludes that there are two editions of the decree, "one for circulation and the other for officials only." Cyrus's decree does provide for financial support, however, coming from those Jews who remained in Babylon. Possibly the records given in Ezra simply summarize the original decree, or each record in Ezra focuses on different aspects of the decree.

priests," v. 9. The Jews were to offer their sacrifices that brought "sweet savours," i.e., a pleasant smell as from incense (cf. Dan. 2:46), to "the God of heaven." At the same time, Darius asked that they make special prayers for him and for his sons.

While this request from Darius was selfish, it is still appropriate that God's people pray for their leaders (Jer. 29:7; 1 Tim. 2:1–2). First Maccabees 7:33 and 12:11 (as well as 2 Maccabees 3:32) show that the Jews followed this practice. Josephus, *Antiquities* 12.2.6, also refers to sacrifices being offered on behalf of the king, v. 10.

Darius clarified his decree. Anyone who violated his orders would have timbers pulled from his house.[76] These would be set up so that he could "be hanged thereon," and his house was to be torn down. From what archaeological evidence we have, hanging here refers to impaling the offender on a sharpened wooden post (cf. Esther 7:9–10). Ancient records from Egypt, Assyria, Persia, and India describe impalement as a form of execution practiced in those countries. Herodotus refers to execution by impalement.[77] An Assyrian relief from the palace of Sennacherib, now in the British Museum, shows the impalement of Jewish captives taken at Lachish. In addition, the homes of these transgressors would be razed and "made a dunghill" (*n*ᵉ*walîû*). This word occurs again in Daniel 2:5 and 3:29. It describes houses being left as heaps of refuse. Public degradation of a person's possessions after his death was a way of showing his disgrace. Second Kings 10:27 illustrates this practice, v. 11. Darius invoked a curse on anyone violating his edict, calling on Israel's God to destroy anyone who would "alter" this decree. This curse would apply broadly. The enemies of the Jews were not to interfere with the building of the temple. The king's decree

[76]Batten, p. 146, states, "The idea is not to punish the one who interferes with the execution of the decree, but the one who would venture to change its terms." Interfering with the execution of the decree, however, would have been the equivalent of changing its terms. The purpose of the decree was to bring about the construction of the temple. Interfering with that purpose opposed the purpose of the king in making the decree.

[77]Herodotus, *Histories*, trans. A. D. Godley (Cambridge, MA: Harvard University Press, 1963), 3.159; 4.43.

was to be carried out "with speed" (*ʾasparnaʾ*, better "diligently," see 5:8), v. 12.

3. Completion of the Temple 6:13–18

Tattenai, the governor "beyond the river," Shetharboznai, and their "companions" (cf. 4:7, 9; 5:3) did, in fact, carry out the instructions in Darius's letter "speedily" (*ʾasparnaʾ*, better "diligently"). This cooperation by the government undoubtedly helped the Jews complete the temple earlier than would otherwise have been possible, v. 13. The "elders of the Jews," the leaders among the people, "builded" primarily through their leadership but also by helping as they were physically able. The prophesying of Haggai and Zechariah stirred the people into action. They finished their building as "Cyrus, and Darius, and Artaxerxes king of Persia" had commanded. We know about the decrees by Cyrus and Darius. The Artaxerxes mentioned here is Artaxerxes Longimanus, who ruled 465–425 BC.[78] Although he initially stopped the work on the walls of Jerusalem (4:17–22), he later showed favor to the Jews by allowing the second return and providing support for their temple worship. Ezra 7:11–26 summarizes his decree, v. 14.

The Jews finished building on the "third day of the month Adar," the twelfth month of the Jewish calendar and equivalent to our mid-February to mid-March. This was in "the sixth year of the reign of Darius" (516 BC), about twenty-one years after the original decree by Cyrus (ca. 536 BC) and a little less than four and one-half years after Darius's decree (Hag. 1:1, 14–15), v. 15.[79]

The Jews rejoiced at the dedication of the newly built temple, v. 16. They offered sacrifices that were meager in comparison to those offered by Solomon at the dedication of the first temple (1 Kings 8:63). When we consider, however, the reduced number and prosperity of the people, the sacrifice was adequate. The Lord looks at the attitude of the heart, not the size of the offering

[78]Since Ezra served into the time of Nehemiah, he includes the work on the walls authorized by Artaxerxes. Ezra does not always confine himself to a strict chronological discussion. See p. 46, n. 55.

[79]Second Maccabees 1:18–23 records that Nehemiah "built the temple and the altar." The context of this passage, however, is fanciful, having Nehemiah bring fire out of muddy water. This makes the accuracy of the account suspect.

(cf. 2 Cor. 8:12). In addition to the freewill offerings, there was a sin offering for the twelve tribes. This hints that representatives of all of the tribes were then living in the land (cf. also 8:35), v. 17.

Jeshua (Joshua), fulfilling his high priestly role, divided the priests into their twenty-four courses (cf. 1 Chron. 24:4–19). He divided the Levites into their groups as well (1 Chron. 23:3–24). These men carried out their duties at the temple as described in the "book of Moses," the Pentateuch. This verse ends the Aramaic section that began in 4:8, v. 18.

4. Restoration of the Ritual 6:19–22

The first feast kept by the Jews who returned with Zerubbabel was the Passover. It was appropriate for them to celebrate Passover since it was the first feast of the royal year (Exod. 12:2–3). Ezra returns briefly to using Hebrew rather than the Aramaic in which he wrote 4:8–6:18. He will adopt it again in 7:12–26, where he records the decree made by Artaxerxes, and then return to Hebrew for the remainder of the book, v. 19.

The priests and Levites first purified themselves, making themselves ritually clean.[80] This qualified them to make sacrifices for the people and for other priests who had not ritually prepared themselves. They killed the "passover [sacrifices]" (Num. 28:16–25) for the people, v. 20. Not only did the returned Jews keep the feast but so did "all such as had separated themselves to them," proselytes to Judaism from among the heathen. These abandoned "the filthiness of the heathen" in order to worship the Lord, v. 21. All kept the week-long "feast of unleavened bread," the feast that immediately follows the Passover (Exod. 12:15–20). They did this with a "joyful" heart. The Lord had moved "the king of Assyria" to help them finish the building of the temple. This is the only place that the title *king of Assyria* refers to the Medo-Persian ruler. We do not know if this means Cyrus, Darius, or Artaxerxes, all of whom had contributed in

[80]Rawlinson, p. 88, translates the first sentence of v. 20 as "the priests purified themselves" while the Levites "were all pure, as one man." On this basis he suggests that the Levites were more upright in heart than the priests. The translation is possible, but it is not likely. While the accents are not conclusive, they do show that the Jews took "priests and the Levites" together. The NASB, NIV, and NKJV translate it similarly to the KJV.

some way to the rebuilding of the temple. In any case, it must refer to the region once ruled by the Assyrian enemies of Israel but now ruled by the Persian king. This freedom from the Assyrian domination had let the Jews return to Palestine, where they could worship God once more in His temple, v. 22.

EZRA 7

The final four chapters of the book focus on the second return from Babylon and the ministry of Ezra. In contrast to the longer period of c. 1–6, about eighty years, this section covers only a single year. Ezra began his journey to Jerusalem on "the first day of the first month" (7:9). The record (in this book) of Ezra's ministry ends exactly one year later on "the first day of the first month" (10:17). Nehemiah 8 and 12, however, mention his later ministry.

II. Ministry of Ezra 7:1–10:44

A. Second Return from Babylon 7:1–8:36

1. Background of Ezra 7:1–10

Verses 1–5 give an abbreviated genealogy of Ezra. From several sources we see that the record omits some generations. The genealogy from Nahshon (prince in the time of Aaron, Num. 1:7; 2:3) to Zerubbabel (1 Chron. 2:10*b*–15; 3:5, 10–19) has twenty-seven generations. Ezra's genealogy over roughly this same period shows only sixteen generations. Verse 1 calls Ezra the "son of" Seraiah, who was the high priest at the time of Israel's fall to Babylon. Seraiah was taken prisoner and brought to Nebuchadnezzar, who sentenced him to death (Jer. 52:24–27). Since this took place ca. 586 BC, about 130 years earlier, there was enough time for several additional generations to have lived. There are six names omitted between Azariah and Meraioth, v. 3 (cf. 1 Chron. 6:7–10). The omission of names from genealogies in the Bible is not unusual (cf. Matt. 1:8*b,* where the names of Ahaziah, Joash, and Amaziah are omitted; see 1 Chron. 3:11–12). The phrase "son of" often means "descendant of." This genealogy is complete enough to show Ezra's qualifications as the spiritual leader of the people.[81]

About fifty-eight years after the dedication of the temple, Ezra led the second return from Babylon to Palestine during the reign of Artaxerxes (465–425 BC), sometimes called Artaxerxes I or Longimanus.[82] Verse 8 places this event in 458 BC. Ezra was the "son" (or descendant) of Seraiah, high priest at the time of Zedekiah (2 Kings 25:18). Since the narrative does not indicate that Ezra held the office of high priest, and since the record does not give the names of the intervening generations between Ezra and Seraiah, it is likely that Ezra was descended from a younger son of Seraiah.

Seraiah was the "son" of Azariah (1 Chron. 6:13–14), who in turn was the "son" of Hilkiah, high priest in the reign of Josiah, at the time of Josiah's revival (1 Chron. 6:13; cf. 2 Kings 22:1–23:15), v. 1. Hilkiah was the "son" of Shallum (also called Meshullam, 1 Chron. 6:13; 9:11; Neh. 11:11), also a high priest. Shallum was the "son" of Zadok (1 Chron. 6:12; 9:11; Neh. 11:11) who was the "son" of Ahitub (1 Chron. 6:7–8, 12), v. 2.

[81]Blenkinsopp, p. 136, considers the genealogy to be "a fiction designed to convey the message that Ezra's function with respect to the law and the cult continued that of the preexilic priesthood." Bowman, p. 622, similarly describes "the genealogy . . . as an unhistorical reflection of the conviction . . . that so important a person as Ezra must have had a significant ancestry." The comments are ludicrous. The Jews would not have accepted Ezra's priestly leadership without the knowledge that he had the right to lead them spiritually. Othniel Margalith, "The Political Role of Ezra as Persian Governor," *ZAW* 98, no. 1 (1986): 110–12, describes Ezra as a political leader, sent by Artaxerxes to govern Judea after the conquest of Egypt by the Greeks in 460 BC. The Persians needed a strong Judea to counter any further hostile moves by the Greeks. While Ezra may have had some political responsibilities, the book of Ezra portrays him as a spiritual leader. The fact that the city walls still lay in ruins thirteen years later (Neh. 1:3) indicates that Ezra did very little to strengthen Judea against any potential foe.

[82]Batten, p. 303, identifies Artaxerxes as Artaxerxes II, king of Persia 404–358 BC. This would place the events of the chapter into the intertestamental period, too late to agree with the account of Ezra in the book of Nehemiah, which even Batten places in the reign of Artaxerxes I. After examining the biblical and extrabiblical evidence, J. Stafford Wright, *The Date of Ezra's Coming to Jerusalem* (1947; repr., London: The Tyndale Press, 1958), p. 6, concludes that Ezra came to Jerusalem in 458 BC. As part of this evidence, a letter from Elephantine, an island in the Nile River near Aswan, written to the governor of Judea ca. 408 BC mentions "Sanballat, the governor of Samaria."

Ahitub was the "son" of Amariah (1 Chron. 6:7, 11),[83] who was the "son" of Azariah (1 Chron. 6:11), who was the "son" of Meraioth (1 Chron. 6:7), v. 3. Meraioth was the "son" of Zerahiah (1 Chron. 6:6) who was the "son" of Uzzi (1 Chron. 6:6). Josephus relates that he "received the priesthood," i.e., the high priesthood (*Antiquities* 5.11.5). Uzzi was the "son" of Bukki (1 Chron. 6:5), v. 4, who was the son of Abishua, the fourth high priest of Israel (1 Chron. 6:5). Abishua was the son of Phinehas, the third high priest (1 Chron. 6:4) who was the son of Eleazar, the second high priest (1 Chron. 6:4), who was the son of Aaron, the "chief priest," i.e., first high priest of the nation (1 Chron. 6:3), v. 5.

Ezra returned to Palestine from "Babylon." As in 6:1 (and 7:9), the word *babel* refers to the city of Babylon but may also be taken as representing the nation of Babylonia. The variations among modern translations reflect this possibility. The CEV, ESV, GNB, and NRSV translate it as "Babylonia." The CB, NASB, NIV, and NLT translate it as "Babylon." Because of Ezra's access to the king, it is more likely that the city is in view here.

Ezra had been a "ready scribe" in Babylon, knowledgeable in the law and therefore concerned with the teaching, preservation, and transmission of God's Word. This had been given to Israel by God Himself and was therefore of supreme importance. We do not know the details of Ezra's request that he be allowed to lead a group returning to Palestine. Verses 12–26 give the decree that he must have solicited from the king. Ezra gives full credit to the Lord for leading the king to grant his request. The statement that this occurred "according to the hand of the Lord his God upon him" is characteristic of Ezra (in varying forms, it appears elsewhere in 7:9, 28; 8:18, 22, 31). In every case it indicates the power of God giving success to His servant, v. 6.

Ezra led a group of exiles returning to Jerusalem. The group included "the children of Israel," ordinary people, (cf. 2:2–35), priests (cf. 2:36–39) and Levites (cf. 2:40–42), singers (cf. 2:41), porters (cf. 2:42), and Nethinim (see the discussion of 2:43). These groups, which are the same categories mentioned in the

[83]Josephus, *Antiquities* 8.1.3, calls Amariah by the name of Arophaeus.

original return of the Jews under Zerubbabel's direction (cf. 2:70), returned in the "seventh year of the king," 458 BC, v. 7.

Ezra arrived in Jerusalem in the "fifth month," the month Ab, roughly mid-July to mid-August today. This is also in the king's seventh year, v. 8. The group left Babylon "on the first day of the first month," Abib, corresponding to mid-March to mid-April today. From 8:15, 21, 31, we see that they journeyed only to the river Ahava, either an unknown tributary of the Euphrates or an irrigation canal, where they waited for twelve days. The approximately eight-hundred-mile trip then took the rest of the four months. Excluding the twelve days at Ahava and assuming they did not travel on the Sabbath, the group of returnees averaged a little over eight miles each day. In view of the size of the group, this is a reasonable distance for daily travel.

The group completed the trip safely "according to the good hand of his God upon [Ezra]." We do not know what this refers to. Statements in 8:21–23 and 31 support the idea that it indicates that they were spared any attacks by marauders, v. 9. The real key to their experiencing God's favor lay in Ezra's preparation and goal. He sought to know God's Word, to obey God's Word, and to teach others the "statutes and judgments" of God's Word. While there may be a distinction between "statutes" (*ḥoq*) and "judgments" (*mišpaṭ*) at times, the two words occur together thirty-six times to summarize all of the responsibilities of Israel under God's law. The phrase has that general sense here, v. 10.

2. Decree of Artaxerxes 7:11–28

The king, Artaxerxes Longimanus (see v. 1), gave the decree to Ezra, who is called both a "priest" and a "scribe." His genealogy in vv. 1–5 shows his qualifications for both positions. The text records his priestly work in c. 9–10 and in Nehemiah 8 and 12. He was "a scribe of the words of the commandments of the Lord and of his statutes." This statement by the king likely indicates that Ezra had been active at the court. The king therefore had some knowledge of him and his ministry among the people. It is possible that Ezra had served as an advisor to the king in matters relating to the Jews.

Jewish tradition credits Ezra with introducing the square Aramaic form of the Hebrew alphabet. The Talmud, *Sanhedrin* 21*b*, claims that the Torah was originally given to Israel in Hebrew written in Hebrew script but was later revealed during Ezra's day in the Aramaic language using Aramaic characters. Ezra supposedly adapted the Aramaic script to represent the sounds of spoken Hebrew, and this became the Hebrew writing system still in use today.[84]

The description of his ministry in the books of Ezra and Nehemiah show his influence on the people, v. 11. Since the passage once more records a decree of the king, 7:12–26 gives the record in Aramaic. Artaxerxes announces himself as the "king of kings." This is a common title used by the Persian kings, reflecting their position as emperors ruling over numerous smaller nations, each with its own king. He begins by calling Ezra a "priest" and a "scribe of the law [*dat*] of the God of heaven."[85] This recognizes Ezra's spiritual leadership in Israel, important even though the decree appoints Ezra as the civil leader of the people. First Esdras 9:40, 49 refers to Ezra as the "chief priest," and Josephus, *Antiquities* 11.5.1, calls him the "principal priest." These overstate the position of Ezra. Nothing in the OT makes him more than a godly priest who served as a civil leader and a spiritual reformer. His appointment by Artaxerxes gave him the authority needed for these responsibilities.

The phrase "perfect *peace*" (*g^emîr*) is awkward. The verb *g^emar* means "to complete." The participle *g^emîr*, found here,

[84]Rabinowitz, pp. 158–59, records the Jewish tradition that Ezra "counted the letters of the *Torah* . . . thereby preserving for posterity a precise count of its contents. . . . Similarly, he counted the words of all of the Books of Scripture. . . . In addition, Ezra counted . . . each of the statutes of the Oral tradition." This tradition is an attempt to justify the scribal practice of counting the words and letters of each text. There is nothing in Scripture, however, to support that view.

[85]Throntveit, pp. 43–44, argues that *dat* refers to a royal decree, not to the Jewish law. He further takes Ezra's title of scribe as a "foreshadowing of his scribal activity in Nehemiah 8:1." He concludes that Ezra's "mission was secular in nature." This argument fails when we examine the word *dat* in Ezra. It occurs only in this chapter (vv. 12, 14, 21, 25, 26 [2x]). In five of these occurrences, it is related to God. The last verse draws a contrast between the *dat* of God and the *dat* of the king. The word is clearly not limited to secular decrees, and Ezra's mission is not secular in nature. Throntveit attributes the theological emphases of the narrative to the unknown compiler who edited the materials included in the book. The view, of course, assumes the existence of an editor, an assumption for which there is no evidence.

most naturally serves as a verb to the phrase "God of heaven," i.e., "the law which the God of heaven completed."[86] The phrase "and at such a time [*keᶜenet*, see 4:10]," better "and now," serves to introduce the next verse, v. 12. The decree gives permission to the Jewish people at Babylon together with the priests and Levites to go to Jerusalem with Ezra, v. 13.

The king and "his seven counsellors" authorized the decree. Esther 1:13–14 describes the "seven princes" as men who "knew the times." This suggests that they were skilled in astrology (cf. Isa. 47:13; Dan. 2:27; 5:15). Herodotus 3.83–84 refers to the seven men who had access to the king. Josephus, *Antiquities* 2.6.1, also mentions them. Ezra is to "inquire concerning Judah and Jerusalem," using as his standard "the law of [his] God," the revealed Word in which Ezra was trained. Since the focus of the command concerns the temple ritual, the "law of thy God" refers here to the Pentateuch, where guidance for the temple ritual appears. It is reasonable that Ezra was to see that the worship at Jerusalem was carried out properly and would make a report back to the king of general conditions there, v. 14.

Further, Ezra was to carry "silver and gold" given by the king and his counselors to Israel's God who dwells "in Jerusalem." This reflects the general conception of localized gods held by the Babylonians. The gift was likely given to secure the blessing of Israel's God on them, v. 15. In addition, Ezra was given the right to solicit "all the silver and gold," given as a "freewill offering," from those Jews who remained behind in the nation of Babylon. This was to be used "for the house of their God" in Jerusalem, v. 16. Ezra could use the money to purchase various offerings "speedily" (*ʾosparnaʾ*, better "diligently," i.e., carefully, see 5:8) for the temple. These included animals for the blood sacrifices, grain

[86]Keil, p. 97, and Ryle, p. 93, relate *gemîr* back to *scribe* and make Ezra a "perfect scribe." It is unlikely, however, that Ezra would have described himself this way. In addition, several words intervene between *gemîr* and *scribe* so that a direct relationship is less likely. Fensham, p. 104, translates *gemîr* as "total contents" and connects it to the following *keᶜenet*; "its total contents are as follows." This is a difficult paraphrase to accept since *keᶜenet* is introduced with a *waw* to signal a new thought. Blenkinsopp, p. 148, understands it "as a conventional contraction for the usual greeting formula." This is speculative. Since the word does not occur elsewhere, there is no support for the view.

for the "meat" (better "meal") offerings, and wine for the drink offerings. The thought is clearly that Ezra should follow the worship ritual of Israel, v. 17. Any gold and silver that remained could be used in other ways "after the will of [his] God," i.e., in connection with the worship of God, v. 18. Additionally, Ezra received "vessels" to use in the worship of God. Since Cyrus had already returned the temple vessels, 1:7–11, these were given in addition. Perhaps Artaxerxes wanted to insure that the worship of Israel's God was done in a worthy manner. He would thus gain greater merit with Israel's God, v. 19. Ezra also received the authority to request additional aid from the "king's treasure house," referring to the one located in Palestine as in 6:8–9, v. 20.

Artaxerxes also ordered the treasurers "beyond [or 'across,' cf. 4:10] the river," on the other side of the Euphrates, to give "speedily" (*ʾosparnaʾ*, better "diligently," see 5:8) to Ezra whatever he required. As in v. 12, he recognized Ezra as "the scribe of the law of the God of heaven," v. 21. He limited the aid to 100 talents of silver, a weighed amount of silver of a little more than 4½ tons. Ezra was permitted to draw up to 100 measures of wheat (about 625 bushels), 100 baths of wine (a little more than 600 gallons), and 100 baths of oil (again a little more than 600 gallons). In addition, he could request as much salt as he needed since salt could be produced in abundance from the deposits around the Dead Sea. These gifts would come from tribute paid to Assyria from that part of the world and stored in Palestine, v. 22. Whatever Ezra's God commanded was to be "diligently done" so that the temple worship could be carried on. The question "why should there be wrath against the realm of the king and his sons" gives the reasoning behind the decree. Artaxerxes wanted the favor of Israel's God for himself and his descendants, not opposition, v. 23.

In addition to these gifts and the freedom from taxation, no "toll, tribute, or custom" (see 4:13) could be imposed on the religious leaders of Israel. Once more, Artaxerxes was trying to gain favor with Israel's God. The use of the plural *we* is simply the royal prerogative as the king speaks for the nation, v. 24.[87]

[87]Rawlinson, p. 111, suggests that the plural pronoun refers to Artaxerxes "and his successors" or that the king "had asked and obtained the assent and consent of his council." It is unlikely that the king would have attempted to

The king gave Ezra the right to act according to the divine "wisdom of [Ezra's] God" that was "in [his] hand." This idiomatically describes Ezra's ability to apply God's Word to specific situations. He was to appoint "magistrates [*šᵉpaṭ*] and judges [*dayyanîn*]" to assist him in this work. We cannot make a clear distinction between *šᵉpaṭ* and *dayyanîn*.[88] These words occur only here in the Aramaic portions of the OT. Both words occur more often in Hebrew. The word *dîn* in both its verbal and noun forms refers to aspects of judgment. The word *šapaṭ*, however, has an additional component of administration. Since we do not have enough of a sample, we cannot say certainly if this distinction carries over into Aramaic, but it is certainly possible.

The qualification for these offices was that the men needed to know God's Word. They could then apply it to the various disputes that came before them. These men would act with legal power in Palestine "beyond the river," west of the Mesopotamian Valley. The king charged Ezra with the responsibility of teaching other judges, who lacked knowledge of the divine law. All of this is in keeping with the Persian view of localized gods. Artaxerxes regarded Israel's God as the supreme authority in that land, v. 25. These men had full authority to execute judgment "speedily" (*ʾosparnaʾ*, better "diligently"), to put to death, or to banish, fine, or imprison. This verse ends the second major Aramaic section of the book (7:12–26), v. 26.

Ezra reverts to Hebrew again, appropriate as he records a doxology of praise, giving thanks to God for giving Artaxerxes the desire to "beautify" the temple, i.e., to bring it into a state worthy of the God it served, v. 27. Further, he recognizes the "mercy" (or "loyal love," *ḥesed*, see 3:11) given him by the king

---

bind his successors to a decree of this nature or that he would have included his council as authorizing his decree.

[88]See Robert Baker Girdlestone, *Synonyms of the Old Testament* (Grand Rapids: Wm. B. Eerdmans, 1951), p. 252. *TWOT*, vol. 1, p. 188, notes that *dîn* is "poetic, probably also an archaic and more elegant term." Since both words occur early in Genesis and in non-poetic contexts, this conclusion is open to question. Rabinowitz, p. 165, cites the view that the phrase "magistrates and judges" refers to "the two types of judges recognized by Jewish law," experts who are qualified to judge civil cases alone and laymen who in groups of three may preside over a civil tribunal. Nothing in the OT supports his view.

and his "counsellors" (cf. v. 14) and "mighty princes" (or "powerful officials," *śar*), the king's advisors and other highly placed leaders. The word *śar* occurs widely in the books of Ezra, Nehemiah, and Esther. It indicates a leader of some kind, with the context usually helping to describe the type of leader (e.g., royal, civil, military, religious, household). We cannot make a clear distinction between the "counselors" and "mighty princes," v. 28.

EZRA 8

This chapter completes the description of the return from Babylon led by Ezra and introduced in c. 7. After listing the various groups joining the return, Ezra describes the steps he took to provide the spiritual leadership needed by the people after their arrival in Palestine. The chapter also reveals Ezra's concern for God's blessing by describing his call for fasting and prayer before setting out. A brief summary of the journey occurs at the end of the chapter.

3. List of the Families 8:1–14

The list of the families accompanying Ezra in c. 8 is similar but not identical to the list of families returning with Zerubbabel in 2:3–19. The order of the families differs and the numbers are much smaller. Apparently, part of some families stayed in Babylon while others returned to Palestine. Then, at the time of Ezra, some or all of the remaining family members journeyed to Palestine. In addition to these, the list does not mention several previous families but names some new families. The list of those who returned groups 1,496 men under several heads of houses. In addition, an unknown number of women and children returned, which means this group included six or seven thousand individuals. The return took place during the reign of Artaxerxes Longimanus (see 7:1). From 7:7, we can date this as 458 BC, v. 1.[89]

a. Priestly Families

This brief list gives only the "chief of their fathers," i.e., the heads of the various priestly families. It is clear from v. 24 that there were other priests.

- Gershom, a priest, descended from Phinehas, the son and successor of Aaron as high priest (Num. 25:11–13)—We know nothing more about him except that he belonged to the same family of descendants as Ezra did (cf. 7:1–5).
- Daniel, a priest, descended from Ithamar, Aaron's youngest son (Exod. 6:23) and possibly the same Daniel who later joined in the covenant (Neh. 10:6)

b. David's Family

- Hattush, a descendant of David, v. 2, and the grandson of Shechaniah (1 Chron. 3:22)—The genealogy reads more clearly if we translate it as "Hattush, [who is] of the sons of Shechaniah." From the more complete genealogy in 1 Chronicles 3:19–22, we know Hattush was a descendant of Zerubbabel.

c. Other Families

- Zechariah, descended from Pharosh (or Parosh, see 2:3); the leader of 150 men—This group was unusual in that they possessed complete genealogies, v. 3.
- Elihoenai, son of Zerahiah and grandson of Pahath-Moab, 2:3; the leader of two hundred men, v. 4

[89]In contrast to the first list of returnees in c. 2 (see p. 26, n. 35 at 2:1), Shumate sees this list as emphasizing the need for continuing faithfulness by God's people as they respond to God's promises. In support of this, Shumate observes that this return began with Ezra as he took the initiative to gather others. There was also the rejoining of families, part of whom had stayed in Babylon but now returned to Palestine. Finally, Ezra sent men to gather Levites and Nethinim for the return.

- Shechaniah, according to the LXX (and 1 Esdras 8:32) the son of Zattu; the grandson of Jahaziel; the leader of three hundred men, v. 5
- Ebed, son of Jonathan and grandson of Adin; the leader of fifty men, v. 6
- Jeshaiah, son of Athaliah and grandson of Elam; the leader of seventy men, v. 7
- Zebadiah, son of Michael and grandson of Shephatiah; the leader of eighty men, v. 8
- Obadiah, son of Jehiel and grandson of Joab; the leader of 218 men, v. 9
- According to the LXX (and 1 Esd. 8:36), Shelomith, the son of Josiphiah and grandson of Bani; the leader of 160 men, v. 10
- Zechariah, son of Bebai; the leader of twenty-eight men, v. 11
- Johanan, son of Hakkatan and grandson of Azgad; the leader of 110 men, v. 12
- Eliphelet, Jeiel, and Shemaiah, the "last sons," i.e., younger sons, of Adonikam; the leaders of sixty men, v. 13[90]
- Uthai and Zabbud, the sons of Bigvai; the leaders of seventy men, v. 14

4. Recruitment of Temple Workers 8:15–20

Ezra led the group to the river that flowed by Ahava, a place named for the river in that area (vv. 21, 31). This was a small river or canal with an unknown location. If we include the fast of v. 21 in the three days of v. 15, the river was located a nine-day journey from Babylon (7:9 cf. v. 31). It was situated near Casiphia (v. 17), a town whose location is also unknown. The people

[90]Ryle, p. 102, tentatively suggests that the older branches of the family had returned to Palestine with Zerubbabel while this "last" group, i.e., the younger group, returned with Ezra. The view is possible although it is speculative. Fensham, p. 112, refers the phrase to "the last three heads of the family of Adonikam who had returned to Judah." This is also a possible interpretation.

camped there in their tents while Ezra surveyed them and found that no Levites had joined the return, v. 15.

Ezra sent for several "chief men," the leaders within the group, and two "men of understanding," likely knowledgeable in the role of the Levites in Israel's worship, v. 16.[91] They went to Iddo, the leader of the Levites and Nethinim (see the discussion at 2:43) located at the "place" (*maqôm*) Casiphia.[92] It is possible that Casiphia was the location of a school for Levites and that Iddo presided over the training there. It may also have been the location of a large group of Jews, where a significant number of Levites would have been expected to live.[93] Either of these suggestions could explain the large number of Levites located there. Ezra gave his representatives a message for Iddo and for the Nethinim (see the discussion at 2:43) that some should join the return to serve in the temple at Jerusalem, v. 17. God graciously brought a "man of understanding [or 'prudence']," Sherebiah (omit *and*), a descendant of Mahli, the grandson of Levi (Exod. 6:16–19), the son of "Israel," here referring to Jacob. His family totaled eighteen men, v. 18. In addition, Hashabiah and Jeshaiah, the descendants of Merari, the third son of Levi (Gen. 46:11), and twenty of their sons agreed to return, v. 19. Two hundred twenty

[91]Kidner, p. 65, considers Joiarib and Elnathan, "men of understanding," as chosen for their diplomatic skill. While this is possible, the *hipʿîl* participle of *bîn*, "men of understanding," occurs elsewhere referring to teachers or men exceptionally knowledgeable in some field, e.g., 2 Chron. 26:5; Neh. 8:7, 9; Prov. 8:9. We cannot tell whether their field here is diplomacy or Levitical service.

[92]Henry, p. 1055, understands Casiphia as the name of "a street or square in Babylon" devoted to a college for training Levites. The view is speculative. The word *maqôm* occurs more than 400x in the OT, never clearly referring to a street.

[93]Blenkinsopp, p. 166, and Ryle, pp. 104–105, suggest that Casiphia was the location of a school to train Levites. Batten, p. 321, and Bowman, p. 636, adopt the view that Casiphia held a large Jewish colony. Lawrence E. Browne, "A Jewish Sanctuary in Babylonia," *JTS* 18 (1916): 400, gives *maqôm* the meaning of "sanctuary." He finds support in 2 Kings 5:11, where *maqôm* occurs. He translates the phrase there as "wave his hand toward the Sanctuary." It is, however, arbitrary to translate *maqôm* as "sanctuary" in both 2 Kings 5 and here. Radmacher and Allen, p. 309, note that the word "place" (*maqôm*) occurs in Deut. 12:5 "as a synonym for the holy place." From this, they conclude, "there was a Jewish sanctuary or temple in Casiphia." Since *maqôm* in Deut. 12:5 does not indicates anything more than a location, this view seems weak. The word *maqôm* is translated "place" almost 400x in the OT. There is no reason to deviate from the common usage here.

Nethinim, previously appointed to this office by David and his "princes" (*śar*, see Ezra 7:28), also joined the group. These were "expressed by name," i.e., written down in a list, v. 20.

5. Intercession with God 8:21–23

Ezra decreed a time of fasting so that the group could seek God's blessing on their travels. The phrase "afflict ourselves" refers to fasting, v. 21. Ryle refers the phrase "afflict ourselves" to "a moral not a physical discipline." The NASB, NIV, and NKJV support this view by translating the phrase "humble ourselves." While this translation is possible, it faces the problem that humility cannot be commanded. In addition, the *hitpaᶜel* theme does not require "humble" (e.g., "afflicted," 2x in 1 Kings 2:26; "chasten," Dan. 10:12). Fasting with humility is desirable, but it is more likely that the "affliction" connected with fasting simply refers to the physical act of refraining from food.

The people carried out the fast to ask God's guidance for them, their "little ones" (*ṭap*),[94] and their "substance" (the wealth they were bringing for use in the temple worship). In the OT, fasting gave opportunity for additional time in prayer. The need for prayer was so great that the people did not take time to eat. The Bible often joins fasting together with prayer (Neh. 1:4; Ps. 35:13; Dan. 9:3; Matt. 17:21 [cf. Mark 9:29]; Luke 2:37; 5:33; Acts 10:30; 13:3; 14:23; 1 Cor. 7:5). The only fast required by the OT law was the fast on the Day of Atonement: "ye shall afflict your souls" (Lev. 23:27).

Christians today no longer keep this fast or the other fasts added by the Jews. These fasts included one in the fourth month, remembering the capture of Jerusalem (Jer. 39:2); one in the fifth month, remembering the burning of the temple (Jer. 52:12–13); one in the seventh month, remembering the death of Gedaliah (Jer. 41:1–3); one in the tenth month, remembering the beginning of the attack on Jerusalem (Jer. 52:4); and the fast of Esther 4:16.

[94]Fensham, p. 116, translates *ṭap* as "weak" and refers this to "all the weak returnees" including "women, children, and the aged." This word, however, occurs more than forty times in the OT, always referring to the young. In particular, the word occurs in four verses (2 Chron. 20:13; 31:18; Esther 3:13; 8:11) that were all written in this same period of Israel's history, and in each of these cases it refers to children.

While the NT does not require Christians to practice these fasts of the Jewish ritual, voluntary fasting is still appropriate.

Ezra had previously told Artaxerxes Longimanus (see 7:1) about God's power to bless them and to defeat their enemies. For this reason he did not feel that he could ask the king to provide an armed escort for them. To do so would have caused him to be "ashamed." We cannot identify "the enemy in the way" other than to suggest marauding bands of men who threatened travelers.[95] From v. 31, it seems as though a definite enemy is in sight, v. 22. The people cast themselves wholly on the Lord for protection. Later, looking back on the completed trip, Ezra recorded that God had answered their prayers, v. 23.

6. Offering for the Temple 8:24–30

Ezra appointed twelve of the "chief [*šar*, see Ezra 7:28] of the priests." In addition to the priests, he assigned Sherebiah, Hashabiah, and ten other Levites (cf. vv. 18–19), v. 24, to take charge of the temple offering. The Hebrew is grammatically difficult at this point. The NAB, NIV, and REB separate the priests from Sherebiah and Hashabiah, while the CEV, NASB, and NKJV identify Sherebiah and Hashabiah with the priests. Verses 18–19 and Nehemiah 12:24 identify Sherebiah and Hashabiah as Levites, not priests.

Ezra weighed the gold, the silver, and the temple vessels that had been given by the king and other Persian leaders, v. 25. This totaled 650 talents of silver (a little over 30 tons), 100 talents of silver vessels (a little over 4½ tons), 100 talents of gold, v. 26, 20 golden basins valued at 1,000 "drams" (or "darics"; see the discussion at 2:69).[96] There were also two fine "copper" (better "bronze") vessels as valuable as gold. We do not know why these two vessels had such an unusual value. They may have been

[95]As Myers, p. 71, mentions, some suggest that "there is here a subtle hint of the superiority of Ezra's method over that of Nehemiah." The situation, however, is different. Nehemiah was a governmental leader, for whom a military escort was appropriate. Ezra is primarily a spiritual leader, who had already expressed his faith in God's power to watch over him.

[96]The values of weights differed in the biblical nations. For this reason, estimates of weight must be understood as approximations. The values mentioned here come from the relationships given in Unger, p. 722.

made from an unusual alloy that gave them a higher value than other bowls, but we cannot be certain, v. 27.

Ezra charged the men he had appointed to oversee the offering. Just as they were "holy," dedicated to the Lord, so the vessels were also dedicated to Him. The silver and gold were a freewill offering to the Lord, v. 28. These Jewish leaders were therefore to watch them carefully to see that nothing was lost or broken. This responsibility would continue until everything was weighed, to verify the amount, before the religious and civil leaders in Jerusalem. This would take place in the "chambers" of the temple. The chambers were rooms built on either side of the temple for storage for the priests and the temple (1 Kings 6:5; Neh. 13:5), v. 29. The appointed priests and Levites accepted the responsibility of bringing the vessels and offering to Jerusalem, v. 30.

7. Summary of the Trip 8:31–32

The group set out from the river of Ahava (cf. vv. 15, 21) "on the twelfth day of the first month." Comparing these verses to 7:9, we see that the journey to Jerusalem took about three and one-half months, not including the time between Babylon and Ahava. The Lord watched over them to keep them safe from attacks by marauders along the way. We cannot tell whether the deliverance came by God's allowing the Jews to fight off attacks or by His keeping them from experiencing any attacks, v. 31. After arriving in Jerusalem, the group rested for three days. This time was likely spent in meeting with the leaders at Jerusalem and in arranging for the settlement of the travelers, v. 32.

8. Delivering the Offering 8:33–36

On the fourth day, the priests and Levites delivered the vessels and the offering to the temple. The phrase "by the hand of Meremoth" is better translated "into the hand of Meremoth," one of the priestly leaders who received the treasure for its use in the temple. Meremoth later helped to repair the wall in two places after Nehemiah's return (Neh. 3:4, 21). Eleazar may have been the priest who participated in the dedication of the wall (Neh. 12:42). He was a "son of Phinehas" in that he was descended from Phinehas, but it is unlikely that his father had this name. Jozabad and Noadiah were the chief Levites. Only

Jozabad is mentioned again (10:23; Neh. 8:7; 11:16). These oversaw the weighing of the offering and the vessels and recorded the number and weight of the vessels, vv. 33–34.

The "children of those that had been carried away," i.e., the returned exiles, made a large burnt offering at the temple. The twelve bullocks, ninety-six rams, and twelve male goats, all multiples of twelve, reflect offerings on behalf of the twelve tribes. They also offered seventy-seven lambs at this time, v. 35.[97]

The Jewish leaders also delivered the "king's commissions," his orders that these representatives assist the returnees (cf. 7:21–26). These went to the "king's lieutenants [or 'satraps', *ᵓaḥašdarpan*], and to the governors [*peḥâ*] on this side the river [better 'across the river,' i.e., southwest of the Euphrates]." The Persian title *ᵓaḥašdarpan* is the word that refers to satraps, those who ruled over provinces. It occurs elsewhere (Esther 3:12; 8:9; 9:3), referring to leaders in the nearby provinces. The determinative form in Aramaic occurs nine times in Daniel. The title *peḥâ* is foreign, possibly an Akkadian loanword that gained wide use in the OT. It occurs twenty-eight times in the OT, referring to leaders of smaller districts or even to a group of men. In response, "they [the governors] furthered the people, and the house of God," supporting them in getting settled and giving them offerings for the temple, v. 36.

EZRA 9

The final two chapters of the book focus on a spiritual problem, intermarriage between the Jews and the pagan people who also lived in the land. In the almost sixty years since

[97]Bowman, p. 643, considers the number seventy-seven as corrupted from seventy-two, the number given in 1 Esdras 8:66 and Josephus, *Antiquities* 11.5.2. This makes all of the sacrifices multiples of twelve. No Hebrew mss support this view. Since the number seven has great symbolic value in the OT, there is no reason to question the multiple "seventy and seven." Ryle, p. 113, calls it "a magnification of the perfect number." Keil, p. 113, refers to it as an "intensified seven."

Zerubbabel's return, he and Jeshua the high priest had passed off the scene. The nation had been left without strong spiritual leadership. While civil tranquility had been maintained, the people had regressed spiritually. Intermarriage with the heathen took place among both the leaders and commoners. By recording Ezra's actions in resolving this problem, the book shows his concern that the marriage relationships of the returned people be governed by the standards set in God's Word. As such, these chapters demonstrate an important principle for the people of God. The standards of the world should never replace the clear standards set down in the Bible.

B. Reforms of the People 9:1–10:44

1. Sin of the People 9:1–2

Some "princes" (or "chiefs," *śar*, see Ezra 7:28), i.e., leaders of the Jews, came to Ezra. From the continuous nature of the narrative in c. 9–10, Ezra was located in the court of the temple "before the house of God" (10:1). The leaders brought the news to Ezra that there was sin among the people, the priests, and the Levites. Some of them had "not separated themselves from the people of the lands." Intermarriage with the heathen violated the Mosaic law (Exod. 34:12–16; Deut. 7:1–4). The list of heathen nations involved serves to illustrate that Israel had followed a worldly practice rather than the principle taught by God's Word. The danger of this lay in its potential for further departure from the Lord. Marriage to the heathen would naturally introduce Israel to the worship of heathen deities and additional heathen practices.

Ezra 10:8–9 dates the effort to correct the problems as taking place on the seventeenth day of the ninth month. The four and one-half months since arriving (cf. 7:8–9) had no doubt been occupied with a variety of other matters. Ezra might have been occupied with setting up the worship of the Jews properly. He may have traveled to other cities to inform them of the changes. He could have been occupied with leadership responsibilities. It might have taken time for the "princes," i.e., the leaders, to realize the magnitude of the problem. It may have required time for those holding high positions among the Jews to develop confidence in Ezra's spiritual leadership.

At some point toward the end of this period, the leaders made Ezra aware of the marriages that had taken place with the heathen. The people were following the abominable practices of the surrounding heathen nations by intermarrying with the Canaanites, Hittites, and so forth. While some of the nations mentioned no longer existed at this time, some individuals still identified themselves with their national heritage. Through the marriages Israel had become entangled with many of these nations' practices.

The Canaanites descended from Canaan, the fourth son of Ham (Gen. 10:6). At one time, they resided throughout Palestine (Gen. 10:18–19). They later became associated more with Phoenicia and Syria. The Hittites descended from Heth, the son of Canaan (Gen. 10:15). From archaeology, we know that non-Semitic people formed the basis for the development of this nation. They were one of the earliest dominant empires, ca. 1600–1450 BC. The Hittite Empire came to its end ca. 1200 BC. We know little about the Perizzites. They first appear living alongside the Canaanites ca. 2080 BC (Gen.13:7). The OT mentions them sporadically, primarily in the early history of the Pentateuch, Joshua, and Judges. The Jebusites have an uncertain origin. From Jerusalem's early name of Jebus (Judg. 19:10), we know that they founded that city. The OT also mentions the Jebusites sporadically, but they receive more attention in the later history of Israel (e.g., 2 Sam. 5:8; 1 Kings 9:20).

The Ammonites and Moabites both came from Lot's incestuous relationship with his daughters (Gen. 19:36–38). The Ammonites generally lived east of the Amorites between the Arnon and Jabbok Rivers. They were defeated by Israel (2 Sam. 12:26–27), and later by Babylon and Egypt. In the third and second centuries BC, the Arabs absorbed them. In OT times, the Moabites generally occupied the territory south of the Arnon River, east of the Dead Sea, and north of the Brook Zered at the southern end of the Dead Sea. They were also defeated by David (2 Sam. 8:2) but later regained their independence. Still later, they fell to the Assyrians and the Babylonians.

The Egyptians earlier had been a strong nation. At this time, however, they had first come under Babylonian rule and later under Persian control. Undoubtedly, small groups of Egyptians had migrated to Palestine. The Amorites were early settlers in Palestine, apparently coming out of the Syrian Desert about the time of Hammurabi, ca. 1700 BC. This people group is mentioned in heathen documents (e.g., a treaty between them and Mursilis, a Hittite king; a wall in the Temple of Karnak, describing a campaign of Seti I) from that time as *amurru*. They occupied territory west of the Dead Sea and the Jordan River between the Arnon and Yarmuk Rivers. Israel defeated them with the aid of God's miraculous intervention (Josh. 10:1–27), v. 1.

The result of this intermarriage had been the joining of the "holy seed" with the heathen. Some of the civil leaders had been "chief," i.e., foremost, in entering into such marriages.[98] Rather than setting a godly example, the "princes [*śar*] and rulers" had flagrantly violated the law. Verses 10–12 refer to this disregard of God's commands, v. 2.[99]

2. Prayer of Ezra 9:3–15

Ezra reacted emotionally, tearing his "garment" (his clothing) and his "mantle" (his robe or outer garment). In addition, he plucked out hair from his head and beard. Both of these actions indicate his grief. Ripping the garments indicated a heart that was torn by grief (cf. 2 Chron. 34:27; Job 1:20; 2:12; Joel 2:13). Plucking the beard indicated humiliation (cf. Isa. 15:2; 50:6). Ezra sat there "astonied" (stunned) at the news, v. 3. Other godly leaders gathered together with Ezra because of this sin of the people. Ezra continued to sit there shocked at the actions of "those that had been carried away," i.e., those who had returned from their Babylonian captivity.

Ezra does not minimize the sinfulness of the people in his description of their actions, which he calls "abominations" (*tôᶜebâ*), vv. 1, 11, 14. This word occurs 117x in the OT and refers to gross

---

[98]Rabinowitz, p. 195, asserts that the nation's leaders were guilty only in that they "did not use their power and influence to restrain the practice." The fact that the list of the guilty given later in the chapter includes the names of priests and Levites argues against his view.

[99]Keil, p. 117, understands the word *chief* as stating that the leaders "were the first to transgress." Their example led the people to follow this practice. This is also a possible view, but with 113 men named as guilty in 10:18–44, it is unlikely that anyone actually kept track of who had first violated the law by marrying outside of Israel.

sin, including such matters as homosexuality (Lev. 18:22; 20:13), human sacrifice (Deut. 12:31), false worship (Deut. 18:9–14), and ritual prostitution (1 Kings 14:24). Ezra further describes their behavior as "trespass," v. 2, (*maᶜal*, also translated "transgression," v. 4), a word that occurs twenty-nine times, almost always referring to the violation of some religious precept. The word may carry the nuance of unfaithfulness (e.g., Lev. 26:40; Num. 5:12). The people had committed "iniquities" (*ᶜawon*), vv. 6, 7, 13, a word coming from a root meaning "bent" or "twisted" and thus indicating deviation from the path of righteousness. Ezra repeatly says that their actions were a "trespass" (*ʾašmâ*), vv. 6, 7, 13, 15, a word that emphasizes their guilt (translated as "guilt" in 1 Chron. 21:3 and Ezra 10:10, NASB, NIV). Their deeds have been "evil" (*raᶜ*). v. 13, a word used over 400x to indicate all kinds of evil, including physical harm (Gen. 26:29, "hurt"), emotional problems (Neh. 2:1, "sad"), and spiritual wickedness (Neh. 13:17). Verse 14 refers to "break[ing]" God's commands, a summary statement that describes all sin.

Ezra sat there for several hours until time for the evening sacrifice. From the mention of this in vv. 4–5 (cf. 10:1), it is likely that these events took place in the outer court of the temple, a natural meeting place for people. It is possible that Ezra used this time for prayer as he considered how best to handle the situation, v. 4.

The evening sacrifice involved offering a lamb as a burnt offering, flour as a meal offering, and some wine as a drink offering (Exod. 29:38–41). The burnt offering symbolized complete dedication to God, giving Him all of the sacrifice as the priest burned the whole animal on the altar. The meal and drink offerings recognized God as the giver of all that was necessary for life. These were offered after sunset but before dark each day. This was an appropriate time to pray since Ezra was going to confess the sin into which the people had fallen. He rose from his "heaviness" (or grief, *taᶜᵃnît*), having torn his garment and his mantle (cf. v. 3). The word *taᶜᵃnît* is from the root *ᶜanâ*, "to be afflicted." It occurs only here in the OT and is variously taken as referring to Ezra's grief (GNB, GW, NLT) or to his fasting before and during his prayer (ESV, NKJV, NRSV). The lexicons also differ, with BDB presenting the idea of fasting and KB understanding it as self-humiliation. I have suggested it means "grief" because of the short time between his hearing of the sin (vv. 1–3) and the beginning of his prayer (v. 5).[100]

Still wearing the torn clothing, Ezra fell to his knees and lifted up his hands to the Lord as he began to pray. The lifting of the hands with the palms upward pictured the need to receive an answer from the Lord, v. 5. Ezra began by confessing his shame over the sin of the people. He "blush[ed] to lift up [his] face." This idiomatic expression indicates the greatness of his shame was such that he could not even look upward toward God (cf. Jer. 6:15; 8:12). Ezra pictured the sin of the nation as rising like a flood of water over their heads. It was large enough to rise into the heavens, where it would attract the attention of God.

Notice that Ezra identified himself with the nation in saying "our iniquities" and "our trespass." In this he followed the pattern of other national leaders, e.g., Moses (Exod. 34:9), David (Ps. 103:10), Isaiah (Isa. 53:5), and Daniel (Dan. 9:16). There is a sense in which every individual believer should identify himself with the larger group—a family, a church, a city, a state, a nation. Because we have failed to evangelize lost souls around us and to help them grow spiritually, we bear some responsibility for the sins of others, v. 6.

Ezra acknowledged the long-standing nature of the people's sin. The people had been doing wrong "since the days of [their] fathers," causing them to be defeated by the "kings of the lands." This included numerous defeats by Egypt, Assyria, and Babylon (e.g., 2 Kings 15:17–20, 29; 17:3–4). Israel's sin had caused them to go into captivity, to be spoil for other nations, and to experience the "confusion [better 'shame'] of face" that the nation faced "this day," v. 7. God had freely given them "grace" (*ḥanan*) that had allowed "a remnant" (omit "to escape") to return to the land. The root *ḥanan* and its derivatives occur widely in all parts of the OT to indicate a display of kindness, sympathy, favor, pity, or grace. While the subject is most often God, the term may also be used of man. This grace was like "a nail in [God's] holy place," i.e., a tent

[100]Breneman, p. 151, and Larson and Dahlen, p. 105, focus on Ezra's humiliation, while Slotki, p. 165, and Bowman, p. 647, refer to fasting. Either view is acceptable.

peg driven into the ground, thus representing a secure dwelling (cf. Isa. 22:23).[101]

God had given this period of grace to "lighten [their] eyes," an idiom for giving them clear directions for life. The lighting of the eyes occurs several times as an idiom, not always with the same sense. In 1 Samuel 14:27, 29, it simply indicates refreshing. In Psalm 13:3 and Proverbs 29:13, it indicates the giving of life. Here and in Psalm 19:8, it refers to giving directions as to how one should live.[102]

God would give His people "reviving in [their] bondage," lifting them out of the slavery in which they were bound, v. 8. "We were bondmen" is lit. "we are bondmen [slaves]," still under the authority of their Persian ruler. Yet God had extended "mercy" (loyal love, *ḥesed*, see 3:11) in that He had given new life to them as a nation. He had let them rebuild the temple and repair many of the ruins in the city and had given them a "wall" (*gader*). Since the wall of Jerusalem was not completed until the time of Nehemiah, Ezra cannot be referring here to the wall of defense surrounding the city. The word *gader* is never used for Nehemiah's wall but occurs eleven times in other places, several times having a metaphorical sense (Ps. 80:12, "hedges"; Isa. 5:5; Ezek. 13:5 and 22:30, both "hedge"; Hos. 2:6). It is reasonable to understand the wall metaphorically here as indicating God's protection of the people.

Wright thinks that Ezra is referring to a wall "actually being built when he spoke" and that some destruction of this took place, later causing Nehemiah to mourn over the lack of a defense for the city (Neh. 1:3–4). It is doubtful that a wall would have been built and destroyed without some mention of it in the books of either Ezra or Nehemiah. Throntveit notes that the word *gader* occurs elsewhere in agricultural contexts referring to a "fence" or "hedge." While *gader* does often refer to

[101]Pope, p. 46, considers the "nail" a reference to the rebuilt temple. He understands the nail symbolically, the temple being "the nail on which [Israel's] hopes were hung." This is also a possible view; cf. Isa. 33:20.

[102]Batten, p. 333, relies on the translation in 1 Esd. 8:79 to conclude that God had "enabled his people . . . to worship him in his holy temple." Keil, p. 120, and Bowman, p. 649, understand the light as "new vitality" as a nation. Breneman, p. 153, and Slotki, p. 166, suggest the reviving of individual spirits. These are also possible views.

a "hedge" or fence around a field, it may also refer to a literal wall, Ezekiel 42:7. The context here refers to rebuilding and repairing the temple. There is no warrant for introducing an agricultural sense at this point. A literal wall serves as a better metaphorical picture of safety, v. 9.[103]

"What shall we say after this?" The rhetorical question implies that the people had no excuse for turning from the commands of God, v. 10, given through the prophets. We do not have any specific statement in the prophets as is given in v. 11. Ezra was undoubtedly referring to general teaching given by the prophets (e.g., Hag. 2:14; Zech. 1:3–4). They had warned that the land was "unclean" spiritually, that the heathen dwelled in "filthiness," and that their "abominations" (their idols) had filled it with spiritual uncleanness, v. 11. In addition, earlier teaching by Moses had warned against intermarriage with the heathen (Exod. 34:11–16). Joshua had warned against intermarriage (Josh. 23:12–13). The prophets had followed this by commanding the people not to intermarry with the heathen. They were not to seek the good of the heathen because they were wicked and God had determined to give their land to Israel "for an inheritance to [their] children for ever" (cf. Deut. 7:1–4), v. 12.

In view of past judgments on sin, in view of God's grace in punishing the people less than they deserved, and in view of His grace in giving them a remnant to possess the land, v. 13, should they have broken His commandments? Should they have joined with the heathen in marriage? Would God not punish them so thoroughly that none would be left and none would escape, v. 14?

Ezra concluded his prayer by recognizing the righteousness of God in fulfilling all His promises to Israel in the past. A remnant still remained. They were guilty before God, however, "in [their] trespasses." They could not stand before God because of their sin (cf. Pss. 76:7; 130:3), v. 15.

---

[103]Wright, p. 18; Throntveit, p. 53

EZRA 10

This chapter completes the narrative begun in c. 9. While Ezra confessed the nation's sin (9:6–15), the people gathered together in the court of the temple. They devised a plan for putting away the heathen wives. The plan took into account the weather, the travel necessary for those living in other towns, and the amount of work involved in the process. The chapter records this plan and lists the men who divorced their wives.

3. Covenant of the People 10:1–9

Since Ezra's purpose in writing this was to show the actions of the people, he writes in the third person, thus minimizing his own role in the matter. The word *when* is better translated as "while." It was Ezra's act of public prayer that drew the people to him. As he "prayed" (*palal*) and confessed the sin of the people (9:6–15), he wept and threw himself on the ground, prostrating himself before God. The word *palal*, which occurs widely to indicate prayer, has the sense of asking someone to intervene or arbitrate in a situation. That sense is appropriate here and in each of the four times the word occurs in Nehemiah (Neh. 1:4, 6; 2:4; 4:9).[104]

The prayer took place "before the house of God," in the outer court of the temple (2 Chron. 4:9), where the people could see and hear him. This was near the brazen altar, on which a burnt offering was made each evening. During this time a large number of men, women, and children gathered around Ezra,[105] and his emotional response impacted the people. Many of them also wept over the sin of the nation, v. 1.

---

[104]See Girdlestone, p. 219; Merrill F. Unger and William White, eds., *Nelson's Expository Dictionary of the Old Testament* (Nashville: Thomas Nelson Publishers, 1980), p. 303.

[105]Rabinowitz, p. 194, gives a rabbinical explanation for the presence of women among those weeping. This may refer to the Jewish wives of those who had also taken Gentile wives, which could indicate that their wives "had been superseded in their husbands' affections by gentile women." Ryle, p. 126, more reasonably explains that the gathering was of those who "were of the same mind with Ezra."

Shechaniah was the son of Jehiel, one of the "sons of Elam" (cf. 2:7; 8:7; v. 26). Since a Jehiel is mentioned later as one who had taken a heathen wife (v. 26), Shechaniah was likely the son of a different Jehiel.[106] He admitted to Ezra that the people had "trespassed" (*maᶜal*, better, "acted unfaithfully") in marrying "strange" (*nokrî*) women from among the heathen people living in the land. The verb *maᶜal* is used frequently in all parts of the OT to refer to unfaithful behavior, most often of man against God (e.g., 2 Chron. 28:19, 22) but also of a wife against her husband (e.g., Num. 5:12). The word *nokrî* refers to something that is "foreign" to a group, not something peculiar. This may be a foreign country (Exod. 2:22), a foreign city (Judg. 19:12), an adulteress (Prov. 5:20), a stranger (Prov. 27:2), a weed (Jer. 2:21), a false god (Gen. 35:2, 4) or, as here, a person not of Israelite background. The word occurs seven times in this chapter but nowhere else in Ezra. It also occurs in Nehemiah 13:26, 27, where it again refers to pagan wives.

Israel had been unfaithful to God in that they had spurned His Word in marrying heathen women. Possibly drawing on the visible sorrow of the people, Shechaniah pointed out that there was "hope" for the nation, v. 2. He suggested that the people make a covenant with God to put away their heathen wives. In addition, "such as are born of them," the children of these marriages, were to be "put away" with their mothers. The mothers were the best to rear the younger children. Any older children were likely already indoctrinated in the pagan worship of their mothers. The Talmud, *Yebamoth* 17*a*, 23*a*, asserts that the child born to a Jewish father and a Gentile mother is considered non-Jewish. This may also be a reason why the children had to stay with their mothers.

The "put[ting] away" would be done according to the counsel of Sechaniah's "lord" Ezra and other godly individuals in the land. The phrase "my lord" is *ᵓᵃdonay*, a phrase that refers often to God elsewhere in the OT. When it refers to a human lord, the

---

[106]Authors differ in identifying Jehiel. Barnes, 454; Bowman, p. 652; and Rawlinson, p. 152, are among those who consider Shechaniah the son of the same man mentioned in v. 26. Keil, p. 126; Larson and Dahlen, p. 116; and Ryle, p. 126, consider the two Jehiels different men. I have followed this view since it would be more usual for Shechaniah to take the lead in confessing the people's sin if he himself had not grown up in this environment.

phrase is *ʾădonî*. There is, however, no OT command of the Lord relating to separation from heathen wives. In fact, in the NT, Paul urges that such marriages be preserved (1 Cor. 7:12–14). The phrase must therefore refer to Ezra. For these reasons, it is best to read *ʾădonî* at this point, which involves a change only in the vowel pointing of the word.

Special covenants are not unusual in the Old Testament. In 2 Kings 23:3, Josiah and the people agreed to obey God's Word. In 2 Chronicles 15:12–13, Asa led the people to agree that they would worship only the Lord. In 2 Chronicles 23:16, after putting Athaliah to death, Jehoiada led the nation to promise to "be the Lord's people." From their subsequent actions in opposing Baal worship and fostering the worship of God, the people accepted the authority of the Mosaic law over them. In 2 Chronicles 29:10, Hezekiah directed the nation to turn from sin and thus to avoid God's wrath. In Jeremiah 34:8, Zedekiah directed the people to release their Jewish slaves, a covenant that they later ignored.

The divorcing of the wives here was to be done permanently "according to the law." Since there is no OT command ordering divorce from a heathen mate, the idea here must be as expressed in Deuteronomy 7:3 and 24:1–4. In 7:3, the Lord forbade Israelites to intermarry with the heathen, and in 24:1–4, the wife with "some uncleanness," which may refer to her heathen beliefs, could be divorced. It is also possible that Shechaniah considered the divorce as bringing the offenders back into agreement with the law they had violated by their marriage (see the discussion at 9:1), v. 3.[107]

When Shechaniah urged Ezra to rise from his prostrate position and to take his leadership role in judging the people (cf. 7:25–26), v. 4, Ezra responded to his plea. He assembled the religious leaders and the people and made them swear that they would accept this solution to the problem. They agreed to the

[107]Brown, pp. 174–75, notes that divorce was actually "a merciful remedy for the wives." Their pagan beliefs in Israel actually made them subject to the penalty of stoning (Deut. 13:6–11). Divorce both extended mercy to the wives and removed the spiritual wickedness from the families involved.

action, giving Ezra public support for a measure that would be difficult for some individuals to accept, v. 5.

Ezra went to the chamber of Johanan (called Jehohanan in NASB, NIV, and ESV) in the temple, possibly a room named to honor the high priest's grandson. This may have been one of the chambers under the care of the priest Eliashib and mentioned in Nehemiah 13:4–5, 7–9. Ezra stayed there and fasted, eating no food and drinking no water. He grieved over the "transgression" (*maᶜal*, see 9:2) of the people. While it is not mentioned specifically, Ezra undoubtedly used this time for prayer to seek the Lord's guidance in settling the matter, v. 6.

Ezra consulted with "the princes and the elders," the leaders of the nation. As the result, a proclamation went throughout the land that the people should gather at Jerusalem, v. 7. The "princes [*śar*, see Ezra 7:28] and the elders" decided that anyone not coming within three days would have his possessions "forfeited" (*ḥaram*), devoted to the Lord. This is one of only three times in the OT that the word *ḥaram* occurs in the *hopal* theme (see also Exod. 22:20; Lev. 27:29). The word refers to something placed under a ban, devoted to God either for His use or for total destruction. The idea here is of giving the possessions for use by the religious leaders in their service to the Lord. Further, the offender would also be excluded from the community. While not everyone was guilty of the sin of marrying with the heathen, the sin is important enough that all must know of its seriousness, v. 8.

The men of Judah and Benjamin gathered at Jerusalem within the three-day period. It was the "ninth month," the month of Chisleu, corresponding to the period from mid-November to mid-December. This was wintertime, the period of the "former rain" (Hos. 6:3; Joel 2:23) during the growing season in Palestine. The people gathered in the "street" (open space, *rᵉḥôb*), likely the court outside the temple. This is the only time that *rᵉḥôb* occurs in Ezra. It does occur four more times in Nehemiah, however (8:1, 3, 16 [2x]), and three times in Esther (4:6; 6:9, 11). The noun *rᵉḥôb* refers to an open area, always something like a courtyard, town square, or marketplace. The people were "trembling" because of both the seriousness of the matter (which might bring God's judgment) and the weather conditions, v. 9.[108]

4. Agreement of the People 10:10–19

Ezra spoke to the gathering as he exercised the leadership given him by Artaxerxes (7:25–26). Initially he told the people that they had "transgressed" (*maʿal*, see v. 2) the law by marrying heathen wives. This caused the "trespass" (*ʾašmâ*, see 9:6) of the nation to increase, v. 10. He urged them to confess their sin to the "Lord God of [their] fathers." This title for God suggests that their actions had revealed that He was not their God. They needed to show their obedience to God by separating from the heathen families and their heathen wives, v. 11.

The people responded in agreement with what Ezra had said, v. 12. There were "many" men involved with this sin, however. Because of the rain, they would not be able to gather in a large crowd outside to take care of the problem. It would not be a matter of merely one or two days to correct the problem. The phrase "we are many that have transgressed" is better rendered "we have transgressed greatly," v. 13. For this reason, they proposed that the "rulers" (or "leaders," *śar*, see Ezra 7:28) of the nation "stand" (or "remain") to make a schedule. Those in a city who had sinned would come at the scheduled time, along with the "elders," the civil leaders, and the "judges" of that city, those who interpreted the law in specific situations. In this way, the "fierce wrath" (or "burning anger") of God would be turned away from the nation, v. 14.

The phrase "Only Jonathan . . . and Jahaziah . . . were employed about this *matter*" is better translated "Only Jonathan . . . and Jahaziah . . . opposed this." Two of the Levites, Meshullam and Shabbethai, also gave aid to this opposition. We do not know

---

[108]Noss and Thomas, p. 237, read too much into the use of different prepositions: "because [*ʿal*] of this matter [*dabar*], and for [*min*] the great rain." They assign *ʿal* an emotional value and refer *min* merely to an outward physical experience. The phrase *ʿal-haddabar* occurs in seven other places. Where there is an emotional quality involved, the verse includes a descriptive word to make this clear: 2 Samuel 19:42 (angry); 1 Kings 21:4 and 1 Chron. 21:7 (displeased); 2 Kings 6:11 (sore troubled). Elsewhere (Gen. 24:9; Deut. 4:2; 1 Kings 11:10, and here), nothing indicates an emotional involvement. The use of different prepositions is likely poetic variation.

the reason for this resistance to correcting the problem. It may have been disagreement over the plan to put away the wives. Or it could have been disagreement with the postponement of the action, arguing for immediate divorces.[109] We cannot be certain which of these positions is correct. I lean toward the first view, that they opposed the idea of mass divorce since this involves the emotions and is therefore more logical to resist.

Meshullam is probably the same man mentioned in v. 29 as having a wife from among the heathen. There is no mention of the others in the list those putting away their wives, v. 15. This opposition, however, did not succeed. The "children of the captivity," i.e., those who had returned from the exile in Babylon, carried out the plan to put away any wives that had come from among the heathen. Ezra and selected individuals who represented the families involved were set apart to lead the work.

Those involved in the marriages are identified by name. The list in vv. 18–44 contains 113 names of guilty men. The work began on the "first day of the tenth month," ten days after developing the plan (cf. v. 9), v. 16. The group examined each case separately and "made an end" (gave their decision) in each case. The investigation and putting away of the heathen wives concluded on the first day of the first month, Nisan, corresponding to mid-March to mid-April. The process took a little less than three months. We may assume that the group did not meet on the Sabbath. They may well have met just one or two days each week. This would have let the men involved continue to work their fields and carry out other responsibilities, v. 17.

[109]Fensham, p. 141, argues that Jonathan and Jahaziah opposed the delay and that Meshullam and Shabbethai supported the proposal made in vv. 13–14. The view is possible since the Hebrew is ambiguous. Breneman, p. 161, and Holmgren, p. 82, mention the view that these men opposed the putting away of the foreign wives. Fensham, p. 141, and Larson and Dahlen, p. 120, mention the view that the group opposed the delay because they wanted an immediate decision. Most authors mention both views as being possible ways of understanding the opposition.

5. List of the Guilty 10:18–44
a. Priests and Levites 10:18–24

The list begins with the names of the priests, who were the greatest offenders because they had violated their responsibility of providing spiritual leadership for the people. Included were the sons of "Jeshua the son of Jozadak," who had returned from Babylon at the time of Zerubbabel's return (2:2; Neh. 7:7; 12:1, 7, 10). Jozadak, contracted from Jehozadak, was the son of Seraiah, high priest at the time of the fall of Jerusalem (2 Kings 25:18). Jeshua (also called Joshua) served as the high priest at the time of the return from the captivity. He was responsible for setting up the altar at Jerusalem so that the people could offer sacrifice (Ezra 3:2). In addition, he helped in the rebuilding of the temple (3:8–9) and resisted the efforts of the Samaritans to join in the work (4:3). After the delay caused by the Samaritan opposition, he helped rally the people to begin building again (5:2). Zechariah 3:1–10 and 6:9–15 involve him in prophecy in such a way as to show him as a type of Christ. The sad lesson from him is that godly Christian parents can lose their children to sinful practices unless they give the rearing of the family a high priority. Although Jeshua was active in godly work, he apparently failed to give his sons proper training.

Four of the sons of "Jeshua . . . and his brethren," had taken heathen wives. We cannot certainly identify the "brethren" of Jeshua. The names of Maaseiah, Eliezer, Jarib, and Gedaliah all occur again in the books of Ezra and Nehemiah, but we cannot be sure that these are the men named later, v. 18. These "gave their hands," shaking hands as binding them to an oath, agreeing that they would "put away their wives." They also sacrificed a ram as an offering for their "trespass" (*ʾašmâ*, see 9:6); cf. Leviticus 5:14–19, v. 19. The additional priests belonged to the families of Immer, Harim, and Pashur (cf. 2:37–39). Once again, several of the names occur elsewhere in Ezra and Nehemiah. There is no way of identifying these men with the other mentions of their names, vv. 20–22.

Several of the Levites had also married heathen wives. The list does not give the names of the families involved. The previous list (in 2:40) gives only Jeshua and Kadmiel as families of the Levites. Jozabad appears again in 8:33, where he assisted in weighing the vessels brought for the temple from Babylon.

Nehemiah 8:7 and 11:16 also mention him. Kelaiah appears again as Kelita in Nehemiah 8:7 and 10:10. Nehemiah 9:5 includes Pethahiah in a list of the Levites. Judah is likely the same one mentioned in Nehemiah 12:8. The names of Shimei and Eliezer do not occur again, v. 23.

The "singers" were a group within the Levites. David had originally appointed these for the purpose of praising the Lord with their music (1 Chron. 9:33; 15:16). Only Eliashib is named as guilty of marrying a heathen wife. The record does not mention him again.

The "porters" were also appointed from among the Levites (1 Chron. 9:18, 26; 2 Chron. 23:4). They guarded the entrances into the temple. They were divided into courses (1 Chron. 26:1–19). Lots were drawn to assign them (1 Chron. 26:13). Three of these had fallen into sin. Only Shallum is mentioned again (2:42; Neh. 7:45), v. 24.

b. Other Men 10:25–44

The remaining verses list the names of other men with marriages to heathen wives. They are grouped by their families. The first is Parosh (v. 25). In Hebrew, the name Malchijah occurs twice in this list of the "sons" (or "descendants") of Parosh, though the KJV has the first occurrence as "Malchiah." The CEV, ESV, and NRSV emend the second mention to "Hashabiah" because of the appearance of this name in 1 Esdras 9:26. But there is no reason why the descendants of Parosh could not have included two men with the same name. The GNB, NASB, NET, and NIV translate both occurrences as the same name.

Also included are Elam (v. 26), Zattu (v. 27), Bebai (v. 28), Bani (v. 29), Pahath-Moab (v. 30), Harim (v. 31), Hashum (v. 33), Bani (v. 34), and Nebo (v. 43). These leaders of the families are mentioned in c. 2, with the single exception of the second Bani (v. 34). With the other families, the list gives only four to eight children each. With the second Bani, the list records twenty-seven names. There is no clear explanation for the listing of Bani twice or for the disproportionately large number of his "sons" involved with marrying heathen women.[110] Verse 44 summarizes the action, even pointing out that some of these families had children (cf. v. 3). This indicates the seriousness of the action since breaking up a home with children is an extreme step.

The abrupt ending of the book is not unusual in the books of the OT. Numbers, for instance, ends with the record of Zelophehad's daughters followed by a brief reference to the commands given by Moses. Joshua ends with the death of Eleazar who has not been mentioned before in the chapter. Nehemiah closes with a record of intermarriage with the heathen followed by a short prayer.

The record of Ezra's ministry closes for a period of thirteen years. He reappears as a spiritual leader of the people in Nehemiah 8 and 12. While the record of his ministry occupies only a small part of the OT, the practical lessons gained from the study of this man's life and character still continue to influence Christians today.

[110]It is possible that Bigvai (either in 2:14 or in 2:29) should be substituted for the second Bani (tentatively, Batten, p. 350; Noss and Thomas, p. 251). It is also possible that two or three family names have dropped out in vv. 35–41. There is no textual evidence to support either of these suggestions. All we can do is speculate, an approach that may lead to error.

INTRODUCTION TO NEHEMIAH

Judah's sins constrained God to bring them into the judgment of captivity. Babylon invaded Palestine three times (605 BC, 597 BC, and 586 BC), each time carrying away some of the prominent people of Judah into captivity (2 Kings 24:1–25:21). This left only the poorer class of people in the land (2 Kings 25:11–12). The captives sojourned in Babylon for seventy years, the remaining time for Babylon's dominance of the biblical world. This captivity fulfilled the prophecies of Jeremiah 25:11–12 and 29:10.

After the conquest of Babylon by the Medo-Persian alliance in 539 BC and the advent of the Persian king Cyrus the Great, the policy changed toward the Israelite captives. Within a year, Cyrus gave his permission for the captives of Israel to return to the land of Palestine (Ezra 1:1–4). The book of Ezra gives the details of this first return. About 536 BC, a group of almost fifty thousand persons returned to Palestine under the leadership of Zerubbabel (also called Sheshbazzar, Ezra 1:8, 11; 5:14, 16). To a limited degree they established there the worship of the Lord once more.

Under the leadership of Zerubbabel and the high priest Jeshua (Joshua) , work began on the reconstruction of the temple. Opposition from the Samaritan inhabitants of Palestine (Ezra 4:1–5, 24), coupled with the selfish interests of the Jews, stopped work on the temple. In 520 BC (Hag. 1:14–15), the prophets Haggai and Zechariah rebuked the people for failing to build the house of the Lord. Under their urging, work again started, and ca. 516 BC (Ezra 6:15) the Jews completed the temple building. The people then resumed their worship of Jehovah under Jeshua's leadership (Zech. 6:11).

From that high point of faithfulness to the Lord, the religious service of the Jews rapidly deteriorated. Their lack of strong leadership, apathy among the people, and opposition from the Samaritans—all of these and more contributed to the failure of the Jews to maintain a thriving religion. In 458 BC (Ezra 7:6–8), Ezra the priest led a second group of Jews from Babylon to reestablish the worship of Israel. After his arrival he helped bring about changes in the moral and spiritual standards of the people, including the abandonment of mixed marriages with the heathen. Rebuilding of the city's walls, however, was not attempted at this time.

Thirteen years after Ezra's return, in 445 BC (Neh. 1:1 cf. Ezra 7:7), Nehemiah learned of the poor physical conditions that characterized Jerusalem. From his brother Hanani and other Jewish officials (1:2–3), he learned that the walls of the city were broken down. This broken-down condition had left the city defenseless and presented a shameful testimony to neighboring countries. This situation stirred Nehemiah's heart. He obtained a commission from King Artaxerxes, also known as Longimanus, to go to Jerusalem to rebuild the walls.[1] This would secure the city from attack by its enemies. Under his leadership the residents repaired and rebuilt the walls. Further, the people returned to a position of obedience to the Lord. The book of Nehemiah tells about the leadership exercised by Nehemiah as he guided the city to accomplish the task of rebuilding the city walls.

After twelve years (2:1 cf. 13:6), in 433 BC, Nehemiah returned to Babylon. After an unspecified period of time away, he came back to Palestine as governor for a second time (13:6–7). This time, he led the nation in spiritual reforms. This is the plot of the book of Nehemiah, a story that should challenge the hearts of Christians as they consider the needs around them for Christian service.

From the nature of the book, we can say confidently that Nehemiah wrote it in Jerusalem. The book is autobiographical, describing many of the actions of Nehemiah as he led the nation. He describes features of the city in connection with his leadership in repairing the wall (3:1–32). He refers to gatherings in a city square (8:1, 3, 16). He describes incidents involving the people of the city (e.g., 8:16–18; 11:1–2). He closes the book by describing several reforms that he made in the city (13:4–9, 10–13, 15–22, 23–29). All of these give the impression that Nehemiah was in the city when he wrote.

The writings of Nehemiah describe historical incidents concerning Israel at the end of the Babylonian captivity and prior to the four hundred silent years of the intertestamental period. In an almost unique way among the books in the Bible, this book emphasizes principles by which people may successfully serve

[1]Artaxerxes received the name Longimanus because his right hand was longer than his left hand.

God. The first part of the book is largely personal, telling of Nehemiah's desire to rebuild the wall around Jerusalem and of the obstacles he overcame in accomplishing that goal. The last part of the book recounts religious reforms among the people brought about by Nehemiah with the aid of Ezra and the Levites. Through recounting Nehemiah's burden to build the walls of Jerusalem and his subsequent completion of the task, the book illustrates many instances of personal faith and implicit trust in the Lord.

The tenure of Nehemiah overlaps the ministry of the prophet Malachi. Both Nehemiah and Malachi denounced the marriage of the people to Gentiles (Neh. 13:23; Mal. 2:11), the withholding of tithes from the Levites (Neh. 13:10; Mal. 3:8), and problems with the priests (Neh. 13:4–8. 29; Mal. 1:6–2:9). It is likely that Malachi rebuked the people during Nehemiah's absence. Nehemiah 12:22 mentions Darius, the Persian king who followed Artaxerxes ca. 425 BC, so the book must have been written after this. A date of 420 BC for the writing is a close approximation, making the book the last of the OT historical books to be written.

Conservatives and liberals alike hold three basic positions as to the authorship. Some attribute the writing of the books of Ezra, Nehemiah and, usually, Chronicles to Ezra.[2] Others posit an unknown editor, generally called the Chronicler, who compiled various sources into one book.[3] Still others consider Nehemiah the author of the book,[4] a view that faces the problem of references in the book that speak of Nehemiah in the third person. This seems to be evidence for an author other than Nehemiah. This argument, also used by those who question Ezra's

---

[2]Radmacher and Allen, p. 302, accept this view. They suggest that Ezra used Nehemiah's memoirs for the passages where Nehemiah speaks in the first person (1:1–7:5; 12:27–43; 13:4–31). Myers, p. lxviii, also makes Ezra the author of Chronicles, Ezra, and Nehemiah. Keil, p. 7, rejects Ezra's authorship of Nehemiah. He notes that there is in the OT "no other instance of a single portion or section of a longer work being distinguished from its other portions by a similar superscription, with the name of the author."

[3]Coggins, p. 2, Fensham, pp. 2–3; and Ryle, p. xxv, adopt this view.

[4]Henry, p. 1067; Keil, p. 140; and Luck, p. 79, all credit Nehemiah with the authorship of the book. Rawlinson, p. ii, accepts Nehemiah's authorship although he sees parts that speak of Nehemiah in the third person (c. 8–10) as contributed by an anonymous writer.

authorship of the book of Ezra, is refuted in my introduction to Ezra (p. 8). It is easiest to defend Nehemiah's authorship. The book uses the first-person pronoun frequently (e.g., 1:1, 2, 4), has its own introduction (1:1), and displays a different emphasis from the book of Ezra.

It is worth noting that Ezra, the man of God, was at Jerusalem some of the time during Nehemiah's leadership (Neh. 8:1–18; 12:26, 36). Ezra's gifts seem to have been confined to teaching the law and exhorting the people to follow spiritual principles. Nehemiah was primarily an administrator, qualified to direct the people in building the city's outer wall. The Lord worked among the people of Jerusalem as He does among believers today, calling individuals with different talents and gifts to perform differing aspects of His work.

We know little about Nehemiah's family background. He was the son of Hachaliah (1:1), born to his parents during the captivity. We do not know from which tribe of Israel he descended. But given that the Babylonian captivity primarily involved Judah and Benjamin, it is likely that he came from one of these two tribes. Unsupported church tradition says that he was from the tribe of Judah. The mention of his ancestors being buried at Jerusalem (2:3, 5) together with other references to Judah (1:2 cf. 7:2) support this. Others suggest that he was from the tribe of Levi, since 7:2 refers to the appointment of his brother Hanani at the same time as the appointing of "the porters and the singers and the Levites."[5] The name *Nehemiah* means "the Lord comforts." *Hanani* is a shortened form of Hananiah ("the Lord is gracious," 1:2; 7:2). By using the shortened form, Nehemiah differentiates his brother from Hananiah (7:2), who was also a leader in Jerusalem.

As the book opens (1:11), Nehemiah occupies the important position of cupbearer to King Artaxerxes Longimanus, the

---

[5]Cyril J. Barber, *Nehemiah and the Dynamics of Effective Leadership* (Neptune, NJ: Loizeaux Brothers, 1976), pp. 13–14, and Pope, p. 55, accept the view that Nehemiah was from Judah. Ryle, p. 146, raises the possibility that he was a Levite and gives two arguments in its favor: (1) the mention of his brother's appointment (7:2) at the same time as the porters, singers, and Levites (7:1), and (2) the emphasis given by Nehemiah to the interests of the priests and Levites. Ryle himself, however, does not draw a conclusion about his background. In my judgment the support for a background from Judah is better.

Persian ruler (465–425 BC). From Hanani's recognition of the reproach that Jerusalem was experiencing because of its ruined condition, it is clear that he was a spiritual man, concerned about the glory of God. It is obvious from Nehemiah's reactions in the book that he also held this characteristic. The names of both Nehemiah and his brother Hanani reflect the family's connection to the Lord. In addition to the meanings of their names, the response of Nehemiah and Hanani to the plight of Jerusalem and their actions described in the book suggest that the two had been reared in a godly home. Undoubtedly Hachaliah and his wife had consistently taught the family to trust God and to seek His ways. This is borne out by Nehemiah's concern over the desolation of Jerusalem and by his leadership in the spiritual reforms that followed the completion of the walls.

Some have concluded that Nehemiah was a priest, primarily based on 2 Maccabees 1:18, 21, which says he offered sacrifice. Others, however, also offered sacrifices, e.g., David (2 Sam. 24:25) and Solomon (1 Kings 3:4; 8:63). Although the priests may have done the actual sacrificial work, the Lord credited the sacrifice to the one bringing it. Since the book does not clearly present Nehemiah as a priest but does call others by this title (e.g., 8:2; 13:4), it is best to accept Nehemiah as a layman, used by God to accomplish His will. Nehemiah thus fulfilled the role played by so many down through the years. Godly laymen, using their unique talents for the glory of the Lord, have always been and will always be vitally necessary to successfully accomplish the Lord's work.

In recognition of his godly actions, the Talmud, *Berakoth* 13*a*, calls Nehemiah a prophet. While he was not a prophet in the usual sense of the term, the Talmud explains the title as appropriate "because he was speaking under the guidance of the holy spirit."

God uniquely prepared Nehemiah for his responsibilities by placing him in his position as cupbearer (1:11) to the Persian king. This was no ordinary servant's task, but one given only to a responsible and faithful individual. Nehemiah had privileged access to the king, even to the extent of being admitted in the presence of the queen (2:6). Herodotus 3.34 refers to the cupbearer as a "very honourable office" among the Persians. Tobit 1:22 says that Ahikar was "cupbearer and keeper of the signet and had charge of administration and of the accounts" before adding that "Esarhaddon appointed him second to himself."

One of Nehemiah's tasks would have been to taste the king's wine to ensure that it was free from poison. This position demanded a man of faithfulness, one to whom the king could entrust his life. That Nehemiah's service met with the king's approval is shown by his willingness to grant him letters of commission to guarantee his safety and access to the king's supplies (2:7–8).

Not only did Nehemiah's position bring him into contact with the king, it also gave him opportunity to observe the working of the government, which gave him the qualifications to rule as governor of Jerusalem after leaving the king's court. Just as God gave Moses experiences in Pharaoh's court and David lessons in Saul's household, so Nehemiah had a rich background of varied governmental experience to aid him in the later years of his service.

Outline of Nehemiah

I. Nehemiah's Burden 1:1–11
- A. Jerusalem's Problem 1:1–3
- B. Nehemiah's Prayer 1:4–11

II. Nehemiah's Preparation 2:1–20
- A. Request of the King 2:1–8
- B. Arrival at Jerusalem 2:9–20

III. Nehemiah's Coworkers 3:1–32

IV. Nehemiah's Opposition 4:1–23
- A. Ridicule of the Work 4:1–6
- B. Defense of the Work 4:7–23

V. Nehemiah's Example 5:1–19
- A. Problem of the People 5:1–5
- B. Proclamation of the Solution 5:6–13
- C. Pattern of Nehemiah's Leadership 5:14–19

VI. Nehemiah's Victories 6:1–19
- A. Accusation of the Enemies 6:1–9
- B. Deceit of the Prophet 6:10–14

- C. Completion of the Wall 6:15–16
- D. Spying of the People 6:17–19

VII. Register of the People 7:1–73a
- A. Organization of the City 7:1–4
- B. Inhabitants of the City 7:5–73*a*

VIII. Instruction of the People 7:73*b* –8:18
- A. Explanation of the Law 7:73*b*–8:8
- B. Response to the Law 8:9–12
- C. Obedience to the Law 8:13–18

IX. Repentance of the People 9:1–37
- A. Worship of the People 9:1–5*a*
- B. Prayer of the People 9:5*b*–37
  1. Deliverance from Egypt 9:5*b*–15
  2. Sustenance in the Wilderness 9:16–25
  3. Rebellion in the Land 9:26–31
  4. Affliction of the People 9:32–37

X. Covenant of the People 9:38–10:39
- A. Signers of the Covenant 9:38–10:27
- B. Summary of the Covenant 10:28–39

XI. Settlement of the People 11:1–36
- A. Increasing the Population of Jerusalem 11:1–24
- B. Enumerating the Cities of Israel 11:25–36

XII. Dedication of the People 12:1–13:3
- A. List of Priests and Levites 12:1–26
- B. Dedication of the City Wall 12:27–43
- C. Provision for the Temple Service 12:44–47
- D. Separation from the Heathen 13:1–3

XIII. Separation of the People 13:4–31
- A. Cleansing of the Temple 13:4–9
- B. Provision for the Levites 13:10–14
- C. Keeping of the Sabbath 13:15–22
- D. Defilement of Marriage 13:23–29
- E. Closing Prayer 13:30–31

The Theology of Nehemiah

As with the book of Ezra, the book of Nehemiah is a historical narrative, primarily focusing on Nehemiah's work as the leader of the nation. It records no miracles and no prophecies. There are no direct speeches from God. The book does contain, however, many accounts of the actions of Nehemiah and others that serve to illustrate spiritual truths.

One of the primary lessons is the preeminence of prayer in the believer's life. The book mentions twelve different prayers, ten by Nehemiah (1:4–11; 4:4–5, 9; 5:19; 6:9, 14; 13:14, 22, 29, 31) and two by the Jews or their religious leaders (9:2–3, 5–37). In addition the book records the offering of praise to God in 5:13 and 8:6. The priests thank the Lord at the dedication of the walls (12:31, 38, 40). Nehemiah 11:17; 12:8, 24, and 46 refer to those who were appointed to lead prayer and praise in the worship service. It is clear that prayer, praise, and thanksgiving played a major part in the nation at this time.

As in the book of Ezra, God's showed His providential care of the nation. He placed Nehemiah in a key position in the Persian court. Having aroused Nehemiah's burden for the broken-down condition of Jerusalem, the Lord used circumstances to give Nehemiah authority to rebuild the city's wall (2:1–20). When Israel began to work on the wall (3:1–32), heathen opposition to the work sprang up (4:1–3, 7–8; 6:1–7, 10–13). In each case the opposition failed and the people completed the wall (6:15–16).

The book repeats the need for religious and moral purity found in Ezra. Nehemiah found the genealogy of those who had returned under the leadership of Zerubbabel. This list included those who could not prove their heritage as priests and were therefore put out of the priesthood (7:61–64). Later the people agreed to avoid intermarriage with the heathen (10:28–30). During Nehemiah's absence the people lapsed into sinful practices. After his return, however, he ousted the heathen from the temple (13:4–9) and took steps to see that the Levites received financial support once more (13:10–13). He also acted to stop intermarriage with the heathen (13:23–30) and to end violations of the Sabbath (13:15–22).

Primarily in the latter part of the book, the people worshiped the Lord. The Levites reminded the people of God's uniqueness and power (9:6). This is significant in view of the Persian background of the book. Early Persians accepted the gods of the different nations as having control only over the lands occupied by their people. Cyrus, the first great Persian king, restored the various gods to their lands in hopes that they would speak to Marduk, the chief god, in his favor. The religious leaders of the Jews, however, showed no hint of accepting this view.

Israel's God was faithful to His covenant with the people and extended mercy to them (1:5; 9:17, 31–32). He overcame His enemies (4:15) and guided individuals to accomplish His will (2:12–13; 7:5). He had given His Word to the people (8:1) and had chosen them as His own people (9:7).

Ezra and his assistants explained God's law to the people (8:1–13). Hearing its teaching about the Feast of Pentecost, the people took steps to observe the celebration (8:13–18). The people confessed their sins and worshiped the Lord (8:6; 9:1–3). They offered praise to Him (5:13) and entered into a covenant to keep His Word, i.e., to keep the Sabbath (10:31), and to make offerings to support the temple service (10:32–39). The Levites took up their responsibilities in the temple once more (12:22–29). The priests, Levites, and people were ritually purified before offering worship to God (12:30–31). They separated the "mixed multitude" of heathen from Israel (13:1–3).

There is a continuing emphasis in the book on the authority of God's Word. Nehemiah condemned the usury of the wealthy (5:7, 10–11 cf. Exod. 22:25; Deut. 23:19–20).[6] When some of the priests could not prove their descent from Aaron (7:63–65), they were put out of the priesthood so that they could not offer sacrifices (Num. 16:40; 18:1–3). The people gathered to hear Ezra read the law of Moses (8:1–13; 9:3). They kept the Feast of Tabernacles as commanded in the Mosaic law (8:14–18), acknowledged the commands of God (9:14), and showed their knowledge of Israel's recorded history (9:7–31). They entered into a covenant to obey God's law (10:29–39). They stopped the heathen from worshiping in the temple (9:2; 13:3 cf. Deut. 23:3–6). They agreed to support the Levites with their tithes (13:10–13 cf. Num. 18:24). Nehemiah

[6]Gary R. Williams, "Contextual Influences in Readings of Nehemiah 5: A Case Study," *Tyndale Bulletin* 53, No. 1 (2002): 57–74, analyzes the social responsibility of the relatively wealthy toward the poor.

rebuked the people for working on the Sabbath. He appointed Levites to guard the gates to keep people from buying and selling on the Sabbath (13:22; cf. Exod. 20:10). He took steps to prevent further intermarriage of the people with the heathen (13:23–28; cf. Exod. 34:14–16). Without emphasizing the various teachings of the Mosaic law, the book's account of Nehemiah's practices places a clear emphasis on the need to obey God's Word.

Perhaps the major lesson of the book lies in the role of individuals in accomplishing the work of God. Nehemiah, of course, stands out in his position of leading the Jews. His ability to remain devoted to the Lord in the face of opposition is remarkable. In the course of finishing the wall, he overcame scorn (2:19–20; 4:3–6), the threat of violence (4:7–9), the discouragement of the people (4:10–15), greed among the people (5:1–13), the deceitful plans of his enemies (6:1–4), false accusations (6:5–9), and attempts to cause him to fear (6:10–14).

In addition to Nehemiah's leadership, the book credits other specific people with their accomplishments in a variety of activities. Individuals within the nation joined their work together to rebuild the wall (3:1–32). We see Hanani and Hananiah holding responsibilities in the city. Later we find Ezra and other priests teaching the people the laws of God (8:1–18) and leading the people to renew their relationship to the Lord (9:1–10:39). Other individual returnees voluntarily moved to Jerusalem to improve the security of the nation's capital (11:1–19). The book names more than one hundred separate individuals in describing the various positions of leadership and work undertaken by the nation.

Nehemiah also demonstrates qualities of leadership that are less obvious.[7] He wrote about his burden for the nation (1:4), a

[7]Numerous authors have taken note of Nehemiah's leadership. The following are typical. Joseph Maciariello, "Lessons in Leadership and Management from Nehemiah," *Theology Today* 60, no. 3 (October 2003): 397–407, uses Nehemiah as an example of Christian leadership. He summarizes several key elements in the leadership of Nehemiah that apply to Christian leaders today. Cyril J. Barber, *Nehemiah and the Dynamics of Effective Leadership* (Neptune, NJ: Loizeaux Brothers, 1976), devotes the entire work to elements of leadership found in the book of Nehemiah. Mark D. Roberts, *Ezra/Nehemiah/Esther,* vol. 11 in *The Preacher's Commentary Series* (Nashville: Word, Inc., 1993), pp. 216–18, also takes note of several leadership qualities evidenced by Nehemiah.

burden he carried for several months (1:1 cf. 2:1). He showed his concern for purity by confessing his own sins as well as the sins of the nation (1:6). He was bold, asking for a major commitment from the king (2:5–8) and challenging the people to take up a major project (2:17–18). He wisely divided the responsibilities of the work (3:1–32). He anticipated difficulties and took action to meet them (4:13, 16–18, 20, 21). He relied on the Lord (e.g., 2:5; 4:4–5; 6:9, 14). He took his stand against other leaders of the people when they erred (5:7, 10). He was generous (5:14, 17–18). He delegated responsibilities (7:2–3). He did not let opposition stop him (4:1–6, 7–9, 10–23; 6:1–14).

NEHEMIAH 1

I. Nehemiah's Burden 1:1–11

The opening chapter of the book sets the stage for the events described in the later chapters. Nehemiah occupied a responsible position of service to the Persian king. His situation was comfortable as he enjoyed the benefits available to those who occupied high places of service in a royal environment. Despite this, upon hearing of the broken-down condition of Jerusalem's walls, he experienced deep grief and began to pray that God would use him to correct this situation.

A. Jerusalem's Problem 1:1–3

The events narrated in the book began "in the month Chisleu," the ninth month of the Hebrew calendar and mid-November to mid-December in the modern calendar. This was in the "twentieth year" of king Artaxerxes, ca. 445 BC. Nehemiah, the son of Hachaliah, an otherwise unknown individual,[8] was at

---

[8]The meaning of *Hachaliah* is unclear. The name literally would suggest something like "the Lord is dark," a meaning with no logical sense. BDB, p. 314, and *ISBE*, vol. 2, p. 1313, tentatively suggest "wait for Jehovah." Others suggest something like "afflicted of the Lord."

"Shushan the palace [*bîrâ*]." The noun *bîrâ* occurs widely in later Hebrew—Chronicles, Nehemiah, Daniel, and primarily Esther. It refers to the temple at Jerusalem (1 Chron. 29:1, 19), to a place of defense at the corner of the north and east walls apparently meant for defending the temple (Neh. 2:8; 7:2), and to the palace at Shushan (e.g., Esther 1:2; 2:5, 8). The word has the same sense here as it does every time it occurs elsewhere. Since it is most likely that the palace of Ahasuerus was a defensible structure, the translation "citadel" or "fortress" is appropriate here.

The phrase "Shushan the palace" is often translated "Shushan the capital," e.g., ESV, GNB. NASB. This is also possible. The NIV and NKJV translate *bîrâ* as "citadel," while the CEV and GW translate it as "fortress." Both the Akkadian and Aramaic cognates can be rendered "fortress" or "citadel."

This fortress was located at "Shushan," the biblical name of Susa, in the province of Elam, about 150 miles north of the tip of the Persian Gulf. Shushan also figures in the records of other biblical figures. Daniel received a vision while at Shushan (Dan. 8:2). Esther, the queen of Ahasuerus, was in Shushan at the time of the events recorded in the book of Esther (e.g., 2:8; 4:16; 9:12). Xenophon, *Cyropaedia* 8.6.22, states that Shushan was the winter residence of the Persian kings. The city was located on the Coaspes River, east of the lower Tigris River. Archaeological excavations have shown that the royal residence there occupied about two and one-half acres, v. 1.

We can only speculate as to the reason for the group of "certain men of Judah" coming to Shushan. The text gives us no information about their purpose in coming. The purpose may have been routine, a regular reporting of conditions in that part of the Persian Empire. It may also have had some unknown special purpose in view.

Hanani, one of Nehemiah's "brethren" (cf. 7:2), naturally seeks out his brother.[9] In the course of the conversation, Nehemiah asks about the Jews "that had escaped, which were

[9]Ryle, p. 149, notes that *brethren* may refer to cousin or relative; cf. Gen. 13:8; 29:15. For this reason he considers Hanani a relative of Nehemiah rather than his actual brother. The view is possible; however, the use of the term twice, here and 7:2, supports the closer family relationship of siblings.

left of the captivity." This phrase refers to those Jews who had returned earlier from their captivity. At this time there had been two groups that had come back to Palestine. About 536 BC, Zerubbabel had led the first group of returnees (Ezra 2:1–70). In 458 BC, Ezra led a smaller group from Babylon to Palestine (Ezra 8:1–36). Although the Jews had been back in Jerusalem for almost ninety years, the walls of the city still lay in ruins, and its gates had been burned (2 Kings 25:8–10). Hanani gave Nehemiah the news about Jerusalem's plight.

From the very first, the example of Nehemiah furnishes a rich challenge to Christians. Even though he served in a responsible position, far removed from the homeland of his people, his concern for his nation is clear. When the opportunity came to him, he immediately wanted to know the state of those who had returned to Jerusalem. When Hanani, his brother, told him about the desolation of the city, Nehemiah was overcome with grief.[10] The significance of the broken-down wall lies in that this was a characteristic of a city so weak and disorganized that it would be unable to defend itself against marauders or aggression by other cities round about. Proverbs 25:28 uses this as an illustration. Solomon describes there a city without walls as a picture of a man whose spirit is not self-controlled and who therefore has no defenses. Nehemiah saw the lack of walls as a reproach to the testimony of the Jews. It implied that their God was not able to defend them.

This picture of God as weak was the source of Nehemiah's grief. He was jealous for the glory of God. He realized, as Moses had before (Num. 14:13–19), that the sins of the people dishonored God before the heathen. For this reason he took this burden on himself and expressed the grief that it caused, vv. 2–3.

---

[10]Laney, p. 37, draws on the opposition of the Samaritans in which they claim that the Jews are building their walls (Ezra 4:12, 16) to conclude that the Samaritans carried out the decree of the king (Ezra 4:17–22) by destroying the walls and gates of the city. Laney says that it is this news that stirred Nehemiah to prayer regarding the rebuilding of the city. Since Nehemiah showed his concern almost two decades later, the view is doubtful.

B. Nehemiah's Prayer 1:4–11

The thought that the city had no defenses shocked Nehemiah. He began to fast, taking this time to mourn and pray (*palal*, see Ezra 10:1) to God, v. 4. His deep concern is evident in that he continued his mourning "certain days." From 2:1 we see that Nehemiah's anxiety lasted until the month Nisan, four months later. This was not a fleeting impulse of grief. Nehemiah carried a burden, revealing himself to be a man who had deep feelings of sorrow for his people.

Nehemiah's compassion is characteristic of a great many servants of God. Jesus wept over Jerusalem (Matt. 23:37–39). Paul wished that he were "accursed from Christ for [his] brethren, [his] kinsmen according to the flesh" (Rom. 9:3). Jeremiah was the "weeping prophet." The psalms reveal David's burdens. Moses showed his compassion by claiming God's forgiveness for the people (Exod. 32:31–32). The psalmist wrote: "He that goeth forth and weepeth . . . shall doubtless come again with rejoicing, bringing his sheaves with him" (Ps. 126:6). And so Christians today must seek a greater burden for others. We must realize that spiritually blind people who do not know where they are going fill this world. We must grieve over the lost around us and over Christians who are indifferent to the lost around them.

As Nehemiah took up his burden, he knew God was his resource and went to Him in intercessory prayer. Verses 5–11 record his petition. The various elements of the prayer are both interesting and instructive. Nehemiah began by addressing the Lord as the Creator God, the maker of the heavens. The name occurs elsewhere (Gen. 24:7; 2 Chron. 36:23; Ezra 1:2), clearly acknowledging the power of God and, therefore, His ability to solve the current problem. Nehemiah then recalled the character of God as "great and terrible [awesome]" (cf. Deut. 7:21). In this way, Nehemiah recognized the exalted position of God. He is the One who "keepeth" (in the sense of exercising great care over) the covenant and "mercy" (loyal love, *ḥesed*, see Ezra 3:11) for His people, v. 5. With these words Nehemiah exalted God as having a nature to love. He approached Him as One who is always faithful and merciful toward those who love and obey Him. Nehemiah affirmed with his words the right of obedient believers to expect answers to their prayers, v. 5.

Consistent with his burden in this matter, Nehemiah "prayed" (*palal*, as in v. 4) day and night. He asked God to hear his prayer on behalf of the nation. Nehemiah confessed that he, his family, and the nation had sinned. They had not kept God's Word; thus their problems were of their own making. The combination of *commandments*, *statutes*, and *judgments* comprehensively refers to God's requirements for the nation. The word *commandments* underscores the authoritative nature of God's Word. *Statutes* refers to unchangeable decrees. The joining of *commandments* with *statutes* suggests that the commandments deal with secular areas while the statutes concern religious matters. The judgments of God make possible the rendering of justice in all areas. The juxtaposition of these words occurs again in 9:13 and 10:29, vv. 6–7.

Nehemiah illustrates a basic principle of prayer. When the Word of God becomes the basis for prayer, we can have assurance that we pray in God's will. Nehemiah reminded God of the promise He had made to Moses. If the people "transgress" (*maᶜal*, see Ezra 10:2) against God, He will disperse them among the nations (Deut. 4:27*a*), v. 8. If, however, they confess their sins and begin once more to obey God, He will bless them (Lev. 26:40–42; Deut. 30:2–4). Nehemiah illustrates this blessing by recognizing God's ability to gather His people back to Palestine from widespread dispersion.

It is worth noting that Nehemiah had evidently studied God's Word. He not only referred to it here (vv. 7, 8, 9), but his actions elsewhere also revealed his knowledge of it. The very act of prayer followed the example of the godly from earlier times (e.g., Abraham, Gen. 20:17; Moses, Num. 11:2; David, 2 Sam. 7:27; Elisha, 2 Kings 6:17). Later Nehemiah rebuked the nobles for their treatment of the poor (5:7–13 cf. Exod. 22:25). In 13:10–13 he took steps to see that people met the needs of the Levites (Num. 18:24). He ordered the people to keep the Sabbath rest (13:15–22 cf. Exod. 20:8–11). He commanded the people to stop marrying the heathen (13:23–28 cf. Exod. 34:14–16), v. 9.

God had "redeemed" the nation from past dispersions. He had brought them out of Egypt (Deut. 9:29) and had also restored some from Babylon (Ezra 2:1–70; 8:31–32. The phrase "strong hand" parallels "great power." As is often the case, the "hand" of God represents His might (e.g., Exod. 32:11; 1 Chron. 29:12), v. 10.

The prayer concludes with the indication that only in God is there deliverance. Nehemiah asked the "Lord" (*ᵃdonay*) to hear his prayer and the prayers of his fellow "servants," other Jews in Babylon who shared Nehemiah's burden for their compatriots in Palestine. The name *ᵃdonay* recognizes God as the master. Nehemiah asked the Lord to "prosper" him, i.e., to give him success, and to grant to him "mercy" (*raḥam*) before "this man," Artaxerxes Longimanus. The word *raḥam* normally refers to deep love or compassion,[11] something Nehemiah would need if he was going to change the situation among the returned Jews.

Nehemiah asked for God's blessing "this day [*yôm*]," i.e., at that time. While the word *yôm* is normally translated "day," it often has the meaning of "time" (e.g., Judg. 20:15; 1 Sam. 1:4; Neh. 4:16; 5:14). From the sequence of time given in 1:1 and 2:1, Nehemiah carried the burden for about four months; hence, the translation of "time" is appropriate here.[12]

By mentioning his position as "cupbearer" (*mašqeh*), Nehemiah gave the reason why he would need to have special grace extended to him from the king. In the Apocrypha, Tobit 1:22 speaks of the cupbearer: "Ahikar was cupbearer, and keeper of the signet, and had charge of administration and of the accounts: and Esarhaddon appointed him second to himself" (trans. from CB). The cupbearer was a high position in the king's administration. Nehemiah undoubtedly had close contact with the king as he carried out his responsibilities. For this reason he needed special favor as he pondered a solution for resolving the condition of Jerusalem.

The manuscripts *Vaticanus* and *Sinaiticus* translate *mašqeh,* "cupbearer," as εὐνοῦχος, "eunuch." *Alexandrinus*, however, translates the word as οἰνοχόος "one who pours wine," i.e., a "cupbearer." The Vulgate translates *pincerna*, "cupbearer" or "butler." The Hebrew is consistent in giving *mašqeh*. It is likely that the

[11]E.g., Gen. 43:30 ("bowels"; Dan. 1:9 and Amos 1:11, "pity."

[12]Raymond Brown, *The Message of Nehemiah*, in *The Bible Speaks Today*, ed. J. A. Motyer (Downers Grove, IL: InterVarsity Press, 1998), pp. 43–44, considers Nehemiah's prayer as impulsive, "a request he had not considered carefully in advance." As the days went by, he came to realize that "today" might not be the right day for his request. While the view is possible, it would show Nehemiah in a bad light, something not seen elsewhere in the book.

thought that Nehemiah was a eunuch comes from (1) his position at the court coupled with (2) the failure to mention any wife. Neither argument is persuasive. Positions in the court were filled by eunuchs and non-eunuchs alike. Nehemiah may or may not have been married. Since a wife did not enter into his responsibilities as governor of the land, there was no need to mention her.

Origen, writing *To Africanus*, combines both ideas of cupbearer and eunuch when he refers to "Neemias, a cupbearer and eunuch of the king."[13] Coggins tentatively suggests that Nehemiah was a eunuch. He bases this on his position as a cupbearer (1:11) and his appearance here before the queen. Batten and Levering also support the view that Nehemiah was a eunuch.[14] There is no OT evidence, however, to support the view. The word referring to eunuchs (*sarîs*) occurs elsewhere (e.g., 2 Kings 9:32; 20:18; Isa. 56:3, 4), but it does not occur here. It is therefore unlikely that Nehemiah was a eunuch. The *hipʿîl* participle *mašqeh* occurs often enough in the OT that it clearly refers to a position of service rather than a physical condition that may or may not have been associated with the position (see Gen. 40:1 ["butler"]; 1 Kings 10:5 and 2 Chron. 9:4 ["cupbearers"]; Hab. 2:15 ["him that giveth . . . drink"]). In 6:10, Shemaiah tries to get Nehemiah to seek refuge in the temple. This would have been an unlikely tactic if Nehemiah was a eunuch since eunuchs were barred from the temple (Deut. 23:1).[15]

With his prayer Nehemiah took the only step available to him. He had no human way to help his people. Several hundred miles separated him from Jerusalem, and he had no great resources of his own on which to draw. He held a position with the king that required his presence. He was not an influential leader of the Jews who could influence others. All that he could claim were the resources of God. It was in this spirit that he came to God in prayer, v. 11.

---

[13]http://www.newadvent.org/fathers/0414.htm, accessed June 11, 2009.

[14]Coggins, p. 73; Batten, p. 190; and Levering, p. 164

[15]Edwin M. Yamauchi, "Was Nehemiah the Cupbearer a Eunuch?" *ZAW* no. 1 (1980), 132–42, examines a wide array of evidence and concludes that while Nehemiah may have been a eunuch, that conclusion is "only a possibility and not a probability."

NEHEMIAH 2

II. Nehemiah's Preparation 2:1–20

With the Lord's help, Nehemiah successfully gained an appointment from the king to correct the problems at Jerusalem. He traveled to Jerusalem, where he could take the right actions. After arriving, he introduced himself to the Persian representatives in the area. This brought the first hint of opposition, an opposition that shows up repeatedly through the first half of the book. Nehemiah approached his task carefully, first examining the walls himself to determine the scope of the necessary building, and then meeting with the Jewish leaders, where he obtained their agreement to undertake the work.

A. Request of the King 2:1–8

1–3 Four months had passed (1:1 cf. 2:1), and it was now the month of Nisan, corresponding to March-April in the modern calendar. (The name *Nisan* is a loan word from the Akkadian *nisannu* "first" which often refers to the first month. It is therefore appropriate here for the first month of the Jewish religious calendar.) While this was earlier "in the twentieth year of Artaxerxes [ca. 445 BC]" than the month Chisleu (1:1), the seeming discrepancy can be explained in several ways. It is possible that the reign of Artaxerxes began with the month in which he became the emperor. If this took place in any month between Nisan and Chisleu, then Nisan would follow Chisleu. If Artaxerxes began his reign after Chisleu, the month of Nisan would fall before Chisleu in his twentieth year. Although this is a possible view, there is no evidence that the reigns of the Persian kings were counted this way.[16] Nehemiah may have used the agricultural year followed in Judah, beginning the year in the month Tishri. This would allow Nisan, now the seventh month, to follow Chisleu, the third month. This is the easiest view to accept.[17]

---

[16]Although he rejects this view, Ryle, p. 147, mentions this as a possibility.

[17]This is the solution proposed by Edwin Thiele, *Mysterious Numbers of the Hebrew Kings* (Grand Rapids: Wm. B. Eerdmans, 1965), pp. 30, 161. Fensham, p. 150, Keil, p. 164, and Laney, p. 79, adopt this view.

Normally Nehemiah would carry out his responsibilities before the king in a happy frame of mind. On this day, however, the burden that he had carried for four months affected his behavior. He was so concerned about Jerusalem that he displayed his sorrow in the king's presence.[18] Apparently, Nehemiah had not previously allowed the state of Jerusalem to affect him outwardly. On this day, however, he had been thinking about the city, and his emotions overwhelmed him. At the time he "took up the wine" to give it to the king, he was close enough to let the king sense his emotional state. It is possible that Nehemiah had tears in his eyes or that his eyes were red from previous tears, v. 1.

Whatever the nature of his expression of grief, Nehemiah's sorrow was apparent to the king. Artaxerxes asked Nehemiah the reason for his sadness. This spontaneously caused Nehemiah to fear. Showing sorrow in the presence of the king was a serious offense (cf. Esther 4:1–2). God, however, overruled in this situation, v. 2. Nehemiah began his answer with a customary phrase, "Let the king live for ever" (1 Kings 1:31; Dan. 2:4; 3:9). He then proceeded to describe the plight of Jerusalem that had caused his sadness. He referred to "the place of [his] fathers' sepulchres." Apparently Nehemiah's family had been wealthy enough to have their own private burial places in caves within the city or cut out from the nearby rocks (cf. 3:16), v. 3.

4–8 The king responded by asking Nehemiah what he wanted. This invited Nehemiah to ask to correct the situation at Jerusalem. Nehemiah quickly "prayed" (*palal*, see Ezra 10:1) to ask the Lord's blessing. This kind of prayer was characteristic of Nehemiah (see also 1:4–11; 4:4–5; 4:9; 5:19; 6:9; 6:14; 13:14, 22, 29, and 31), v. 4. Nehemiah had apparently been thinking about the plight of Jerusalem ever since his brother had revealed it to him (1:2–3). Now, having prayed, he requested the king to commission him to rebuild "the city."

Nehemiah's request had to be made tactfully since Artaxerxes had earlier ordered that work on the city be stopped (Ezra 4:17–22). While the Jews had completed their work on the

[18]Maxwell, p. 69, suggests that Nehemiah deliberately looked sad in order to solicit the king's question. In view of Nehemiah's integrity displayed throughout the book, this is highly unlikely.

temple (520 BC), they had not continued to work on the walls, the primary defense of the city. Nehemiah now hoped to end this halt in building the walls, v. 5. The king asked Nehemiah for the details of his commission—how long it would take, when he would return—and Nehemiah set a time. We find out later (5:14; 13:6) that Nehemiah remained at Jerusalem for twelve years. It is doubtful that his original request covered this period of time. He apparently obtained extensions from the king to let him continue the work.

The mention of the queen probably indicates that this conversation took place in a private session rather than at a public dinner. Persian history records that Artaxerxes Longimanus had one primary wife, Damaspia, and that she was the mother of Xerxes II, his only legitimate son. In addition, he had many concubines, by some of whom he had additional children. We know little about Damaspia. She died on the same day as her husband, between December 24, 424 BC and January 10, 423 BC, possibly suggesting that both succumbed to a plague of some kind. There is no record of where they died. Their bodies were carried back to Persia.[19] The mention here of the queen may indicate that her presence influenced the king's decision by prompting him to act in a kindly manner. It is also possible that the earlier influence of Queen Esther and Mordecai remained. This had ended at least twenty years earlier (1:1; 2:1) but could well have affected Artaxerxes during his childhood, v. 6.

Nehemiah asked for letters commissioning him so that the "governors" (*peḥâ*, see Ezra 8:36) "beyond the [Euphrates] river" would help him by providing safe conduct. Nehemiah's response was different from that of Ezra thirteen years earlier (2:1 cf. Ezra 7:8). Ezra had refused help to insure safety (8:22). That situation, however, differed from the circumstances here. Ezra had testified of God's power to the king and therefore did not think he should ask for a guard to protect him. Nehemiah was a highly placed governmental official who would normally travel with an escort. In addition, the presence of the king's guard would

[19]Information taken from Photius's excerpt of Ctesias's *Persia*, http://www.livius.org/ct-cz/ctesias/photius_persica2.html#%A747. Accessed June 12, 2009.

have served to establish his credentials as the newly appointed governor over Israel, v. 7.[20]

Nehemiah also asked for a letter to Asaph, the keeper of the royal forest (lit. "park" or "enclosed garden"). Josephus, *Antiquities* 8.7.3, describes this place: "Very pleasant it is in fine gardens, and abounding in rivulets of water." While this is possible, it is also speculative. We do not have enough information to identify the place certainly although it logically would have been near Jerusalem. It would have been extensive enough to furnish wood for the gates of the "palace" (or "fortress," *bîrâ*, see 1:1), beams used in repairing the gates of the city, and lumber "for the house that [he would] enter into," Nehemiah's own house, which undoubtedly would have included governmental offices. Henry places this park or garden in "the forest of Lebanon" (cf. 2 Kings 19:23). This suggestion has the advantage of following the earlier example of Ezra 3:7. Keil locates the gardens as a "sycamore forest in the low plains" south of Jerusalem. Ryle identifies it with Solomon's Garden in Etham, about six or seven miles south of Jerusalem.[21]

While Nehemiah says nothing about his office, his request clearly implies a formal position as governor over the Jews in Palestine. The king granted Nehemiah's entire request. Although it was the king who granted the request, Nehemiah recognized that it was God who had directed in this. The reference to God's hand occurs often in the books of Ezra and Nehemiah (Ezra 7:6, 9, 28; 8:18, 22, 31; Neh. 1:10; and 2:18), v. 8.

B. Arrival at Jerusalem 2:9–20

9–10 Accompanied by a royal guard, Nehemiah traveled across the regions between Babylon and Palestine. He presented his letters to the "governors" (*peḥâ*) to announce the royal policy that he would carry out, v. 9. Sanballat was the governor of Syria. The name *Sanballat* means "Sin [the Akkadian moon-goddess] gives life." He is called "the Horonite," probably a

[20]Myers, p. 71, mentions that some suggest "there is here a subtle hint of the superiority of Ezra's method [no military guard, Ezra 8:22] over that of Nehemiah." The Lord, however, does not lead everyone the same way. Nehemiah was a governmental leader, and a military escort was appropriate.

[21]Henry, p. 1072; Keil, p. 166; Ryle, p. 162.

reference to where he was born. We know of a town named Beth-Horon, on the border between Ephraim and Benjamin (Josh. 16:5; 18:13), which could have been his birthplace. We cannot be certain that this was the location, however.

Evidence of Sanballat's position comes from Egypt. For several hundred years a Jewish colony had liveved on the island Elephantine at the first cataract of the Nile River, opposite Aswan. Letters from there dated ca. 410 BC mention Sanballat as the governor of Samaria.[22]

Tobiah was "the servant, the Ammonite," a vague description.[23] He may have been the king's servant or the servant of Sanballat. He may also have come from a servant's background, much the same as Nehemiah. Some think that Tobiah was the governor of Ammon at that time.[24] In this case a weak Israel would have been to his advantage. Whatever his background, his role in the opposition to Nehemiah shows him to have been one of the leaders.

At this point Nehemiah had not revealed to the Jews his purpose in coming to Jerusalem. He had only shown his royal commission to the political leaders of the region. Their response suggests that it was to their advantage to keep the region weak and thus firmly under their control. In all likelihood the opposition was due at least partially to the rivalry between Samaria and Judah.[25] The NT develops more fully the rivalry between Judah and Samaria (e.g., Luke 9:52–53; John 4:9). While nothing is said openly about this, it is also a reasonable conclusion that

[22]Coggins, p. 72, refers to papyri dated in the early fourth century BC that mention another Sanballat. For this reason he concludes that we cannot date Nehemiah certainly in the fifth century BC. The references to Zerubbabel (7:7; 12:1, 47), Artaxerxes (2:1; 5:14; 13:6), and the high priest Eliashib (3:1, 20; 13:4, 28), whose service can be approximately dated from 12:10, support the earlier date for the book.

[23]Rawlinson, p. 17, suggests that Tobiah was Sanballat's servant, "perhaps his secretary." Luck, p. 90, adopts the same position. From the mention of Tobiah later (6:12, 14, 17, 19; 13:4, 7, 8), it seems that Tobiah held a position of leadership.

[24]Coggins, p. 74, and Kidner, p. 15, suggest this possibility.

[25]John G. Butler, *Nehemiah the Wall Builder* (Clinton, IA: LBC Publications, 1998), p. 55, adopts this view.

these leaders resented the loss of their power and, in all probability, the loss of revenue received from the Jews, v. 10.

11–16 After arriving in the city, Nehemiah waited three days before taking any steps toward his goal. This time was likely spent in meetings with various leaders to introduce himself as the new representative from the king. Although he did not reveal his purpose in coming at this point (cf. v. 16), this interval would have allowed him to learn which leaders were most influential and who held the responsibilities that he would need to draw on. It is also possible that Nehemiah required some time to refresh himself physically after the rigors of the long journey, v. 11.

Perhaps anticipating some opposition to his plans, Nehemiah made an inspection tour of the city by night. He rode an unidentified animal, probably a horse. The presence of the "horse gate" (3:28) suggests that horses had at one time been common in the city. Nehemiah 2:9 refers to "horsemen" that accompanied Nehemiah to Jerusalem. Nehemiah 7:68 mentions a large number of horses that had come to Jerusalem at the time of Zerubbabel's return. While it is also possible that Nehemiah rode a mule (Neh. 7:68), these were not as common as horses in Zerubbabel's return. Nehemiah took with him only a few men, either servants or soldiers, v. 12.

There is uncertainty about the exact identification of the places mentioned in his inspection. Much of ancient Jerusalem has been destroyed and rebuilt. The "gate of the valley" (2 Chron. 26:9) was fifteen hundred feet from the "dung port" (3:13). Both of these must have been in the southern part of the city, opening toward the Valley of Hinnom, where the people dumped their refuse. The "dung port [lit. 'gate']" is probably the same as the "potsherd gate" (Jer. 19:2, ESV, NASB, NIV), a gate for the disposal of refuse. The "dragon well" is usually identified with En Rogel, a well serving as a source of water in the fuller's field for cleaning garments (Isa. 7:3; 36:2). It was near the intersection of the valley of Hinnom and the Kidron Valley. After going out, Nehemiah "viewed" (better "inspected") the broken-down condition of the walls, v. 13. The "gate of the fountain" seems to be the gate in the south end of the eastern wall that led to the "king's pool." This was undoubtedly the pool of Siloah (Siloam) (3:15). It is here called the "king's pool," probably so named because of Hezekiah's part in its construction (2 Kings 20:20). At this point the debris was so great that Nehemiah could no longer continue to follow the wall on horseback, v. 14.

Probably leaving the animal with one of the men with him (v. 12), Nehemiah then continued on foot along the brook that runs through the Kidron Valley, east of the city. From there, he "viewed" (again, "inspected") the wall of the city. He then "turned back," reentering at the Valley Gate where he had left the city, v. 15. Nehemiah did not speak of the inspection immediately to the city's leaders. These leaders probably came from the council of elders that governed the Jewish inhabitants. Nehemiah waited until his plans were complete before telling others, v. 16.

17–18 Having completed his inspection, Nehemiah met at some later time with the leaders of the people. He proposed rebuilding the walls in order to remove the "distress" of the city, its reproach (cf. Prov. 25:28), v. 17. He persuasively told them of God's blessing on his work and of the authority from Artaxerxes Longimanus (see 1:11) to proceed with the rebuilding of the city and its walls. These leaders agreed to begin the work and "strengthened their hands," beginning their preparations for the task, v. 18.

19–20 The local Samaritan officials scoffed at the plans of the Jews. This opposition apparently came from the ongoing enmity between the Samaritans and the Jews. In addition to Sanballat and Tobiah (v. 10), Geshem appears here for the first time. The name *Geshem* appears on a silver vessel dated in the late fifth century BC. The inscription on the vessel reads "Qaynu, son of Geshem, king of Qedar."[26] This identifies the one who has dedicated the vessel to the Arabian goddess Han'lat. Other evidence suggests that Geshem and his son controlled a league of Arabian tribes that ruled Moab, Edom, and part of Arabia, v. 19.[27] Nehemiah replied to their accusations with a statement of confidence in God, and he reminded them that they had "no portion (*ḥeleq*), nor right (*ṣᵉdaqâ*), nor memorial (*zikkarôn*)" in

[26]F. M. Cross, Jr., "Geshem the Arabian, Enemy of Nehemiah," *Biblical Archaeologist* 18 No. 2 (February, 1955), 46–47.

[27]Ryle, p. 170, identifies Geshem as the chief of an Arabian tribe, some group to the south of Judah or the Arabian community set up by Sargon in Samaria. Luck, p. 92, follows Rawlinson, p. 19, in tentatively suggesting that he was head of a group of Arab troops in Samaria.

the city. The three terms cover the various bases on which the Samaritans might claim authority in Jerusalem. They did not have a *ḥeleq* (a legal claim), a *ṣ*ᵉ*daqâ* (an ethical or moral claim), or a *zikkarôn* (a historical claim). Nehemiah thus repelled the first round of a great deal of opposition to him and his work described in the book, v. 20.

NEHEMIAH 3

This chapter records the work of various individuals and groups in rebuilding the wall of Jerusalem. Beginning with the Sheep Gate, the chapter recounts in order the work done on the wall between the gates of the city. The work began at the Sheep Gate, with the building continuing to the Fish Gate, vv. 1–2. It continued to the Old Gate, vv. 3–5, on to the Valley Gate, vv. 6–12, and then to the Dung Gate, vv. 13–14. The work on the Fountain Gate came next, v. 15, followed by that on the Water Gate, vv. 16–26. The work moved next to the Horse Gate, v. 27–28, moved on to the East Gate. v. 29, to the gate called Miphkad, v.v. 30–31, and then continued to where the work had started at the Sheep Gate, v. 32.

III. Nehemiah's Coworkers 3:1–32

There is a slight peculiarity in how each man or group is introduced. In vv. 1–15, the standard phrase is "next unto him [or 'them']" and then the name or names of the men involved. In vv. 20–32, the words "after him [or 'them']" introduce the ones involved. In vv. 17–19, both phrases occur by way of introduction. This change of phrases has caused some to assume the involvement of different authors or sources for the information.[28] Bailey argues cogently against this view.[29] He makes three

[28]Batten, p. 207, understands these different introductions as evidence for editing of the chapter.

[29]Nicholas Andrew Bailey, "Nehemiah 3:1–32: an Intersection of the Text and the Topography," *PEQ* 122 (January–June 1990): 36–38.

points. (1) The usage agrees with the text and the topography since 3:1–15 describes the building on the west side while 3:16–32 treats the activity on the east side. (2) There is logic to the passage. The list begins with the work at the Sheep Gate, the most important gate since it was nearest the temple and animals to be sacrificed came through this gate. It was also the only gate repaired by the priests, the most important group involved in the work and therefore logically mentioned first. (3) The phrase "next . . ." is lit. "on his hand." As the work moves to the southern end of the city, the hand would be the right hand. When the work turns northward, the phrase "after . . ." is lit. "behind . . . ," a normal distinction in view of the change in the direction of the work. The use of both phrases in 3:17–19 may well reflect changes in the topography or configuration of the wall (see "angle," v. 19).

1–2 The account of the rebuilding of the walls begins with the work of the priests. This group was under the leadership of Eliashib, the high priest (v. 20; 13:28). The priests worked in the area of the Sheep Gate, located on the northeastern part of the city walls near the temple area. The name likely came from the use of the gate to bring sheep into the city, possibly for sacrifice. The gate receives mention only in Nehemiah (also 3:32; 12:39) and John 5:2, where the supplied word "market" should be "gate."

The character of the work at this point appears in that "they sanctified [*qadaš*, or "consecrated"] it," dedicating it to the Lord. The word *qadaš* occurs widely in the OT but only five times in Nehemiah (3:1 [2x], 12:47 [2x], 13:22). The word refers primarily to that which is set apart to God for His service. When *qadaš* occurs in the *piᶜel*, as here and in 13:22, it normally refers to the consecration of someone or something to God. They set up the "doors," the two leaves of the Sheep Gate. Moving counterclockwise around the walls, they built to the "tower of Meah" (*hammeʾâ*, lit. "the hundred," possibly indicating an office used by the centurions in previous times). It is mentioned again in 12:39.[30] They built also to the "tower of Hananeel" ("God is gra-

[30]*The Jewish Encyclopedia*, ed. Isidore Singer (New York: Ktav Publishing House, Inc., n.d.), vol. 6, p. 197, suggests other suppositions, "that the tower was either garrisoned by one hundred men, or was one hundred cubits high, or had one hundred steps." Coggins, p. 82, suggests that the Tower of

cious"), also mentioned in 12:39, Jeremiah 31:38, and Zechariah 14:10. This work also was "sanctified" (or "consecrated"). Both of these locations were at the northeastern corner of the wall.

It is appropriate to list first the contribution of the priests. Those who are involved in the Lord's work ought always to lead the way in His service. The "Nethinims" (better "Nethinim"), also involved in the temple service, are listed in vv. 26 and 31. In addition, the chapter lists men from other vocations. These included goldsmiths and apothecaries (v. 8), political leaders (vv. 9, 12, 14, 15, 16, 17, 18, 19), a gatekeeper (v. 29), and merchants (v. 32). There were undoubtedly other vocations involved. The chapter reveals a cooperative effort involving men with different abilities and strengths. This is a picture of God's work in every age (Rom. 12:4-8; 1 Cor. 12), v. 1.

Men from Jericho built the next section of the wall. They worked on the northern part of the wall, the area they would normally have entered when traveling from their own city. Zaccur, the son of Imri, an otherwise unknown person, worked next to the men of Jericho. Jericho, as mentioned here, was the first of several other cities to send workers. Men also came from Tekoa (v. 5), Gibeon and Mizpah (v. 7), Zanoah (v. 13), Beth-haccerem (v. 14), Beth-zur (v. 16), and Keilah (v. 17). These men recognized that the defenseless condition of Jerusalem, especially since it was the location of the temple, reflected on the nation as a whole. Although Jerusalem was not their home, they joined in the work, v. 2.

3–5 The "sons of Hassenaah"[31] repaired the next section, the Fish Gate. This gate received its name from the fish that were brought through it from the Mediterranean. It is logical that a fish market was located inside the wall near the gate (also

---

Hananeel and the Tower of the Hundred are different names for the same tower. While the two towers were undoubtedly close to one another, the mention of both in 12:39 strongly supports understanding them as different structures.

[31]Kidner, p. 86, understands *Hassenaah* as a place name. The name *Senaah* occurs again at Ezra 2:35 and Neh. 7:38, but in neither place are children named, the only such omissions in the list. If it was a place, we cannot locate it with any certainty. A similar name, *Hassenuah*, occurs as a personal name in 11:9 and 1 Chron. 9:7.

mentioned in 2 Chron. 33:14, Neh. 12:39, and Zeph. 1:10). The men set up the doors together with the "locks" (better, "bolts," *manᶜûl*) and the "bars" (*berîaḥ*). The word *manᶜûl* occurs six times in the OT, five of them in this chapter (3:3, 6, 13, 14, 15; Song of Sol. 5:5), each time here referring to some way for securing the gates. The word *berîaḥ* occurs widely to refer to various kinds of bars, often those holding the upright pieces of the tabernacle (e.g., Exod. 26:26–29), and elsewhere those set across a city's gates to secure them (e.g., 1 Kings 4:13; 2 Chron. 8:5), v. 3.

Continuing in a counter-clockwise direction, "Meremoth, the son of Urijah" repaired the next section. Meremoth was one of the priests who earlier weighed and tabulated the gold and silver vessels brought to Jerusalem at the time of Ezra's return (Ezra 8:33–34). His father "Urijah," also spelled "Uriah" (Ezra 8:33), was later part of an escort for Ezra during the reading of the law to the people (Neh. 8:4). Urijah was the son of Koz (lit. "Hakkoz") about whom we know nothing else certainly. Verse 21 mentions all three of these men again.

Meshullam (cf. v. 30; 6:18) worked on the next section. He was the "son of Berechiah," who was "the son of Meshezabeel." There is no clear mention of Berechiah elsewhere. Meshezabeel is likely the same man mentioned in 10:21 and 11:24. Zadok (10:21), son of Baana, worked on the next section. We know nothing else about Baana, but the name may be a variant spelling of Baanah (Ezra 2:2), v. 4.

Tekoa was a town about ten miles south of Jerusalem. The first group of men from this city (see v. 27) repaired the next area although some of their nobles haughtily refused to support the work. The phrase "put not their necks to the work" comes from the use of oxen drawing the plow with a harness attached to their necks. The phrase "work of their Lord" is ambiguous. It may refer to the Lord's work (e.g., ESV, NKJV),[32] to the work called for by

[32]Butler, p. 82, and Keil, p. 177, adopt this view. Keil considers the word *ᵓadonêhem*, "their Lord," a plural of excellence referring to God. While this is possible, the narrative emphasizes the leadership of Nehemiah. It is therefore more likely that these nobles had been influenced by Sanballat, Tobiah, and Gesshem and rejected any effort to strengthen the city.

Nehemiah (e.g., NET, REB)[33] or, more probably, to the "work of their masters" (e.g., NASB, NIV). Since pride clearly dominated these men, it is best to take the phrase as a reference to their refusal to serve under others who supervised the work, v. 5.

6–12 The "old gate" is mentioned only here and at 12:39. The phrase means lit. "gate of the old [or 'Jeshanah']." Although the words *gate* and *old* differ in gender, the sense is still that of an "old gate." The adjective is likely feminine since it refers to a part of the city, normally a feminine idea in Hebrew.[34] From its place in the narrative, the gate must have been in the northwestern part of the wall. Logically, it was the gate used most often to enter the older part of the city.

Jehoiada, the son of Paseah, and Meshullam, the son of Besodeiah, worked on this gate. They laid the beams to frame it, set up the doors, and install locks. Paseah, called Phaseah in 7:51, was one of the Nethinim in the return under Zerubbabel (Ezra 2:49). We know nothing else about Jehoiada, Meshullam, or Besodeiah, v. 6.

Melatiah and Jadon, again unknown men, built the next part. The men of Gibeon and Mizpah, two small towns north of Jerusalem about six and seven miles respectively, assisted them in the work. They built "unto the throne" (*kisseʾ*, or "to the [official] seat"), a confusing phrase that has been variously interpreted.[35] It likely has the same use as in Psalm 9:4 and Proverbs 20:8,

---

[33]Holmgren, p. 103, Ryle, p. 175, and Throntveit, p. 75, adopt this view. The word *Lord* (*ʾadonêhem*), however, is plural. While it is possible to consider this a plural of majesty referring to Nehemiah, it is more natural here to see it as a reference to the on-site leaders of the work.

[34]Some authors and translators suppose *Jeshanah* refers to a city (2 Chron. 13:19) thought to be located ca. fifteen miles north of Jerusalem. W. F. Albright, "New Identifications of Ancient Towns," *BASOR* 9 (February, 1923): 7–8, relies on the mention of the town in Josephus, *Antiquities*, 8.11.3; 14.15.12, where he locates a town called Isana north of Jerusalem in the vicinity of Bethel and Ephron. Albright suggests a location named Burj el-Isâah that seems to meet the criteria. It is possible that the gate reflects the city's name although it is unlikely that a gate would bear the name of a city so minor that its location is not clearly known and is barely mentioned by name in Scripture.

[35]Keil, p. 179, and Luck, p. 94 consider this "a judgment seat" used by the Persian governor when he was in Jerusalem. Coggins, pp. 82–83, suggests that Gibeon and Mizpah were under the "direct authority of the governor." Noss and Thomas, p. 303, understand it as "the residence of the governor" as

where it refers to a place of judgment. It would indicate here that the Persian "governor" (*peḥâ*, see Ezra 8:36) of the region had a place in Jerusalem to use for the trials he held to decide various matters, v. 7.

After the labor of these men comes the work of Uzziel, the son of Harhaiah, one of the "goldsmiths" (better "refiners"), and Hananiah, "the son of one of the apothecaries" (better, "an apothecary [or 'perfumer']"). Elsewhere these refiners created idols (Isa. 41:7; 46:6) and dishes (Jer. 10:9, "founder"). Logically they would also have created jewelry and ornate decorations for the wealthy. Apothecaries created oils used in worship (Exod. 30:25; 37:29) or for anointing the dead (2 Chron. 16:14). They also compounded perfumes (Exod. 30:35). There are several other Uzziels and Hananiahs in the OT, but we cannot identify these individuals with any of them.

These men "fortified" (*ᶜazab* or "left") the city in the area of the "broad wall." The meaning of this phrase is unclear. The verb *ᶜazab* normally means "to leave or forsake." Twice, however, both times in Nehemiah, it is translated "fortify" (also 4:2). This has led some to translate the verb as "restored," allowing it to refer to the building process.[36] Although suitable in this context, this brings up the question of why a different verb would be used here when *ḥazaq* occurs thirty-five times elsewhere in the chapter referring to various repairs. This suggests that the usual meaning is appropriate here.

The phrase may mean that the builders left that portion of the wall alone since it didn't need much work.[37] It may suggest that part of Jerusalem itself lay outside the wall and so these men left that part outside the newly rebuilt wall.[38] Other views have also

---

though he had a dwelling in the city. This is unlikely since *kisseᵓ* never refers to a place of residence elsewhere.

[36]Keil, p. 200; Kidner, p. 87; Noss and Thomas, p. 304; and *TWOT*, vol. 2, p. 659, adopt this view. Fensham, p. 175, translates it as "repair." The verb *ᶜazab* occurs more than 200x, however, and is never translated in the KJV as "restore" or "repair."

[37]Butler, p. 79; Pope, p. 63, and Rawlinson, p. 28, prefer this view.

[38]Laney, p. 83; Larson and Dahlen, p. 159; and Ryle, p. 179, adopt this position.

been suggested. Since the object of the verb is Jerusalem, the idea of leaving part of the city outside the restored wall seems best.

We do not know the location of the "broad wall" or why it received this name. Rademacher and Allen state that "the Broad Wall was probably built in the seventh century B.C. by Hezekiah to accommodate the influx of refugees from the fall of Samaria in 722 B.C." They support that view using 2 Chronicles 32:5. Noss and Thomas see it as "the pre-exilic wall that branched off between the Ephraim Gate and the Tower of the Ovens . . . extended to the west along the western hill, and rejoined the original wall next to the Siloam Pool." Larson and Dahlen say the name refers to an area inside the city enclosed by that wall. Nehemiah 12:38 locates it near the "tower of the furnaces." This would place the wall in the northwest part of the city, but we cannot be more specific, v. 8.[39]

Rephaiah, "the ruler [*śar*, see Ezra 7:28] of the half part [*pelek*] of Jerusalem," and the son of Hur, built the following portion of the wall.[40] The word *pelek* refers to a district. We can relate it to the Akkadian cognate *pilku*, "circuit, boundary," and thus an area or district. The word *pelek* occurs ten times in the OT, eight of them in this chapter (vv. 9, 12, 14, 15, 16, 17 [2x], 18).[41] The phrase "half part" refers to a part of this district adjacent to the

[39]Rademacher and Allen, p. 314; Noss and Thomas, p. 304; Larson and Dahlen, p. 159.

[40]Henry, p. 1078, notes the different rulers mentioned in the chapter. These include rulers over "the half part of Jerusalem" (vv. 9, 12); "part of Beth-haccerem" (v. 14); "Mizpah" (vv. 15, 19); "the half part of Beth-zur" (v. 16); and "the half part of Keilah" (vv. 17–18). Henry suggests, "The Persian government would not entrust any one with a strong city, but appointed two to be a watch upon each other." This view is possible but also speculative.

[41]Bowman, pp. 687–88, notes that it is unlikely that "depopulated Jerusalem" or a small town such as Keilah (pp. 17–18) would need two rulers. He relates *pelek* to an Akkadian cognate *pilku,* which refers to an "assigned portion." In this chapter, it would refer to the foreman who oversaw "half of the assignment" in the town. The description of the work, however, lists many other men who seemed to have responsibility over various parts of the work. Aaron Demsky, "*Pelekh* in Nehemiah 3," *IEJ* 33, nos. 3–4 (1983): 243–44, relates the word to the Akkadian *pilku*, "work duty" or "tax in the form of conscripted labour." He sees this as referring to the citizens fulfilling the taxation laid on them by the Persians. Aside from the fact that this is not a major use in Akkadian, it does not explain how some refused to join in the work (v. 5). The Akkadian cognate is most often used of an area, i.e., a district.

city even though we cannot identify which portion is in view (cf. v. 12). Since 7:2 refers to Hanani and Hananiah having "charge over Jerusalem," it is not likely that the district here was within the city. We know nothing else of Rephaiah or Hur, v. 9. Jedaiah, the son of Harumaph, both unknown persons, took responsibility for the next section of the wall, located near his house. The name Harumaph means "split nose" and so may indicate a physical deformity. Next to him, Hattush, possibly the priest mentioned in 10:4 and the son of an unknown Hashabniah, or the son of the Levite Hashabniah (cf. 9:5), repaired the wall, v. 10.

Malchiah (Ezra 10:31) was the son of Harim, an unknown individual. Hashub, possibly the same man mentioned in 10:23, was the son of Pahath-moab, the head of a prominent family in Judah (Ezra 2:6; 8:4; Neh. 7:11) and later a signer of Nehemiah's covenant, 10:14. Malchiah and Harub repaired "the other piece" (better, "another section") of the wall, but the exact part is not mentioned. Here and in vv. 20, 21, 27, and 30, no earlier work is described. In vv. 19 (cf. v. 7) and 21 (cf. v. 4), the person is associated with earlier repair of the wall. While it is possible that the list of names in the chapter is incomplete,[42] it is also possible that the narrative omits the earlier work due to its insignificance. This would have freed up the workers to do additional repairs

Malchiah and Harub also worked on "the tower of the furnaces" (cf. 12:38), a tower built into the northwestern wall for defensive purposes. The name likely came from nearby ovens, used by bakers preparing their products, v. 11. Shallum was the son of Halohesh, a signer of Nehemiah's covenant, 10:24. Shallum was the "ruler" (*śar*) of the other half of the "part" (or "district," *pelek*) adjacent to Jerusalem (cf. v. 9). He and his "daughters"[43]

[42]Fensham, pp. 172–73 sees the use of "another" without describing the first work as indicating that the chapter does not give a complete list of those leading the work.

[43]Coggins, p. 83, and Fensham, p. 176, argue that the word *daughters* refers to the inhabitants of some small villages in Shallum's district; cf. Pss. 9:14; 48:11. When used this way, however, the word should be in a construct relationship with the parent, e.g., daughter of Babylon, daughter of Zion. Since it does not have that grammatical relationship here, it is better understood to refer to Shallum's own family. Luck, p. 95, mentions the view that the "daughters" were wealthy women who hired others to do the actual work. This would be a strange way to express their contribution to the work.

worked together in repairing the next part of the wall. While the involvement of daughters in this work is unusual, it is not impossible that Shallum wished to involve his family, v. 12.

13–14 The Valley Gate had been Nehemiah's starting point in his previous inspection (2:12–15). This lay toward the south, in the western wall of the city. Hanun and those who lived in Zanoah, a small town about fifteen miles west of Jerusalem, repaired the gates and a thousand cubits (about fifteen hundred feet) of the wall. Since they worked on such a large section of the wall, it is likely that a large group from Zanoah joined in the work. It is also probable that the repairs were not extensive in that area. Since Nehemiah rode his horse in this area (2:12–13), this supports the conclusion that Hanun and the others carried out only minor repairs, v. 13.

Malchiah, the son of Rechab, an unknown individual, was the "ruler" (*śar*) of "part" (or "district," *pelek*) of Beth-haccerem. Jeremiah 6:1 mentions this as a place for signaling. The location of this town is uncertain. It has been identified with modern Khirbet Salih, a small town two miles north of Jerusalem.[44] It has also been identified with 'Ain Karim, on the top of Jebel 'Ali, a mountain four and one-half miles west of Jerusalem.[45] The Dead Sea Scrolls place it in the Valley of the Kings, southwest of Jerusalem.[46] Yohanan Aharoni suggests a site called *Ramath Raḥel*, the highest point between Jerusalem and Bethlehem.[47] About all we can say now is that this small town and its surrounding region was near Jerusalem.

Malchiah repaired the Dung Gate, generally thought to be located in the southeastern part of the city wall. This name came from the use of this gate for carrying refuse and garbage out of the city to be burned in the Valley of Tophet. As with the

---

44 *Wycliffe Bible Encyclopedia*, ed. Charles F. Pfeiffer, Howard F. Vos, and John Rea (Chicago: Moody Press, 1975), vol. 1, p. 224.

45 Merrill F. Unger, *Unger's Bible Dictionary*. Chicago: Moody Press, 1967, p. 140.

46 Michael Wise, Martin Abegg Jr., and Edward Cook, *The Dead Sea Scrolls: a New Translation* (San Francisco: HarperSanFrancisco, 1996), pp. 83, 195.

47 Y. Aharoni, "*Ramath Raḥel*," *IEJ* 6 (1956): 152–155.

Old Gate, v. 6, this work involved rebuilding the gate as well we setting up doors with locks and bars to secure them, v. 14.

15 Shallun, the son of Colhozeh, probably the same man mentioned in 11:5, was the "ruler" (*śar*) of "part" (or "the district," *pelek*) of Mizpah. This is distinct from the town of Mizpah and probably refers here to the region surrounding the city (cf. vv. 7, 19). Shallun led the group that repaired the Fountain Gate, rebuilding it, covering it (*ṭalal*), setting up the doors of the gate, and installing locks and bars to secure it. The verb *ṭalal*, "to cover," appears only here in the OT. It is a cognate of the Akkadian *ṣalalu*, also "to cover." The related Hebrew *ṣalal*, "to shade," used in 13:19 ("dark"), reflects the idea of some cover blocking the light. The gate was located near the Pool of Siloam, where water flowed into the city through Hezekiah's tunnel, excavated when the spring was sealed (2 Chron. 32:2–4). This same group also repaired the wall by "the king's garden," near the pool of Siloah (or Siloam, John 9:7), and some stairs leading away from the "city of David," the older part of the city captured by David. From their location near the pool of Siloam, it is likely that the "stairs" are those leading into the valley at the south end of the old city, v. 15.[48]

16–26 Nehemiah, the son of Azbuk, was the "ruler" (*śar*) of "part" (or "district," *pelek*) of Beth-zur, a small town approximately fifteen miles south of Jerusalem. We know nothing more about Azbuk. This Nehemiah, likely assisted by men from Beth-zur, rebuilt the wall near the "sepulchres of David" where the descendants of David lay buried. The repairs extended to the "pool that was made," apparently referring to the result of Hezekiah's work in bringing the waters under the city walls and to the "house of the mighty," the barracks of the "mighty men of David." We do not know the locations of these places, v. 16.

Several Levites worked on the next sections of the wall. Rehum was the son of Bani, but we know nothing else about the son. Bani joined Nehemiah in interpreting the law to the people, 8:7, and in exhorting the people to praise the Lord, 9:4–5. He later signed Nehemiah's covenant, 10:13. Hashabiah was a leader

---

[48]Ryle, p. 182, identifies the stairs as those leading up the eastern slope of Mount Zion. While this is possible, these are almost a thousand feet from the Pool of Siloam, so the identification must remain tentative.

of the Levites, 12:24, the "ruler" (*śar*) of "part" (or "the district," *pelek*) of Keilah, fifteen miles southwest of Jerusalem. He also signed Nehemiah's covenant later, 10:11, v. 17.

Bavai, the son of Henadad, an unknown person, was the "ruler" (*śar*) of the other "part" (or "district," *pelek*) of Keilah. Other than being a brother of Binnui, v. 24, we know nothing else about Bavai. It is possible that "Bavai" ("Bavvay" in the MT) is a scribal error for "Binnui," v. 24, also the son of Henadad. There is some manuscript evidence for this. The translations differ. The CEV, GW, NET, and NLT use "Binnui," while the ESV, GNB, NASB, and NKJV follow the KJV in translating the name as "Bavai" or "Bavvai," v. 18.

Ezer, the son of Jeshua, also unknown elsewhere, served as the "ruler" (*śar*) of the town of Mizpah, distinct from the surrounding area (v. 15). He led a second party from Mizpah (v. 7) to repair the wall "up to the armoury," the storage area for the arms and armor of the soldiers. This was probably the "arsenal" showed off by Hezekiah to the Babylonian representatives (Isa. 39:2). The work continued to "the turning [or "angle"] of the wall," an unknown projection in the wall, v. 19.

The account singles out Baruch, the son of Zabbai, for his zeal in working on the wall. He "earnestly repaired" from "the turning [again 'the angle'] of the wall" to the entrance into the house of Eliashib, the high priest. The location of this house seems to have been south of the temple, in the northeastern part of the city. This work was the "other piece" (or "second piece") done by Baruch. The narrative does not mention his first piece of work, possibly an indication that it did not involve a great deal of time or effort.

Meremoth, the son of Urijah who, in turn, was the son of Koz, worked on "another piece" (again, "a second piece") in the next section of the wall. Verse 4 mentions the first part of Meremoth's work on another part of the wall. Here he repaired the wall that extended from the door leading to Eliashib's house to the end of the house. Verse 1 mentions Eliashib as leading the work near the Sheep Gate, v. 21. The next group includes several unnamed priests, "men of the plain [*kikkar*]." The word *kikkar* refers to something round, here a portion of land located in the Jordan Valley (e.g., 1 Kings 7:46; 2 Chron. 4:17). These priests owned land in the area where they worked when not involved with priestly duties, v. 22.[49]

Benjamin, possibly mentioned in 12:34, and Hashub, possibly the same man mentioned in 10:23, carried out the repairs of the next part of the wall. We cannot identify either man with certainty. The fact that they worked on the wall near "their house" suggests a family relationship. Azariah was the son of Maaseiah, who was the son of Ananiah, an otherwise unknown individual. Azariah helped Ezra in expounding the law, 8:7, and signed the covenant, 10:2. He also assisted Nehemiah in the dedication of the wall, 12:33. Maaseiah assisted Ezra at the reading of the law, 8:7, and signed the covenant, 10:25. Azariah repaired the wall by his house, v. 23.

Binnui, the son of Henadad, repaired the next section, beginning by the house of Azariah and continuing to "the turning [or 'angle'] of the wall" and on to the corner. As in vv. 19, 20, and 25, the word *turning* refers to some unidentified projection in the wall. Binnui later signed Nehemiah's covenant, 10:9. We know nothing for sure about Henadad, but he might have been the same man mentioned in Ezra 3:9, v. 24.

Palal, the son of Uzai, served opposite the projection from the wall and the tower of the king's "high house." We may understand the phrase in Hebrew as the "high tower" away from the king's house, or the tower that is away from the king's "high house." The versions translate this in various ways. The majority (e.g., CEV, ESV, GNB, NASB, NET, and NIV) take it to mean "high house," which they render as "upper palace" or "upper house." But others (e.g., CB, GW, and REB) translate it

[49]Bowman, pp. 692–93, places the dwelling of the priests closer to Jerusalem "scarcely as far from the temple as the Jordan Valley." He cites Jeremiah 1:1, which refers to priests living in Anathoth, about three miles northeast of Jerusalem, and Luke 1:39, which places Zacharias in "the hill country" of Judah. Priests, however, served at Jerusalem only one out of every twenty-four weeks (1 Chron. 24:1–19). First Chronicles 13:2 indicates that the priests lived in cities throughout the land. Joshua 21:11 places priests living in Hebron, about twenty miles south of Jerusalem. Second Chron. 31:15, 19, refers generally to the cities occupied by priests. Ezra 2:70 refers to the priests dwelling in "their cities." Cities of refuge, where priests could live, were scattered throughout the land on both sides of the Jordan River. For these reasons, it seems reasonable that a group of priests lived in the Jordan Valley.

as "upper tower." The term *high house* seems to refer to Solomon's palace, located higher on the temple mount than the earlier palace built by David.[50]

For some unknown reason, the "court of the prison [better 'guard']," discussed at 12:39, was associated with the king's house (Jer. 32:2). The OT does not mention either Palal or Uzai again. After Palal, Pedaiah, the son of Parosh, worked. We cannot certainly identify Pedaiah elsewhere in the OT. The name of his father, Parosh, occurs frequently in Ezra and Nehemiah (Ezra 2:3; 8:3, "Pharosh"; 10:25; Neh. 7:8; 10:14). While it is likely that this refers to Pedaiah's father in at least some of these places, it is impossible to determine whether any of these instances refer to him, v. 25.

Nehemiah inserts a parenthetical remark to describe the nature of the dwellings in this area. The Nethinim (see the discussion at Ezra 2:43) were temple servants who carried out the menial aspects of the work, cutting wood and drawing water for the temple service. The name means "given," indicating that these had been given to help in the ministry. In Nehemiah's time they lived in "Ophel" ("swelling"), a hilly area on Mount Moriah by the Water Gate and near the temple (cf. 11:21), v. 26.

27–28 The phrase "after them" is lit. "after him," referring back to Pedaiah (v. 25). A second group of Tekoites repaired the next part of the wall (cf. v. 5). Their work began at the projecting tower and continued as far as "the wall of Ophel," near the home of the Nethinim (v. 26). Josephus, *The Wars of the Jews*, 5.6.1, places this wall between the Kidron Valley and the temple mount. Since this was an inner wall of the city, it was not worked on at this time, v. 27. After them, the priests repaired the wall above the Horse Gate. This gate was near the king's palace (2 Chron. 23:15) in the eastern wall of the city (Jer. 31:40). Each of the priests worked on the wall near his house, v. 28.

29 Zadok, the son of Immer, also worked on the wall near his residence. We know nothing specific about either Zadok or

[50]Barnes, p. 464, Fensham, p. 178, and Larson and Dahlen, p. 161, say *high house* refers to Solomon's palace. But Myers, p. 117, Pope, p. 65, and Ryle, p. 186, believe the upper tower that projected out from the king's palace is the referent of the phrase.

Immer. After Zadok, Shemaiah, the son of Shechaniah, worked on the wall. He was a descendant of Zerubbabel (1 Chron. 3:19–22) and was charged with opening and closing the East Gate, which was in the northeast part of the city, at the appropriate times. Shemaiah is thought to be the Semei of Luke 3:26. We know nothing else for certain about Shechaniah, v. 29.

30–32 Hananiah, the son of Shelamiah, repaired the next section of the wall. We know nothing definite about either of these men. Hanun, the sixth son of Zalaph, both otherwise unknown persons, worked on the next part. The detail about being a "sixth son" differentiates him from the Hanun mentioned earlier (v. 13). We do not know if his older brothers still lived in the area. In addition to his earlier work (v. 4), Meshullam, the son of the otherwise unknown Berechiah, worked near his living quarters. Meshullam's daughter later married the son of Tobiah the Ammonite (6:17–18), v. 30.

Malchiah, the "goldsmith's" (or "refiner's," see v. 8) son, worked on the next part, continuing to the "place" (or "house") of the Nethinim (v. 26), and of the merchants. Since this place used by the Nethinim is near the temple, it is possible that those actively serving there at any particular time used the place. This area of work is in front of the Miphkad Gate, mentioned only here and uncertainly located in the city's north wall. Malchiah also repaired as far as "the going up of the corner," apparently a room located on the wall at that point, v. 31.

Nehemiah completes his description of the building by ending where he began. The "goldsmiths" (or "refiners") and merchants rebuilt the section from the room to the Sheep Gate, near the northeastern corner of the city, v. 32.

Among others, H. A. Ironside draws a spiritual application from the ten gates and their order as mentioned in this chapter.[51] The Sheep Gate suggests the cross, the sacrifice of the Lamb of God, and God's judgment on Him as He bore the sins of mankind. The Fish Gate reminds those who receive this sacrifice that they should be fishers of men. The Old Gate suggests subjection to God's will. The Valley Gate suggests humility, the

---

[51]H. A. Ironside, *Notes on the Books of Ezra, Nehemiah and Esther* (Neptune, NJ: Loizeaux Brothers, Inc.,1976), pp. 24–32.

Dung Gate cleansing from sin, and the Fountain Gate sanctification by the Holy Spirit and God's Word. Ironside equates the Water Gate with the Word of God. The Horse Gate refers to war and thus suggests the conflicts of the Tribulation. It also reminds believers that the Lord will one day come from heaven on a white horse. The East Gate suggests the coming of the "Sun of righteousness" (Mal. 4:2), and the Miphkad Gate refers to the "Judgment Seat of Christ" (2 Cor. 5:10).

While this application of the gates is devotional, it is also highly subjective. Nehemiah 12:39 mentions two additional gates, the Gate of Ephraim and the Prison Gate, for which Ironside makes no spiritual applications. Other applications could also be suggested, depending on what someone might imagine that these gates mean. However, it is best to see them as simply entrances through the wall into the city. Since the chapter mentions the gates only to indicate locations of the workers, there is no need to seek spiritual significance in them.

NEHEMIAH 4

IV. Nehemiah's Opposition 4:1–23

In the MT, vv. 1–6 belongs to c. 3, numbered as vv. 33–38 there. This is generally followed by the LXX, while the Vulgate follows the same grouping that is found in most Bibles today. The association with c. 4 is better since the anger of Sanballat and Tobiah (vv. 1, 3) connects well to v. 7, which mentions these two men again.

A. Ridicule of the Work 4:1–6

1–3 Sanballat (see 2:10) became "wroth" (*ḥarâ*) at the news of the plan to rebuild the city's walls. The word *ḥarâ* is graphic. The verb means "to kindle, be hot" and thus refers to the heat of anger. The context here suggests a burning anger, strong enough to lead Sanballat to work against the decree of Artaxerxes. Sanballat also experienced "great indignation," the adjective *great* indicating a high degree of vexation. This led him to "mock" the Jews, speaking of them with derision, v. 1. Sanballat spoke before an assembly of "his brethren," fellow officials of Persia in various capacities, and the "army of Samaria," soldiers assigned to insure peace in the region. He tells them about the Jews' plans, speaking contemptuously of them as he does.

Sanballat asked five rhetorical questions to show his belief that the Jews would not succeed in carrying out their plans. The first question is general—what are these "feeble" (*ʾamelal*) Jews doing? This expressed his belief that the Jews could not succeed. The word *ʾamelal* occurs only here. It comes from the verb *ʾamal*, "to wither, waste away, languish," which elsewhere describes dried up fields (Isa. 16:8; 24:7) and faint-hearted men (Ezek. 16:30).

In asking this question, Sanballat poetically scorned the Jews rather than literally assessing their abilities. Thus Sanballat bought into the common belief that only strength and resources can bring about accomplishments. God, however, delights in using the weak to accomplish His will (cf. 1 Cor. 1:27–29). It is more important to be yielded to God so that He can work through you by His power than to have power in yourself and in your own resources.

The second question, "Will they fortify themselves?" is taken in different ways. It literally means "Will they leave [*ʿazab*, see 3:8] for themselves?" The word *ʿazab* occurs twelve times in Ezra and Nehemiah. With two exceptions, here and 3:8, the KJV translates it as "leave" or "forsake." Some understand *ʿazab* with a secondary meaning, "to repair" (CEV, ESV, NASB). This faces the problem stated at 3:8, that the word never has this meaning elsewhere. The question asks if the Jews will leave the building of the fortified wall to themselves, i.e., will they be able with their poor resources to finish the work?[52] Sanballat's question, then, again suggests the inability of the Jews to succeed in their work.

The three remaining questions continue with a sarcastic tone. Would the Jews offer sacrifice, as though this could secure divine aid? Sanballat clearly did not expect this to happen. Would the Jews complete the work in a single day? No! This was a work too

[52]Authors accepting a liberal view, e.g., Ryle, p. 191, often suggest a textual error. This leads to speculation with no textual support as to a correct reading. Batten, p. 226, and Pope, p. 67, are among those who understand the verb in its normal sense of "to leave or forsake."

large for them to attempt. Would they bring back to full strength the stones that had been burned and were therefore now only unusable rubble? The limestone commonly used in buildings in Jerusalem loses its strength when burned. These words overstate the work required by the Jews. While the gates of the city had been burned (1:3; 2:17), there is no indication that the walls had been. The Babylonians had broken them down (2 Kings 25:10; Jer. 52:14), thereby leaving usable rock for the repairs, v. 2. Tobiah the Ammonite (see 2:10) joined Sanballat in mocking the Jews. He suggested that even the footsteps of a fox, a relatively light animal, would break down the work of the Jews, v. 3.

4–6 News of the mockery reached Nehemiah. In response he spontaneously prayed. In view of the contempt shown to them, he asked God to turn the reproach of their enemies back on them. He asked the Lord to bring them under judgment in "the land [better 'a land'] of captivity," i.e., in a land where their foes would be taken into captivity, v. 4.

The next imprecation is equivalent to saying, "Don't overlook their iniquity [*ᶜawon*, see Ezra 9:6], or don't let them get away with this." Nehemiah thus prayed that God would vindicate the Jews because their enemies had publicly provoked Him to "anger" (*kaᶜas*). Although the verse does not mention God as the object of the provocation, the KJV rightly supplies the word *thee*. The *hipᶜîl* of the verb *kaᶜas* occurs six more times, with five of them (1 Kings 15:30; 21:22; 2 Kings 23:26; Jer. 8:19; Hos. 12:14) referring to the anger of God and the remaining one (Ezek. 32:9) to the anger of men caused by God, v. 5.

The people ignored the threats of their foes and continued working on the wall. They finished "unto the half thereof," i.e., to half of the full height, leaving no gaps through which an enemy could enter the city. Although the wall was undoubtedly uneven in its height, the word *half* is an appropriate approximation to describe it. This accomplishment was possible because of the willingness of the people to work, v. 6.[53]

[53]Myers, p. 123, proposes various interpretations without drawing any conclusion. He suggests that half the wall was built, that it was built only to half of its width, or that it was built to half of its height. We can reject the first two suggestions since walls are customarily built as a whole, not partially.

B. Defense of the Work 4:7–23

7–9 The representatives of four Persian provinces now joined in the attempt to stop the work of the Jews. Sanballat, leading the Syrians, joined Tobiah and the Ammonites, the Arabs (probably led by Geshem, 2:19), and the Philistines (represented by the Ashdodites). Ashdod joined Gaza, Gath, Ashkelon, and Ekron as the five principal cities of the Philistines. The city was three miles from the Mediterranean, almost due west of Jerusalem. The alliance of these four groups represented the surrounding territories—the Syrians to the north, the Arabs to the south, the Ammonites to the east, and the Philistines to the west.

When these enemies of the Jews heard of the progress in rebuilding the walls, they became "wroth" (*ḥarâ,* see v. 1), v. 7. They conspired to fight against the Jews with the intent "to hinder it" (lit., to "work error"), i.e., to bringing such confusion that it would lead the Jews to make mistakes, v. 8. In response to the threat, Nehemiah first led the people to pray, appropriating God's power for protection. He then set a watch "because of them," thereby countering the threat of attack. This added the human element of protection to warn the people if the enemy showed up, v. 9.

10–12 Another problem confronted Nehemiah. No doubt fearful of the opposition, "Judah," the people of the nation involved in the building, lamented their weakness in the face of so much work. Too much "rubbish," dirt and rock from the broken-down wall, remained. The workers' "strength [had] decayed," i.e., they were worn out from removing the rubble. This was going to keep them from finishing the wall, v. 10. In addition, their foes threatened them with sudden attack that would kill them and stop the building of the walls, v. 11.

Even other Jews discouraged them. Those who lived in surrounding towns, where there would have been more contact with the heathen, had said "ten times," i.e., again and again, that they were going to attack the builders regardless of which way they might turn. The same phrase "ten times" also occurs in Numbers

---

Bowman, p. 699, understands the verse to say that half the work was finished. While this view is possible since v. 7 refers to stopping the breaches, it suggests rather that only the initial stages were completed, establishing protection.

14:22 and Job 19:3. In all three cases it idiomatically expresses the idea of a repeated thought or action. This follows the use of the number *ten*, which may indicate "many" (e.g., Gen. 31:7, 41; Num. 14:22; Mic. 6:7). In this situation, the people expressed their fear that the foes would attack all of the places in Jerusalem where the men have returned to help with the repairs of the wall v. 12.[54]

13–15 The phrase "therefore set I . . ." reads better "then I stationed men in the lowest places behind the wall, the exposed places [*baṣṣᵉḥiḥîyîm*], and I stationed the people. . . ." The verb *ṣaḥah*, "to be dazzling," lies behind the noun *ṣᵉḥîḥîm*, which elsewhere means "top," referring to the sunlit surface of a rock (Ezek. 24:7, 8; 26:4, 14). The word refers to open places in the wall, scorched or dazzled by the sun. It is variously translated "holes" (CEV), "open" (ESV), "unfinished" (GNB), or "exposed" (NASB), all of which give the same idea. The sense is that Nehemiah set defenders at those points where the wall was most likely to be breached by the enemy. Further, he armed them with weapons with which to confront attackers. The sword mentioned here is the short sword that would be readily handled by the workers. In addition, the people carried spears and bows for their defense, v. 13. After surveying the preparations, Nehemiah exhorted the people not to fear the enemy. They were to remember the "great and terrible [or 'awesome']" Lord (*ʾᵃdonay*, see 1:11) who was on their side as they fought for their families, v. 14. The enemy, hearing that the people knew about their plans and that Israel's God had made their counsel of no avail, abandoned their thought of attack. At this the people returned to their work. Verses 17–21 make it clear that they maintained a state of readiness for battle at the same time they worked, v. 15.

16–18 Nehemiah made provision for work and for defense. Half of his "servants," Nehemiah's personal guard (cf. 4:23; 5:10, 16), were occupied in building the wall, and half of them were prepared for defense. Those had spears, shields (*magen*, the

[54]Keil, p. 203, and Ryle, p. 197, understand the phrase "from all places" to refer to the nearby towns which no longer had men to defend them in case of attack. They implore the men to return to give safety to their homes. While this is possible, Nehemiah's future actions (vv. 13–14, 16–23) show that he is concerned about the defense of Jerusalem. Since this is not a likely answer to a threat to surrounding towns, I have adopted the above sense.

small round shield carried by a soldier), bows, and "habergeons" (breastplates, coats of mail, or some form of body armor). By setting his personal guard as a watch, Nehemiah allowed the work to proceed as swiftly as possible while still maintaining the safety of the city. The "rulers" (or captains) were behind the people, ready to give direction in case of an attack and to direct the work of building the wall, v. 16.[55] The phrase "they which builded [or 'who built'] on the wall" completes v. 16. It clarifies those included in "the house of Judah."

The phrase "and they that bare burdens . . ." begins a new thought. Those involved in carrying material, either supplies for the work or removing rubbish, did so with one hand involved in the work and the other hand carrying a "weapon" (*šelaḥ*). This introduces the problem of explaining how work can be done with one hand at the same time the other hand carries a weapon. Various explanations have been given. Matthew Henry states the phrase "cannot be understood literally" but indicates the people were equally involved with both work and defense. Radmacher and Allen suggest the swords were hung on the sides of the men as they carried out their responsibilities in the work. Rawlinson, combining the thought here with v. 18, divides the workers into two groups. The builders use both hands in their work but have a sword hung by their side. The ones carrying materials did so with one hand and kept a sword in the other hand. Laney offers the possibility that the weapons were kept near at hand. Since the work and the carrying of materials require both hands at times, this seems to be the best explanation.[56]

There is no agreement as to what kind of weapon the word *šelaḥ* refers to. KB simply gives "weapon." BDB gives "missile, weapon." Keil suggests a "sword." Myers following the AB, which uses "spear." Bowman relates the word *šalaḥ* to something thrown, as if the workers had a hand free to throw stones at their enemies. Fensham gives "missile," also thinking of a stone that

---

[55]Rawlinson, p. 42, and Luck, p. 101, understand "rulers" as the princes of Judah. While this is possible, I have taken the word to refer to captains because of the emphasis on defense in the verse.

[56]Henry, p. 108; Radmacher and Allen, p. 315; Rawlinson, p. 42; Laney, p. 89.

could be thrown at an attacker.[57] Most translations (including NASB, NIV, and ESV) simply use "weapon," v. 17. The builders, needing two hands for their work, had their swords nearby as they worked. Nehemiah's aide with his "trumpet" (*šôpar*, referring to the trumpet made from the curved horn of a ram) remained with him, ready to signal the people if needed, v. 18.

19–21 Nehemiah spoke to the leaders and the people. He reminded them of the scope of the work and that they were separated from each other, v. 19. The "trumpet" (*šôpar*) call would therefore signal them if there were any need to assemble for defense. He encouraged them with the words "our God shall fight for us," v. 20. The people continued their work from the first light of the morning until the stars appeared. The work was done in the early part of summer (cf. 6:15), the time of the year when the days are the longest. The people, however, had a "mind to work" (v. 6) and thus willingly put in the long hours required for building the wall. Following the example of Nehemiah's servants (v. 16), half of them labored while half remained ready for defense, v. 21.

22–23 As an additional precaution, Nehemiah urged the people from the outlying towns and their servants to remain in Jerusalem at night. This enabled them join in the work by day with some of them helping to guard against an attack at night, v. 22. Nehemiah set an example of carefulness. He, his "brethren" (other Jews involved in the administration of the nation), his servants, and his personal guard did not change their clothes at night. The final phrase "*saving that* every one put them off for washing" is lit. "every one his weapon the water," i.e., they took their weapons with them when they went for water, v. 23.[58]

---

[57]KB, vol. 4, p. 1517; BDB, p. 1010; Keil, p. 205; Myers, p. 124; Bowman, p. 703; Fensham, p. 188.

[58]The NIV and NASB support this view, but many versions translate the clause as something like "each one kept his weapons at his hand [or 'right hand']" (ESV, GNB, GW), as do Keil, p. 207, and Kidner, p. 94, , reading the Hebrew as *hêmîn* (or *hêmînû*), "at his right *hand,*" rather than the MT *hammayim*, "the water." While this is a logical translation, there is no textual support for it, and the LXX and the Vulgate support the MT. Rawlinson, p. 42, gives the literal translation as "each man's weapon was his water." He understands this to mean "a man's only bath was his weapon," which would be a peculiar way to phrase the fact that the workers did not bathe during this time.

NEHEMIAH 5

V. Nehemiah's Example 5:1–19

Up to this point, the threat to the nation in opposing their work had come from outside the people. The leaders of surrounding nations saw a weak Jerusalem as being to their advantage and so attempted to hinder the work. A problem now developed from within the nation as some of the people sought to gain personal advantage from the situation. Such problems are not unique to the OT. Satan is always ready to lead Christians into some activity or attitude that will hinder the Lord's work from going on.

A. Problem of the People 5:1–5

1–2 A situation from within the Jewish community came to Nehemiah's attention. The people cried out against some of the wealthier Jews, not merely murmuring but with a "great cry" to indicate their distress. This expression of grief naturally involved the "wives" since it had affected their children (vv. 2, 5), v. 1.[59]

The problem came from three areas, all of which related to the poverty of the Jews. This poverty reflected the circumstances faced by the people. With the Syrians, Arabs, Ammonites, and Philistines allied against them, normal trade had undoubtedly suffered. In addition, men from the nearby towns were staying in Jerusalem (4:22) and therefore not able to carry on their normal income-producing work. The growth of Jerusalem from these additional people would have naturally exhausted their resources more quickly than normal.

The writer introduces each complaint with almost the same words ("there were those that said," vv. 2, 3, 4). In the first place, because of large families, some needed to obtain grain. The presence of an enemy outside the city walls had undoubtedly driven up the price of grain within the city. Because of this, "therefore we take up corn [*dagan*]. . . ." The word *dagan* refers to cereal grain. In Palestine this could include wheat, barley, millet,

---

[59]Throntveit, pp. 61, argues that c. 5 is out of position. It interrupts his structural analysis of c. 1–7. He sees the chapter as following c. 13. Since there is no textual support for his view, there is no need to reposition the chapter.

beans, lentils, and several other lesser-known grains. It did not refer to maize, the corn commonly eaten today but not raised in biblical times, v. 2.

3–5 The second problem was a "dearth," a famine, that had caused a shortage of "corn" (*dagan*). This apparently had taken place prior to Nehemiah's return and the building of the city walls. Some of the people had borrowed money, mortgaging their possessions to buy grain because of this difficulty, v. 3.

The third problem required mortgaging property, borrowing money (*kesep*, see Ezra 3:7) to pay the annual tribute to Persia. Herodotus 3.91 gives the annual tribute as almost fifteen thousand talents, v. 4. Even though they were Jews akin to "their [wealthy] brethren," some had sold their children into slavery to others to pay the mortgages.[60] It is clear that this sale of the children into bondage had not taken place voluntarily. The sale of the children was the result of the extreme interest charged by the lenders. Some of the parents had now lost their lands and had no way of redeeming their children from their servitude.

The lament mentions twice (vv. 1, 5) that "brethren" had been involved in causing the plight of the Jews. This greed on the part of the wealthier Jews violated both the letter and the spirit of the Mosaic law. The Jews were forbidden to exact interest from other Jews who were forced to borrow (Exod. 22:25). Further, they were to display a spirit of love for one another (Lev. 19:18). Israelites could voluntarily sell their children into slavery (Exod. 21:2, 7; Lev. 25:39–40). They could also voluntarily sell their property (Lev. 25:25, 29). The charging of interest here, however, had forced some to sell their children into bondage. This oppression of others by those who loaned money was wrong, (Lev. 25:14). By failing to act charitably toward others, the wealthier class had created problems for other Jews, v. 5.

[60]Bowman, p. 708, notes that the text mentions daughters twice. He concludes that the second mention must differ from the first. Since the phrase "brought unto bondage" (*nikbašôt*) refers to rape in Esther 7:8 ("force"), he gives it that sense here. The more common meaning of this word is "subdue." This occurs 14x, while the reference to rape occurs only once where the context makes the sense clear. It is more likely that the double reference here is simply a means of giving emphasis to show the enormity of the problem.

B. Proclamation of the Solution 5:6–13

6–7 Nehemiah therefore became "angry" (*ḥarâ*, see Neh. 4:1) when he heard of these problems, v. 6. He "consulted with [him]self," thinking the matter through before acting. He then charged the wealthy with "usury" (*maššaᵓ*), burdening their countrymen unfairly.[61] Nehemiah called an assembly of the people to discuss publicly the problem caused by the usury.

The meaning of *usury* has changed over the years. Today, it refers to a burdensome charge laid on the borrower. In biblical times, however, it had the simple meaning of "interest." Although the charging of a reasonable interest rate may seem fair, in this case it violated the more important responsibility of showing love to others. Nehemiah rightly inveighed against those who had added this burden to their fellow Israelites, v. 7.

8–11 Nehemiah pointed out the inconsistency of the actions of the Jews. He and others who had recently come from Babylon had "redeemed [their] brethren the Jews," buying them out of slavery from the surrounding nations as they had means. He gives no details about this, but apparently he and others had assisted poverty-stricken Jews in Babylon to keep them from being sold as slaves to heathen masters. Now these moneylenders were causing their brethren to be sold back into bondage. The question "Shall they be sold unto us?" suggests that Nehemiah and others loyal to him would be forced to buy them back.[62] The guilty people had no answer to Nehemiah's charge, v. 8.

Nehemiah reminded them of the need to "walk in the fear of [their] God" (cf. Deut. 10:12) by dealing kindly with their countrymen. This would forestall the "reproach of the heathen," the taunts that would come from the nation's enemies, v. 9. Nehe-

[61]Rawlinson, p. 47, argues against translating *maššaᵓ* as "usury." He notes that the complaint had not mentioned usury. He prefers to translate v. 7*b* as "Ye lend upon pledge." By requiring pledges of land, houses, or children, the lenders had imposed a burden on the people. While the noun *maššaᵓ* does not necessarily mean "usury," the context here shows that the loans had proved burdensome, and thus usurious, to their fellow Israelites. The NASB, NIV, and NKJV all use *usury*.

[62]Fensham, p. 194, gives the possible view that "unto us" should be understood as "concerning us," i.e., as far as the Jews were concerned, they were still being sold. Even if the purchasers were Jews, it was still wrong. I have adopted the above view as being a more normal translation of the *lamed* preposition.

miah included himself as one who had lent "money" (*kesep*, see Ezra 3:7) and "corn" (*dagan*) to others. The act of loaning was not wrong. It was wrong, however, to exact interest from poor fellow Israelites (Lev. 25:35–37; Deut. 23:19) although interest could be charged to non-Israelites (Deut. 23:20).

Because of the circumstances at this time, Nehemiah urged all to quit this practice of charging interest, v. 10. In this emergency he exhorted the others to return the lands, vineyards, olive yards, and houses that had been seized. The lenders should also give back "the hundredth part of the "money" (*kesep*), i.e., the one percent monthly interest on what they had loaned. This had been paid in money, "corn" (*dagan*), wine, and oil, v.11.

12–13 The wealthy individuals agreed to restore what they had taken through their lending and interest practices. Further, they would "require nothing" of the people in the future. To ensure this, Nehemiah required "them," the nobles, to take an oath before the priests, v. 12. To illustrate God's curse if they did not keep their word, Nehemiah shook out his "lap," i.e., the loose-fitting mantle in which things could be carried. This visible action demonstrated that they would be so emptied by God of their possessions if they failed to carry out their promise. The people responded by saying "Amen," a word meaning "verily" or "truly." This gives the sense of "so be it" as they express their agreement with what has been said. They also offered their praise to the Lord for being able to work out this situation, v. 13.

C. Pattern of Nehemiah's Leadership 5:14–19

14–15 Perhaps as an encouragement to the wealthy, Nehemiah appended his own fiscal practices to the record of the earlier difficulty faced by the people. During the twelve years of his leadership (445–433 BC), neither he nor his "brethren," other Jews who served with him in the administration, had eaten "the bread of the governor [*peḥâ*, see Ezra 8:36]," i.e., the food due him and paid for from the local taxes on the people. *Brethren* here refers to fellow-servants occupied with the administration of the people, v. 14.[63] This was contrary to the practice of the "governors" (*peḥâ*) who had gone before him. In all likelihood Nehemiah was referring to the Samaritan governors who had served prior to his coming. They had been "chargeable" (better, "heavy," i.e., burdensome) to the people. They had received their expenses from the local taxes of "bread and wine, beside forty shekels of silver," i.e., a total of "forty shekels" per day required for the expenses of the office. In addition, the servants of the office "bare rule" over the people, i.e., lorded it over them, causing oppression. He does not explain the nature of this oppression. In view of the context, it likely involved additional financial burdens, perhaps inflicted as they assisted in collecting the taxes. Nehemiah had refrained from this because of "the fear of God," his reverence toward the Lord, v. 15.

16–17 Rather than looking for opportunities to purchase land from individuals in need, Nehemiah and his servants had joined in the work on Jerusalem's wall, v. 16. He had also entertained 150 of the Jewish leaders, as well as foreign dignitaries from surrounding heathen nations, v. 17.

18–19 These entertainment needs required that an ox, six choice sheep, and a variety of fowls be prepared each day for Nehemiah's table. Periodically the stores of wine needed to be replenished. Despite this heavy need for food and wine at his own table, Nehemiah had not required the "bread of the governor [*peḥâ*]," cf. v. 14. He had not required them to furnish this because he knew that the burden of the Persian tribute was heavy (cf. v. 4), v. 18. In view of his relationship with the people, Nehemiah asked the Lord to remember him with goodness. This is a characteristic prayer of Nehemiah (cf. 13:14, 22, 31), v. 19.

[63]Luck, p. 104, views *brethren* as referring to family members of Nehemiah. Since the book mentions only one family member (Hanani, 1:2; 7:2), the word is likely broader than this.

NEHEMIAH 6

VI. Nehemiah's Victories 6:1–19

The work continued on the wall. The enemies of the Jews, however, did not abandon their opposition to this work. Since Nehemiah was the one leading the Jews to strengthen their capital city, they focused their opposition on him. This chapter records three separate attacks on Nehemiah. It also records the completion of the work on the city's walls.

A. Accusation of the Enemies 6:1–9

1–4 Nehemiah's enemies heard that the Jews had completed the wall, except for setting "up the doors upon [or 'in'] the gates." Although there is an apparent conflict between 3:1, 3 ("set up the doors"), and the events of this chapter, there is actually nothing to concern us here. Chapter 3 gives an overview of the whole building project. Chapters 4, 5, and 6 describe other matters that took place during the same period of time. This chapter fills in details of the building process that have not yet been discussed, v. 1.

Nehemiah's foes invited him to meet with them in "one of the villages," better "Chephirim" (cf. 7:29). Chephirim was a city located in the plain of Ono in the area occupied by the tribe of Benjamin. The plain of Ono lay northwest from Lod (Neh. 7:37), known in the NT as Lydda, and ran toward Joppa. The area was also known as the "valley of craftsmen" (cf. 11:35). The word translated "villages," *k*[e]*parîm*, occurs in related forms eight times elsewhere. In 1 Samuel 6:18, 1 Chronicles 27:25, and Song of Solomon 7:11, the translation "villages" is appropriate. Joshua 18:24 compounds the word to refer to a different location. Other instances (Josh. 9:17; 18:26; Ezra 2:25; Neh. 7:29) use this word to refer to a specific location ("Chephirah"). In view of this, I prefer to translate the word as the proper name *Chephirah* here.

Brown leaves the translation as "villages" and places this "a full day" away from Jerusalem. Keil asserts that "there is no valid ground for regarding [*k*[e]*pirîm*] as the proper name of a special locality" but then suggests a locality near Lod, more than twenty miles from Jerusalem.[64] The distance involved in these suggestions makes them unlikely. Why would Nehemiah's foes ask him to travel so far? They could work whatever harm they planned in a private location much nearer. In addition, to make sense of the phrase *the villages*, we must supply words such as *one of* to clarify it. Since Chephirah occurs elsewhere in Ezra and Nehemiah, it is reasonable to see this name occurring here.[65]

This town lay about eight miles northwest of Jerusalem, in the area that had belonged earlier to Benjamin. The invitation was deceitful, part of a plan to harm Nehemiah, possibly even killing him to stop his leadership, v. 2. He responded that he was involved with an important work and could not leave since the work would stop in his absence. He no doubt made decisions regarding the work that could not be delegated to others, v. 3. Despite the refusal, Nehemiah's enemies repeated the invitation four times. These invitations likely varied the meeting place and time of meeting, but Nehemiah refused each time, v. 4.

5–9 Sanballat then changed his tactics by sending his servant to circulate an open letter, i.e., one that is readily readable by others. The letter likely would have been written on parchment or papyrus and left unsealed so that anyone could read it, v. 5.[66] The letter quoted unnamed heathen and "Gashmu" (a variant spelling of Geshem) who accused Nehemiah of rebellion by building the wall to fortify the city in preparation for pro-

[64]Raymond Brown, p. 100; Keil, p. 216.

[65]Richard Schiemann, "Covenanting with the Princes: Neh VI 2," *VT* 17 (1967): 367–69, argues that *kᵉpirîm* has a metaphorical use, standing for "princes," in Nah. 2:12–13 and Ezek. 19:2–6. He therefore sees this as an invitation to Nehemiah to meet "with his opponents who are governors, or tribal chiefs, or princes of local districts" for the purpose of establishing a covenant with them. While the word *kᵉpirîm* may have a metaphorical use elsewhere, this is rare. The word normally refers to a lion but has a secondary meaning of "village." The view also requires interpreting the phrase "let us meet together" to refer to establishing a covenant. It leaves unanswered the question as to why Nehemiah should enter into an agreement with leaders who had already made clear their opposition to rebuilding the walls, an action that had the sanction of the Persian king.

[66]Bowman, p. 716, suggests that the letter was written on clay so that it could not be folded or sealed. While this is possible, the addition of the adjective "open" stresses the changed nature of the letter. There would be no need to so describe an ostracon since its nature would be obvious.

claiming himself king, v. 6. The letter also accused Nehemiah of appointing prophets to proclaim him king. This part either misunderstood the prophecy of Zechariah 9:9, given at about this same time, or more probably was an outright false charge against Nehemiah. Nehemiah's enemies had likely gained the cooperation of Noadiah and other false prophets (v. 14) in making this charge. Sanballat urged Nehemiah to meet with him to consider these charges, v. 7. The Jewish leader denied the truth of the charge and accused Sanballat of making up the accusation, v. 8.[67] Nehemiah recognized that his foes had tried to make the Jews afraid and to turn them from the work. The expression "the hands shall be weakened" is an idiom that indicates a lack of power (cf. 2 Chron. 15:7; Ezra 4:4; Jer. 38:4). Spontaneously Nehemiah prayed that the Lord would "strengthen [his] hands" (cf. 2:18), v. 9.[68]

B. Deceit of the Prophet 6:10–14

10 We know nothing of Shemaiah except that Ezra 2:60 mentions his father's house. He is generally thought to be a priest or a prophet.[69] Based on v. 12 ("prophecy") and v. 14 ("rest of the prophets"), Shemaiah likely held the office of a prophet although at this point he had sold out to the enemies of the Jews. He apparently called for Nehemiah to visit him while he, Shemaiah, was "shut up" in his house. The phrase is understood differently.

---

[67]Holmgren, pp. 117–18, tentatively suggests that Nehemiah did have plans to make himself Judah's king. He sees 2:3, 5 ("my father's sepulchres") as indicating a royal family background. The fact that Nehemiah served in the Persian court also supports his royal background. The view is weak since there is no evidence that only members of the royal family were buried in Jerusalem. Second Chronicles 21:20 and 28:27 indicate there were burial places in Jerusalem not normally used by the kings. Ecclesiastes 8:10 likely refers to the burial of the wicked in Jerusalem. In addition, Nehemiah's denial, v. 8, would be an outright lie if he had planned to rule as king.

[68]Ryle, pp. 223–24, notes that God's name is supplied in the KJV. He prefers to take the verb as an infinitive and translate this expression as "I will strengthen my hands." The LXX and Vulgate support this interpretation. While this view is possible, most translations generally follow the KJV, e.g., CEV, ESV, NASB, NIV, NKJV. In addition, Nehemiah frequently prayed spontaneously, e.g., 2:4, 5:19; 6:14; 13:14, 22, 31.

[69]Rademacher and Allen, p. 316, identify Shemaiah as a priest. Henry, p. 1087, refers to Shemaiah as a "pretended prophet."

He may have been ritually defiled.[70] He may have been pretending to fear that his life was in danger from the enemies.[71] He may have prophesied symbolically that Nehemiah should shut himself up.[72] While any one of these suggestions may serve to explain the phrase, it is clear that his condition was temporary since he asked Nehemiah to meet him at the temple. We cannot dogmatically choose one explanation over another. Shemaiah urged Nehemiah to meet him in "the house of God, within the temple." Although the phrase "house of God" normally indicates the temple, here it is a specific location within the temple, inside "the doors of the temple" where Nehemiah was not permitted by the law to go (Num. 3:10, 38; 18:7).

11–14 Nehemiah refused to hide himself in the temple. The phrase "such a man as I" points out that he is not a Levite. Had he gone into the temple to hide "to save his life," he would have been subject to divine punishment (cf. 2 Chron. 26:16–21). It is true that an innocent person could take hold of the horns of the brazen altar to claim divine protection (e.g., 1 Kings 1:50–53), but such an action would not protect a guilty person (1 Kings 2:28–36). The brazen altar, however, was located in the temple courtyard. Nehemiah later went into the court of the temple to oversee the casting out of Tobiah's possessions (13:7–9). From the actions of Jeremiah in bringing the Rechabites into the chambers of the temple court (Jer. 35:2–4), it is clear that laymen could go into this area. The court of the temple, however, is not in view here. Shemaiah proposed they should go into the Holy Place, where they could "shut the doors of the temple," v. 10. This would clearly have violated the law, v. 11.[73]

---

[70]Barnes, p. 468, and Slotki, p. 217, refer to some legal uncleanness that kept Shemaiah from serving in the temple. This view has the problem that such uncleanness would have continued to keep him from entering the temple.

[71]Rayond Brown, p. 105, and Butler, p. 166, make this suggestion.

[72]Breneman, p. 212; Fensham, p. 205; and Keil, p. 219, mention this view as a possibility.

[73]Henry, p. 1088, understands Nehemiah's refusal as based on his position of leadership among the people. How could he desert the work while expecting the people to continue? This is a possible view that may also have been in Nehemiah's mind as he answered Shemaiah.

Since Shemaiah's invitation was contrary to the law, Nehemiah perceived that Shemaiah's warning was not of God. Sanballat and Tobiah therefore must have hired him, v. 12. They had tried to make him fearful and to lead him into a sinful response. He would then have had an evil "report" (*šem*, better "name"). The word *šem* occurs nineteen times in the books of Ezra, Nehemiah, and Esther, everywhere else translated "name." Such a bad name would have let his enemies accuse him before the others who stood guard against a possible attack, v. 13. In recalling the incident, Nehemiah spontaneously prays that God will frustrate his enemies who try to make him afraid. He mentions Noadiah, a prophetess about whom nothing else is known, and "the rest of the prophets," an indication that other false prophets had cooperated with Israel's enemies in opposing the rebuilding of the walls, v. 14.

C. Completion of the Wall 6:15–16

After only fifty-two days of work, the Jews finished the wall in the month Elul (mid-August to mid-September). The "twenty and fifth day of the month" would have been in early September. From Nehemiah's later concern for keeping the Sabbath (13:15–22), it is certain that the fifty-two days did not include the Sabbath days. Josephus, *Antiquities* 11.5.8, gives "two years and four months" as the time involved in building the wall. Since the LXX and Vulgate both support the MT by giving fifty-two days as the time, there is no reason to accept the record of Josephus on this matter. Josephus is not always accurate in giving historical information.

Some have argued that the time period of fifty-two days is too short to be plausible. There are several possible answers to this criticism. (1) At least thirty-seven separate groups worked on the project. Many of these were larger groups from nearby towns, e.g., 3:7, 13, or groups of priests, e.g., 3:22, 28, and could accomplish correspondingly more work than could individuals. (2) The Jerusalem of Nehemiah's day was not very large in circumference. Kathleen Kenyon's excavation of the preexilic city led her to estimate that the length of the wall in Nehemiah's time was about one and one-half miles or, if the northern end of the western hill is included, about three miles.[74] This would mean that each group needed to repair only about three yards per day to finish in fifty-two work days. (3) Material for the repairs would have been near at hand in the ruins of the old wall. (4) Nehemiah urged the people to hasten their work, 2:17; 6:3. (5) The people worked from early morning until late at night, 4:21. (6) In many places the wall still stood and did not need extensive repairs. Any one or a combination of these reasons, coupled with the fact that the people relied on God (4:9) and received His blessing on their work (e.g., 4:15; 6:16), can explain the short time required for the repairs, v. 15. When the enemies of the people saw the results, they "were much cast down in their own eyes," becoming discouraged over their failure to stop the work of the Jews. They recognized that God had blessed the work of the people, v. 16.

D. Spying of the People 6:17–19

Nehemiah recounts one more danger faced during the building of the wall. The phrase "in those days" refers to the time before the wall's completion. Although Tobiah represented Ammon, 2:10, he had connections in Israel through his marriage into the family of Shechaniah, and the marriage of his son into the family of Meshullam. It is sad that Meshullam, a man who at one time had served faithfully (3:4, 30), had a son who turned away from the Mosaic law by marrying a heathen woman.

Through these connections Tobiah kept up with events in Jerusalem as he received letters from some of the "nobles," civic leaders in the city, vv. 17–18. These faithless individuals spoke favorably of Tobiah, trying to change Nehemiah's attitude toward him. At the same time, they reported Nehemiah's words to Tobiah. Using this information, Tobiah wrote several threatening letters to Nehemiah in an attempt to make him afraid to continue his work, v. 19.

---

[74]Kathleen M. Kenyon, *Jerusalem: Excavating 3000 Years of History* (New York: McGraw-Hill Book Company, 1967), p. 110.

NEHEMIAH 7

VII. Register of the People 7:1–73*a*

Once the completion of the wall provided security for the city, Nehemiah turned his attention to other matters. As he organized some elements of the city's daily life, he took a census. In doing this, he found a listing of the people who had returned to Palestine after Cyrus's decree authorizing the first return from captivity almost a century before (Ezra 1:2–4). Since Nehemiah needed a record of the people for the various decisions that he faced, the chapter gives this listing. It essentially repeats the earlier list of Ezra 2, the discussion of which notes minor differences (see pp. 25–37).

A. Organization of the People 7:1–4

After completing the wall and setting up the gates (cf. 6:1), Nehemiah appointed porters, singers, and Levites to carry out various responsibilities. The porters kept the gates of the temple (1 Chron. 9:22–23). The singers added a note of joy to the worship ceremonies (1 Chron. 15:16; 2 Chron. 5:13). The Levites held numerous positions of service in the temple, including singing and guarding the gates. Since Nehemiah mentions those offices separately, the emphasis here is on the support role of the Levites in assisting the priests (e.g., 1 Chron. 26:20; 2 Chron. 24:11; 29:5), v. 1.

Nehemiah also appointed his brother Hanani (1:2) and Hananiah as rulers of the city.[75] We know nothing of Hananiah except that he was the ruler over the "palace" (or "fortress," *bîrâ*, the same word used in 1:1). This was a fortress at the corner of the north and east walls for the defense of the temple. Hananiah is described as "a faithful man" who "feared God" more than other men. Undoubtedly these two men handled the routine

[75]Bowman, p. 724, asserts, "It is improbable that two officials bearing the same name would rule Jerusalem simultaneously." He understands the *waw* joining the names as explicative, "my brother Hanani, that is Hananiah." Since 3:9, 12 indicates that two men divided the governing of the area outside Jerusalem, it is not surprising that the area within the city would be similarly assigned.

day-to-day business while Nehemiah retained control over major decisions, v. 2.[76]

Nehemiah ordered that the gates of the city not be opened until later in the day. The verb *said* is actually the third person singular masculine form, "he said." While it is possible that the verb refers to Hananiah in v. 2, it is normally understood as referring to Nehemiah as do vv. 1–2 since he held the authority. Modern versions, e.g., ESV, GW, NASB, NIV, NKJV, translate it as "I said."

The preposition *until* (*ᶜad*) can also mean "during." By translating it this way, as do GW and the NLT, the meaning changes so that the gates were shut during the hottest part of the day when people may have stayed inside to rest. The city would have been more vulnerable at this time. The meaning "during," however, is rare in the OT and is therefore unlikely here.

It is likely that the gates of a city would open at sunrise. Nehemiah's order to delay their opening guarded against a surprise attack. Since the population of the city was small at that time (cf. 11:1), this was a necessary precaution. Further, Nehemiah ordered the guards, the gatekeepers of v. 1, to "stand by" and to shut and bar the gates at night. After that, watchers from among the people would patrol the areas around the walls "in his watch," i.e., his post, or in the area near their homes, v. 3. This was necessary because of the limited number of people living in the same space the former city had occupied. The word *large* translates the Hebrew idiom *raḥᵃbat yadayim*, lit. "wide of hands." Although phrased in an unusual way, the term is descriptive and occurs elsewhere (1 Chron. 4:40; Ps. 104:25; Is. 22:18; 33:21). New houses also "were not builded," leaving large areas of the city empty of inhabitants. The small city population was the reason for the later action of 11:1, when Nehemiah took steps to increase the population, v. 4.

[76]Luck, p. 110, suggests that Nehemiah makes these appointments in preparation for his return to Persia. While this is possible, it is clear from the events of c. 7–12 that Nehemiah was in the city and did not leave until later. Nehemiah 5:14 indicates that he stayed at Jerusalem twelve years before returning.

B. Inhabitants of the City 7:5–73*a*

In response to the Lord's leading, Nehemiah took a census of the people. This census prepared the people for worship by identifying those who were true Israelites. The census also identified those who were qualified to carry out the priestly rituals, v. 5*a*. In taking steps toward this, Nehemiah discovered the census record of those who "came up at the first" in Zerubbabel's return (Ezra 2:1–70), vv. 5*b*–6. The list is similar to the lists in Ezra 2 and the apocryphal book of 1 Esdras. The discussion at Ezra 2 (pp. 25–37) notes the differences.

The first group contains the names of twelve men, the same listed in Ezra 2:2 with the addition of Nahamani. These twelve men were probably the leaders of those in the twelve tribes who had returned to Palestine, v. 7. A listing of family groups and groups from various towns and regions comes next, vv. 8–38. A list of the priests, vv. 39–42, and Levites, v. 43, including singers, v. 44, and porters, v. 45, is followed by a list of the Nethinim (discussed at Ezra 2:43 and Neh. 3:26), which is given by family groups, vv. 46–56. The "children of Solomon's servants," vv. 57–60, and several individuals who could not prove their descent from Israel, vv. 61–62, follows.

A second list of priests includes those who could not prove their descent from Aaron. Zerubbabel, the "Tirshatha," had earlier excluded them from the benefits of the priesthood until the high priest could use the Urim and Thummim to find God's will in the matter (cf. Ezra 2:61–63), vv. 63–65. A total of 42,360 returned, v. 66, together with 7,337 servants and 245 singers, v. 67. In addition, the returnees brought horses, mules, camels, and asses to assist in the various forms of work after they settled the land, vv. 68–69.

Nehemiah records some of the contributions made to the work by "some of the chief of the fathers," leaders among the people, and the "Tirshatha," the Persian title for governor, here referring to Zerubbabel. His earlier contribution had included "a thousand drams [probably referring to the Persian *dari*ᶜ, equivalent to the later Greek *drachma*] of gold," about seventeen pounds (CEV, GNB). In addition he gave fifty basins and five hundred thirty priestly garments.

It is widely speculated that something has dropped out of the text following the phrase "five hundred." Often, the phrase is given as "five hundred minas of silver." Breneman, Noss and Thomas, and Ryle adopt this position,[77] as do the CB, ESV, and NAB. Most translations, however, follow the MT. There is no textual support for inserting extra words, and no change is needed. While the phrasing in Hebrew is awkward, it is entirely possible that Nehemiah gave five hundred thirty garments for the use of the priests. Since the census of priests given in vv. 39–42 lists more than 4,289 men in four families, this number of garments would not have been excessive. The people had given one hundred garments before the return (Ezra 2:69) and another sixty-seven garments at this time (Neh. 7:72). Elsewhere the basins used in Israel's worship are made of either silver (e.g., Num. 7:13, 19, 85, all translated "bowl") or gold (e.g., 1 Kings 7:50; 2 Chron. 4:8), v. 70. Some members among the "chief of the fathers" gave 20,000 "drams" (again "darics") of gold, about 337 pounds, and 2,200 "pound" (or "minas") of silver, about 3,215 pounds (CEV, GNB), v. 71. The rest of the people gave an equal amount of gold, 337 pounds, and 2,000 minas of silver, about 2,923 pounds (CEV, GNB, GW), v. 72. All of these groups settled in cities throughout the land. This continued the practice of the first group of returnees (cf. Ezra 2:70), v. 73*a*. The final part of v. 73 introduces c. 8 and is discussed in the next chapter.

[77]Breneman, p. 220; Noss and Thomas, p. 395; Ryle, pp. 36–37.

NEHEMIAH 8

VIII. Instruction of the People 7:73*b*–8:18

Most modern translations indicate in some way that v. 73*b* begins c. 8, e.g., GNB, GW, NASB, NIV, NKJV. This follows the early translations of the LXX and Vulgate, which also attach v. 73*b* to c. 8. In contrast, Laney argues that 73*b* belongs with c. 7. He states that connecting it with c. 8 ignores the chapter division of the MT as well as the fact that 73*b* "appears to be a direct quotation of Ezra 3:1."[78] But neither argument is strong. The chapter divisions of the MT were adopted in the 15th century from work done earlier by leaders of the Roman Catholic Church. The divisions were incorporated into the Vulgate and later transferred into the Hebrew Bible. The chapter divisions of the MT often differ from those of English Bibles, e.g., Nehemiah 9:38 (MT) is 10:1 (English); Isaiah 8:23 (MT) is 9:1 (English); Isaiah 63:19*b* (MT) is 64:1 (English). On the other hand, the well-known Isaiah 52:13–15 (English) clearly belongs with 53:1–12. The similarity of 73*b* to Ezra 3:1 does not change if we attach the verse to c. 8.

A. Explanation of the Law 7:73*b*–8:8

7:73*b*–8:3 The people completed the settlement of their cities by the beginning of Tishri, the seventh month of the Hebrew calendar (mid-September to mid-October). This was the month in which the Jews to celebrate several feasts at Jerusalem, as commanded by the law. In addition to the new moon festival (Num. 28:11–15), observed in the seventh month as the Feast of Trumpets (Lev. 23:23–25), the Jews also observed the Day of Atonement (Lev. 23:26–32) and the Feast of Tabernacles (Lev. 23:33–43) during this time, v. 73*b*.[79] The people left their cities in order to gather at Jerusalem to worship the Lord.

Ezra again assumed spiritual leadership of the people. This was thirteen years after his original journey to Palestine (Ezra

[78]Laney, p. 98.

[79]Since Ezra is the chief character in the chapter, many liberal commentators (e.g., Bowman, p. 731) assume that v. 73 was originally a part of the book of Ezra. Some copyist or editor transposed the material here, but no manuscript evidence supports this view.

7:7–8 cf. Neh. 2:1). The lack of any mention of Ezra until this point in the book of Nehemiah suggests that he may have been absent. In addition, the development of additional spiritual problems (renewed need to organize the temple service, 12:44–47; separating the mixed multitude from the temple worship, 13:1–3; cleansing the temple, 13:4–9; failure to give to support the Levites, 13:10–13; violation of the Sabbath, 13:15–22; intermarriage with the heathen, 13:23–28) supports the absence of Ezra. We do not know his whereabouts, however, during this time.[80]

The people gathered in the "street" (or "open space," *reḥôb*, see Ezra 10:9) near the Water Gate (cf. 3:26). This gate is thought to have been located south of Ophel, part of Mount Moriah, on the eastern side of the city. At the people's request, Ezra brought the "book of the law of Moses" in order to read it to the assembly. The public reading reflected the lack of personal copies of God's Word. Today it is common for an individual to have several copies of the Bible. In that day, however, it was rare to have a copy of even part of God's Word. The people requested Ezra to read the law to them. This was the first day of the month (v. 2), the time to observe the feast "which the Lord had commanded to Israel" (Lev. 23:23–25).

"The book of the law of Moses" was likely the entire Pentateuch although the only part we can identify (vv. 14–15) comes from the legal section (Lev. 23:40–43). Later references to Israel's history (9:6–31) and to the elements of the new covenant made by the people (10:30–39) followed the second reading of the law later in the month (9:1–3), v. 1.

Ezra brought the book to read portions to "all that could hear with understanding," i.e., the men, women, and older children, who gathered for the reading. It had been God's plan from

[80]Leslie McFall, "Was Nehemiah Contemporary with Ezra in 458 BC?" *WTJ* 53 (Fall 1991): 270–273, seeks to place Ezra and Nehemiah together at this time with no extended absence by Ezra. He argues that Nehemiah made two visits to Jerusalem, the first as governor of Judah from 465–454 BC and a brief second visit to repair the walls of the city in 445 BC. To support the view, McFall requires that the dates given in Neh. 2:1; 5:14; and 13:6–7 be reckoned differently from one another. The first (5:14; 13:6–7) is a dynastic date, commencing with the reign of Xerxes (although Xerxes is not known to have founded a new dynasty), while the second date (2:1) is based solely on the reign of Artaxerxes. The view is interesting but complicated by many assumptions.

the beginning to teach the children (Deut. 4:10; 6:6–7; 11:18–19). This took place at the beginning of the "seventh month" (mid-September to mid-October), v. 2. The group gathered in the "street" (*reḥôb*), and Ezra read "from the morning" (lit., "from the light," i.e., from daybreak) until midday, about six hours. Verses 4–8 make it clear that the reading was not continuous but rather was broken up with explanation. In all of this, the "ears of all the people were attentive unto the book of the law." Not having ready access to God's Word, the people did not grow tired quickly of hearing it, v. 3.

4–8 Ezra stood on a "pulpit" (*migdal-ᶜeṣ*, lit. "a tower of wood," i.e., a "platform") made for this reading. Thirteen men, six on his right and seven on his left, stood by him. This group was apparently an escort to show their respect for Ezra and for the law from which he would read. We do not know how or from what groups they were selected. It is a reasonable assumption that these were not priests or Levites since v. 7 refers to those groups. These may well have been civic leaders in Jerusalem and in the nearby cities (cf. v. 15), v. 4. As Ezra opened the book of the law, unrolling the scroll, the people stood to show respect for the Word of God.

The Bible general says little about the position of the people during the public reading of the Word. Here and in Joshua 8:33–35, the people stood for its reading. In Luke 4:16 (cf. v. 29, "rose up") and Acts 13:15–16, the people sat. While asking people today to stand for the reading of the Bible appropriately shows respect, it is not consistently a biblical practice, v. 5.

All of them worshiped the Lord. Ezra blessed the Lord, appropriately called "the great God." The people answered, "Amen, Amen," i.e., "verily, verily," or "so be it, so be it." They lifted their hands, a visual symbol of reaching out to God for His blessings. The raising of hands is also a preference rather than a command. On other occasions, people prayed in a variety of positions, with nothing said about lifting the hands, e.g., kneeling (1 Kings 8:54); bowing the head (1 Chron. 29:20); lying down (Isa. 38:2). The attitude of the heart in prayer is far more important than the position of the body.

The people also bowed with their faces toward the ground, v. 6. As Ezra read, a group of men "and the Levites" (i.e., "and the rest of the Levites") helped the people understand. Of the men named in the verse, seven are elsewhere named as Levites. Nehemiah 9:5 mentions Jeshua, Bani, Sherebiah, and Hodaiah as Levites. Nehemiah 10:9–14 mentions the Levites Jeshua, Bani, Sherebiah, Hodijah, Kelita, Hanan, and Pelaiah. Verse 9 refers to the group as "Levites." They served to paraphrase, restate, and otherwise explain the law as it was read.

The Levites first read the law "distinctly," communicating it clearly to the people. The word *distinctly* is understood in two basic ways. The *puʿal* verb *paraš* simply means "to declare distinctly." Many translations take it in this way, e.g., ESV, NKJV, NIV. Some, however, understand the verb as meaning "to translate," e.g., NASB, GNB, NJB. There is no indication in the text, however, that the people needed a translation into Aramaic at this time. Twelve years later, after the intermarriage with the heathen and the development of children who could not speak Hebrew (13:24), there was a problem. Since Ezra and Nehemiah as well as Haggai and Zechariah, active prophets at this time, wrote in Hebrew, it is clear that this language was still in use by the Jews. The wording here ("gave the sense, and caused them to understand the reading") indicates that there was explanation of the law and, probably, application to daily life of the Jews. In several places the Talmud (*Sanhedrin* 21*b*; *Nedarim* 37*b*; *Megillah* 3*a*) connects the Targums, Aramaic explanations of the Hebrew, to this reading of the law, vv. 7–8.

B. Response to the Law 8:9–12

The people responded with tears when they heard the law. The cause of their grief is not clear. It may have been an emotional reaction to hearing the Word of God openly proclaimed. While the rebuilt temple had been in use for about seventy-five years, it is clear from vv. 14–18 that the people had not been practicing the commands of the law. This suggests that they had not heard it in many years and had fallen away from their religious practices. Hearing it read at this time, they responded emotionally with tears.[81]

While this is a possible view, the words *mourn* and *weep* suggest a cause for their grief. This leads to the thought that

[81]Holmgren, p. 125, and Slotki, p. 230, adopt this view.

the people wept as they realized that some of their practices were sin, v. 9. Nehemiah was now the "Tirshatha," the Persian governor, having taken the place of Zerubbabel (Ezra 2:63; Neh. 7:65, 70) and others who followed him. Ezra and the Levites joined Nehemiah in urging the people not to weep over what they had heard. The day was holy, a time for festival observances.

The first day of the month was not only a time for keeping various festivals, it was more importantly a time when the people had understood God's Word. They should therefore celebrate it with rejoicing rather than grief, v. 9. Ezra told the people to celebrate by eating the "fat" (*mašman*), i.e., richly prepared food.[82] The plural word *mašmannîm* refers to different kinds of fat or richly prepared food, evidence of God's blessing (cf. Gen. 27:28, 39). The word is not *ḥeleb*, which may refer to the fat of animals forbidden to the people (Lev. 3:17). The people should also drink sweet liquids, i.e., date syrup or apple juice.

They were to send portions of food to those "for whom nothing is prepared." This is variously understood as referring to the poor or to those who had no food prepared.[83] The day was holy, one in which they should honor their God by charitable service. Rather than sorrowing, they were to rejoice in the Lord as they engaged in their daily activities.[84] The "joy of the Lord," i.e., their joy in the Lord, would give them "strength" (*maᶜôz*) to do these things. While the noun *maᶜôz* normally refers to a place of strength, i.e., a fortress, the context here supports better the idea of "strength,"

[82]Keil, p. 231, understands Nehemiah as the spokesman, but he also sees Ezra and the Levites as concurring in the command. The NIV and NLT similarly make Nehemiah the one speaking. While this is possible, the religious content of the command seem more likely to relate to Ezra; cf. v. 13, where Ezra is clearly the speaker.

[83]Barnes, p. 472, and Breneman, p. 228, understand this to mean the poor. In addition to the poor, Larson and Dahlen, p. 219, would include foreigners living among the Jews.

[84]G. C. I. Wong, "A Note on 'Joy' in Nehemiah VIII 10," *VT* 45, no. 3 (July 1995): 383–85, argues that the phrase "joy of the Lord" should be understood as a subjective genitive, "the Lord's joy over his people" that will protect them. While the view is possible, the context relates more to Israel's emotions (sorrow, vv. 9, 11; mirth, v. 12; gladness, v. 17). Further, it seems that the emotions result from the people's understanding of God's Word. This persuades me that *joy* here is an objective genitive, the joy possessed by the people.

v. 10. The Levites also urged the people not to grieve because the day was holy, set apart to the Lord, v. 11. Now that "they," the people, understood the meaning of the "words of the law" (v. 9), they responded by returning to their homes to carry out their celebrations, v. 12.[85]

C. Obedience to the Law 8:13–18

13–15 The "chief of the fathers," the leaders of the various families, returned for a second day to hear "the words of the law" so they could understand it. The priests and Levites joined in this. Apparently, the first day had focused on general principles known to the priests and Levites by virtue of their knowledge. Ezra then began to take up lesser-known elements of the law, information that the priests and Levites needed to know. Having devoted himself to God's Word (Ezra 7:10), Ezra was prepared to read and discuss it, v. 13. While studying the law, the people found the command regarding dwelling in "booths." This was a part of the Feast of Tabernacles that commemorated Israel's sojourn during the wilderness wanderings (Lev. 23:34–43), v. 14. They were to go to the nearby hills and gather the branches of various shrubs and trees—the olive, "pine" (lit. "oil trees," an unidentifiable tree),[86] myrtle shrub, palm, and "thick trees," i.e., other trees with heavily interwoven branches. These trees are all heavily leaved and serve well to make booths to provide shade, v. 15.

16–18 The people had kept the Feast of Tabernacles earlier (Ezra 3:4), but they had not built booths to live in during the week. They now made their booths on the flat roofs of their houses, in their courtyards, in the court of the temple, and in the "street" (i.e., the open area, *rᵉḥôb*, Ezra 10:9) near the Water Gate in the eastern wall of the city (8:1), and the "street" (*rᵉḥôb*),

[85]Myers, p. 151, understands the pronoun *they* to refer to Nehemiah, Ezra, and the Levites as they urged the people to be calm. The antecedent to the pronoun, however, is *people*. Further, the people are the ones understanding "the words that were declared unto them."

[86]Noss and Thomas, p. 412, suggest it is "a member of the pine or cypress family." The majority of translations and authors use some term related to the wild olive tree. Rawlinson, p. 89, suggests "oleaster branches." Keil, p. 233 agrees, using "wild olive (oleaster)." Barnes, p. 473, and Coggins, p. 105, similarly give "wild olive." Fensham, p. 220, is more detailed, relating it "to the small tree *Elaeagnus augustfolia* [i.e., wild olive], which is plentiful in the Holy Land."

again an open area, near the Gate of Ephraim in the western wall, v. 16. All the people made booths from branches, a practice that had not been followed "since the days of Jeshua [a variant spelling of Joshua]." Although the Jews had kept the feast earlier during Solomon's reign (2 Chron. 8:13) and following Zerubbabel's return (Ezra 3:4), they had not followed the practice of making and living in booths. Doing so now reminded them of God's provision since the wilderness wanderings and served to spark a new joy in the Lord.[87]

The knowledge that they were obeying God's Word gave them joy, v. 17. Throughout the feast, Ezra ("he") read from the law daily. This carried out the command of Deuteronomy 31:10–13 for the sabbatical year. We do not know whether or not this was the seventh year. Ezra may have chosen to read the law since the Jews had not kept the Sabbath year in such a long time. The Talmud, *Baba Kamma* 82*a*, *Megillah* 31*a*, recognizes Ezra as ordaining the public reading of the Torah but also looks back to Moses (Exod. 24:7; Deut. 31:12) as instituting this practice among the Jews. The distinction, supposedly, is that Moses read the law on Sabbaths, festivals, and new moons. Ezra, says the Talmud, instructed the people on Mondays and Thursdays, when they came to the markets, and on the Sabbath afternoons when they could take time for studying.[88]

The feast climaxed with a solemn assembly on the eighth day "according unto the manner," i.e., carrying out the ordinance concerning the feast (Lev. 23:36). The "solemn assembly" elsewhere was a day of fasting devoted to the Lord, with no work permitted (Joel 1:14; 2:15; Num. 29:35). This prepared the people for the confession of their sins and making a covenant expressing their determination to turn from them (9:1–10:39), v. 18.

---

[87]Bowman, p. 740, sees a difference here from the command in Leviticus. He understands the people to begin keeping the feast on the third day here, following the gathering of v. 13. But Leviticus (23:34, 39) commands the feast to begin on the fifteenth day of the month. The narrative here does not specify the starting point. Since time was involved in gathering and weaving together the branches to make booths, a period of time must have passed. It is reasonable that people began the feast at the proper time.

[88]Geoffrey Wigoder, ed., *The New Encyclopedia of Judaism* (New York: New York University Press, 2002), p. 636.

NEHEMIAH 9

IX. Repentance of the People 9:1–37

The reading of the Mosaic law by Ezra and the consequent obedience of the people in living in booths while observing the Feast of Tabernacles had a continuing impact on the nation. The people separated from the heathen, confessed their sins, and worshiped the Lord. The Levites recounted God's mercies to the nation throughout its history. Although their sin had brought judgment, God had still extended grace to His people.

A. Worship of the People 9:1–5*a*

1–3 In "this month," still the seventh month of Tishri (8:2), two days after the "solemn assembly" of 8:18 (cf. Lev. 23:34), the people gathered again. The gathering was not commanded in the Mosaic law. It is likely that the keeping of the Feast of Tabernacles had caused the people to realize how far they had strayed from keeping God's Word.[89] The gathering also prepared them for entering into a new covenant with God (10:30–39). This time they showed outward signs of their inward grief by fasting, wearing sackcloth (a coarse garment made from the hair of a camel or goat), and putting dirt on their heads. Fasting often expresses grief in the OT (e.g., Judg. 20:26; Joel 2:12), as do the wearing of sackcloth directly against the skin (e.g., Gen. 37:34; 1 Kings 21:27; Isa. 32:11) and the placing of "earth," i.e., dirt, on the head (e.g., 1 Sam. 4:12; Job 2:12), v. 1.

In their worship, the people separated themselves from the "strangers" (*nokrî*, see Ezra 6:2). These were the heathen in the city who could not appropriately join in the worship. The people confessed their sins and the "iniquities" (*ᶜᵃwon*, see Ezra 9:6) of their fathers. The exclusion of foreigners from Israel's worship assumes that there had been no true conversion. It was entirely possible for a foreigner to convert to Judaism (Josh. 2:11 cf. 6:25; Ruth 1:16; 2 Kings 5:17; Isa. 14:1). He would show this by

[89]Bowman, p. 743, asserts "the idea that the mood of 8:9 returned after the brief festival . . . is psychologically improbable." The festival of c. 8, however, ended with a "solemn assembly" (see discussion at 8:18). This naturally prepared them for the actions of c. 9.

his willingness to keep the law, including undergoing the rite of circumcision. Without this, however, it was necessary to exclude the heathen from Israel's worship (Neh. 13:3), v. 2.

The Levites stood once more to read the law, continuing the practice begun in 8:7–8, when Ezra and the Levites led the worship of the people. While there is no mention of it again, the practice of explaining the law was undoubtedly continued by the Levites. This reading and explanation lasted for "one fourth part of the day," three hours. An additional three hours were given over to confession and worship, v. 3.[90]

4–5*a* One group of Levites stood on the "stairs." The translations understand this in two ways. The CEV, GNB, and NASB assume it is the platform used earlier (8:4) even though this is a different word. The ESV, NET, NIV, and NKJV translate it as "steps" or "stairs." This is possible, although we do not know where the stairs were located in the city. Also, standing on a flight of stairs seems an unusual place from which to lead the people. Some elevated area, possibly the stage earlier built for proclaiming the Word to the people, would have been more appropriate.

The Levites led the people in crying out to God as they confessed their sins. Since the prayer of confession and praise lasted three hours (v. 3), it is likely that different Levites led, praying one after another, v. 4. A second group of Levites, including five of those in the first group, led the people in offering praise to God. There is no explanation given for the exclusion of seven Levites and the inclusion of their replacements. It is possible that the five who participated in both the confession and praise held positions of leadership, v. 5*a*.

B. History of the People 9:5*b*–37

1. Deliverance from Egypt 5*b*–15

5*b*–8 The Levites exhorted the people to "stand up and bless the Lord," i.e., to take their stand for their God by ascribing blessings to Him "for ever and ever." The superlative phrase

[90]Laney, p. 105, and Slotki, p. 234, equate the phrase "one fourth part of the day" with a six-hour period of time). The phrasing in 8:3 does suggest six hours. Here, however, where two periods of time are in view, it is better to limit the phrase to a fourth of the daytime hours, making each period about three hours.

indicates that God's people should offer praise to Him throughout eternity to come. His "name," representing His nature, is exalted far above what can be spoken in "all [manner of] blessing and praise." The statement in the verse briefly summarizes the praise offered to the Lord by the Levites. Verses 5*b*–37 are poetic, and many modern translations (e.g., CEV, NASB, NCV, NJB, NKJV) indicate this by formatting them as poetry. Some of the translations include v. 38 in the poem since it draws a logical conclusion to the poetry, v. 5*b*.

The poem is similar to the five historical psalms (78, 105, 106, 135, and 136), which also praise the Lord for His work on behalf of the nation. While other psalms also mention incidents from Israel's history (e.g., Ps. 114), additional themes or the style of writing place them into different categories of psalms. The psalms mentioned above, however, focus almost totally on Israel's history. By reviewing this history, the psalmist shows the gracious activity that God has extended to Israel. The poem here follows that same approach.

In v. 6, a single voice, likely that of Ezra, begins speaking.[91] He acknowledges God as the only Lord. He recalls the creative work of God in making the atmospheric heavens and the "heaven of heavens," the stellar heavens with its "host" of stars, nebulae, and other heavenly objects. In addition, He has made the bodies of water on the earth with all the creatures that inhabit them. He has preserved the creation. In response to His obvious power, the "host of heaven," the angels, worship Him.

The OT regularly emphasizes the uniqueness of God (e.g., Deut. 32:12; 2 Chron. 6:14; Isa. 43:10; 44:6, 8). The implied significance is that the idols, symbols of other gods worshiped by the heathen, represent nothing and therefore should not receive the worship of mankind. There is only one God worthy of worship, v. 6.

In continuing to work out His plan for mankind, God called "Abram" ("high [i.e., 'exalted'] father") from "Ur of the

[91]Luck, p. 115, understands the entire group of Levites as offering the prayer, one that had earlier been composed by Ezra. This ignores the fact that the Levites were divided into two groups, which had differing responsibilities (vv. 4 and 5). The prayer does use plural pronouns (*we*, vv. 33, 36, 37, 38; *our*, vv. 9, 16, 32, 34, 36, 37, 38; *us*, vv. 32, 33, 37), but this is natural when an individual prays on behalf of a group.

Chaldees" south of the Euphrates in lower Mesopotamia. He later renamed him "Abraham" (Gen. 17:5, "father of a multitude"), v. 7. Because Abraham was faithful (Gen. 15:6; 18:19), God made a covenant with him (Gen. 15:18–21; 17:6–8) to give his descendants the land of Palestine. The promise was "to his seed," Abraham's descendants, not to Abraham (cf. Gen. 12:8; 15:18). While Abraham did live in the land, it was not his alone. At that time several other heathen nations resided in Palestine. God later fulfilled His promise and thereby showed His righteous nature. Although even now Israel still does not possess all of the land promised them, the promise assures us that it will one day be theirs (e.g., Ps. 105:8–11; Isa. 60:21), v. 8.

9–15 Ezra continues to summarize Israel's history. God had seen the affliction of the nation in Egypt and heard their cry at the Red Sea (*yam-sûp*) for relief (Exod. 14:10). Strictly speaking, the Hebrew phrase *yam-sûp* refers to the Sea of Reeds, the place where Israel crossed the waters dividing Egypt from the Sinaitic peninsula. The common name *Red Sea* comes from the LXX translation of this phrase. While we do not know the location of this body of water, it is clear from v. 11 and the narrative in Exodus 14 that it was not merely a swampy area because it was deep enough to drown the Egyptian army, which attempted to stop the Israelites as they left Egypt, v. 9.

God showed "signs and wonders" to Pharaoh and the Egyptians by means of the plagues (Exod. 7:14–12:30), sent to bring about Israel's release. In doing this, God received "a name, as it is this day," i.e., a reputation that continued to be held in Israel, v. 10. Ezra recalls the language of Exodus 15:4–5 as he describes Israel's deliverance from Egypt. The Lord brought the nation through the Red Sea, while the Egyptians that followed them were drowned, v. 11. He then led Israel through the wilderness with a cloud having a pillar-like shape during the daylight hours and by a similarly shaped fire at night (Exod. 13:21–22). These showed the direction the nation was to travel, v. 12.

The Lord met with His people on Mount Sinai, speaking to them from "heaven" through Moses (Exod. 19:18–31:18). The word *heaven* here refers to the heights of Mount Sinai (Exod. 19:20), from which God communicated His will to the people. He gave them "right judgments . . . true laws, good statutes and commandments" from there. The gift of "right judgments" made possible the rendering of justice in all areas. The term *true laws* refers to true teachings, not limited to legal matters but broadly applying to every area. The "good statutes" were unchangeable decrees. The combination here with "commandments" probably limits *good statutes* to religious matters, while *commandments* refers to "precepts, statutes, and laws" in more general areas. Verse 34 adds the failure to hear God's "testimonies." His "testimonies" are those matters in which God testifies of their truth and rightness, vv. 13–14. He also gave them "bread from heaven," manna (Exod. 16:14–22), to satisfy their hunger and water out of the rock to quench their thirst (Exod. 17:2–7). He assured them of victory over the inhabitants of the land that He had "sworn" (lit., "lifted [His] hand") to give them, v. 15.

2. Sustenance in the Wilderness 9:16–25

16–19 Despite God's goodness to the people, "they and [their] fathers" arrogantly resisted God's commands. The phrase "they and our fathers" should be understood as "they, even our fathers," a reference to the leaders of Israel in the days of Moses. The hardening of the neck regularly indicates a rebellious spirit (e.g., 2 Kings 17:14; Prov. 29:1), v. 16. The first generation refused to obey God's commands. When they perceived themselves as having to fight against insurmountable odds in Canaan, they "hardened their necks," again referring to a rebellious spirit among the people. They appointed a "captain" (better "leader") to lead them back into Egyptian bondage (Num. 14:4, 40–44). The word translated "rebellion" (*miryam*) differs from the word *Egypt* (*miṣrayim*) by only the consonant *ṣadê*. Since the middle part of verse 17 is based on Numbers 14:4, where the word *Egypt* occurs, several translations (e.g., ESV, GNB, GW, NASB) assume that the *ṣadê* has dropped out and that the correct translation should read, "They appointed a leader to return to their bondage in Egypt." The LXX, Vulgate, and several Hebrew manuscripts support the change.

Quick to pardon this rebellion, God was "gracious" (*ḥanun*, see Ezra 9:8) and "merciful" (*raḥûm*, see Neh. 1:11), slow in becoming angry, and great in His "kindness" (or "loyal love," *ḥesed*, see Ezra 3:11). He did not forsake them, v. 17. They rebelled again, making a molten calf to worship and attributing their deliverance to it (Exod. 32:4). By this, they committed great "provocations" (or "blasphemies"), v. 18. God in His "mercies" (*raḥam*, see Neh. 1:11) still did not forsake them in the wilderness of Sinai. He continued to lead them by the cloud and the fire (cf. v. 12), v. 19.

20–25 God had given His "good spirit," i.e., the Holy Spirit (Ps. 143:10), to teach them. He continued to give them manna (Exod. 16:14–22) and water (Exod. 17:6; Ps. 105:41), v. 20. He sustained them for forty years in the wilderness, meeting their needs for food, water, clothing, and health (Deut. 2:7) so that "they lacked nothing," v. 21. He gave them victory over the nations in Canaan, dividing up the land among them "into corners" (or "by boundaries," cf. GNB, GW, NASB). This included possessing "the land of Sihon and [better 'even'] the land of the king of Heshbon and the land of Og." Sihon was the Amorite king who ruled over the territory east of the Jordan River between the Arnon and Jabbok Rivers. Heshbon, located about fifteen miles east of the northern tip of the Dead Sea, was his capital. Og was also an Amorite king. He ruled sixty cities in the territory of Bashan, north of the Jabbok River (Josh 13:30), v. 22.

The Israelite "children" multiplied "as the stars of heaven," i.e., into an uncountable number. This new generation of children came into Canaan, the land promised to their fathers before the sin that brought God's judgment and caused them to die in the wilderness, v. 23. They conquered the land, defeating the heathen nations who lived in it, and doing with the people "as they would," putting them to tribute, v. 24. They took over the "strong [or 'fenced'] cities" in the "fat land," i.e., productive land. They occupied houses filled with good things. They dug wells, planted crops, ate and became "fat," i.e., prosperous.[92] They "delighted" (*ᶜdn*) in the goodness of the land. The root

[92]Barnes, p. 475; Bowman, p. 753; and Noss and Thomas, p. 447, say that the verb *become fat* has a negative sense associated with turning away from God. While the word may sometimes have that connotation, it may also indicate prosperity, e.g., Gen. 49:20; 1 Chron. 4:40. Since the word has a good meaning in the first part of the verse and since the phrase immediately following this one is also positive, it is unlikely that it takes a negative sense here.

ᶜdn is related to the Eden of Genesis 2:8–3:24. While the verb occurs only here, it strongly conveys the meaning of "reveled" (NASB, NIV), v. 25.

3. Rebellion in the Land 9:26–31

Despite God's goodness to them, the people turned away from Him and His Word. Casting the law "behind their backs" placed it where it could not be seen (cf. 1 Kings 14:9; Ezek. 23:35). They killed some of His prophets and committed great "provocations" (again, "blasphemies," cf. v. 18), a reference to their worship of false gods, v. 26. As judgment, God delivered the people into the hand of their enemies until they cried out to Him for deliverance. He then showed His "mercies" (*raḥam*, see Neh. 1:11) by raising up "saviours" (judges) who led them to gain deliverance from their enemies, v. 27.

This cycle repeated itself "many times." The book of Judges gives the record of this cycle. The sin of the people brought God's judgment. Their confession brought His "mercies" (*raḥam*), v. 28. The people continued to rebel. They refused to obey God's Word (His "law . . . commandments . . . judgments"). They "withdrew the shoulder," a picture drawn from an ox who refuses to bear the yoke. They "hardened their neck" (see v. 16), rebelling against God's direction, v. 29.

The Lord graciously sent His prophets to rebuke them. When they would not hear this rebuke, He delivered them over to "the people of the lands," their heathen enemies, v. 30. Because of God's "great mercies [*raḥam*]," He did not completely destroy or abandon His people. He is a "gracious" (*ḥanun*, see Ezra 9:8) and merciful (*raḥum*) God, v. 31.

4. Affliction of the People 9:32–37

Ezra prayed to the great, mighty, and "terrible" (awesome) God, One who keeps His covenants and extends "mercy" (or loyal love, *ḥesed*, see Ezra 3:11) to His people. He asks that God not look upon Israel's trouble as "little" but as great and burdensome. These have come on their "kings . . . princes . . . priests . . . prophets . . . fathers, and . . . all [God's] people," i.e., on the leaders of the nation and on the nation itself.

Ezra emphasized the trials they had faced since the days of the "kings of Assyria," Tiglath-pileser III (2 Kings 15:29; 16:7, 10), 745–726 BC; Shalmaneser V (2 Kings 17:3; 18:9; Hos. 10:14), 726–722 BC; Sargon II (mentioned only in Isa. 20:1 but, judging from his inscriptions, responsible for the conquest of 2 Kings 17:4–6), 722–705 BC; Sennacherib (2 Kings 18:13–19:36), 705–681 BC; and Esarhaddon (2 Kings 19:37; Ezra 4:2; the "king of Assyria" in 2 Chron. 33:11), 680–669 BC. Other Assyrian kings also warred in Palestine, e.g., Shalmaneser III (858–824 BC) and Adad-nirari III (810–782 BC), but the OT does not mention these events, v. 32.

God had justly brought judgment on the people of Israel because of their sin, v. 33. Their civil and religious leaders and their ancestors had failed to keep God's "law" and had ignored His "commandments." As before (v. 13), this juxtaposition of terms indicates God's Word as it governs all of life. The "law" stresses His religious teachings, while the "commandments" focus on more secular areas.

In addition, the people had spurned God's "testimonies" given against them (e.g., 1 Sam. 8:7–20; Isa. 7:10–12), v. 34. They had not served God in the land that He had given them, and they had not turned from their sinful ways, v. 35. They were now in bondage to Persia. Even though they occupied and enjoyed the fruits of the land promised to their ancestors, they were still servants, v. 36. The land yielded its increase to the Persian kings as tribute. The Persian kings controlled the people and their "cattle" (*b^e^hemôt*),[93] and they were in great distress because of it, v. 37.[94] Verse 38 is better connected to c. 10. The KJV has followed the chapter division given in the LXX and Vulgate translations. The MT has it as the first verse of c. 10.

---

[93]Bowman, p. 756, mentions 2:12, 14, where the word *b^e^hemôt* refers to animals that were ridden. He suggests the possible view that the word here refers to animals taken for use by the cavalry during war. While *b^e^hemôt* may refer to riding animals, it almost always refers to cattle specifically or to farm animals generally. In 10:36 it clearly refers to sacrificial animals.

[94]Holmgren, p. 129, asserts that the Persian rule over the Jews "was not oppressive." While the captivity of the people under Persia was not as oppressive as that under the Babylonians, the Jews were nonetheless slaves to Persia. Some returned, but many stayed in Mesopotamia under the Persian rule. Even the ones returning were still obligated to send tribute to Persia. This caused "great distress" in the form of financial pressures.

NEHEMIAH 10

X. Covenant of the People 9:38–10:39

Apparently, this rehearsal of the record of God's mercies to Israel throughout its history had a profound impact on those who had assembled. The people agreed to make a renewed covenant with God. This chapter records the names of those who enter into the new covenant. In addition, the chapter summarizes the main points agreed to by the people.

A. Signers of the Covenant 9:38–10:27

38 This verse is 10:1 in the MT, beginning the chapter. Many modern translations have a break after v. 37 to show this connection (e.g., CEV, NET, NRSV, REB). "Because of all this," meaning their recognition of Israel's sins and God's subsequent judgments (9:16–37), the leaders of the people now made a "sure [*ᵓᵃmanâ*] *covenant*" in which they agreed to keep the provisions of the law. Although the word *covenant* is supplied, it is appropriate in view of the verb *make* (*karat*). This word means "to cut," and regularly occurs when a covenant is "cut" (e.g., Ezra 10:3; Neh. 9:8). The cutting refers to the slaughter of an animal that sealed the making of the covenant. The modifying word *ᵓᵃmanâ* occurs in the OT only here and at 11:23 ("certain portion"). It comes from a root meaning "to be faithful." This gives the sense here of something fixed and therefore reliable. To show the official nature of this covenant, the "princes [better 'leaders']," the civil leaders of the nation, and the "Levites . . . and priests," the religious leaders of the nation, now set a seal on it, v. 38.

1–8 Nehemiah, the "Tirshatha," the Persian governor, also the "son of Hachaliah" (cf. 1:1), heads the list of those who signed the covenant. Zidkijah (better "Zedekiah"), probably Nehemiah's secretary (cf. Zadok, 13:13), followed Nehemiah in signing. Ezra 4:8–9 and 17 furnish an example of associating a scribe with the leader. These two represent the civil leadership of the city.

Henry identifies Zidkijah as one of twenty-two priests.[95] While this is possible, the MT places the conjunction *and* be-

[95]Henry, p. 1104.

tween *Nehemiah* and *Zidkijah*. This grouping of Zidkijah with Nehemiah supports better an association with him, probably representing the civil government, rather than with the priests. The identification of Zidkijah with Zadok is possible but speculative, v. 1.

The heads of twenty-one priestly families (cf. v. 8) follow. Nehemiah 12:2–7 lists most of these again. Seraiah, listed first, was likely "the ruler of the house of God" (11:11). Azariah had worked on the wall (3:23) and helped Ezra in expounding the law after its reading (8:7). He later assisted at the dedication of the wall (12:33). Jeremiah also assisted at the dedication of the wall (12:34), v. 2. We know nothing else about Pashur. Amariah may have been the father of Jehohanan (12:13). Malchijah assisted Ezra at the reading of the law (8:4) and later participated in the dedication of the wall (12:42), v. 3.

Hattush may have accompanied Ezra on his return to Jerusalem (Ezra 8:2). He had helped in the building of the wall (Neh. 3:10). We know nothing about Shebaniah except that he had a son named Joseph (12:14). We know nothing for certain about Malluch, v. 4, or about Harim, Meremoth, or Obadiah, v. 5. Daniel was probably the priest who returned from Babylon with Ezra (Ezra 8:2). We know nothing about Ginnethon other than the name of his son (12:16). Baruch earlier helped repair the wall (3:20), v. 6. The name Meshullam occurs thirteen times in the book. This is likely the one who assisted Ezra during the reading of the law (8:4) and helped repair the wall (3:4, 6, 30) but we cannot be certain. We know nothing about Abijah other than the name of his son Zichri (12:17). Similarly, we know nothing else about Mijamin, v. 7, Maaziah, or Bilgai. Shemaiah was likely the father of Jonathan and the son of Mattaniah (12:35).

We can only speculate why Ezra was not among those who signed the covenant. It is possible that he was not in the city at the time. From 8:18 and 9:1, we gather that the events of this chapter occurred more than two weeks after Ezra's last mentioned spiritual activity. Since c. 12 mentions him several times, however, any absence must have been temporary. It is also possible that Ezra was ill at this time. Perhaps he did not sign because, although respected for his knowledge of the law, he did not hold a formal position of leadership in the city. Another explanation is that, since Ezra was a member of the family of Seraiah (Ezra 7:1), Seraiah represented the family with his signature, v. 8.

9–13 The names of seventeen Levites who signed the covenant occur next. The phrase "and their brethren" in v. 10 separates the first three of these—Jeshua, Binnui, and Kadmiel—from the others. This probably lays emphasis on these men as the heads of the orders of the Levites (cf. 12:8, where the same three are among those who are "over the thanksgiving"). Jeshua earlier assisted Ezra in explaining the law to the people (8:7) and in leading the public repentance of the people (9:4–5). Binnui helped repair the city's walls (3:24). Kadmiel helped lead the people in their public repentance (9:4–5), v. 9.

Either this Shebaniah or the one mentioned in v. 12 was one of those leading the public repentance of the people (9:4–5). The narrative gives no information about the second Shebaniah. Similarly, either this Hodijah or the one mentioned in v. 13 assisted Ezra at the reading of the law (8:7) and was one of those leading the people at the time of their repentance (9:4–5). We know nothing else with certainty. Kelita, Pelaiah, and Hanan assisted Ezra at his reading of the law (8:7). Hanan later was one of the faithful men appointed as treasurer to distribute offerings to the Levites (13:13), v. 10. We know nothing about Micha other than the names of his father and his son (11:17, 22) and that they were descendants of the singer Asaph (11:17, 22). This is the only occurrence of Rehob as a personal name in Israel. Hashabiah was a leader among the Levites (12:24). Both he (3:17), v. 11, and Zaccur (3:2) worked on the wall. Sherebiah came with Ezra from Babylon (Ezra 8:18, 24). He had assisted at the reading of the law (Neh. 8:7) and led in the public confession of sins (9:4–5). He later assisted in the public service of thanksgiving (12:8). For Shebaniah, see v. 10, v. 12. For Hodijah, see v. 10. Bani assisted Ezra at the reading of the law (8:7) and was one of those leading the people in their confession of sins (9:4–5). We know nothing else about Beninu, v. 13.

14–27 The list of the heads of the various families signing the covenant now follows. Many of the names in vv. 14–20 are repeats from the lists of Ezra 2 and Nehemiah 7. But of the names in vv. 21–27, only Harim, v. 27, occurs in the earlier lists, likely a coincidental repetition of the name. The latter half of the list apparently records the names of new families. These would include those families that had come into being as significant branches of older families as well as those who were new arrivals into the land.

We know nothing about most of these men in vv. 14–20 except their inclusion in the two earlier lists. Elam may have been one of the priests who assisted Nehemiah in the dedication ceremony (12:42), v. 14. Bunni was apparently the same man who joined in the public confession of sins (9:4), v. 15. Hodijah earlier helped explain to the people the law at its reading (8:7). Later, he was one of the leaders in the public confession of sins (9:5). Hashum stood with Ezra in his reading of the law (8:4), v. 18.

Zadok was one of those who repaired the wall (3:4). He later became a treasurer of the Levites charged with distributing offerings to other Levites (13:13). Although the name Hanan occurs five times in the book, including vv. 22, 26, we cannot certainly identify him. Anaiah stood with Ezra at the reading of the law (8:4), v. 22. Hananiah (3:8, 30), Hashub (3:11, 23), v. 23, and Rehum (3:17) may have helped in working on the wall. Rehum appears again as one of those joining in Nehemiah's covenant (12:3). The name Maaseiah occurs twelve times in the books of Ezra and Nehemiah. Among other activities, he stood by Ezra during the reading of the law (8:4) and explained it to the people (8:7), v. 25.

B. Summary of the Covenant 10:28–39

28–29 These verses give a general statement of the covenant. The "rest of the people" included different groups of people in the land. Since there were too many to name individually, Nehemiah refers to them generally. These include others associated with the worship of the people (priests, Levites, porters, singers, Nethinim [discussed at Ezra 2:43 and Neh. 3:26]). In addition, there were proselytes, some who had separated themselves among from the heathen to follow God's Word. There were also wives, sons, and daughters. The children who had knowledge, i.e., who were old enough to understand, agreed to the covenant, v. 28. These followed the guidance of the leaders and agreed to obey God's law. As in 9:13 and 34, "the commandments . . . judgments and . . . statutes" included both the religious (*judgments*, *statutes*) and secular (*commandments*) areas of life (cf. 1:7; 9:13), v. 29.

30–39 These verses summarize the more significant aspects of the covenant. (1) The people agreed to avoid intermarriage with the heathen. Such marriage had long been forbidden by the Mosaic law (Exod. 34:14–16; Deut. 7:3–4) because of its potential for introducing false gods into the home. Israel had violated this in the past and had been led into apostasy (Num. 25:1–2; 1 Kings 11:2–4; Ezra 9:1–2). It is appropriate that they agreed now to avoid these relationships, v. 30.

(2) The people pledged not to desecrate the Sabbath or other holy days by buying "ware or any victuals [*šeber*]," goods or foodstuffs, from "the people of the land," heathen vendors. While *šeber* refers primarily to grain, it has a wider significance here. In 13:15 we find that other food as well could not be sold on the Sabbath. The "holy days" in Israel were other days devoted to the Lord on which no work was to be done (e.g., Num. 28:25, 26; 29:7). With this provision the people set aside a day to specially devote themselves to the Lord. The rest gave them time for both physical and spiritual renewal.

(3) There is next an agreement to keep the Sabbath year, not exacting the payment of debts during that time (Deut. 15:2). This interval allowed the land to rest, which was necessary for the increased growth of crops. It also forced the people to rely on God for His provision during the year. Foregoing the "exaction of every debt" (lit., "burden of every hand") during the year was a natural step in view of the lessened harvest from the fields. The word *hand* here has a poetic use, referring to the loans that had been passed from the hand of the wealthy to the poor. The willingness to pass by these debts showed concern for those who were materially less fortunate, v. 31.

The final points of the covenant all relate to supporting "the house of [their] God" (vv. 32, 34, 35, 39). By giving of their means, the people enabled the work of the priests to continue. This was vital in maintaining the nation's worship of God. When this support failed, as it later did, the priests abandoned their service at the temple in order to work in their fields (13:10). The pledge to give faithfully here reflected a love for God and His service.

(4) The nation accepted a special tax, one-third of a shekel, to support the temple service. Israel had earlier done this (Exod.

30:11–16). With the coming of the monarchy, the priests had come to rely on royal support (2 Chron. 31:3; 35:7). This support had stopped at time of the captivity. The people now took on this responsibility themselves again. The earlier tax had been one-half shekel (Exod. 30:13–16). Later (Matt. 17:27), it is a "piece of money" (lit., "stater," equivalent to the Hebrew shekel). (Since this was enough to pay the tax for both Jesus and Peter, the tax again would have been one-half shekel.

There is no clear explanation for the lesser tax imposed here, vv. 32. Fensham and Myers offer the plausible suggestion that the shift to a third of a shekel was due to "the fact that the Persian monetary system was based on ten silver shekels for one gold shekel, whereas the sacred shekel was in the proportion of fifteen to one." Bowman is similar, making the one-third shekel based on the Babylonian standard while the one-half shekel is based on a later Phoenician standard. Kidner explains the difference by noting that this was an annual tax whereas the earlier amount was imposed only when a census was held. Keil suggests the lessened amount is "in consideration . . . of the poverty of the greater portion of the community." Slotki considers the third part as "in addition to the half-shekel required by the Mosaic law." While any of these views may be true, no reason is recorded in the biblical text, so any explanation must therefore be considered speculative.[96]

The tax would pay for various offerings used in the temple worship. These offerings included the "shewbread" (or "row bread," i.e., loaves of bread arranged in two rows on the table). They provided for the regular "meat" (or meal) offerings, the burnt offerings, the "holy things" (i.e., special offerings) and the sin offerings. These were offered on Sabbath days, the new moon feasts, and the special feasts commanded throughout the year, v. 33.

(5) The people cast lots to organize themselves to provide wood for the temple sacrifices. Since the Mosaic law does not mention wood offerings, the phrase "as it is written in the law" must refer to the continually burning fire on the temple altar (Lev. 6:12–13) and therefore the implied provision of wood, v. 34.

[96]Fensham, p. 240; Myers. pp. 178–79; Bowman, p. 764; Kidner, p. 118; Keil, p. 263; Slotki, p. 246.

(6) In addition, the signers of the covenant agreed to bring the firstfruit offerings to the temple. These included the first fruits of the harvest, v. 35; the redemption of their firstborn sons and the offering of their firstborn animals as sacrifice, v. 36; and offerings from the harvest to be stored for use by the priests plus tithes from the harvest for the Levites, v. 37. The high priest, a descendant of Aaron, had to join the Levites as they collected the tithes. This was probably for the purpose of collecting the "tithe of tithes" (cf. Num. 18:26) from the Levites for the priests, v. 38.[97] The faithful giving of the people and Levites included the offerings of "corn" (*dagan*, see 5:2), wine, and oil for the use of the priests.

(7) In the final point of the covenant, the people pledged not to "forsake the house of [their] God." The offerings of corn, wine, and oil were stored in the storehouse chambers of the temple under the oversight of the Levites (1 Chron. 9:26; 23:28). This would have made the provisions available to the priests and Levites as needed. It would also serve as a continuing reminder of the faithfulness of the people in giving to the Lord that which He required. v. 39.

NEHEMIAH 11

XI. Settlement of the People 11:1–36

Nehemiah now dealt with a practical matter. The lack of inhabitants in the city of Jerusalem, mentioned earlier in 7:4, was still a problem.[98] The "rulers" (or "leaders," *śar*, see Ezra 7:28) of the nation lived there since they needed to consult with

[97]Raymond Brown, p. 192, suggests that the presence of the high priest guarded against "any possibility of suspicion or accusation regarding the misappropriation of funds." This is also a possible view. With human nature being sinful, even those involved in God's service may sometimes give in to greed.

[98]Henry, p. 1108, suggests that the people avoided living in Jerusalem because the holy city required greater strictness of life or because the hatred of the heathen living in the region made it dangerous to reside there. Neither of these reasons was in force at the time of the original return under Ezra. At that

one another. The people, however, had scattered throughout the land. This left the security of the city in doubt and also meant the city did not have enough people to occupy the sales and service positions necessary for everyday life. In addition, since Jerusalem was the "holy city" and the site of the temple, the worship center of Israel, it was a disgrace for it to be relatively uninhabited. Augmenting the number of residents would keep Israel's God from the reproach connected with a city that did not function well.

A. Increasing the Population of Jerusalem 11:1–24

1–2 To solve the population problem in the capital city, the people adopted a plan to cast lots for the purpose of selecting ten percent of the families to move to Jerusalem.[99] The remaining ninety percent would "dwell in other cities," i.e., towns and villages of all sizes scattered throughout the land, v. 1. Some families willingly offered to move to Jerusalem. This elicited praise from the others, v. 2.

3–6 The "chief" (or "heads") of the "province" naturally located at Jerusalem where they could participate in governmental decisions. The "province" is the land of Judah, one of many such divisions in the Persian Empire. In addition, many different people from the priests, Levites, Nethinim (discussed at Ezra 2:43 and Neh. 3:26), and royal servants resided in various cities in the land, v. 3. Some of these same groups lived in Jerusalem. The first of these were from the tribe of Judah. Athaiah, a descendant of Perez (Gen. 38:29), headed one family, v. 4. Maaseiah (called Asaiah, 1 Chron. 9:5), a descendant of Shilonia (or "Shelah," the youngest son of Judah, Gen. 38:5), headed

---

time the people settled in cities throughout the land, most likely returning to the regions where they had some previous family connection (Ezra 2:70).

[99]Bowman, pp. 731, 769–70, thinks c. 10 is connected "neither chronologically nor in substance." For this reason he considers c. 8–10 out of order, taken by some copyist from Ezra and mistakenly placed here. There is no manuscript evidence to support his view. Further, there is a logical reason for c. 8–10 to follow 7:73. Those chapters describe the worship of the people in the "seventh month," mentioned in 7:73. With that description completed, Nehemiah now returns to the thought suggested in 7:4, the sparse population of Jerusalem. To resolve that problem, he gathered a large convocation of people (7:5), an action that led to finding the genealogy given in 7:5–72.

a second family. All together, the men of Perez (probably also including the descendants of Shelah) numbered 468, v. 6.

7–9 There were also families from Benjamin. Sallu, v. 7, a descendant of Jesaiah, an unknown individual, headed the first family, v. 7. After him came "Gabbai, Sallai" (better "Gabbai *and* Sallai"). The total number of Benjamites included 928 men, v. 8. The overall leader of the families in Jerusalem was Joel, with Judah serving as his assistant. While this seems to contradict the leadership of Hanani and Hananaiah (7:2), it is clear that a period of time had passed. The former leadership reflects an appointment by Nehemiah.[100] With the increased population, the people now selected their own leaders, v. 9.

10–14 The priestly inhabitants of the city followed next. In 1 Chronicles 9:10 we see the names of three families—those of Jedaiah, Jehoiarib (Joiarib), and Jachin. The phrase "son of" here indicates a family relationship between Jedaiah and Joiarib but not a father-son relationship, v. 10. Seraiah was a descendant of Ahitub, a former high priest (1 Chron. 9:11). He was thus qualified to serve as "ruler of the house of God," i.e., the high priest. First Samuel 14:3 presents Ahitub as the son of Phinehas and the grandson of Eli, the high priest that brought up Samuel. Ahitub likely replaced Eli as high priest after his death. Nehemiah 12:12 gives Meraiah as head of the family descended from Seraiah. This suggests that Seraiah died shortly after the events of this chapter. The fact that Eliashib was high priest when Nehemiah returned from Babylon (13:7) supports this, v. 11.

There were 822 priests for "the work of the house," the ceremonial observances. These included 242 members of the family led by Adaiah, vv. 12–13*a*, and 128 in the family led by Amashai. Their brethren were "mighty men of valour," a description that likely indicates that these men in some way guarded the city against attack.[101] Zabdiel, the son of "one of the great men," was over this group.

---

[100]Kidner, p. 118, explains Judah's position as leading the "second quarter" (2 Kings 22:14, "college") of the city. The view is speculative with little to commend it.

[101]Rawlinson, p. 118, understands the phrase to refer to very able men for their service in the temple. This phrase, however, occurs 15x elsewhere (e.g., Josh. 6:2; 1 Chron. 7:9, 40), normally having a military context.

The phrase "one of the great men" translates the word *hagg^edôlîm*. The AB and GNB connect the name to a "leading family." Fensham and Kidner understand the phrase the same way. The majority of modern translations, e.g., ESV, NASB, and NLT, translate this as a personal name, making Zabdiel the son of "Haggedolim." Rawlinson and Keil also take it as a personal name.[102] Variations of the word *gadôl* occur more than five hundred times, none of them elsewhere a personal name. For this reason, it is best to follow the KJV's translation. While we do not know who the "great man" was, the fact that his son occupied a position of leadership supports his inclusion in a prominent family, vv. 13*b*–14.

15–18 Several Levitical families also lived in the city. These included Shemaiah, v. 15, plus Shabbethai and Jozabad, who were over the "outward business" of the temple, i.e., ordering supplies and supervising the maintenance, v. 16. Mattaniah, a descendant of Asaph, carried on the family tradition of music by leading the temple singers in a song of thanksgiving in prayer. Bakbukiah was his assistant, and Abda was an additional assistant, v. 17. There were 288 Levites, v. 18.

19–24 The "porters" (or "gatekeepers," those charged with the security of the temple area, necessary because of its sacred nature), under Akkub and Talmon, included 172 men, v. 19. Other priests and Levites lived on their inherited property throughout the land, v. 20. In contrast, the Nethinim, being set apart for work in the temple (see 3:26), lived in Ophel on the southern slope of Mount Moriah. Their leaders were Ziha and Gispa, v. 21. Uzzi, another descendant of Asaph, was in charge of the Levites as they took care of "the business of the house of God," the internal affairs of the temple. These included preparations for the daily and special worship times together with the assignment of priests and Levites to their responsibilities. The "singers" were "the sons of Asaph," early Levitical leader of "the singers" (1 Chron. 16:5). The supplied helping verb *were* should be omitted. Uzzi was "over the business of the house of God," v. 22. His responsibilities also included dispersing the "certain portion" earlier commanded by King Artaxerxes to be provided to the singers for

[102]Fensham, p. 246, Kidner, p. 119; Rawlinson, p. 118; Keil, p. 260.

their daily work (Ezra 6:9–10; 7:21–23), v. 23. Pethahiah represented the king in matters concerning Palestine, v. 24.

B. Enumerating the Cities of Israel 11:25–36

25–30 Some of the people lived in cities throughout the land. The first part of the listing here includes cities that, for the most part, were located in Simeon and Judah. Kirjath-arba is the ancient name for Hebron (Gen. 23:2). The town and "the villages thereof," nearby smaller settlements dependent to some degree on the larger town, lay about twenty miles south of Jerusalem, in the area occupied by Judah (Josh. 15:13). Dibon and its surrounding settlements were east of the Dead Sea, about three miles north of the Arnon River. This was an area once occupied by Gad (Num. 32:34). Jekabzeel is another name for Kabzeel. The city and the smaller settlements close to it were in Judah near the border of Edom (Josh. 15:21). We cannot give a more precise location, v. 25. We do not know the location of Jeshua other than to put it in the southern part of the land, near the other cities in this list. Moladah was in the area given to Judah (Josh. 15:26). Later, however, the people of Simeon occupied it as well as Beth-phelet, Hazar-shual, and Beersheba (the southernmost town in Palestine), which were somewhere in the territory given to Simeon (Josh. 19:1–8), v. 26.

Ziklag also lay in the area occupied by Simeon (Josh. 19:5). We do not know the location of Mekonah and its land. It was probably situated near the other towns mentioned in this section, v. 27. En-rimmon seems to have begun as two small towns, Ain and Rimmon (Josh. 15:32; 19:7). With time, they grew together into a single town. This is generally identified today with Khirbet Umm er-Rummanmin, nine miles north of Beersheba. This would place it in the area occupied by Simeon. The town of Zareah, also spelled Zoreah, was in the region occupied by Simeon (Josh. 15:33). Jarmuth was about six miles south of Zareah in the lowlands of Judah (Josh. 15:35), v. 29.

The final cities of this section were all located near Jerusalem. The inhabitants of Zanoah had earlier helped repair the wall of Jerusalem (3:13). The town lay about fifteen miles west of Jerusalem. We know Adullam mostly for the cave located near it (1 Sam. 22:1; 2 Sam. 23:13). The town and its fields were about fifteen miles southwest of Jerusalem. Continuing to the southwest, Lachish and its surrounding fields were fifteen miles past Adullam. Azekah and the land near it lay in the lowlands of Judah (Josh. 15:35), about ten miles north of Lachish. The final phrase summarizes the settling of the land at this time. The people were living in the area between Beersheba, at the southern border of Judah, and the valley of Hinnom on the south side of Jerusalem, v. 30.

31–36 The enumeration now lists cities generally located in Benjamin. The phrase "from Geba *dwelt* at" is better rendered "from Geba *and beyond*." The *min* preposition indicates some kind of separation. Here, the separation is away from Geba, giving the sense that the people of Benjamin lived at Geba and then spread to other cities. Geba was located about six miles north of Jerusalem.

Michmash was seven miles north of Jerusalem. Aija, better known as Ai, lay about ten miles north of Jerusalem. Bethel with its surrounding fields was about twelve miles north of Jerusalem, v. 31. Anathoth was a small city about two and one-half miles northeast of Jerusalem. The location of Nob is unknown. From Isaiah 10:28–32, we know that it was the final town northeast of Jerusalem before entering the city. The OT does not mention Ananiah elsewhere so we cannot certainly locate it other than to place it somewhere in Benjamin's territory. It is often identified as the NT town of Bethany, v. 32.[103]

The Hazor mentioned here is not the one-time major city in Palestine (Josh. 11:10). Its location is unknown, but from its association with the other cities in this passage, it likely lay to the north of Jerusalem. Ramah is a city located five miles north of Jerusalem. Another Ramah lay in the region given to Naphtali (Josh. 19:32, 36). Since most of these other towns were in Benjamin, it is probable that Ramah was in that region also.

From its mention in 2 Samuel 4:1–3, Gittaim must have been located in Benjamin, but we cannot place it precisely, v. 33. Hadid is thought to be modern Haditheh, about twenty-two miles northwest of Jerusalem. The town lay in Ephraim, near

---

[103]Bowman; Myers, p. 192; p. 783; Unger, p. 48; *Wycliffe Bible Encyclopedia*, vol. 1, p. 64. Slotki, p. 253, identifies it with Beit Hannina, a village located two miles north of Jerusalem.

Dan. The location of Zeboim is not known. From its association with Hadid and Neballat, it may have been in the same area. Neballat was about a mile north of Hadid and was also in Ephraim, v. 34.

Lod, the town called Lydda in Acts 9:32–38, was situated on the Ajalon River eleven miles southeast of Joppa. Ono was also on the Ajalon about seven miles from Joppa. Ono was a city located in the "plain of Ono" (6:2). This region is the same as that designated as the "valley of craftsmen." The term refers to the specialized crafts carried out there, v. 35. The closing verse means that "of the Levites were [better 'with'] divisions in Judah" some were assigned to "Benjamin," v. 36.

NEHEMIAH 12

XII. Dedication of the People 12:1–13:3

The early part of this chapter completes the listing of the priests and Levites involved in the worship of God at Jerusalem and in the care of the city. The major topic dealt with here, however, is the dedication of the wall, previously completed (6:15) but never formally dedicated with an activity recognizing the blessing of God on the nation.

A. Listing of the Priests and Levites 12:1–26

1–9 Nehemiah supplements the earlier summary of the priests and Levites who had returned to Palestine (7:39–45).[104] Initially the list mentions the heads of the various courses of priests and Levites. The list includes many of those who signed the covenant (10:2–8) or who headed the priestly courses under the high priest Jehoiakim (12:12–13). Most of the names in these lists are the

[104]Fensham, p. 250, understands the list as giving "family names, and not names of individuals." It is difficult to account for v. 8 with this explanation since it clearly refers to an individual.

same. In this initial list the names of the priests occur in vv. 1–7 and the Levites in vv. 8–9.

The priests who returned with Zerubbabel and Jeshua (Ezra 2:2) included Seraiah and Jeremiah (both also mentioned as signing the covenant, 10:2). The chapter introducing the book by his name discusses Ezra, v. 1. Many of the remaining priests also signed the covenant. Among these were Amariah (10:3), Malluch, and Hattush (10:4), v. 2. Shechaniah and Shebaniah were apparently the same person. The *kap* and the *bêt* being similar in appearance, the *kap* has been misread for the *bêt*. The similar sequence of names in 10:5 suggests that Rehum (12:3) was the same person as Harim (also 12:15), the first two consonants being transposed. Other variations in spelling are relatively minor.

The list of covenant signers also included Meremoth (10:5), v. 3. We know nothing else about Iddo. Ginnetho ("Ginnethon," 10:6), Baruch (10:6), v. 4, and Miamin (10:7) earlier signed the covenant. Though neither Maadiah nor Bilgah is mentioned elsewhere, v. 5, Shemaiah is listed in 10:8. We know nothing else about Joiarib, Jedaiah, Sallu, Amok, or Hilkiah. Jedaiah served at Jerusalem (11:10). These men were the leading priests during the time that Jeshua served as the high priest.

The names of the last six priests are set off in the MT by the conjunction *and* before Joiarib. The significance of this is not clear. Noss and Thomas suggest that the last group included men who were "not yet chiefs or family heads at the time of the return from captivity in Babylon." Rawlinson explains that the final six families "did not seal to the covenant, whereas the other sixteen courses did so." Bowman tentatively makes the final group of names a Maccabean addition, a suggestion with no manuscript support.[105] We can only speculate on the reason for distinguishing them. These priests held leadership positions over the other priests and their "brethren," a reference to the Levites, vv. 6–7.

The Levites included Jeshua, Binnui and Kadmiel (10:9), and Sherebiah (10:12). We know nothing certain about Judah. From his position as being "over the thanksgiving," Mattaniah is mentioned in 11:17 as a descendant of Asaph. He is over the

[105]Noss and Thomas, p.500; Rawlinson, p. 127; Bowman, p. 785.

"thanksgiving" (or "songs of praise"), sung by "[him] and his brethren," v. 8. Bakbukiah, the assistant director (11:17) and Unni (correctly spelled as Unno), a person not mentioned elsewhere, were also among "watches" (or "services") of the Levites. The fact that they were "over against" (or "opposite") "Mattaniah . . . and his brethren" suggests that Bakbukiah and Unno led a second choir, making antiphonal responses possible in the worship services (see also v. 24), v. 9.[106]

10–11 These verses give a short genealogy of the high priestly office. First Chronicles 6:3–15 gives an earlier genealogy of the high priests up to the Babylonian captivity. At the time of Zerubbabel's return (Ezra 3:2) from the captivity, Jeshua was the high priest. Joiakim served as high priest during the gap in time between Ezra 6 and 7 (Neh. 12:10, 12, 26). Eliashib was the high priest during the time of Nehemiah's work (3:1, 20). Joiada, Jonathan, and Jaddua later served in that office. Apparently, Joiada's brother Johanan succeeded him but only briefly and is therefore omitted from this list (see vv. 22–23), vv. 10–11.

Jaddua presents a problem for the conservative dating of the book. The only Jaddua mentioned in history as a high priest served at the time of Darius Codomannus (336–330 BC). Josephus mentions a Jaddua who was high priest at the time of Darius (*Antiquities* 11.8.4) and who died after the death of Alexander the Great (11.8.7), 323 BC. This suggests a late date for the book or later editorial activity.[107]

The Jaddua mentioned here, however, was the son of Jonathan and the grandson of Joiada. Both Jonathan (or Johanan, 12:22) and Joiada (13:28) served during the time of Nehemiah. This leads to the conclusion that "Darius the Persian" (12:22) is Darius Nothus, who reigned 423–404 BC. The Jaddua mentioned by Josephus must either be a second Jaddua or simply a historical error by Josephus. In the same passage he mentions Sanbal-

[106]Ryle, p. 295, suggests that Mattaniah represents the descendants of Asaph, while Bakbukiah and Unno represent descendants of other families of the singers. While there is no proof of the view, it is possible.

[107]Ryle, p. 297, identifies Darius as Darius Codomannus (336–331). This identification supports his view of a later compiler who wrote the book from various documents. If we accept Nehemiah as the author, this Darius cannot be Codomannus.

lat and his son-in-law Manasseh. There is no question that these were both contemporaries of Nehemiah. Josephus must therefore have been wrong in his dating of these individuals.

12–21 The next section gives the names of the heads of the priestly courses during the time that Joiakim was the high priest. Meriah was born to Seraiah (v. 1), Hananiah to Jeremiah (v. 1), v. 12, and Meshullam to Ezra (v. 1). Jehohanan was the son of Amariah (v. 2), v. 13, Jonathan the son of Melicu (or "Malluch," v. 2), and Joseph the son of Shebaniah, v. 14.[108] Harim (10:27) was the father of Adna, and Meraioth (spelled Meremoth in some manuscripts of the LXX) the father of Helkai, v. 15. Zechariah was born to Iddo (v. 4), Meshullam to Ginnethon (v. 4), v. 16, and Zichri to Abijah (v. 4). The name of the son of Miniamin (v. 5) has dropped out of the MT. The son of Moadiah (v. 5) was Piltai, v. 17, and Shammua the son of Bilgah (v. 5). Shemaiah (v. 6) was the father of Jehonathan, v. 18, Joiarib (v. 6) the father of Mattenai, and Jedaih (v. 6) the father of Uzzi, v. 19. Kallai was born to Sallai (v. 7), Eber to Amok (v. 7), v. 20, Hashabiah to Hilkiah (v. 7), and Nethaneel to Jedaiah (v. 7), v. 21.

22–26 The final part of the list includes the heads of the Levites, singers, and porters during the time of Joiakim's priestly leadership. Eliashib, Joiada, Jonathan, and Jaddua were the high priests mentioned earlier in vv. 10, 11. "Darius the Persian" refers to King Darius II Nothus (423–404 BC), v. 22. The names of these Levitical chiefs come from "the book of the chronicles," a record of day-by-day events, not the biblical book with the same name. This record covers the years until Johanan took office, apparently serving as high priest after his brother Joiada (12:10) for only a short time. The shortness of his office is deduced from the succession of Joiada's son Jonathan, v. 23.[109]

Hashabiah was probably the same man who repaired the wall (3:17) and signed Nehemiah's covenant (10:11). Sherebiah was also a signer of the covenant (10:12). The phrase "Jeshua, the

---

[108]Several Hebrew mss, some mss of the LXX, and the Syriac version give Shechaniah, v. 3, instead of Shebaniah.

[109]It is also possible that the names *Johanan* and *Jonathan* are used to refer to the same man by mistake. While "son" in v. 23 could well mean the grandson of Eliashib, it seems less likely in my judgment that a scribal error has interchanged the names.

son of Kadmiel" is puzzling. This is the only place that refers to a relationship between Jeshua and Kadmiel. In Ezra 2:40 and 3:9 and in Nehemiah 7:43, Jeshua and Kadmiel occur without mention of a relationship between them. Jeshua, Binnui (or Bani), and Kadmiel occur as a sequence (Neh. 9:4, 5; 10:9; 12:8) with no relationship indicated between Jeshua and Kadmiel. The LXX translates *ben*, "son," as *ui^{c}oi*, "sons (plural), which may suggest *b^{e}nê* as the original. This, in turn, is close to *banî*, "Bani," mentioned elsewhere in connection with Jeshua and Kadmiel.[110] It is also possible that "son" refers to the relationship between Jeshua and Kadmiel, both being singers (cf. "sons of the singers," v. 28).

These men led the people in praising and thanking the Lord according to David's command (e.g., 1 Chron. 23:30; 25:1, 6). As in v. 9, this was done "ward over against ward" (or "service corresponding to service"). This also refers to the antiphonal singing of the two Levitical choirs commanded by David, v. 24.

Mattaniah, Bakbukiah, and Obadiah were singers (cf. 11:17) and should be considered separately from the other names. The names continue the thought of singing from the previous verse. Meshullam, Talmon, and Akkub were porters, responsible for guarding the entrances into the temple (cf. 1 Chron. 9:17). They stood at the "thresholds" (better "storehouses") of the gates, rooms located there for storage, v. 25.

All of these men served in the times when Joiakim was the high priest, Nehemiah the Persian "governor" (*peḥâ*, see Ezra 8:36), and Ezra the "scribe," v. 26.

B. Dedication of the City Wall 12:27–43

27–30 Nehemiah arranged a ceremony for dedicating the wall. Although c. 6 records the completion of the repairs on the wall in the sixth month of Elul, four days before the end of the month (6:15), there was a relatively short period of time between the completion and the dedication. Since c. 7, c. 11, and the first part of c. 12 are primarily lists of people, they involve no passage of time, but c. 8 describes the keeping of the Feast of Tabernacles in the seventh month. This was an important feast that could not

[110]Ryle, p. 297, and Rawlinson, p. 129. Keil, p. 273, deletes *ben* ("son") as a gloss.

be set aside for the dedication of the wall. The revival described in c. 9 follows in the same month. The resettlement of the people into Jerusalem required a short period of time (11:1–2). Even though several chapters of the book have intervened, the time involved was only a few weeks. Nehemiah now scheduled the dedication ceremony. This was a time for recognizing the blessings of God on the nation ("gave thanks," vv. 31, 38, 40; "rejoiced, joy," v. 43; "great sacrifices," v. 43).

Nehemiah brought the Levites dwelling in the country regions around Jerusalem to the city to help with the public "thanksgivings" (*tôdôt*)[111] and the music. The word *tôdôt* occurs widely in the OT, especially in Psalms. While it normally refers to a sacrificial offering, it frequently indicates gratitude (e.g., Pss. 100:4; 147:7; Isa. 51:3; Jer. 30:19; Jon. 2:9). All four times the word occurs in Nehemiah (vv. 27, 31, 38, 40), it is translated as a plural, appropriately giving emphasis to the thankful attitude manifested by the two processions as they traversed the wall on their way to the temple.

Cymbals, "psalteries" (or "lyres"), and harps accompanied the singing, v. 27. The "sons of the singers," individuals among the Levites involved with the singing, came from around Jerusalem. The "plain country [*kikkar*, see 3:22]" refers to the southern part of the Jordan Valley (cf. 3:22). The "villages of Netophathi" were located near Bethlehem (Neh. 7:26) south of Jerusalem, v. 28. The "house of Gilgal" (or "Beth-Gilgal") lies about twenty miles northeast of Jerusalem. Geba is about six miles north of Jerusalem. We cannot locate Azmaveth, called "Beth-Azmaveth" (7:28), although, from its associations here, it was also north of Jerusalem, v. 29. The priests and Levites engaged

[111]Several translations, e.g., NAB, REV, NJB, render *tôdôt* as "choir" or "choirs." Some commentators, e.g., Blenkinsopp and Raymond Brown, also follow this translation. M. J. Boda, "The Use of *Tôdôt* in Nehemiah XII," *VT* 44, no. 3 (July 1994): 387–93, correctly rejects this translation. He concludes instead that the two groups on the wall "were led by the sacrifices that were to be offered in the temple." While his view is remotely possible, it is difficult to think of priests carrying the sacrifices while walking along the recently completed wall. The sacrificial animals themselves would not have willingly walked along the wall.

in purification rituals, offering sacrifices for themselves, the people, and the city's wall and gates, v. 30.

31–37 Nehemiah led "the princes [*śar*, see Ezra 7:28] of Judah," the tribal leaders, to the wall. He divided them into two groups to give "thanks" (*tôdôt*) and then to walk to their starting points. Beginning on the south wall, one group led by Ezra (v. 36) went to the right, then along the eastern wall, moving counterclockwise until meeting the second group at the temple, v. 31. This group included Hoshaiah and "half of the princes [*śar*] of Judah." We know nothing of Hoshaiah except that, since he headed the group, he must have held a leadership position among the Jews, v. 32. His group included Azariah, Ezra (not the same as the author of the book by this name), Meshullam, Judah, Benjamin, Shemaiah, and Jeremiah. Although these names occur elsewhere, we cannot certainly identify them other than to place them in leadership positions among the Jews, vv. 33–34. Some of the "sons" of the priests accompanied the singing with music. Zechariah, a descendant of Asaph, v. 35, and other priests sounded their "[silver] trumpets" (*ḥ^{a}ṣoṣ^{e}rôt*, see Ezra 3:10) and the "musical instruments of David," likely stringed instruments (cf. 1 Sam. 16:23). Ezra "the scribe" (the author of the book of Ezra) went in front of them, v. 36. The group ascended the "going up," the stairs at the Fountain Gate, in the southeastern part of the wall, and traveled north past "the house of David"[112] to the Water Gate in the eastern wall of the city, v. 37.

38–43 Nehemiah followed behind the second group of princes as they gave "thanks" (*tôdôt*) to the Lord. They began near "the tower of the furnaces" (3:11) in the northwest corner and proceeded clockwise along the Broad Wall, v. 38. They passed by the Gate of Ephraim (8:16), the Old Gate (3:6), the Fish Gate (3:3), the Tower of Hananeel (3:1), the Tower of Meah (see the discussion at 3:1), the Sheep Gate (3:1, 32), and to the Prison Gate (better "Gate of the Guard"), v. 39. This is the only

[112] We cannot certainly identify the "house of David." Most authors do not mention it, e.g., Coggins, Laney, Myers. Some, e.g., Barnes, p. 481, and Rawlinson, p. 29, consider this a reference to David's palace. While the identification must remain speculative, the association of the term with David's palace is reasonable. Cf. 3:25.

time that Bible mentions the Prison Gate or Gate of the Guard, so its location is unknown. Since the Sheep Gate was at the northeastern part of the city, this gate likely was in the north or northeastern wall. Nehemiah 3:25 mentions the "court of the prison ['guard']," located near the palace on the temple mount. It is possible that the gate mentioned here should be associated with this court.

The two companies met in this area, v. 40. The priests sounded their "[silver] trumpets" (*ḥ^{a}ṣoṣ^{e}rôt*), v. 41, and the singers under Jezrahiah sang their "thanks" (*tôdôt*) to God, v. 42. The leaders offered "great sacrifices" to the Lord. Their wives and children joined the rejoicing. The degree of joy was such that it was "heard even afar off," v. 43.

C. Provision for the Temple Service 12:44–47

Nehemiah acted to organize the support for the temple-servants.[113] Some of these had been appointed to receive the offerings of grain, and so forth that came into the temple. Others went through the land to receive the tithes of the people for the priests and Levites. These offerings reflected the rejoicing of the people in those who served God in the temple, v. 44. The phrase "both the singers . . . purification" should be translated "they [i.e., the priests and Levites] performed the service of their God and the service of purification, together with the singers and the gatekeepers." This followed the commands given by David and Solomon, v. 45. This practice had begun in the days of David and Asaph, the chief musician under him (1 Chron. 16:4–5), and continued under Solomon, v. 46. During the time of Zerubbabel and Nehemiah's leadership, all of the people gave offerings for the temple servants. The singers and porters took these and "sanctified" (or "set apart") portions for the Levites. The Levites, in turn, set apart portions for the priests, v. 47.

[113]Keil, p. 283, understands Nehemiah's second return (13:6) as taking place before v. 44, with the reforms of vv. 44–47 taking place afterward. This is possible. The chronology of Nehemiah's leadership of the people is not clearly described.

NEHEMIAH 13

D. Separation from the Heathen 13:1–3

The phrase "on that day" refers to the actions taken in 12:44–47. For that reason, the discussion of these verses logically follows here. In reading from "the book of Moses," the Pentateuch, during one of the festival times, the priests read in Deuteronomy 23:3–6 about the treachery of Ammon and Moab in hiring Balaam to curse the people. In 1967, excavations at Deir 'Alla, Jordan, in an area originally belonging to Moab revealed plaster fragments from a wall inscription stating "Inscription of Balaam son of Beor, the prophet, man of the gods." The inscription is written in an older Aramaic. Radiocarbon dates and analysis of the style of the writing place it between 800 and 600 BC. That dates it to two hundred to four hundred years before Nehemiah's time.[114]

Despite this to attempt to hurt Israel, God had blessed the nation. Because of the sin of Ammon and Moab, God had commanded that these heathen nations be excluded from the assembly of the people, vv. 1–2. Thus, "they" (Nehemiah and the leaders of the nation) acted to correct this problem, separating the people in their worship from the "mixed multitude," the foreigners among them.

Though it is left unstated, there was a practical purpose in this. These non-Israelites were still worshiping heathen gods. There was no true conversion among them such as had been shown by Ruth the Moabitess (Ruth 1:16). The presence of heathen worshipers would tend to draw Israel away from the Lord. The people had earlier separated the heathen from their worship (9:2), but during Nehemiah's absence the foreign inhabitants of the land had again joined with Israel in keeping the ceremonies, v. 3.

XIII. Separation of the People 13:4–31

After twelve years of service as the governor (5:14; 13:6), Nehemiah returned to the court in Persia for unknown reasons.

[114]http://www.aish.com/society/Work/sciencenature/Biblical_Archaeology_Prophet_and_the_Earthquake0.asp (accessed December 26, 2008).

At some point later in time, he came back to take up his position again. Several problems had developed during his absence, and he took steps to correct them. This chapter describes four distinct actions taken by Nehemiah as he led the people to renew a right relationship with their Lord.

A. Cleansing of the Temple 13:4–9

4–5 Eliashib, the priest in charge of the "chamber [lit., 'chambers'] of the house of [their] God," caused the first problem. This Eliashib was not the same as the high priest Eliashib who is mentioned frequently elsewhere (3:1, 20, 21; 12:10, 22, 23; 13:28).[115] The word *oversight* is a passive participle, lit. "was appointed" (as in the ESV and NASB). The CEV, GW, and NIV translate it as "had been put in charge." This indicates that someone else had given him this responsibility. The overseeing of the temple's storage chambers differed markedly from the responsibilities held by the high priest.

"Before this," at some time in the past during Nehemiah's absence, Eliashib had been allied in some unknown way to Tobiah, one of the leaders who had opposed the building of the wall (4:3). The word translated "allied" (*qarôb*) sometimes refers to a family connection (e.g., Lev. 21:2, 3; Num. 27:11; Ruth 2:20; 3:12). It may also refer to a marriage of family members here, but we cannot be certain, v. 4. Whatever the connection, the priest had made available areas in the temple for Tobiah's personal use. In addition to the "great chamber" of the temple, there were other chambers involved, as v. 9 makes clear. The priests used these rooms for storing "meat-offerings" (better "meal offerings"), frankincense (used in preparing incense for the altar of incense, Exodus 30:34–36; also used with meal offerings, Leviticus 2:1–2), vessels used in the temple service, and the offerings of "corn" (*dagan*, see 5:2), wine, and oil for those serving in the temple. To assist Tobiah, Eliashib had made these storage chambers available for his use when he was in Jerusalem. The unstated tragedy in this is that at one time Eliashib must have been faithful to

[115]Butler, pp. 74, 300–302; Henry, p. 1115; Keil, p. 287; and Rademacher and Allen, pp. 321–22, identify Eliashib with the high priest mentioned earlier. Bowman, p. 805; Fensham, p. 260; Larson and Dahlen, p. 271; and Myers, p. 212, understand the mention of Eliashib as referring to another priest.

the Lord, allowing the high priest to assign him responsibility for these storage chambers. Past faithfulness, however, does not guarantee future faithfulness, and Eliashib was now participating in a wicked relationship, v. 5.

6–9 This misuse of the temple had taken place while Nehemiah was in Babylon. He had returned to Persia in the thirty-second year of Artaxerxes Longimanus, twelve years after his original commission by the king (2:1). That this text calls Artaxerxes the "king of Babylon" is not a mistake.[116] The title simply uses the capital city, Babylon, to represent the whole empire. Similar uses of a capital city occur elsewhere, e.g., 1 Kings 21:1 (Samaria representing Israel); 2 Chronicles 24:23 (Damascus representing Syria); Ezra 5:13 (as here, Babylon representing the capital of Persia); Jonah 3:6 (Nineveh representing Assyria).

We cannot tell how long Nehemiah had been gone from Jerusalem. The phrase "after certain days" probably indicates several years, enough time for the sins mentioned in the chapter to have developed. After this period of time, Nehemiah received permission to return to Judah, v. 6.

On arrival, Nehemiah became aware of the wicked actions of Eliashib in letting Tobiah stay in the temple chambers when he was in the city, v. 7. He took action to evict Tobiah and threw out his "household stuff," i.e., the vessels used by Tobiah, from the temple chamber, v. 8. He then had the area purified. From other examples (e.g., 2 Kings 23:4–6; 2 Chron. 29:16–19; Matt. 21:12), the purification involved ridding the temple of all vestiges of Tobiah's occupancy. After this Nehemiah had the temple vessels, the grain and flour used in meal offerings, the frankincense, and the shewbread (Lev. 24:7) returned to the chamber, v. 9.

B. Provision for the Levites 13:10–14

Despite the pledge made at the previous renewal of the covenant, 10:39, the people had stopped bringing their tithes and offerings to the temple. The Mosaic law commanded the nation to support the Levites with offerings (Num. 18:24). Because of this failure by the people, some of the Levites and singers had

---

[116]Batten, p. 289, sees the inclusion of "Babylon" as an addition "from a later hand." Breneman, p. 269, calls the use of the title "strange."

left their temple responsibilities and had gone to their fields, where they could work to grow food for themselves and their families, v. 10. Nehemiah rebuked the leaders of the people for their failure in this matter. He then gathered the Levites back to their "place," the temple area where they served, v. 11. Under this influence the people once more began supporting the service at the temple with the offerings of their tithes of "corn" (*dagan*, see 5:2), wine, and oil. They brought them to the "treasuries," the temple storage areas, v. 12. To oversee the distribution of the offerings, Nehemiah appointed four treasurers—Shelemiah and Zadok, both priests, and Pedaiah and Hanan, both Levites. All these were faithful men. Since the tithes were meant for both the priests and Levites, having representatives of both groups served to insure the accuracy of the distributions, v. 13. Nehemiah prayed that the Lord would look favorably on his "good [or 'loyal,' *ḥesed*, see Ezra 3:11] deeds", v. 14.

C. Keeping of the Sabbath 13:15–22

15–16 The next problem concerned the keeping of the Sabbath. Some of the people were working at treading the juice from the grapes, bringing "sheaves" (lit., "heaps") of various produce into the city, loading donkeys, and carrying a variety of materials into Jerusalem for sale. Undoubtedly this list represents other work at various tasks done also by the people. Nehemiah "testified" (or "warned") them against the sale of food on the Sabbath, v. 15. Some of the people from Tyre also sold fish and other merchandise on the Sabbath. All of this violated the command to keep the Sabbath as a day of rest (Exod. 20:8–11). It also represented a violation of the covenant entered into earlier by the people (10:31), v. 16.

17–18 Nehemiah rebuked the leaders of Judah who had allowed the people to profane the Sabbath, v. 17. He reminded them that God had judged the nation in the past for this very reason (Lev. 26:14–39, especially vv. 34–35; Jer. 17:21–23; Ezek. 20:13, 16, 20, 24). He accused them of bringing more punishment on the people by letting them profane the Sabbath, v. 18.

19–22 Nehemiah ordered the city gates to be closed as the gates "began to be dark" (or "shadowed," *ṣalal*, see 3:15), i.e., as the sun went down. Based on the biblical account of the creation week ("the evening and the morning," Gen. 1:19, 23, 31), the Jews begin each day in the evening (Lev. 23:32) although they do not agree among themselves as to whether the day begins with sunset or with nightfall. The gates remained closed during the Sabbath, opening only after evening came, marking the beginning of the next day. In addition Nehemiah placed some of his own servants as guards at the gates to insure that the merchants did not bring their wares in for sale, v. 19.

The merchants adjusted to this situation by setting up their shops outside the walls and simply waiting for the day to pass. After the second time this took place, v. 20, Nehemiah warned them that he would "lay hands" on them if it happened again, arresting them for violating the law. While they may not have sold their goods on the Sabbath, their packing up and traveling to the city involved work, an open violation of the Sabbath laws. Nehemiah's threat to "lay hands" on them is described with a phrase that can refer to inflicting serious harm (Esther 2:21; 6:2; 8:7). This warning solved the problem, v. 21. Nehemiah commanded the Levites to cleanse themselves, which indicates that the problem was a sacred matter. The Levites were to post a permanent guard at the gates on the Sabbath so the day would remain a holy one. This would "sanctify" (or "consecrate," *qadaš*, see 3:1) the day to the Lord. Briefly Nehemiah committed himself to the Lord by asking His blessing according to His great "mercy" (or "loyal love," *ḥesed*, see Ezra 3:11), v. 22.

D. Defilement of Marriage 13:23–29

23–24 The final problem concerned the intermarriage of the people with the heathen. Despite the covenant made earlier to avoid such marriage (10:30), the people had once more entered into marriages with the foreigners living in the area. Some of the Israelite men had taken wives from among the women of Ashdod, a Philistine city. Others had intermarried with women from Ammon and Moab, v. 23. As a result the children from these marriages spoke the languages of their mothers and not Hebrew. While the speech of Ashdod is the only language mentioned, the children undoubtedly learned the speech of their mothers and spoke the languages of Ammon and Moab also. While we have few samples of these languages, what little exists shows that these languages were cognate to Hebrew, i.e., similar to Hebrew but sufficiently different to keep the children from understanding Hebrew. This situation not only attacked the spiritual relationship of the people with God but it also threatened the very existence of Israel as a nation, v. 24.

25–27 Nehemiah contended with those who had sinned in this way. He "cursed" them, reviling them and exposing them to shame for their disobedience. He struck some of them, physically castigating them to show his contempt for their actions. He punished others by plucking out some of the hair in their beards. This action openly shamed them (2 Sam. 10:4–5; Isa. 50:6). He forced "them" (the Jews) to swear that they would not let their sons and daughters intermarry with the heathen, v. 25.

Nehemiah reminded the people that Solomon had sinned in this way. Even though Solomon was the recipient of God's love, he had yielded to the temptation to marry "outlandish (or 'foreign,' *nokrî*, see Ezra 10:2) women," an action that caused him to sin (1 Kings 11:4–5; 2 Kings 23:13). Although Nehemiah did not say it explicitly, his words imply that Solomon's sin hadbrought judgment on the nation, v. 26. Nehemiah asked if the people ("we") should listen to those who had "transgress[ed]" (*maᶜal*, see Ezra 10:2) God's command by marrying "strange [*nokrî*] wives," heathen women (cf. Exod. 34:14–16)? Clearly the answer to this rhetorical question was no, v. 27.

28–29 Even the high priestly family had participated in this sin. One of the grandsons of Eliashib had married the daughter of Sanballat. Nehemiah "chased him" away, excluding him from further priestly service, and likely excluding him from Jerusalem, v. 28. Nehemiah asked the Lord to keep his actions in mind, actions that he had taken because of the defilement of the priesthood and the "covenant of the priesthood" (Lev. 21:7; cf. Ezek. 44:22). These actions had defiled the Levites, bringing the priesthood into disrepute, v. 29.

E. Closing Prayer 13:30–31

Nehemiah recalled his work of cleansing the priesthood by forbidding them to marry "strangers" (*nekar*, see Ezra 10:2), 13:23–29. He had also made provision for the priests and Levites to be organized in their temple duties. The book does not mention this, but the references to those who oversaw certain temple functions imply it, e.g., 11:16, 17, v. 30. Further, Nehemiah had arranged for the wood offering (10:34) and the firstfruit offerings to be brought to the temple (10:35). He asked the Lord to remember him for good (cf. 5:19; 13:14, 22). This is a fitting climax to the book since Nehemiah's prayers are so frequent elsewhere (1:4–11; 2:4; 4:4–5; 5:19, 6:9, 14; 13:14, 22, 29), v. 31.

INTRODUCTION TO ESTHER

The book of Esther is one of the most controversial of the Old Testament books. It is one of only two books in the Bible that do not mention clearly the name of God. The Song of Solomon also does not mention God by name, aside from the name *yah* occurring in 8:6 as a suffix in the word *šalhebetyâ*, "Yahweh flame," i.e., a powerful flame.

In addition, Esther is the only OT book not found among the scrolls at Qumran.[1] It is not quoted in the New Testament. Its purpose has been widely misunderstood. For these reasons some have questioned whether the book belongs in the canon of Scripture. Martin Luther did not consider Esther canonical. In his *Table Talk* he said, "I am so great an enemy to the second book of Maccabees, and to Esther, that I wish that they had not come to us at all, for they have too many heathen unnaturalities."[2]

In his commentary on the Esther, Lewis Paton says, "The book is so conspicuously lacking in religion that it should never have been included in the Canon of the OT, but should have been left . . . among the apocryphal writings." Bernhard Anderson says that it "seems strangely out of place in the Christian Bible." He goes so far as to say, "As we turn to [Esther] from other books of the Bible, 'we fall, as it were, from heaven to earth.'" He then quotes Ewald favorably, "How, then, does Esther deserve a place in the Christian Bible?"[3]

---

[1]Sidnie White Crawford, "Has Every Book of the Bible Been Found Among the Dead Sea Scrolls?" *BR* 12, no. 5 (October 1996): 28–33, 56, discusses four fragments found at Qumran (4Q550) and publicized by J. T. Milik ("Les modèles araméens du livre d'Esther dans la Grotte 4 de Qumran," *Revue de Qumran* 15 [September–March 1991–92]: 364) as a model or source for the book of Esther. Crawford does not go quite this far, but she still sees the Qumran fragments as "part of a larger cycle of royal courtier tales set in the Persian or some other foreign court, a genre . . . upon which the author of proto-Esther drew when constructing his narrative." She bases this conclusion on fragmentary evidence which in no way gives a clear connection to Esther.

[2]Martin Luther, *The Table Talk of Martin Luther*, trans. William Hazlitt (Philadelphia: The Lutheran Publication Society, n.d.), p. 13.

[3]Lewis Paton, *A Critical and Exegetical Commentary on the Book of Esther* (Edinburgh: T. & T. Clark, 1976), p. 97; Bernhard Anderson, "The Place of Esther in the Christian Bible," *Journal of Religion* 30, no. 1 (January 1950): 32.

Browne expresses a typically low view of the book: "Gentile and Jew alike are represented in the book as actuated by the basest motives of pride, greed, and cruelty. If the book fills any useful place in the Bible it is as a picture of unredeemed humanity." Pfeiffer draws the conclusion that "we must regard the Book of Esther as a work of fiction and all characters in the book, with the exception of Xerxes, as purely imaginary." Michael Heltzer blatantly calls the book "fiction" but to bolster his view gives no evidence that cannot be explained in a way that supports the historicity of the book. Heltzer dates the book "not long after 340 B.C.E.," when the Persian armies suppressed a rebellion among the Jews. He suggests that "to console themselves, the Jews invented a story set in an earlier Persian reign that told of a persecution that they had gloriously overcome."[4] The suggestion has no merit. The Jews did not need to invent a story about overcoming persecution. They already had the OT records telling of deliverance from Egypt, from a variety of nations in the time of the Judges, and from Assyria.

There were questions even among the Jews as to whether or not the book should be included among their sacred Scriptures. *Megillah 7a* records the following debate. "Rab Judah said in the name of Samuel; [the scroll] of Esther does not make the hands unclean. Are we to infer from this that Samuel was of the opinion that Esther was not composed under the inspiration of the Holy Spirit? How can this be, seeing that Samuel has said that Esther was composed under the inspiration of the Holy Spirit?—It was composed to be recited [by heart] but not to be written."[5] *Sanhedrin* 100*a* reads, "Levi b. Samuel and R. Huna b. Ḥiyya were repairing the mantles of the Scrolls of R. Judah's college. On coming to the Scroll of Esther, they remarked, 'O, this Scroll of Esther does not require a mantle.'" The statement suggested that the book was

[4]L. E. Browne, "Esther," *Peake's Commentary on the Bible*, eds. Matthew Black and H. H. Rowley (1919; repr., Camden, NJ: Thomas Nelson and Sons, 1967), p. 381; Robert H. Pfeiffer, *Introduction to the Old Testament* (New York: Harper & Brothers Publishers, 1948), p. 739; Michael Heltzer, "The Book of Esther: Where Does Fiction Start and History End?" *BR* 8, no. 1 (February 1992): 25.

[5]*Megillah*, trans. Maurice Simon, in *The Babylonian Talmud*, ed. J. Epstein (London: The Soncino Press, 1938).

of lower grade, so it would not be defiled by hands touching it. The mantle kept a person from touching the book. Rabbi Judah reproved them, saying, "This too savours of irreverence."[6]

The failure of the NT to quote the book is not a serious problem. The NT also does not quote either Ezra or Nehemiah.[7] In addition, while not direct quotations, there may be allusions to Esther in the NT. Matthew 1:11 may be drawn from Esther 2:6. In Hebrews 11:34, the phrase "escaped the edge of the sword" may refer to the deliverance of the Jews brought about by Esther's plea to the king.

Several explanations have been advanced to explain the absence of God's name. H. D. Kennedy suggests that the book omits God's name since the "story is Persian" and the author did not want to cast pearls before swine. Archaeological evidence from Persia, e.g., the Cylinder of Cyrus, refers frequently to the "gods." Giving the book a Persian flavor would not be an adequate reason to avoid using God's name. J. Vernon McGee explains the lack of God's name by asserting that the book records the story of a people who were out of His will. God had provided a way for them to return to Palestine, but they had remained in Persia.[8] This view overlooks the fact that the last return had taken place more than fifty years earlier, when many of the Jews in Esther's time had not yet been born. It would be another twenty years before the return led by Ezra. While some of the people were undoubtedly out of God's will by not returning, there may have been legitimate reasons for many

[6]*Sanhedrin*, trans. H. Freedman, in *The Babylonian Talmud*, ed. J. Epstein (London: The Soncino Press, 1938).

[7]James Elder Cumming, *The Book of Esther: Its Spiritual Teaching* (London: The Religious Tract Society, n.d.), p. 6, mentions several other books also not quoted in the NT. These include Ruth, 2 Kings, 1 and 2 Chronicles, Song of Solomon, Lamentations, Daniel, Obadiah, Jonah, Nahum, and Zephaniah. Some of these are debatable, e.g., Daniel (Matt. 26:64 cf. Dan. 7:13) and Jonah (Matt. 12:40-41), but it is clear that the NT does not mention many of the OT books.

[8]H. D. Kennedy, *Does God Care?* (New York: Christian Alliance Publishing Co., 1920), p. 7; J. Vernon McGee, *Exposition on the Book of Esther* (Wheaton, IL: Van Kampen Press, 1951), p. 12. John C. Whitcomb, *Esther: The Triumph of God's Sovereignty* (Chicago: Moody Press, 1979), p. 26, is similar with his statement that the Jews were not only out of the Promised Land but "were not even concerned about God's theocratic program centered in that land."

of the people to remain behind. In addition the actions of Esther and Mordecai reflect a desire to honor the Lord—refusing to give reverence to Haman, placing faith in God to deliver the nation—and would naturally be a setting where God's name could be used.

Rod Mattoon gives two other suggestions. He mentions that the writer leaves out God's name because the book may have been for the royal records of Persia or that God's name was omitted to keep the Persians from giving credit to their heathen gods. Rawlinson offers the view that the author "may have viewed it as irreverent to introduce the name of God without necessity into a history which was addressed as much to Persians as to Jews, and was not so much intended for sacred history as for secular." Gordis explains the omission of God's name by saying that "a Jewish author undertook to write his book in the form of a chronicle of the Persian court, written by a Gentile scribe."[9] While Gordis does give evidence to support his view, it is interpretive, making his view speculative.

Gevaryahu asserts that the author did not mention God's name as "a subtle form of intentional protest" over the fact that "an innocent daughter of Israel [is given] to an uncircumcised Gentile king." Again, the view is speculative. Jackowski thinks "the silence and stillness (not absence) of God forces the Jewish community to rely on traditions of communal prayer and fasting for strength; to confront life alone according to the faith that holds them together." The absence of God gives Esther the "willingness to trust in the unseen workings of God."[10]

Paton mentions briefly the additional view that the author may have been a skeptic.[11] It is hard to interpret the action of fasting (4:3, 16; 9:31) without understanding an accompanying prayer to God. Mordecai's challenge to Esther that she was "come to the kingdom for such a time as this" (4:14) seems clearly to refer to

---

[9]Rod Mattoon, *Treasures from Esther* (Springfield, IL: Lincoln Land Baptist Church, 2002), pp. 4–5; Rawlinson, p. v; Robert Gordis, "Esther—a New Solution," *JBL* 100 (September 1981): 375.

[10]Haim M. L. Gevaryahu, "Esther is a Story of Jewish Defense, Not a Story of Jewish Revenge," in *JBQ* 21, no. 1 (January 1993): 12. Karol Jackowski, "Holy Disobedience in Esther," in *Theology Today* 45, no. 4 (January 1989): 406.

[11]Paton, p. 95.

God. Paton concludes that the author wrote the book to be read at the feast of Purim. Since the celebration at this time involved extensive drinking—the Talmud gives a rule that the people should drink until they cannot distinguish between "Blessed be Mordecai" and "Cursed be Haman"—the people might well profane the name of God if it occurred in the reading. It therefore was omitted completely. Since the Mishnah was written about six centuries after Esther, it is likely that the drunken observance of the feast evolved over a period of time.[12] The OT elsewhere warns against excess in "strong drink" (e.g., Prov. 20:1; Isa. 5:22).

Bell notes that the major Jewish players in the historical events, Mordecai and Esther, both engage in conduct unbecoming to Jews. Mordecai encourages Esther to enter the contest to marry an uncircumcised pagan king. Esther keeps her ethnicity secret. This may play a minor part in keeping God's name out of the book. More importantly, "God often chooses to work silently behind the scenes, without miraculous means and occasions of direct revelation."[13] Since we cannot dogmatically explain why God's name does not occur in the book, these views are all speculative.

Sabua discusses rabbinical efforts to find acrostics using the first letters of consecutive words to form the name of YHWH in 1:20, 5:4, 13, and 7:7. In 5:4, the acrostic uses the initial letters of four consecutive words. In 1:20, the acrostic uses the initial letters of four consecutive words when read backwards. In 5:13 and 7:7, the acrostic uses the final letters of four consecutive words. Since nothing in these verses refers to the work of the Lord, the occurrence of these letters is purely random rather than by design. The rabbis were seeking something to justify including the book in the OT canon. Sabua notes that Moore, using the same technique, found two places where Satan's name occurs in the book. In Esther 2:3, the initial letters of three consecutive words spell *Satan* when read forward. In 2:4, the next-to-last letters of three consecutive words spell *Satan* when

[12]Gordis, p. 363, notes that this view contradicts "twenty centuries of Purim observance, during which Jews might imbibe liquor and be merry on Purim but never to the point of blasphemy."

[13]Robert D. Bell, *The Theological Messages of the Old Testament Books* (Greenville, SC: Bob Jones University Press, 2010), p. 194.

read forward. These results show such letter sequences to be coincidental and not intentional.

Sabua proposes a new way of finding God's name in the book. She notes that *yhwdym*, the traditional way of spelling the name of the Jews, occurs thirty-two times. In six places (4:7; 8:1, 7, 13; 9:15, 18), however, the name occurs with an extra *yodh* before the final *mem*. She argues that the *yodh* refers to a "hand," representing "the hand of God." In each case, she sees this as God delivering "either a Jew, or the Jews as a whole."[14] However, this suggestion of Sabua's simply plays with the facts. The six references do not all clearly refer to delivering a Jew or all of the Jews. Further, there are other places that do refer to such deliverance (e.g., 6:10; 8:17; 9:1) where the extra *yodh* does not occur. The spelling of the name with a double *yodh* is simply a variant spelling with no special significance.

There are several possible reasons why Esther was not among the books found at Qumran. Its omission may be due purely to chance.[15] It may be that the Essenes reacted against the failure of the book to use God's name.[16] It is also possible that the Essenes did not observe the feast of Purim since God did not command it.[17] The Essenes also may have reacted against the account of a Jewish maiden entering the harem of a heathen king.[18]

There are no valid reasons to question the inclusion of Esther in the canon of Scripture. The Jews accepted it before the time of Christ. The LXX, translated about 250 BC, included the book. The Talmud, *Baba Bathra* 15*a*, dated in the sixth century AD,

[14]Rachel B. K. Sabua, "The Hidden Hand of God," *BR* 7, no. 1 (February 1992): 31–32; Carey A. Moore, *Esther*, in *The Anchor Bible*, ed. William Foxwell Albright and David Noel Freedman (Garden City, NY: Doubleday & Company, 1971), p. 50.

[15]Frank Moore Cross Jr., *The Ancient Library of Qumran and Modern Biblical Studies* (Garden City, NY: Doubleday & Company, 1958), p. 121, takes this position.

[16]Both Joyce Baldwin, *Esther: An Introduction and Commentary* (Downers Grove, IL: InterVarsity Press, 1984), p. 49, and Moore, *Esther*, in *The Anchor Bible*, p. xxii, mention the absence of God's name as a possible reason for the failure to find the book at Qumran.

[17]Reid, p. 21, agrees with this position.

[18]Robert H. Eisenmann and Michael Wise, *The Dead Sea Scrolls Uncovered* (Rockbury, MA; Element, Inc., 1992), p. 101, suggest this view.

states, "The men of the Great Synagogue wrote . . . Ezekiel, the twelve Minor Prophets, Daniel, and the scroll of Esther." The "men of the Great Synagogue" formed a tribunal in the period between the OT and NT, ca. 400–170 BC. They traced their origin to Ezra and Nehemiah. Since they were not present in Persia at the time of Esther, the statement must refer to the preserving of an earlier written Esther. Second Maccabees 15:36, dated in the late second century BC, refers to Mordecai.

Josephus, writing in the first century AD, tells the story of Esther (*Antiquities* 11.6). The church leader Origen, in the early third century AD, accepted it as canonical and included it in his list of the books in the OT.[19] In his first letter to the Church at Corinth, written about 96 AD, Clement the bishop of Rome referred favorably to the book of Esther.[20] The Council of Jamnia in 90 AD included Esther in its list of accepted books. Early Jewish rabbis quoted from it.

In the Hebrew Bible the Jews grouped Esther with the Song of Solomon, Ruth, Lamentations and Ecclesiastes. These were called the five *Megilloth*, from the Hebrew verb *galal*, "to roll," and thus referring to the rolled-up scrolls containing these books. The book of Esther normally comes last in this group since it is read during Purim, the last of the Jewish feasts. Among the Jews it is a popular book due to the nature of Purim as a feast of rejoicing. This popularity leads the Jews to call the book *hamm^{e}gillah*, "the scroll." Maimonides, a twelfth-century Spanish rabbi, also known as Rabbi Moses ben Maimon (or Rambam), ranked it next to the Pentateuch in importance. He stated, "All the books of the Prophets, and all the Hagiographa shall cease in the days of the Messiah, except the volume of Est; and, lo, that shall be as stable as the Pent, and as the constitutions of the oral law which shall never cease."[21] Jewish families read it each year during the feast of Purim.

[19]N. R. M. De Lange, *Origen and the Jews* (New York: Cambridge University Press, 1976), p. 52.

[20]Cyril C. Richardson, trans. and ed., *Early Christian Fathers* (Philadelphia: The Westminster Press, 1953), vol. 1, p. 68.

[21]John Urquhart, "Esther, book of" in *The International Standard Bible Encyclopedia*, vol. 2, ed. James Orr (Grand Rapids: Wm. B. Eerdmans Publishing Co., 1952.

The popularity of the book among Jews led the Nazis to ban its reading in the concentration camps of World War II. The Jewish inmates in the camps at Auschwitz, Dachau, Treblinka, and Bergen-Belsen recalled the book from memory. They wrote it out and read it secretly on Purim. They understood the lesson that Jewish resistance to annihilation by the heathen "represents the service of God and devotion to His cause. . . . [They viewed] it not merely a record of past deliverance but a prophecy of future salvation."[22]

The LXX translation of Esther includes more than a hundred verses not found in the MT. These verses are distinguished from the MT by letters rather than verse numbers. These portions generally have the name "Additions to Esther." There are six sections that apparently were added to the book to give it a spiritual dimension. Jerome, the translator of the Vulgate, doubted the canonicity of these additions and so moved them to the end of the book. The Vulgate includes the passages as 10:4–16:24 with notes to indicate the place of each section in the story of Esther.

Section A (11:2–12:6) precedes Esther 1:1 and thus serves as an introduction to the book of Esther. It describes a dream experienced by Mordecai and also tells of the plot of two palace servants against the king. Section B (13:1–7) follows Esther 3:13. It gives the text of the king's decree authorizing Haman to kill the Jews throughout the empire. Section C (13:8–14:19) follows Esther 4:17. It gives the prayer of Mordecai on behalf of Israel and the prayer of Esther asking for courage and deliverance as she approaches the king. Section D (15:1–16) replaces Esther 5:1–2 in the MT and follows immediately after the previous section. It describes Esther's entrance into the king's throne room. Section E (16:1–24) following Esther 8:12, gives the king's decree allowing the Jews to defend themselves. The final section, F, follows Esther 10:3 as 10:4–11:1. It gives additional details about Mordecai's dream and also explains its symbolism.

Jews and Protestants reject these additions. Even though there is no Hebrew text to support the additions, the Roman Catholic Church declared them canonical at the Council of Trent in 1546. This was largely a reaction to the criticisms of

[22]Gordis, pp. 13–14.

Martin Luther. Some Roman Catholic versions of the Bible (e.g., NAB) include these passages as part of Esther.[23] The Eastern Orthodox Church also accepts the additions as canonical. Other translations of the Bible (e.g., The Complete Bible, The Holy Bible: New American Catholic Edition) place the Additions to Esther in the Apocrypha. In the Apocrypha, the 10:4–11:1 passage serves as a conclusion to the Additions.

We do not know who wrote Esther. The author was familiar with the Persian culture and language. He likewise was thoroughly familiar with Jewish culture. Archaeology confirms the accuracy of the book. Archaeological and historical records confirm the extent of the empire, the location of the capital at Shushan, the use of couriers and horses (3:13; 8:10), execution by impaling (5:14), and the use of lots (3:7). Different possibilities have been suggested regarding authorship, but we cannot know for sure who the writer of the book was. Several Jewish rabbis held that "the roll of Esther was spoken to Moses from Sinai."[24] Some commentators (e.g., Matthew Henry, Thomas M'Crie, and Joseph Parker) have misunderstood the statement "Mordecai wrote these things" (9:25) as identifying Mordecai as the author of the book.[25] The author, however, never uses the first person. Further, it is unlikely that Mordecai would have praised himself as in 10:2–3. While we may speculate as to the author, there is not enough information given to let us identify him with certainty.[26]

[23]Roger L. Omanson and Philip A. Noss, *A Handbook on the Book of Esther: The Hebrew and Greek Texts* in the *UBS Handbook Series* (New York: United Bible Societies, 1997), p. 5, perceptively note, "From a literary point of view, this approach is problematic because it mixes the Greek and Hebrew versions, and the resulting translation is true neither to the Greek version nor to the Hebrew version."

[24]George Foot Moore, *Judaism in the First Centuries of the Christian Era: the Age of the Tannaim* (Cambridge, MA: Harvard University Press, 1927), vol. 1, p. 245.

[25]Henry, p. 1121; Adam Clarke, *A Commentary and Critical Notes* (New York: T. Mason & G. Lane, 1840), vol. 2, p. 806; Thomas M'Crie, *Lectures on the Book of Esther* (1875; repr., Birmingham, AL: Solid Ground Christian Books, 2006), pp. 13–15; and Joseph Parker, *The People's Bible: Discourses upon Holy Scripture* (New York: Funk & Wagnalls, Publishers, 1889), vol. 10, p. 302.

[26]David Talshir and Zipora Talshir, "The Double Month Naming in Late Biblical Books: A New Clue for Dating Esther?" in *VT* 65, no. 4 (2004): 551–

Judging from the style of the Hebrew, the book is earlier than the second century BC and the Qumran literature in the Dead Sea Scrolls. The frequent occurrence of Persian words, including the names, and Aramaisms argues for an early date. The lack of any Greek vocabulary supports an early date. The author clearly has an intimate knowledge of the palace (1:5–6; 7:7–8). At the end of the book, Xerxes, the Persian ruler from 486–465 BC, was still in power. For this reason, conservatives generally date the book in the late fifth century BC.

Authors vary widely in dating the book. Anderson and Paton note that Ben Sirach fails to mention the book, implying that the book is later than the early second century BC. This argument is weak since Ben Sirach does not mention Ruth, Ezra, any of the poetical books, or any of the Minor Prophets. Bechtel more reasonably dates the book "at least eighty years after the time it describes" although she gives a broader range of 400–200 BCE. Gordis dates it at 400 BCE. Rawlinson dates it "when Xerxes had been dead about twenty years," ca. 445 BC. Baldwin dates the book in the last part of the fifth century or early fourth century BC. Fox interprets the linguistic features of the text as dating it in the third century BC.[27]

Friedberg notes the way in which Ezra, Nehemiah, and Esther name the months as illustrating the Babylonian lunar system of dating. Esther, however, illustrates an earlier system than that used in Ezra and Nehemiah. Friedberg concludes that Esther must be placed in the early Persian period, the late fifth century BC, and earlier than the rule of Darius the Great, 521–485 BC. While his comments are of interest, the book cannot be placed earlier than the end of the reign of Xerxes (Ahasuerus, 10:1) in 465 BC. Talshir and Talshir point out some errors in

---

52, argue that Nehemiah's familiarity with the Persian court and the eastern culture suggests that he was the author.

[27]Bernhard W. Anderson, *The Book of Esther*, in *The Interpreter's Bible*, ed. George Arthur Buttrick (Nashville: Abingdon Press, 1954), vol. 3, p. 867; Paton, p. 61; Carol M. Bechtel, *Esther* in *Interpretation: Bible Commentary for Teaching and Preaching* (Louisville: John Knox Press, 1989), p. 3; Gordis, p. 8; Rawlinson, p. iv; Baldwin, p. 49; Fox, p. 140.

Friedberg's reasoning. Unfortunately, their liberal presuppositions cause them to assign a late date to the book.[28]

While admitting the imperfection of the literary structure of Esther, several authors have taken note of a chiasmic structure in the book.[29] Although slightly modifying the views of these

A Greatness of Xerxes *1:1–2*	**A'** Greatness of Mordecai *10:1–3*
B Two Persian banquets *1:3–8*	**B'** Two Jewish banquets *9:20–32*
C Esther, a part of the Gentile group *2:10–20*	**C'** Gentiles, a part of the Jewish group *8:17*
D Elevation of Haman *3:1*	**D'** Elevation of Mordecai *9:15*
E Decree to kill the Jews *3:12–15*	**E'** Decree to defend the Jews *8:9–14*
F Exchange between Mordecai and Esther *4:1–17*	**F'** Exchange between Ahasuerus and Esther *7:1–6*
G Banquet with Esther, Xerxes, and Haman *5:5–8*	**G'** Banquet with Esther, Xerxes, and Haman *7:1–6*

H' Royal procession honoring Mordecai *6:1–11*

authors, the following chart shows the parallels that contribute to the chiasm.

The book is historical. Liberal authors, however, deny the book's historical accuracy.[30] Bechtel is typical of this view:

---

[28]Albert D. Friedberg, "A New Clue in the Dating of the Composition of the Book of Esther," in *VT* 50, no. 4 (2000): 561–65; Talshir and Talshir, pp. 550–54.

[29]Bechtel, pp. 5–6; Michael V. Fox, *Character and Ideology in the Book of Esther* (Columbia: University of South Carolina Press, 1991), p. 157; Jon D. Levenson, *Esther: A Commentary* (Louisville: Westminster John Knox Press, 1997), pp. 5, 8.

[30]George A. F. Knight, *Esther, Song of Songs, Lamentations* in *Torch Bible Commentaries*, ed. John Marsh, Alan Richardson, and R. Gregor Smith (London: SCM Press Ltd., 1955), considers the accuracy or inaccuracy of the book as having no meaning. The biblical authors "were not primarily concerned whether their characters or events were real or fictitious." The information given serves as "mere channels for the truth of the doctrines they were proclaiming." Similarly, Adele Berlin, *Esther* in *The JPS Bible Commentary*, ed. Michael Fishbane (Philadelphia: The Jewish Publication Society, 2001),

> There is some reason to doubt the historicity of the book of Esther. We know from extrabiblical sources, for instance, that Xerxes I was off fighting the Battle of Salamis at the time when, according to the book, Esther was brought into the harem (2:16, 480 B.C.E.). The Greek historian Herodotus [9.108–13] reports that, for at least several months after that famous battle, the king was involved in a disastrous dalliance with his daughter-in-law. Also, we know that his queen was named Amestris and that she probably came from one of the seven noble families of Persia [Herodotus 3.84].[31]

Bechtel makes other charges against the accuracy of the book, but these are enough to illustrate her reasoning.

Bechtel's objections all have answers. Esther 2:16 dates Esther's entrance into the harem in the "seventh year" of Xerxes' reign. This places it in 478 BC, two years after his loss to the Greeks at Salamis. This also allows time for a short-lived involvement with his daughter-in-law. As for the queen being named Amestris, Xerxes, like all kings of that era, had more than one wife, each of whom could claim at times the role of queen. Since Esther's role in the preservation of the Jews was the major event of her life, and Xerxes' decision to let Haman annihilate them was foolish, it is understandable that the Persian records do not mention her or the event. As for the queen coming from one of the seven noble families, that was likely a general rule. Herodotus 3.88 refers to Darius, who "took wives from the noblest houses of Persia." He then refers to daughters of Cyrus and Smerdis, neither of whom were of the seven leading families. Amestris, known to be the chief wife of Xerxes, was the daughter of Otanes, one of the seven leaders of the empire,[32] but his passion for other women was widely known. The king's lust no doubt overruled policy when he desired to bring additional women into his harem. The commentary on the individual chapters answers additional charges made by Bechtel and other liberal authors

---

p. xv, states, "The story itself is implausible in history and, as many scholars now agree, it is better viewed as imaginative storytelling." These views ignore inspiration as unimportant. A book filled with errors cannot be trusted as to its message.

[31]Bechtel, p. 3.

[32]Herodotus 7.61.

In addition, the fact of Esther's inclusion in the Old Testament argues that it is accurate. The idea that God would allow a historically flawed book into the canon of Scripture is unthinkable. Esther is not a fable written to illustrate general principles; it is historically reliable. The book records the deliverance of the Jews from a threat to their national existence. As an incidental addition, the background of the Feast of Purim is explained. While the book does not mention God by name, the record of Israel's deliverance clearly illustrates God's providential care for His people.[33] We see His work on behalf of Israel to preserve a people for Himself.

Outline of Esther

I. The Threat to Israel 1:1–3:15
- A. The Banquets at the Palace 1:1–9
- B. The Refusal by the Queen 1:10–22
- C. The Choice of a New Queen 2:1–18
- D. The Deliverance of the King 2:19–23
- E. The Plot Against Israel 3:1–15
    1. Haman's Anger Toward Mordecai 3:1–6
    2. Haman's Plot Against the Jews 3:7–15

II. The Deliverance of Israel 4:1–10:3
- A. The Plan of Mordecai 4:1–17
    1. Mordecai's Grief 4:1–3
    2. Mordecai's Request 4:4–9
    3. Esther's Decision 4:10–17
- B. The First Banquet of Esther 5:1–8
    1. The First Invitation 5:1–5
    2. The Second Invitation 5:6–8
- C. The Plot of Haman 5:9–14

[33]Alexander Carson, *God's Providence Unfolded in the Book of Esther* (Swengel, PA: Bible Truth Depot, 1962), p. 111, aptly comments, "God is everywhere seen in [Esther], though he is not named. Just so God is every moment manifesting himself in the works of his providence, though he works unseen to all but the eye of faith. . . . The book of Esther, from the beginning to the end, proclaims the providence of God, though it does not expressly name him."

- D. The Humiliation of Haman 6:1–13
  1. Xerxes' Sleeplessness 6:1–3
  2. Haman's Suggestion 6:4–9
  3. Mordecai's Honor 6:10–11
  4. Haman's Mourning 6:12–13
- E. The Second Banquet of Esther 6:14–7:10
  1. The King's Request 6:14–7:4
  2. The King's Decision 7:5–10
- F. The Promotion of Mordecai 8:1–17
  1. Possession of Haman's House 8:1–2
  2. Plea of the Queen 8:3–6
  3. Decree by the King 8:7–14
  4. Rejoicing of the Jews 8:15–17
- G. The Vengeance of Israel 9:1–16
  1. Destruction of Israel's Enemies 9:1–11
  2. Death of Haman's Family 9:12–16
- H. The Feast of Purim 9:17–10:3
  1. The Jews' Celebration 9:17–19
  2. Mordecai's and Esther's Instructions 9:20–32
  3. Exaltation of Mordecai 10:1–3

The Purposes of Esther

There are both historical and spiritual applications of the book of Esther. Historically, the book recounts numerous details of Israel's life under Persian rule.[34] While we know that only a small number of Jews returned to Palestine from the captivity, the rest of the Bible is silent regarding the life of those who remained behind. The book of Esther gives us a brief glimpse of these people.

The book also relates for us the background of the Feast of Purim. The Lord never commanded Israel to observe this feast. Despite this lack of divine sanction, it has become the most

[34] Sandra Beth Berg, *The Book of Esther: Motifs, Themes and Structure* (Missoula, MT: Scholars Press, 1979), p. 123, states that Esther "can no longer be considered an accurate, historical account of events at Susa. . . . Any historical core in Esther has been overlaid with novelistic elaborations and accommodated to the storyteller's narrative style. Berg, however, cites no inaccuracies or historical distortions. Her comment is subjective, based on her liberal viewpoint toward the Old Testament.

popular of the Jewish observances today. When we read the historical background, we understand more fully the popularity of the celebration. The threat to Israel was real, and the deliverance was dramatic. Observing the feast each year expresses Israel's gratitude to the Lord.

The book also illustrates several spiritual principles. The attempt by Xerxes to parade his wife before the men at his feast (1:10–11) illustrates the carnality of the natural man. His angry response (1:12) is typical of those who have their goals frustrated. The king removes his queen from her position for fear that other women in the kingdom will act independently of their husbands (1:15–22). The selection of a new queen shows no indication of love. It is rather based on the ability of the prospective brides to gratify the king's sensual desires (2:2–17).

Haman's reaction to Mordecai's refusal to bow vividly shows the power of pride to control a person (3:1–5; 5:14). He also responded in anger when his will was frustrated (3:5; 5:9). His expectation that others should bow before him (3:5), his boasting over his accomplishments (5:10–11), and his anticipation of honor from the king (6:6) show his pride. Haman wanted to eradicate the entire Jewish nation, an extreme form of vengeance (3:6–15). As part of this desire for revenge, we see the element of greed entering in. Xerxes was willing to sell an entire nation for the income it will bring him (3:9–11). Haman not only satisfied his anger against Mordecai, he entered into an investment that he believed would profit him greatly (3:12–15; see discussion in c. 3). The Jews responded to this threat by turning to God. Along with other indications of their grief, they entered into a national fast (4:3). While there is no mention of prayer in the book, this often accompanied fasting (1 Sam. 7:5–6; Neh. 1:4; Ps. 35:13; Dan. 9:3).[35] Mordecai's message to Esther clearly shows his faith that God would deliver His people (4:14). Esther also fasted before going in to the king (4:16).

[35]M'Crie, p. 286, understands the word *cry* in 9:31 as the prayer of the Jews that accompanied their fast. This word translates the noun *zaᶜaq*, which also occurs in 4:1. The OT uses this word 18x, but nowhere else does it refer to prayer. It normally indicates a cry of distress over some difficult situation facing the people.

The overwhelming value of the book, however, lies in its demonstration of God's providential care for His own.[36] The removal of Vashti as queen (1:15–22), the God-given beauty and personality of Esther that led to her selection as queen (2:16–17), Mordecai's discovery of the plot to assassinate Xerxes (2:21–23), the latter's willingness to receive Esther and to attend her banquet (5:1–8; 7:1), the king's insomnia, followed by the exaltation of Mordecai at the very time that Haman plotted to take his life (6:1–11), and other details all build to the climax of the deliverance of the Jews (8:5–9:16). In many ways we see in Esther the display of God's sovereignty. Over and over again the book describes providentially arranged events that culminated in the deliverance of Israel.

This is a spiritual lesson for believers today. Just as the Lord watched over His people in Esther's time, so He watches over His people today. Just as He providentially cared for Israel then, so He providentially cares for Christians today. We may trust the Lord to supply our needs. In turn we should praise God for His care and should live in such a way as to show our gratitude to God.

ESTHER 1

The opening chapters introduce the theme of the book. Through a series of circumstances, the Persian king Xerxes divorced his wife, which led (as later chapters recount) to the choice of Esther as his new wife, placing her in a position to neutralize the threat against the Jews that later developed.

God had chosen Israel to be His own people. Their sin, however, had caused Him to punish them. They had been in

[36]A. Boyd Luter and Barry C. Davis, *Ruth & Esther: God Behind the Seen* (Fearn, Ross-shire, Scotland: Christian Focus, 2003), p. 364, give the additional view that the book "shows the depth of the spiritual morass into which the Jews had stumbled." This lets us see how God deals with His people when they fall out of a right relationship with Him. This is certainly a right value illustrated in the book, but in my judgment the providential care of God is the major message of Esther.

captivity in Babylon. At the time of the events in this book, however, those deported by the Babylonians were now under the Persian conquerors of Babylon. Some years earlier, the decree of Cyrus the Great (Ezra 1:1–4) had permitted the Jews to resettle in Palestine. Many of them, however, remained and found their place in the Persian Empire. The history recorded in Esther focuses on this group.

I. The Threat to Israel 1:1–3:15

A. The Banquets at the Palace 1:1–9

The word *Ahasuerus* is a title meaning "mighty man." It refers here to the Persian ruler Xerxes. *Xerxes* is the Greek version of *Khshayârsha* (the Persian equivalent of *Ahasuerus*) and is thought to mean something like "he who rules over men." He ruled Persia 486–465 BC.[37] Xerxes was the son of Darius I (520–486 BC), the king who authorized the rebuilding of the temple (Hag. 2:1–9 cf. 1:1, ca. 520 BC). Xerxes' mother was Atossa, a daughter of Cyrus the Great, making Xerxes the grandson of Cyrus (550–530 BC). Herodotus 7.187 describes him: "Of all those tens of thousands of men, for goodliness and stature there was not worthier than Xerxes himself to hold that command."

Xerxes is the wealthy fourth king referred to in Daniel 11:2. His empire was divided into 127 "provinces," a term that is not fully understood.[38] The basis for these regions may have been political, geographical, racial, or some combination of factors. The term differs from the Persian satrapies, limited to twenty

[37]Others identify Ahasuerus differently. Josephus (*Antiquities* 11.6.1) and the LXX name him as Artaxerxes I, who ruled Persia 464–423 BC. Henry, p. 1122, follows this view. Symon Patrick, *The Book of Esther*, in *A Critical Commentary and Paraphrase on the Old and New Testament and the Apocrypha* (Philadelphia: 1859), vol. 2, p. 684, identifies him as Darius Ochus, also known as Artaxerxes III, who reigned over Persia 359–338 BC. Meir Zlotowitz, *The Megillah: The Book of Esther* (Brooklyn, NY: Mesorah Publications, Ltd., 1987), p. xxiv, seems to identify Ahasuerus with Cambyses, although he gives the wrong date for his ascension.

[38]Among others, Fox, p. 15, thinks the number of satrapies "had become vague in historical memory, and their number is here greatly inflated." He objects that the word *ʾaḥašdarpani* (refers to "satraps" but translated "lieutenants" in Esther 3:12; 8:9; and 9:4; see Ezra 8:36) refers to "officials of a lower order" in the book. In no case does the occurrence require us to understand this as a minor official.

by the description in Herodotus 3.89–94.[39] The provinces ranged from India to Ethiopia. A tablet from the reign of Xerxes found at Persepolis reads: "Thus speaks king Xerxes: These are the countries—in addition to Persia—over which I am king under the 'shadow' of Ahurumazda, over which I hold sway, which are bringing their tribute to me." This is followed by a list of countries, including "India" and "Ethiopia" (or Cush).[40] First Esdras 3:2 also refers to "the hundred and twenty-seven provinces from India to Ethiopia."

In giving the detailed description of the region ruled by Ahasuerus, the author indicates that he knows of more than one ruler with this name. The name *Ahasuerus* also occurs in Ezra 4:6 and Daniel 9:1. In Ezra 4.6, it also refers to Xerxes. The king cannot be certainly identified in Daniel 1.9, but the verse likely refers to Astyages or Cyaxares, kings ruling over Media, part of the Persian Empire. By mentioning the scope of the empire, the author makes it clear which Ahasuerus he refers to.

The historical information given in the book agrees with our knowledge of Xerxes. This includes the extent of his empire (1:1); the mention of Persia before Media (1:3, 14, 18, 19), implying that the Persians had risen to greater power in the alliance; the feast in his third year (1:3–4), reasonably a time for planning his invasion of Greece; his self-indulgence in his seventh year (2:1–17), after his defeat by Greece; and his need of money after the disastrous campaign, causing him to respond to Haman's bribe (3:9). In addition the comments of Herodotus in books 7–9 concerning Xerxes agree with the details given in Esther.

The empire reached eastward to "India" (*hoddu*, referring to "dwellers on the Indus River"), the northwestern part previously conquered by Darius I and generally covering the area occupied

[39]Carey A. Moore, "Eight Questions Most Frequently Asked About the Book of Esther," in *BR* 8, no. 1 (Spring 1987): 18–20, answers the questions "Is the story true? Did it really happen?" by stating that "most modern scholars do not believe the tale reflects actual history." He cites the number of satrapies as differing from that given by Herodotus as twenty. He draws this conclusion after admitting that a great deal of "literary and archaeological evidence . . . illuminates the Esther story." Moore ignores the possibility that the word *provinces* in 1:1 does not mean the same as the Persian word *satrapies.*

[40]*ANET*, p. 316.

today by Pakistan. On the south it reached to "Ethiopia," (or Cush, *kuš*), the region in Egypt south of the first cataract on the upper Nile, a region brought under control earlier by Cambyses. In an inscription Xerxes referred to himself as "the great king, the . . . king of kings . . . the king of (all) countries (which speak) all kinds of languages, the king of this (entire) big and far (reaching) earth," v. 1.[41]

Shushan, the Hebrew name of the city more commonly called by the Greek name *Susa*, was the old capital of Elam and the winter palace of the Persians. It was one of several capital cities used by the Persians. The initial capital built by Cyrus the Great was Pasargadae, about forty miles northeast of modern-day Shiraz in Iran. Later Darius built Persepolis, about twenty-five miles southwest of Pasargadae. Later kings used Shushan as the winter residence and Ecbatana, north of the Zagros Mountains, as their summer residence.

Susa is often called "Shushan" (meaning "palace" or "fortress," *bîrâ*, see Neh. 1:1). This name distinguishes the royal buildings, located to the west, from the city itself (4:16; 9:12–15). The city dated back to ca. 4000 BC. According to Xenophon, Shushan served as the king's residence during the early three months of the year.[42] It was located about 150 miles north of the Persian Gulf. The name *Shushan* means "lily," apparently referring to the abundance of lilies that grow in the area. The main city occupied about five thousand acres, with the surrounding area being inhabited as well. It was strategically located on the roads to Persepolis, Sardis, and Ecbatana (or Achmetha). Excavations of the city found the palace. Inside excavations revealed large monuments, the throne room, and the location of the harem. v. 2.

In the third year of his reign, ca. 483 BC, Xerxes hosted a "banquet" (*mišteh*) for "all his princes [*śar*, see Ezra 7:28] and his servants." The word *mišteh* occurs widely in the OT to refer to a banquet or feast. Where the context is clear (e.g., 1 Sam. 25:36; Ezra 3:7), it may also refer to the drinking of wine or some other beverage. Where the context does not emphasize drinking, there

[41] *ANET*, p. 316.

[42] Xenophon, *Cyropaedia* 8.6.22.

is no need to make the feast into a drunken orgy.[43] The princes at the banquet were political appointees and not necessarily sons of Xerxes. They include the "power," i.e., the leading officers of his army, as well as nobles and princes from the provincial divisions of the empire.

The banquet lasted for 180 days.[44] While this sounds like an enormous feast, it is not unusual for kings of that period of history. It was customary for ancient kings to hold great feasts (cf. Dan. 5:1). The Greek doctor and early historian of Persia and India, Ctesias, born ca. 416 BC, records that the Persian king provided food for fifteen thousand persons daily in his royal court.[45] The Roman poet Statius, in a poem offering thanksgiving to the Emperor Domitian, refers to Caesar hosting the Roman chieftains and knights "reclin[ing] together at a thousand tables."[46] Pliny the Elder, also Roman, writing in his *Natural History*, mentions the Roman General Pompey, who gave "a lavish feast to a thousand guests." He also mentions the Bithynian king Pythes who "gave a banquet to the forces of Xerxes" which amounted to 788,000 men.[47] Ashur-banipal of Assyria is said to have hosted 69,574 guests for ten days.[48]

The feast is for the military leaders of "Persia and Media." The listing of Persia before Media is appropriate since the Persians held greater authority in the alliance of the nations at this time (see also vv. 14, 18, 19). The Assyrian and Babylonian

---

[43]Bechtel, p. 21, and Payton, p. 126, make *mišteh* emphasize the drinking. At this point this emphasis is unnecessary.

[44]Among others, Keil, pp. 324–25, thinks that the feast described in vv. 5–8 is the same as the feast mentioned in vv. 2–4. Xerxes gathers the leaders of his empire for six months to plan the coming war against Greece. When the planning is complete, he then hosts a feast. The natural reading of the passage is against the view. In addition the attendees in v. 3 are different from those mentioned in v. 5. The view also requires a forced interpretation of v. 5*a*, "when these days were expired."

[45]Referred to in Athenaeus, *The Deiphnosophists*, trans. Charles Burton Gulick (Cambridge, MA: Harvard University Press, 1967), 2.4.146.

[46]"Silvae," in *Statius*, trans. J. H. Mozley (Cambridge, MA: Harvard University Press, 1961), 1.4.4.31–33.

[47]Pliny, *Natural History*, trans. H. Rackham (Cambridge, MA: Harvard University Press, 1968), 9.33.47.

[48]*ANET*, p. 560.

inscriptions after the ninth century BC mention the Medes as a people occupying the area between the Caspian Sea and the Zagros Mountains. The Persians lived in the plateau area between the Indus and Tigris rivers. Initially the Medes dominated the alliance between the two groups. Joining with Babylon, the alliance overthrew the Assyrian Empire. With the ascension of Cyrus as ruler of Persia, the Persians acquired the dominant role in the alliance with the Medes. Cyrus led the Persian army to defeat Astyages, the Median king. He next led the combined army to victory over Croesus, the king of Lydia. With the subsequent defeat of Babylon, the Persian-Median alliance became the leading world empire for a little more than two hundred years.

From the timing of Xerxes' feast and the inclusion of military leaders, the feast may have been for the purpose of planning the military campaign into Greece that began about this time. Herodotus 7.8 describes such a gathering: "Xerxes held an assembly of the noblest among the Persians, convened with special intent, that he might learn their opinions and himself declare his will before them all." After hearing counsel for and against such a campaign and having several dreams about the matter, Xerxes decided to invade Greece, v. 3.

The feast described here lasted for 180 days, enough time to allow for mixing business and pleasure, v. 4.[49] Afterward Xerxes hosted another "feast" (*mišteh*). He invited "all the people . . . present in Shushan the palace." This likely refers to those holding positions of service in Shushan the "palace" (or "fortress") at this time. This included both the "great and small," i.e., those having both important and unimportant responsibilities.[50] The

[49]Luter and Davis, p. 112, comment that bringing all of the officials of the empire would have resulted in the inefficient functioning of government. They suggest "more likely, they attended in shifts, with only one group being at the banquet at any given time." While this is possible, the narrative reads as if all of the leaders were present. If the purpose of the gathering was to plan the coming invasion of Greece, it is likely that the leaders of the provinces left their governing responsibilities to lesser officials.

[50]Levenson, p. 46, suggests that this feast was for the purpose of celebrating the king's marriage to Vashti. If this was the case, the king's order to Vashti to appear "is less abrupt than otherwise seems the case." While the suggestion is possible, the text does not give a reason, and so we may only speculate about the purpose for the feast.

banquet was limited to men. It lasted seven days and was held in the "court of the garden," an area within the city watered by a nearby river, v. 5.

The decorations at the court where the banquet took place included "white" [*ḥûr*, some kind of white cloth], green [*karpas*, "cotton or fine linen"], and blue [t^{e}*kelet*, a dye made from mollusks and giving a purplish blue color] hangings." Cords tied to silver rings fasten the decorations to marble pillars. Beds inlaid with gold and silver rested on the multicolored pavement. The people reclined on these while they ate. The phrase "a pavement of red, and blue, and white, and black, marble" is better "a mosaic of porphyry and marble and mother of pearl and precious stones." Other than the word *marble*, the translations of these terms are tentative. Several versions offer different suggestions: "[the courtyard] paved with white marble, red feldspar, shining mother-of-pearl, and blue turquoise" (GNB); "a mosaic pavement of purple rock, white marble, pearl-like stone, and black marble" (GW); "a mosaic pavement of alabaster, turquoise, and white and black marble" (NKJV). Whatever the exact meaning, it is clear that the courtyard was a colorful place, v. 6.

The guests drank an abundant supply of wine from golden goblets. Xenophon refers to Persians drinking at banquets to the point where "they themselves are carried out when they are no longer able to stand straight enough to walk out." Athenaeus refers to "wine, which has the strength of fire when it enters into men; it swells them as the north or south wind swells the Libyan sea, and brings to light the hidden things in the deep; so wine drives the wits from men in complete upheaval." Strabo also speaks of the drinking of the Persians: "They carry on their most important deliberations when drinking wine; and they regard decisions then made as more lasting than those made when they are sober." Herodotus mentions the drinking habit of the Persians. "They are greatly given to wine. . . . It is their custom to deliberate about the gravest matters when they are drunk; and what they approve in their counsels is proposed to them the next day by the master of the house where they deliberate, when they are now sober and if being sober they still approve it, they act thereon, but if not they cast it aside. And when they have taken counsel about a matter when sober, they decide upon it when they are drunk."[51]

The differing nature of the goblets emphasizes the king's wealth, v. 7. The drinking was "according to law [*dat*, or 'decree']," with no one being compelled to drink.[52] They might rather drink as much as they wished, doing "according to every man's pleasure." Each could drink as little or as much as he wished. According to the Talmud, *Megillah* 12*a*, each guest received wine from his native land, v. 8.

At the same time, Vashti ("beautiful"), the queen, holds another "feast" (*mišteh*) for the women in the palace. History does not record the name of any queen by the name of Vashti or, later, Esther. Jewish tradition, in the Talmud, *Megillah* 10*b*, identifies Vashti as the "[grand]daughter" of Nebuchadnezzar. While this may have been the case, we have no way of verifying it.

The only known wife of Xerxes is Amestris, the daughter of a Persian general named Otanes.[53] Various solutions have been suggested to explain the different wives in the book. Xerxes undoubtedly had more than one wife at that time. *Vashti* may be a variant spelling or another name of Amestris.[54] She might have been a recent wife, added to the harem for unusual beauty that the king now wished to show off. Esther could have been considered a concubine or a secondary wife or may have died young and not gained a prominent place in Persian history. We do not have a clear answer to the problem, v. 9.

B. The Refusal by the Queen 1:10–22

On the seventh day of his banquet, Xerxes was "merry with wine," intimating that he was drunk at the time of this incident. He sent seven "chamberlains" (*hassarîsîm*, could be translated

---

[51]Xenophon, *Cyropaedia* 8.8.10; Athenaeus, *The Deipnosophists*, 2.36; Strabo, *The Geography of Strabo*, trans. Horace Leonard Jones (Cambridge, MA: Harvard University Press, 1966), 15.3.20; Herodotus 1.133.

[52]It is also possible that the phrase "none did compel" indicates that the guests were not under the normal constraint of drinking only when the king drank. Moore, p. 7, mentions this possible interpretation of the phrase.

[53]See Herodotus 7.61; 9.108–112.

[54]Mattoon, p. 14, takes this position, but it is difficult to support linguistically.

"eunuchs" or "court officials"), v. 10,[55] to bring Queen Vashti to his feast.[56] He commanded Vashti to leave the feast she was giving for the women and come to him, wearing her crown to emphasize her royal position. He wanted to show off her beauty to the guests at his own banquet. He intended to parade Vashti before the "people," the lesser ranking attendees, and the "princes" (*śar*, see Ezra 7:28), v. 11.[57] She, however, refused to obey his summons. Josephus, *Antiquities* 11.6.1, says that Xerxes "sent oftentimes the eunuchs to her" but that she refused "out of regard to the laws of the Persians, which forbid the wives to be seen by strangers." We do not know if this was Persian law. Both of the Targums, Aramaic comments on the book of Esther, say that Vashti refused because Xerxes commanded her to appear naked before the guests.[58] Other suggestions have been made to excuse Vashti's refusal. *Megillah* 12*b* says that God had caused leprosy to break out on her. It also mentions the view of one rabbi that "Gabriel came and fixed a tail on her." Jobes suggests the possibility that she would have been in the late stage of her pregnancy with Xerxes' son. Knight mentions the views that Vashti was drunk or that she was disgusted at the behavior of

[55]Fox, pp. 19–20, shows his liberal bias by stating that the author of Esther "shows a predilection for lists of Persian names. Such listings are probably an attempt to give the narrative historical verisimilitude, to convey the impression that the narrator has the historical details well in hand." Fox gives no details to justify his conclusion.

[56]Both the Targum *Rishon* and the Targum *Sheni* call Vashti the daughter of Evil-Merodach, the son and successor of Nebuchadnezzar. Since Evil-Merodach died in 560 BC and the feast was in the "third year" of Xerxes, 484 BC, seventy-six years later, it is highly unlikely that this genealogy is correct. Xerxes probably would not have attempted to show off the beauty of a woman who was at least seventy-five years old.

[57]The Talmud, *Megillah* 12*b*, gives an old Jewish teaching that Vashti had made her Jewish maids strip off their clothing and work on the Sabbath and that God put into the king's heart to have her appear in public with her clothing stripped off: "As she had done so it was decreed against her." The interpretation is based partially on taking v. 11, in which the king calls Vashti to come "with the crown royal," to mean that she was to appear unclothed and wearing only the crown. While this is an interesting view, nothing in Scripture supports it.

[58]Bernard Grossfeld, trans., *The Two Targums of Esther* in *The Aramaic Bible: The Targums*, ed. Kevin Cathcart, Michael Maher, and Martin McNamara (Collegeville, MN: The Liturgical Press, 1991), pp. 28, 128.

Xerxes. Streane offers the reason that Vashti was "aware of the insults likely to be put upon her in a scene of drunken revelry."[59]

Some commentators condemn Vashti for her refusal to obey her husband.[60] In my opinion, this is a misapplication of Ephesians 5:22–24. Virtually everyone agrees that Xerxes was wrong in wanting to parade his wife in front of the leaders of the empire. Since we do not know the circumstances relating to the command of Xerxes to Vashti to appear, we should avoid approval or disapproval on her decision. Since the Bible does not condemn her, we should be cautious about expressing an opinion.

Scripture gives no reason for Vashti's refusal to appear. In view of the context, it seems likely that she did not wish to parade herself before a drunken crowd of men. Her refusal to come caused Xerxes to become "wroth" (*qaṣap*) and to burn with "anger" (*ḥemâ*) over the affront to his authority. The word *qaṣap* refers to strong anger. It may legitimately be translated here as "enraged" (ESV) or "furious" (NIV). The companion word *ḥemâ* has the root meaning "to be hot." It refers here to the heated emotional state of anger, v. 12.

Xerxes consulted his "wise men," the counselors to the king. The phrase "knew the times" suggests that these were skilled counselors whose duty was to advise the king (cf. 1 Chron. 12:32).[61] It was Xerxes' custom to consult his advisors on everything relating the laws of the empire, v. 13. The seven "princes" (*śar*) who are named were the closest advisors to the king. Herodotus 3.83–84 refers to the seven men who had access to the king. Josephus, *Antiquities* 2.6.1, also mentions them. Ezra

---

[59]Karen H. Jobes, Esther, in *The NIV Application Commentary* (Grand Rapids: Zondervan, 1999), p. 74; Knight, p. 28; A. W. Streane, *The Book of Esther*, in The Cambridge Bible for Schools and Colleges, ed. A. F. Kirkpatrick (Cambridge, England: University Press, 1907), p. 6.

[60]E.g., McGee, p. 23; M'Crie, pp. 35–36.

[61]Jobes, p. 78, interprets the phrase "knew the times" as indicating that these men were skilled in "astrology and other forms of divination." Omanson and Noss, p. 36, and Whitcomb, p. 39, also suggest this. But the narrative does not mention any delay to consult star charts or other methods used in divination before giving their advice to the king. In addition, their conversation included no references to the heavens or to heavenly powers. The advice was practical, meant to prevent the people from ridiculing the king and to keep wives in subjection to their husbands.

7:14 refers to "the seven counselors" of Artaxerxes, suggesting it may have been common to have such advisors, v. 14. Xerxes posed the problem created by Vashti, v. 15.[62] Memucan spoke before the king and his "princes" (*śar*), agreeing that Vashti had given an affront to the kingdom by her actions, v. 16. Her actions would be spoken of by "all women," women in general, throughout the kingdom, v. 17. This might well cause the wives of the "princes" (*śar*), the nobility of the kingdom, to disobey their husbands, v. 18.

Memucan urged the king to issue a decree that would become unalterable law. According to Persian law, a king's decree could not be set aside (cf. 8:8; Dan. 6:8, 12, 15).[63] Vashti would be set aside as queen, never again to come into the king's presence. Another queen would be put into her place to ensure that all wives would obey their husbands. This included both "great and small," the phrase referring here to social position. There is unintentional humor in this. The emperor was to decree for others what he himself had not been able to achieve. Presumably the threat of punishment would make the difference. Clearly

[62]Bechtel, p. 24, comments, "It seems odd that [Xerxes] does not know the laws of his own empire well enough to negotiate this fairly straightforward infraction." Her comment ignores the setting. Never before had the king hosted such an occasion, and never before had the queen refused such a command of the king. It was not that Xerxes did not know the law; it was rather that Xerxes did not know how best to punish Vashti after this unique violation of his will.

[63]Berlin, p. xvii, asserts, "To govern a country in which a law could never be changed [cf. 1:19; 8:8] would make governing impossible." Moore, p. 11, comments that "such a law seems inflexible and crippling to good government and, hence, improbable." Diodorus Siculus, *Diodorus of Sicily*, trans. C. Bradford Welles (Cambridge, MA: Harvard University Press, 1963), 17.30.5, supports the existence of such a law. He tells about Darius III, who in his anger condemned a man to death. When his anger cooled, however, "he promptly regretted his act and reproached himself for having made a serious mistake, but all his royal power was not able to undo what was done." Reid, p. 72, considers the phrase "hyperbolic rather than literal—'make a decision and stick to it!'" The historical evidence cited above supports taking the phrase literally. Ben Zion Katz, "Irrevocability of Persian Law in the Scroll of Esther," in *JBQ* 31, no. 2 (April–June 2003), p. 94, argues that the word *altered* (*ʿbr*) should be translated "transgressed." While this is a possible translation, the root *ʿbr* overwhelmingly refers to "passing over, through, by," or some related idea. In addition, the reference to the irreversibility of the king's command in 8:8 supports that idea here.

neither the king nor his advisors understood the nature of love in the marriage relationship, vv. 19–20. The suggestion pleased the king and the other "princes" (*śar*), v. 21. The decision was written in the different languages of the kingdom and letters sent throughout the kingdom so all would know.

This is the first mention of the means whereby the king communicated with officials throughout the empire (see also 3:12–14; 4:3; 8:9, 13, 17; 9:20, 30). Herodotus 8.98 describes the express system used by the Persian kings: "There is nothing mortal that accomplishes a course more swiftly than do these messengers. . . . It is said that as many days as there are in the whole journey, so many are the men and horses that stand along the road, each horse and man at the interval of a day's journey; and these are stayed neither by snow nor rain nor heat nor darkness from accomplishing their appointed course with all speed. The first rider delivers his charge to the second, the second to the third, and thence it passes on from hand to hand."

The clause "that it should be published according to the language of every people" is better rendered "and speak the language of his people." In a home where the wife was from a different national group than the husband, the children might naturally grow up speaking her language (cf. Neh. 13:23–24). This decree established the father's language as the dominant one in the family.[64] This part of the decree was an additional step to establish the husband's leadership in the home and to keep the wife in submission to his directions.

We hear no more of Vashti. Rabbinic tradition in the Talmud, *Megillah* 11*b*, 19*a*, and both Targums says she was executed, v. 22. Various authors, e.g., Jobes (tentatively) and Streane, identify her with Amestris, who from historical records continued as the queen of Xerxes until his death.[65] Since this goes contrary to the setting aside of Vashti, it cannot be the correct view. The Bible does not tell us about her fate, so it must remain unknown.

---

[64]Many versions, e.g., CEV, GNB, GW, KJV, and commentators, e.g., Kennedy, p. 23, and Zlotowitz, p. 51, treat the phrase as though the decree was sent in the languages of the various countries in the Persian Empire. This view reads into the Hebrew rather than translating it as given in the MT.

[65]Jobes, p. 74; Streane, p. 5.

ESTHER 2

This chapter introduces Mordecai and Esther, the two main characters of the book. Although the book does not call attention to it, there is a gap of several years between c. 1 and this chapter (1:3 cf. 2:16). During this interval the Persian navy had been overwhelmed by a disastrous storm, and later the Greeks defeated the Persian army at Salamis and Plataea. . Now back in Persian territory, Xerxes recalled the earlier happier days. At the suggestion of his counselors, he followed a plan designed to give him a beautiful queen once more.

C. The Choice of a New Queen 2:1–18

Enough time had passed so that Xerxes' "wrath" (*ḥemâ*, see 1:12) over Vashti's refusal to obey his command had subsided. At some point later he "remembered Vashti," perhaps suggesting some regret over his hasty action. It is possible but not likely that the king actually loved Vashti. Josephus, *Antiquities* 11.6.2, comments that "the king having been fond of her, he did not well bear a separation." Even if there had been love between the king and Vashti, the approximately three years between 1:3 and 2:16 (the difference between the third year and the seventh year, minus a year or so required by 2:12–15) was ample time for that love to have waned. Since the process to replace Vashti depended on the beauty of the women and their ability to gratify the king's sexual desires, it is more likely that his relationship with Vashti was similar. His desire to bring her into his banquet suggests that she possessed unique beauty.

Verse 16 places this in or shortly before the seventh year of Xerxes' reign, ca. 478 BC. The time for the disastrous campaign of Xerxes against the Greeks lies between 1:3 and 2:16. In 480 BC, his navy was defeated off the east coast of Cyprus near the port city of Salamis. About one year later, in 479 BC, his army was routed at Plataea, north of Athens, v. 1.

His servants suggested a program by which Xerxes could choose another queen. He would gather "fair young virgins." While this is not stated, these would have been of good reputation and beautiful, suitable to replace the deposed Queen Vashti. This approach to selecting another wife was in keeping with what we know of Xerxes. Herodotus 9.108 describes him as indulging himself in immoral behavior after his defeat by Greece, v. 2.

Throughout the kingdom, representatives of Xerxes were to find suitable candidates to send to Shushan the "palace" (or "fortress," *bîrâ*, see Neh. 1:1). There they would stay in the "house of the women," the harem. Hege (also called Hegai, vv. 8, 15), the king's "chamberlain" (*s^e^rîs*, lit., "eunuch") would give them "things for their purification [*maraq*]." The word *s^e^rîs* may refer either to an officer (e.g., Gen. 37:36; 1 Sam. 8:15) or to a eunuch (2 Kings 9:32; Dan. 1:3). In many cases we cannot be certain which is in view. Where there is contact with the king's harem, as here, the translation "eunuch" is appropriate. The root *maraq* occurs infrequently but often enough to give the sense of "rubbing" or "scouring." The noun here refers to the application of "ointments." Verse 12 says that they were prepared for "twelve months." This gave time to rid the women of customs that might have offended the king and to teach them Persian customs. In addition, it guarded against bringing to the king an already pregnant woman or one with disease, v. 3. The king would then choose which of the women he wanted as queen, v. 4.[66]

The Lord's hand is evident in the deposal of Vashti as queen. Knowing the events that were about to threaten the nation of Israel, the Lord began the process that would eventually bring Esther to the throne. It was essential that she occupy this position of influence. When the storm raged about the nation, Esther was in place to bring about the calm that would sustain God's people. God's providential care is clear.

The author now introduces Mordecai, Esther's guardian, who was "in Shushan the palace [or 'fortress']." From what we see of Mordecai later (sitting in the king's gate, 2:19; encountering Haman regularly, 3:2–4; leading the city to fast, 4:15-17), he was a resident of the city rather than merely passing through on

[66]Many authors, e.g., Moore, *Esther*, in *The Anchor Bible*, p. xlvi, and Paton, p. 165, accuse the narrative of error at this point. Herodotus 3.84 says that the king could marry a wife only from one of the seven noble families. For an answer to this objection, see the discussion on p. 206 regarding the wives of Darius.

a trip. He undoubtedly held some position in government that placed him where he would encounter Haman frequently.

Mordecai was a Benjamite, descended from Kish through Shimei and Jair.[67] While the names of Kish, Shimei, and Jair occur elsewhere, we cannot dogmatically claim that they refer here to any of these men. It is possible, however, perhaps even probable, that the mention here connects Mordecai with Saul (1 Sam. 10:21). A connection of Mordecai with Saul coupled with a connection of Haman with Agag would foreshadow the enmity we see in the book of Esther between Haman the Agagite and the Jews (3:6 cf. 1 Sam. 15:32–33). If this is the case, however, the next verse introduces a minor difficulty in the chronology, v. 5.

The phrase "who [*ʾašer*] had been carried away from Jerusalem with the captivity" raises the chronological problem. The second captivity of Judah took place in 597 BC, during the reign of "Jeconiah" (also called "Jehoiachin," e.g., 2 Kings 24:6, 8, 12, 15). The reign of Xerxes began in 486 BC. If the phrase refers to Mordecai, it would mean that he was about 120 years old and Esther at least 70. To avoid this problem, we understand the relative pronoun *ʾašer* as referring to Kish, Mordecai's great-grandfather.[68] This gives Mordecai and Esther more reasonable ages. That Kish had been carried away from Jerusalem in Jeconiah's captivity suggests the possibility that he in some way served in

---

[67]Knight, pp. 31, mistakenly understands Benjamin as the royal tribe from which both David and Jesus came. He sees the author of Esther as making Mordecai a Benjamite to enhance his position in Israel. "In this way, the events in the late book of Esther, though set down long after the great days of Israel's story, become firmly grafted into the stem of the vine, Israel." Knight's view comes from his belief that the book is not historical, but rather fiction and not fact.

[68]Anderson, p. 840, has the relative pronoun referring to Mordecai and so gives Mordecai and Esther the advanced ages mentioned above. The nature of Mordecai's name argues that he was born after the captivity began. Further, the position of *ʾašer* in the sentence relates it more naturally to Kish than to Mordecai. Henry, p. 1122, also understands Mordecai as having been taken in Jeconiah's captivity. This leads him to adopt the view that Ahasuerus is Pseudo-Smerdis, "who hindered the building of the temple." Gordis, p. 27, identifies Kish as Saul's father but avoids the chronological problem by not discussing it. Keil, pp. 334–36, proposes that Shimei and Kish are "the names of renowned ancestors." Since OT genealogies frequently skip generations, this is a possible view.

Judah's government (cf. 2 Kings 24:14). Rather than identifying Kish with Saul's father (1 Sam. 9:1–2), it may be that the name is a family name. In that case Mordecai's ancestor Kish has the same name as Saul's father, an indication of the family connection that relates Mordecai to Saul.

Luter and Davis accuse Mordecai of doing the "unthinkable" by encouraging Esther to marry Xerxes "even though he knows that God strictly forbade his people the practice of mixed religious marriage." The accusation is unjust. Based on the narrative in the book, Esther did not volunteer for inclusion in the group being considered. Beautiful women were "sought" for the king, then "gather[ed] together" to the "house of the women" (2:2–3). Esther did not choose to go; she was chosen. Once she was in that position, Mordecai advised her in the way that would give her the best chance of success. Luter and Davis also state that "neither Esther nor Mordecai . . . give any evidence of being particularly religious or spiritual." McGee is similar in saying "when Mordecai and Esther first appear, they do so in a very bad light." This overlooks Mordecai's refusal to bow before Haman, implying worship (see discussion at 3:2); Mordecai's confidence that "deliverance [would] arise . . . from another place" (4:14), a clear statement of his belief in God's power; Esther's desire that the Jews fast three days (4:16), a practice normally accompanied by prayer; and her willingness to risk her life on behalf of the Jews (4:16). There is ample evidence that both Mordecai and Esther were religious and spiritual.[69]

Mordecai's name, a form of *Marduk*, indicates that he was born in Persia and given a Persian name.[70] It may be significant that the name *Marduka* occurs in a table found at Morsippa in Mesopotamia. The table mentions an accountant named *Marduka* who inspected Susa, biblical Shushan, in the last part of Darius's reign or the early part of Xerxes' rule, v. 6.[71]

---

[69]Luter and Davis, p. 100; McGee, p. 30.

[70]Moore, "Eight Questions," pp. 20–21, argues that the names of Esther and Mordecai, being related to heathen gods, are evidence that the book "represents the historization of a myth or myths." This ignores the fact that other captives received names of heathen origin, cf. Ezra 1:8; 2:2; Dan. 1:7.

[71]A. Ungnad, "Keilinschriftliche Beitrage zum Buch Esra and Esther," *ZAW* 58 (1940–41): 240–44; and A. Ungnad, "Keilinschriftliche Beitrage zum

Being older than Esther, Mordecai had brought her up after her parents died. The phrase "took her for his own daughter" may indicate adoption. It may also simply indicate that he took her into his household and cared for her as she grew older. The Talmud, *Megillah* 13*a*, gives the view that *bayit*, "home," should be read for *bat*, "daughter," in the MT. Some Jews interpret this as though Esther was married to Mordecai, a marriage that continued while she lived with Xerxes.[72] The interpretation is fanciful, lacking logic as well as textual support. The narrative states that the Persians gathered "virgins" (2:3) for Xerxes, not married women. Esther was the daughter of "Abihail" (v. 15), a man about whom we know nothing. Her Hebrew name, *Hadassah*, means "myrtle," referring to an evergreen shrub that produces beautiful white flowers. *Esther*, her Persian name, means "star."[73]

The phrase "[Esther] was his [Mordecai's] uncle's daughter" (v. 7) identifies Mordecai and Esther as cousins. Josephus, *Antiquities* 11.6.2, says Mordecai was her uncle. Josephus, however, is not always accurate in his history. Esther was "fair and beautiful," a description giving the reason why she was included in the search for the new queen. The Talmud, *Megillah* 15*a*, says "There have been four women of surpassing beauty in the world—

Buch Esra and Esther," *ZAW* 59 (1942–43): 219. Ungnad identifies the *Marduka* of the inscription with the Mordecai of Esther. Edwin M. Yamauchi, "Mordecai, The Persepolis Tablets, and the Susa Excavations," in *VT* 42, no. 2 (April 1992): 273, mentions several tablets from Persepolis dated 505–499 BC that include over thirty references to the names *Marduka* or *Marduku*, applied to four different men.

[72]Zlotowitz, p. xxxi, adopts this position.

[73]It is possible that *Esther* is a Babylonian name. In this case it is a variant of *Ishtar*, the name of the Babylonian goddess of love and war. She was represented in the heavens by the planet Venus. I have assumed a Persian origin for the name *Esther* because of the length of time the Jews had been in captivity at this time and because of the setting of the narrative at Shushan, the Persian capital. A. S. Yahuda, "The Meaning of the Name Esther," in Carey A. Moore, ed., *Studies in the Book of Esther* (New York: KTAV Publishing House, Inc., 1982), p. 175, argues that both the names *Hadassah* and *Esther* mean "myrtle." He suggests an Old Persian word with this meaning. Since the Old Persian word occurs nowhere else, his argument must remain theoretical and speculative. Ran Zadok, "Notes on Esther," in *ZAW* 98, no. 1 (1986): 107, argues that *str* (Esther) cannot represent Ishtar. He offers two reasons that are valid only if certain assumptions are made.

Sarah, Rahab, Abigail, and Esther."[74] The comment undoubtedly comes from the favorable treatment of each of these women in the OT, v. 7.

After the king's decree was published, Esther was "brought" (or taken) with the other maidens to Shushan the "palace" (or fortress). Josephus, *Antiquities* 11.6.2, says there were four hundred maidens in the group, v. 8. She obtained "kindness" (or "loyal favor," *ḥesed*, see Ezra 3:11) from Hegai, the servant in charge of preparing the virgins. Since his only contact with Esther came in the training process, it is clear that she was likeable, having charm and graciousness. Hegai gave her special beauty treatments. He assigned seven maids to wait on her and gave them the best place in the house for their dwelling.

The phrase "such things as belonged" refers to portions of food. The Talmud, *Megillah* 13*a*, describes Esther as keeping the Jewish dietary laws. However, in all probability, since the Jews have been in captivity well over a century at this point, it is likely that the Jews generally had stopped keeping the dietary laws. It is not so much that Esther failed to keep these laws; it is rather that she didn't know about them, v. 9.

For some unknown reason, Mordecai had told her not to reveal her nationality. He may have feared that she would be publicly disgraced. He may have accepted the fact that she was involved in the search and simply hoped for the best. He may have hoped for personal gain through Esther's advancement. Zlotowitz gives several rabbinic comments explaining the secrecy. In the early twelfth century, Rabbi Eleazar ben Yehudah of Worms stated that Mordecai knew that as queen, Esther would save Israel from some calamity. She therefore hid her nationality to improve her chances of becoming queen. Yosef Lekach, a commentary on Esther written in 1566 by Rabbi Eliezer ben Eliyahu Harole Ashenazy, reasoned that Mordecai had her keep her relationship to him secret so that others would not be secretive when around him. Rashi, an acronym for Rabbi Shlomo ben Yitzchok, an eleventh-century rabbi from France,

[74]One rabbi substituted Vashti for Esther. The inclusion of Vashti, however, is an obvious attempt to explain why Xerxes tried to show her off before the men at the banquet in 1:4–8.

taught that she kept her royal lineage as a descendant from King Saul secret so the king would think her background was too humble and would send her away. Avraham Ibn Ezra, a twelfth-century Spanish rabbi, explained that she kept her background secret so she could secretly observe her religion. Had she been known as a Jew, she would have been forced to violate her convictions. Eliyahu ben Shlomo Zalman of Vilna, who was a sixteenth-century rabbi, thought that Mordecai was afraid his family would be killed for having kept Esther hidden so long and not surrendering her voluntarily when she was discovered.[75]

We cannot be dogmatic as to why Mordecai had Esther keep their relationship secret. We simply do not know why she was charged not to tell of her Jewish background. From his behavior later in the book, it is reasonable to assume that Mordecai's motive was wholesome in this, v. 10. Each day, he walked by the courtyard of the harem to gather information about his ward. Although we do not know how he gathered this information, it is reasonable to assume that Mordecai had some contact in the harem to keep him up to date with the situation (cf. 4:1–16), v. 11.[76]

During the twelve-month waiting period, each of the maidens received special beauty treatments. "Oil of myrrh" was an extract from *Balsamodendron myrrha*, a low tree that grows throughout Arabia. It has a pleasant smell (Ps. 45:8; Prov. 7:17) and may also have been used to soften the skin. Other "sweet odors" and treatments also were used to prepare the women. This process took a full year, with the first six months involving massages with the oil of myrrh and the final six months other spices and ointments, v. 12. William F. Albright describes a cosmetic burner used to scent the body, both for cosmetic and for

[75]Zlotowitz, p. 58.

[76]Carl Armerding, *Esther: For Such a Time as This* (Chicago: Moody Press, 1955), p. 29, suggests that Mordecai was one of the porters who watched the entrance into the palace. This would explain his presence at the gate each day. While this is possible, other events in the book suggest a higher position. His uncovering the plot of the king's servants against the king (2:21–23) and his elevation to the prime minister's position (8:2) argue for a position in government that gave him access to the king's servants and that had prepared him for greater responsibilities.

hygienic reasons. Something similar to this would seem to have been used in the preparation of the maidens for Xerxes.[77]

When the king was ready, one of the maidens would go in to him. She took "whatsoever she desired," clothing, jewelry, perfumes, and so on, chosen to set off her beauty, v. 13. After spending the night with the king, she went into the "second house of the women," where the concubines stayed. Shaashgaz, the king's chamberlain (*s*ᵉ*rîs*, "eunuch," see v. 3), presided over this house.[78] In this context the word *concubine* indicates lesser wives of the king. Unless the king "delighted" in her, having a strong desire to gratify his sexual desires, she remained there, living the remainder of her life with no intimate contact with a man, v. 14.

Esther's turn to go into the king arrived. Since Hegai, "the king's chamberlain" (*s*ᵉ*rîs*, "eunuch"), had favored her, she wisely relied on his guidance, probably referring to her dress and appearance, as she prepared to meet the king. Her demeanor and actions had let her gain "favour" with all others who had interacted with her, v. 15.[79] Her turn took place in "Tebeth," the tenth month of the Jewish ecclesiastical calendar, equivalent to mid-December to mid-January, in the seventh year of the king's reign, 479 BC, v. 16.[80]

---

[77]William F. Albright, "The Lachish Cosmetic Burner and Esther 2:12," in *A Light Unto My Path: Old Testament Studies in Honor of Jacob M. Myers*, ed. Howard N. Bream, Ralph D. Heim, and Carey A. Moore (Philadelphia: Temple University Press, 1974), pp. 26–31.

[78]The "second house" is generally supposed to be a separate harem (Bechtel, p. 32; Paton, p. 180; Rawlinson, p. 40). Paul Haupt, *The Book of Esther: Critical Edition of the Hebrew with Notes* (Chicago: University of Chicago Press, 1908), p. 22, asserts that there was no second house. The woman returned to the same house but was now under the care of another chamberlain. While it is possible that the "second house" was located under the same roof, the text supports its being a separate location. Haupt deletes *šenî*, "second," to support his view. There is little support for this.

[79]Gordis, pp. 30–31, has the other virgins preparing themselves with "ostentatious dress and adornment." Esther, having "either an innate modesty . . . or her confidence in her natural attractiveness," avoids this kind of preparation. While the view may be true, the book does not tell us anything other than that Esther followed the advice of Hegai. We speculate when we go further than this.

[80]Paton, p. 173, dates the process of selecting the virgins in the third year of Xerxes (1:3), right after the expulsion of Vashti. Since Esther's turn came in the seventh year, "the interval of four years . . . during which one girl was presented every day to the King, suggests that there were as many as 1460 girls."

Xerxes responded favorably to Esther. The word (*ʾahab*) ("loved") has a broad sense (in addition to genuine love, cf. Gen. 27:4; Judg. 16:4; 2 Sam. 13:1). Since the king had other concubines, his "love" seems to have been more of a "lust." Nevertheless, Esther obtained "grace [*ḥen*] and favour [*ḥesed*]," impressing him so much that he named her queen in place of the deposed Vashti, v. 17.

Xerxes held a great "feast" (*mišteh*, see 1:3) for his "princes" (*śar*, see Ezra 7:28) and "servants," no doubt limited to the ones holding higher positions at Shushan. This was "Esther's feast [*mišteh*]" in that at this time he raised Esther to the position of queen. In *Antiquities* 11.11.2, Josephus says that the wedding feast lasted "a whole month" and that he commanded the nations within his empire to keep a feast to celebrate his marriage. In honor of the occasion, the king declared a "release" (*hᵃnaḥâ*, or rest), a holiday,[81] and "gave gifts," probably to representatives of other nations who came to celebrate the occasion, v. 18.

D. The Deliverance of the King 2:19–23

The scene shifts back to Mordecai. All of the "virgins" gathered together. This may have been to announce to them the king's choice. The text does not explain the purpose of the gathering. A variety of other explanations have been proposed: moving the women into the second harem (Fox); a second gathering of virgins (Keil, Kennedy, and Rawlinson); a gathering of virgins for Esther's wedding banquet (mentioned by Bechtel); the choice of ladies-in-waiting to assist Esther (mentioned by

---

This assumes that the process began immediately, but since we know that Xerxes was occupied with his campaign in Greece, this cannot be the case. It further assumes that a new girl was given to the king every night, allowing no time for sickness, official trips of government, or just plain tiredness. While we do not know where Josephus obtained his number of four hundred virgins, it is probably much closer to the truth.

[81]There are other interpretations of *hᵃnaḥâ*. The word is variously understood as meaning "a holiday" (NASB, NIV), "relief from taxes" (ESV; Baldwin, p 69), "a release of prisoners" (LXX, Paton, p. 185), or an exemption from military service, which is mentioned as one possibility by Rawlinson, p. 41, and by Eugene Roop, *Ruth, Jonah, Esther*, in *Believers Church Bible Commentary*, ed. Elmer Martens (Scottdale, PA: Herald Press, 2002), p. 187. The root of *hᵃnaḥâ* is *nôaḥ*, "to rest." For this reason I have adopted the first of the above suggestions.

Levenson); the late arrival of virgins from distant regions (also mentioned by Levenson). Paton mentions several other possibilities that various authors have suggested: the king demanded a fresh supply of concubines; the courtiers of the king, jealous of Esther's influence, tried to lead the king to select another favorite; Xerxes made a second gathering to rouse Esther's jealousy so that she would tell him her race; the phrase "second gathering" refers to the gathering of the concubines into the second house of the women; or this is a parenthetical comment that refers to a time previous to the king's marriage to Esther. Robert Gordis suggests that this is a "second procession of the unsuccessful contestants, whose undeniable charms served to set off in more striking relief Esther's beauty."[82]

The word *virgins* refers broadly to the group that included both those who had been with the king and others who had not. During the occasion Mordecai sat at "the king's gate," apparently indicating that he held some official position. From his later advancement to Haman's position (8:2), it is likely that his position was one of significant responsibilities. It is unlikely that the king would have advanced him without knowing something of his ability. From the king's identification of Mordecai in 6:10, it is clear that he knew of him.[83] Herodotus 3.120 mentions that Persian officials sat at the "king's door," v. 19. As instructed by her uncle, Esther had kept her nationality secret. We may speculate that knowledge of this would have kept her from being named queen, v. 20.

Two of the king's "chamberlains" (*sarîsê hammelek*, lit., "king's eunuchs") developed a plot to "lay hand" on the king, i.e., to assassinate him. We are not told why they developed their plan other than that they "were wroth" (*qaṣap*, see 1:12). We do not know how they planned to carry out their plan. The Targum *Rishon* says that they planned to kill Esther with poison and the

---

[82]Fox, p. 38; Keil, p. 341; Kennedy, p. 41; Rawlinson, p. 55; Bechtel, p. 55; Levenson, p. 63; Paton, p. 186; Robert Gordis, "Studies in the Esther Narrative," *JBL* 95 (1976): 47.

[83]Paton, p. 188, suggests that Mordecai was a "man of leisure," who took this position simply to learn of Esther's well-being. From Mordecai's advancement later, it seems rather that he demonstrated his ability at this point, giving the king reason to promote him later.

king "by sword in his bedchamber." The Targum *Sheni* gives the fanciful view that they planned to put a poisonous snake in the king's wine that would strike him when he drank from the jug from which he usually drank.[84] *Megillah* 13*b* states that they planned to poison the king.

At this time Mordecai sat "in the king's gate," holding some undisclosed governmental position, v. 21. In the Talmud, *Megillah* 13*b* states that Bigthan and Teresh spoke in the Tarsian language, thinking that no one would understand it. Mordecai, however, supposedly understood seventy languages and thus gained the knowledge of their plan. Scripture does not tell how Mordecai learned of the planned assassination. In some way it was literally "made known" to him so that he could warn Esther. In his historical record, Josephus (*Antiquities* 11.6.4) says that Barnabazus, a slave of one of the eunuchs, betrayed them to Mordecai, who told Esther of the plot and she, in turn, warned the king, v. 22.

The servants were arrested, an investigation determined their guilt, and they were "hanged." From what we know of Persian justice, this involved impaling them on sharpened wood spikes and leaving them to die from the wound and exposure. Herodotus (3.159 and 4.43) mentions this as the method of execution. A note was made of the matter in "the book of the king's chronicles" (lit., "the book of the acts of the days"), the records giving the history of events during the king's reign. We know from archaeology that both the Assyrians and Babylonians kept historical records of each year. This apparently was a similar book of Persian history, v. 23.

Once again, we see the providential work of God. While we do not know the details of his position, Mordecai at that time "sat in the king's gate" (v. 21). The position allowed him continuing access to Esther so that he could give her guidance during the time when the contest to replace Vashti was going on (v. 11). His position in the court gave him access to the inner workings of the court. This let him uncover the plot against Xerxes, an action that becomes significant in chapter 6. He was able to show his loyalty to Xerxes. The position also allowed him later to find out the details of Ha-

[84] Grossfeld, pp. 49, 140.

man's plot (4:7–8). The Lord placed Mordecai in the position so that he was the right man in the right place at the right time.

ESTHER 3

The earlier chapters have identified the main characters and their positions in the empire. This chapter introduces Haman, an additional character of major importance, whose pride led him to develop a plot to annihilate the Jews. This conflict and its resolution occupy the remainder of the book. It is important since we cannot understand fully the development of the historical record without it.

E. The Plot Against Israel 3:1–15

1. Haman's Anger Toward Mordecai 3:1–6

Sometime between the seventh year and twelfth year of Xerxes' reign (2:16 cf. 3:7), Haman "the son of Hammedatha the Agagite" was promoted over the other "princes" (*śar*, see Ezra 7:28) of the land. We know nothing about Hammedatha, Haman's father. Josephus, *Antiquities* 11.6.5, identifies the land of the Agagites as Amalek (cf. 1 Sam. 15:7–33), v. 1. The OT mentions only two men named Agag. Balaam (Num. 24:7) refers to an unknown king with this name. From his statement the king was apparently a great monarch in his time. The second Agag is better known. He was the king of the Amalekites that was defeated in battle by King Saul. Although Saul attempted to spare his life, the prophet Samuel ended that effort by taking a sword himself and putting Agag to death (1 Sam. 15:32–33).[85]

[85]Zlotowitz, p. xxix, drawing on the Targum *Sheni*, gives a fanciful explanation regarding Haman's ancestry. Supposedly, after Saul spared Agag (1 Sam. 15:9), he lived for a time with his wife, during which time she conceived. This child became the ancestor of Haman. Gordis, p. 95, follows this view. The account in 1 Samuel gives no indication that Agag lived more than a day. Samuel met Saul "in the morning" (1 Sam. 15:12) of the next day. After announcing Saul's rejection as king by the Lord, he killed Agag with his sword (1 Sam. 15:16–35).

In all probability Haman was a descendant of the king who killed by Samuel. This relationship does much to explain Haman's hostility toward the Jews. However, it is also possible that the name "Agagite" reflects Haman's origin in a place named Agag and that his reaction to Mordecai simply reflected his pride.[86] An inscription dated during the reign of the Assyrian king Sargon mentions Agag as a province in Persia. Haman may have come from there or have been the descendant of someone who did.[87] The relationship to King Agag, however, better explains the enmity that developed between Haman and the Jews.

From 3:1 it seems that Haman's appointment probably took place around the twelfth year. It is unlikely that the conflict with Mordecai would have taken long to develop. It is possible that the discovery that Mordecai was a Jew kindled resentment in Haman over the past treatment of his people by Israel.[88] It is also possible that the phrase "the Jews' enemy" (v. 10) refers to a previously held prejudice against the Jews.

At the king's command the officials of the royal court bow to acknowledge Haman's position. The Targum *Rishon* says that Haman had embroidered an "image . . . on his chest," while the Targum *Sheni* places two images on his garment, "one in

[86]Rawlinson, p. 62, states that "a reference to descent from the Amalekite king Agag . . . is scarcely possible." He does not give any other reason for the term *Agagite*, however. Omanson and Noss, p. 89, give four possibilities other than taking the term as a reference to a descendant from Agag: (1) the word is a nickname; (2) it is an official title; (3) it is the name of an unknown country; (4) the Hebrew originally referred to a "Gagean," a northern enemy of the Persians. They recognize, however, that the relationship to the Amalekite king is the most widely accepted view. In my judgment, the most logical reason for mentioning the name is to identify Haman as a hereditary enemy of Israel.

[87]Whitcomb, p. 63, mentions an inscription dating from the time of Sargon, ca. 725 BC, that mentions Agag as a place in the area occupied by the Medes. Jules Oppert, *Les Inscriptiones Assyriennes des Sargonides et Les Fastes de Ninive* (Versailles, 1862), p. 25, was the first to recognize this possibility.

[88]Haupt, pp. 29, 54, asserts that Haman tricked the king into thinking that he, not Mordecai, had saved the king's life (cf. 2:21–23). As a reward for his supposed loyalty, the king elevated him to the position of prime minister. Haman's plan to exterminate all of the Jews is aimed particularly at the death of Mordecai, thus keeping his role in the king's deliverance from being known. This view is without merit.

the front and one in the back."[89] Bowing before this would have implied worship. Mordecai therefore "bowed [*kara*ᶜ] not, nor did [Haman] reverence [*šaḥâ*]." Mordecai's determination not to bow caused Haman to be filled with "wrath" (*ḥemâ*, see 1:12).

The word *kara*ᶜ has a broad range of meaning, "to kneel, crouch, bend down" and, by implication, "to give reverence." When the word refers to a Jew bowing in this sense, it always refers to bowing before God (e.g., 1 Kings 8:54; Ezra 9:5). The word *šaḥâ*, here translated "reverence," is elsewhere normally translated "worship." Zlotowitz notes that when the words for bowing (*kara*ᶜ) and reverencing (*šaḥâ*) occur together elsewhere (2 Chron. 7:3; 29:29; Pss. 22:29; 95:6), they always refer to worshiping God.[90] The heathen may bow before others (2 Kings 1:13), but the people of God may not act in a way that would suggest giving reverence to another. In the case here, there is no question about the sense of the word, v. 2.[91]

The king's servants noticed Mordecai's failure to bow before Haman. They questioned Mordecai about his actions, but he initially gave them no answer, v. 3.[92] In response to their repeated

---

[89]Grossfeld, pp. 51, 165.

[90]Zlotowitz, p. 65.

[91]Baldwin states that Mordecai's being a Jew "would not preclude his bowing down." She gives examples to support her conclusion, but these use a different word to refer to bowing. Baldwin's view leads her to refer to Mordecai's "pig-headed pride" and to "his awkwardness which caused the crisis in the first place," pp. 76–77. Haupt, p. 29, Roop, p. 195, and Keil, p. 343, adopt the same view. They give different OT examples, none of them using the word *kara*ᶜ. Bechtel, p. 37, gives two examples of bowing before others. Once more, these references do not use *kara*ᶜ. The view ignores the use of *kara*ᶜ elsewhere in the OT. Carson, p. 39, thinks that Mordecai's failure to bow was based on Haman's being an Amalekite. Mordecai's unwillingness to bow "arose from ignorance of his duty." Carson refers to 8:3, where Esther falls before the king to justify his position that it was not wrong to bow before Haman. Once again, the verse uses a different word. Reid, p. 90, mentions the view "that Mordecai is obstinate; personally affronted by being overlooked for promotion" or that he shows "loyalty to the king because Haman had been involved in the conspiracy [against him, 2:21–23]."

[92]Ronald T. Hyman, "Esther 3:3: the Question with No Response," in *JBQ* 22, no. 2 (April 1994): 108, explains Mordecai's lack of a response as "understandably silent in order to avoid further trouble." While this is a possible view, Hyman goes too far in concluding that, "though Mordecai expected his silence to calm the situation, the silence has led to Haman's outrage and

questions, he revealed to them his Jewish heritage, v. 4. In some unexplained way, Mordecai interpreted bowing before Haman as an act of reverence. In the Targum *Sheni*, Mordecai tells his questioners, "I only bow down to the ever-existing God who is One in heaven, and who is an all-consuming fire and whose angels are fire." While this is the correct answer, it is also an attempt by the author to show Mordecai in the best possible light. The MT gives no answer. We see Haman's pride in his response of "wrath" (*ḥemâ*, see 1:12), v. 5.

Since Mordecai's position as a Jew kept him from rendering such honor, Haman determined that he would annihilate the entire nation. Since he was called an Agagite (3:1), it was likely that Haman descended from Agag. If Agag was the one of Samuel's time, this would explain Haman's effort to get rid of the Jews. The Targums give Haman an alternative genealogy; both of the Targums make him a descendant of Esau. The Targum *Rishon* derives his anger toward the Jews from the fact that Jacob "took away the birthright and the blessing from Esau." They had attempted to annihilate his people. He now plans the same fate for them, v. 6.

2. Haman's Plot Against the Jews 3:7–15

Haman has "Pur" (*pûr*) cast before him, probably by diviners who used this method to determine the will of the gods.[93] The word occurs only eight times in the OT, here and seven times in c. 9 (vv. 24, 26 [2x], 28, 29, 31, 32). The word *pûr* is an Akkadian loanword from *puru*, "stone." It refers to a single stone, probably cut, marked, and used in the way we would use dice. Its primary significance in the book is in giving its name to the Jewish feast of Purim, discussed at 9:26. The explanation in 9:24 puts it in

---

the proposed vengeful destruction of all the Jews of the kingdom." While Mordecai may initially have refused an answer, v. 4 tells us that he had indeed answered, telling them of his Jewish background, which would not permit him to bow in reverence before Haman.

[93]William W. Hallo, "The First Purim," *Biblical Archaeologist* 46, no. 1 (Winter 1993): 20–23, describes several lots used by the Akkadians, Egyptians, people of India, Assyrians, and Babylonians to determine the will of the gods in legal, commercial, and religious matters. These were generally cubes, made from wood or baked clay, often inscribed on only four sides, but sometimes on all six sides, and cast out from a bowl.

terms of the more common Hebrew word *goral*, "lot." Haman wanted to know the best time for carrying out his plot. From elsewhere in the Bible, we know that lots were used to determine God's will (cf. Num. 26:55; Josh. 14:2; 18:6). Herodotus 3.128 describes the drawing of lots to accomplish a task assigned by the king. Xenophon, *Cyropaedia* 1.6.46 and 4.5.55, also refers to the use of lots. The verb *cast* here has the sense of causing something to fall. From this we conclude that these diviners relied on the throwing of the stone to select the month and day that Haman would exact his revenge.[94]

This consulting of the gods took place in the month Nisan, March-April of our modern calendar and the first month of the Jewish calendar. This was in the twelfth year of Xerxes, ca. 474 BC, five years after the selection of Esther as queen. Haman selected the month Adar, equivalent to February-March, and the last month of the Jewish calendar, as the time when he would exact his revenge on the Jews.

The Midrash has a fanciful explanation for the selection of Adar. Supposedly

> the first day was unfavourable because in it, God made heaven and earth. The second day was unfavourable because in it the waters were separated, as Israel is separated from the nations. The third day was unfavourable because in it seeds were created that the Israelites bring as offerings. The fourth day was unfavourable because in it the heavenly bodies were created to give Israel light. The fifth day was unfavourable because in it beasts were created for Israel to sacrifice. The sixth day was unfavourable because in it the first man was created. The seventh day was unfavourable because it was the Sabbath. Then he tried the months. Nisan was unfavourable because of the merit of Passover; Iyar, because the manna was given in it; Sivan, because of the merit of the law; Tammuz, because of the merit of the land; Ab, because they had already suffered enough in that month; Elul, because in it the walls of Jerusalem were finished; Tishri, because of the merit of the Feast

[94]Paton, p. 201, thinks that the lot was cast to determine "a lucky day for going to the King to make his request." When he found that day, one that was unfavorable for the Jews, he selected it "in the following year as the date for their massacre." Esther 9:24 argues against this view.

> of Trumpets, Day of Atonement, and Tabernacles; Marchesvan, because Sarah died in it; Chislev, because of the Feast of Dedication; Tebeth, because of the merit of Ezra; Shebat, because of the merit of the men of the Great Synagogue. But in Adar no merit was found.[95]

While the view is interesting, it is more probable that the Lord directed the selection process so as to allow time for the elevation of Mordecai to a position that would let him reverse Haman's plan.

Although Haman had followed the accepted practice for his time for finding the will of the gods, it would fail. The failure of his plan illustrates Numbers 23:23. God Himself prevented the success of such a plot against His people. God controls even the fall of the thrown dice (cf. Prov. 16:33).

Haman then approached the king with a report of the Jews as a rebellious people. They had their own laws, laws that differed from those of other nations. Since they kept these laws and not the king's laws, there was no profit in letting them continue in their ways, v. 8. He urged the king to decree that they be "destroyed" (*ʾabad*).[96] As an inducement he offered to "pay" (*šaqal*, lit., "weigh") the king ten thousand talents of silver, equivalent to several million dollars in today's money. He would give this to those over the king's business so that it would go into the royal treasury. Herodotus 3.95 gives the tribute received

---

[95]Quoted by Paton, pp. 201–2.

[96]Berg, p. 102, points out that *ʾabad* can mean "cause to be dispossessed, homeless" and the homonym *ʿabad* refers to "work," arguing that Haman intentionally let the king think he was selling the rebellious people into slavery or homelessness when, in reality, he planned to destroy them. This would explain the king's ignorance in 7:5 when he asked who planned the destruction. There are several arguments against the view. The verb *ʾabad* occurs here in the *piʿel* theme. The five times this *piʿel* verb occurs outside of Esther (Deut. 12:2; Ps. 119:95; Eccles. 3:6 ["lose"]; Jer. 12:17; Ezek. 22:27), it always has the sense of destruction, never that of becoming dispossessed or homeless. Secondly, in the context of Esther 3:9, the same verb clearly means "destruction" (3:13). It is unthinkable that such a letter would go out over the king's seal without his knowing of it. Finally, it is equally unthinkable that Haman would intentionally deceive Xerxes to such a degree. The wholesale slaughter of tens of thousands of Jews—a large enough number to cause the death of more than seventy-five thousand enemies (9:15–16)—would not have been something Haman could keep secret from the king.

by the king each year as almost fifteen thousand talents. Haman was thus offering two-thirds of the annual income, an attractive gift that the king could not refuse. Haman, of course, planned to recover his investment by confiscating the properties of the Jews, v. 9.

Xerxes accepted the proposal. The signet ring was used to press the king's official mark into wax. It was a way of indicating the official nature of royal decrees or proclamations. In giving his signet ring to Haman, Xerxes gave him unlimited authority to write orders with the king's power behind them (cf. Gen. 41:42–44; 1 Kings 21:8). As indicated in the discussion of v. 2, the phrase "the Jews' enemy" probably refers to a long-held enmity of Haman toward the Jews. It is possible that it refers to a newly developed enmity based on a desire to punish Mordecai. His desire to destroy "all the Jews" (v. 6), however, more likely supports a long-held enmity, v. 10. The statement "the silver is given to thee" refers to the value of property to be confiscated from the Jews after they are killed. The king recognized that Haman would prosper from his actions, v. 11.

Several authors consider the phrase "the silver is given to thee" as referring to the amount of money Haman offered to pay, meaing that the king turned down the bribe.[97] Haupt is more reasonable.[98] He understands the king as saying, in effect, "You take care of the silver (by paying it to the royal treasury)." While these are possible views, the context relates it more to the estates of those who will die. The statement that follows—"the people also, to do with them as it seemeth good to thee"—virtually forces the comment about the silver to relate to the wealth of the people about to be killed. In addition, Mordecai's comment in 4:7 about the money being paid to the king and Esther's lament in 7:4 about being "sold" indicate that the king accepted Haman's offer of ten thousand talents of silver.

Haman assembled the king's scribes and told them what to write. The orders went out to the "lieutenants" (or "satraps," *ᵓaḥašdarpan*; see Ezra 8:36), governors (*peḥâ*, see Ezra 8:36), and rulers [*šar*, see Ezra 7:28] in all parts of the empire. The eleven-

---

[97]E.g., Bechtel, p. 41; Berlin, p. 42; and Radmacher and Allen, p. 325.

[98]Haupt, p. 34.

month delay between the "first month" when the orders were written, and "Adar," the last month of the calendar, when they were to be carried out, reflected Haman's confidence from casting the lot that Adar (see v. 7) would be the best time to carry out his plans. Haman may have felt the delay was to his advantage, v. 12.

The letters went out by "posts" (*raṣîm*, or "couriers") to all parts of the empire. The word *raṣîm* is lit. "runners" and is translated that way more than seventy times in the OT. In Esther, however, two occurrences of the word (8:10, 14) clarify that here it means couriers who rode animals. Herodotus describes a system similar to the pony express, with stables along various routes (described in the discussion at 1:22). It may be that runners were used for nearby cities and horses for destinations farther away, v. 13.

The letters went out eleven months in advance of the date for the execution (v. 13 cf. v. 12). This advance announcement was probably intended to frighten the Jews into fleeing the empire and thus leaving their property to be easily seized, v. 14.[99] As the "posts" (or "couriers," *raṣîm*) took the king's decree to the various parts of the empire, it was also publicized in Shushan the "palace" (or "fortress," *bîrâ*, see Neh. 1:1). Xerxes and Haman sat down "to eat and drink," unconcerned about what would happen. The people of Shushan, however, were "perplexed," bewildered by what the king had decreed, because they did not understand the reasons behind it. This is the first time in the book that "Shushan" is distinguished from "Shushan the palace." When the name occurs without the qualifying phrase "the palace" (as it also does in 4:8, 16; 8:15; 9:13, 14, 15 [2x], 18), it refers to the city proper, east of the fortress occupied by the king and other servants, v. 15.

[99]Zlotowitz, p. 72, gives two additional suggestions: (1) Haman published the letters immediately so the king would not have a chance to change his mind; (2) God sovereignly guided in the timing to give the Jews a chance to repent of their sins.

ESTHER 4

II. The Deliverance of Israel 4:1–10:3

The stage for the dramatic rescue of the Jews was now set. The threat had been developed, and the need existed for national deliverance. We see a chain of events put into motion that culminated in the deliverance of Israel. In doing this, the Lord showed His faithfulness to His covenant with the nation. We also see His providential working on behalf of His people.

A. The Plan of Mordecai 4:1–17

1. Mordecai's Grief 4:1–3

After learning of Haman's plan, Mordecai reacted in typical Jewish fashion by tearing his clothing, putting on sackcloth, and sprinkling ashes on his head. Tearing the outward clothing indicated inward grief (cf. Gen. 37:29; 1 Sam. 4:12). Sackcloth was a dark, coarsely-woven fabric made from the hair of a camel or goat. Its name comes from its common usage in making sacks for carrying or storing things (e.g., Gen. 42:25; Lev. 11:32). It was worn next to the skin to indicate grief (cf. 1 Kings 21:27; Job 16:15). Ashes were placed on the body to show sorrow (cf. 2 Sam. 13:19; Jer. 6:26).

Mordecai then went into the city and lit. "cried a cry [*wayyizᶜaq zeᶜaqâ*] loud and bitter." The repetition of the root *zᶜq* gives emphasis to his actions. The ESV and NKJV show the repetition, both translating "he cried out with a loud and bitter cry," v. 1. He came to the king's gate but could not enter because of his grief, v. 2. As the news of the decree spread throughout the empire, other Jews similarly showed their grief. Fasting occurs here as a way of showing grief (e.g., 2 Sam. 1:12; Joel 2:12). At other times it is associated with prayer (e.g., 2 Sam. 12:16; Ezra

8:21). The decree affected the Jews deeply, so much so that many of them put on sackcloth and lay down in ashes, v. 3.[100]

2. Mordecai's Request 4:4–9

Eventually Esther's maids and "chamberlains" (*sarîs*, "eunuchs") told her about Mordecai's actions. She sent clothing to him to replace the sackcloth, but he refused it, v. 4. She then sent Hathach, one of the king's servants who had been assigned to her, to find out what was troubling Mordecai, v. 5. Hathach found Mordecai in "the street [or 'open space,' i.e., a plaza area, *rᵉḥôb*, see Ezra 10:9] of the city," an open area in front of the king's gate, v. 6. Mordecai related to him the details of Haman's plan. Being a highly placed official himself, Mordecai had no doubt learned of the payment of "money" (*kesep*) and so forth, from his contacts in the palace, v. 7. He gave a copy of the decree that had been publicized throughout the city of Shushan (see discussion at 3:15) to Hathach for Esther and urged her to plead with Xerxes for mercy, v. 8. Hathach returned to Esther with this information, v. 9.

3. Esther's Decision 4:10–17

Esther sent Hathach back to Mordecai to explain her limited access to the king. Not having been with him for a month, she perhaps felt that she had lost favor with him. This led to her fear that she would be condemned if she entered his presence without permission. Herodotus 1.99 states that no one could come into the king's presence. In 3.84 and 3.118, however, he mentions that six officials were exempted from this law. This shows that the law was in place, vv. 10–11. On hearing Esther's reply, Mordecai pointed out that she would not escape the threat to the Jews, vv. 12, 13.

God would watch over His people by sending them deliverance "from another place," from some unknown source.[101]

---

[100]Omanson and Noss, p. 119, explain this as spreading ashes on sackcloth and lying down in the cloth, a possible way to understand the passage. Elsewhere mourners both place ashes on the body (2 Sam. 13:19) or sit in ashes (Job 2:8; Isa. 58:5).

[101]Knight, p. 37, understands the word *place* as "a reverential substitute for the divine name" and asserts that by this means Mordecai expressed his faith. This view is speculative. Although the Lord clearly controlled the "enlarge-

Esther, however, and her "father's house" would be caught up in Haman's destruction.[102] While we do not know the extent of Esther's family, there must have been others who perhaps had been taken in by other relatives after the death of her father. Mordecai noted that God had placed Esther in the royal court "for such a time as this." The statement shows Mordecai's reliance on the Lord, v. 14.[103]

Esther sent back her answer, v. 15. She asked Mordecai to gather the Jews in the city of Shushan. The gathering was likely for the purpose of communicating the need to fast, rather than coming together for a joint three-day fast.[104] Since Esther's later actions took place "on the third day" (5:1), this was a fast that would last until the third day rather than one involving three complete days of fasting. From the narrative, the events of the chapter took place on the first day. It is therefore clear that the fast involved parts of the first and last days and all of the second day. The phrase "night or day" indicates that the fast was to be continuous, not broken into periods of fasting followed by times

---

ment and deliverance" of Israel at this point, nothing indicates that "another place" refers to Him.

[102]John M. Wiebe, "Esther 4:14: 'Will Relief and Deliverance Arise for the Jews from Another Place?'" in *CBQ* 53, no. 3 (July 1991): 409–15, argues that "thy father's house" means the family of Esther's stepfather, referring to Mordecai. Since he had been faithful to the Lord, it makes no sense that his house would be destroyed. Wiebe therefore translates the clause as a question: "Will relief and deliverance arise for the Jews from another place?" Wiebe acknowledges that such a translation would normally be introduced in some way—an interrogative particle, pronoun, adverb, or conjunction—none of which occur here. While this is not a fatal flaw in his interpretation, it does point out a weakness in it. In addition, it is Wiebe's belief that the "father's house" is Mordecai's house that requires his reinterpretation. As noted above, there is another possibility that explains this phrase.

[103]Whitcomb, p. 75, states "it is not at all certain that Mordecai was a true believer." His mourning may be no more than a natural reaction to the circumstances. This position is difficult to accept. His statement that deliverance would arrive "from another place" and his pointing out to Esther that she had "come to the kingdom for such a time as this" show spiritual discernment. Although he did not mention God at this point, it is clear that he was relying on God for the deliverance of the nation.

[104]Henry, p. 1135, understands the three-day fast as "only one whole day and two whole nights." There is no good reason for interpreting the fast this way.

when food and drink was permitted.[105] It began at night and continued into the day. This follows the pattern established at Creation (e.g., Gen. 1:5, 8, 13) that led to beginning the Jewish day in the evening and ending it the following day.

Since fasting without prayer would have been meaningless at this point, we may assume that prayer accompanied the fast. Esther and her servants were going to abstain from food also.[106] After this spiritual preparation, she would approach the king. The statement "If I perish, I perish," shows her willingness to accept whatever God had for her in this situation, v. 16.

Mordecai then "went his way" (*ᶜabar*, lit., "passed over"), possibly indicating that he crossed over the Kerhes River, which flowed through the city near the royal palace. *Megillah* 15*a* suggests that Mordecai crossed to the other side of Shushan in order to speak with the Jews who lived in that part of the city. He then carried out Esther's wishes in gathering the Jews to tell them of the need to fast and pray for the queen, v. 17

---

[105]Baldwin, p. 81, states that "the fast could have been confined to certain hours." Levenson, p. 81, similarly suggests that "perhaps we are to imagine a fast during daylight only." The phrase "night or day" could as well be translated "night *and* day." Facing such a crisis as this, it is reasonable to accept the fast as continuing through the whole period concluding with Esther's meeting with the king.

[106]Luter and Davis, pp. 235–36, argue for Esther's lack of spirituality. They note that a three-day fast at this time would have conflicted with observing the Passover and that no purpose would have been served by having her heathen maidens fast since they would pray (if they prayed) to Medo-Persian gods. Their argument concerning the Passover assumes that the fast followed the decree of 3:12 (cf. 3:7). But it is reasonable to assume that some time took place between the proclamation of the decree and Esther's decision. The lamenting of the Jews throughout the provinces (4:3) required time for the decree to reach them. Further, we do not know whether the Jews in Shushan were able to worship as they had done in Palestine. There was no place for them to offer the sacrifices required during Passover. Finally, Luter and Davis assume that Esther's maidens were heathen. Having been queen at this time for five years (3:7 cf. 2:16), she may well have surrounded herself with Jewish maidens to give herself contact with her people.

ESTHER 5

This chapter begins the account of the deliverance of the Jews. The first of Esther's two banquets is described (vv. 1–8 cf, 7:1–2). Following this, Haman saw Mordecai's failure to bow before him (v. 9). This led to his plan to publicly execute Mordecai (vv. 10–14). Chapter six poetically contrasts with this as Haman plunged from the height of his planned punishment of Mordecai to the depths of his assignment to publicly honor the object of his hatred.

B. The First Banquet of Esther 5:1–8

1. The First Invitation 5:1–5

On the third day of the fast, Esther abandoned any hint of her fast by dressing in her royal garments. She thus prepared herself to enter the inner court of the palace, near where King Xerxes was seated on his throne. Excavations of the palace show this to have been a large square, v. 1. When the king saw her in the court, he responded to her presence by holding out his scepter as a sign of his "favour" (*ḥen*, see 2:15). Esther approached him and touched the tip of the scepter, apparently a Persian custom, v. 2.

The king asked Esther to explain her coming, offering to give her up to "half of the kingdom." This last should not be taken literally since this was an idiom reflecting oriental hospitality (cf. v. 6; 7:2; Mark 6:23) v. 3. She invited the king and Haman to a "banquet" (*mišteh*, see 1:3). Although this was not her real reason for approaching the king, Esther probably did not think that the time was right to bring up the subject. There no doubt were numerous servants, guards, and officials present in the throne room.[107]

Haman's presence at the feast was reasonable in view of his position in the government. He carried out the king's wishes.

[107]Levenson, p. 90, mentions several possibilities that have been suggested to explain why Esther did not make her request at this time. She might have wanted the king to forget her uninvited entrance before making her request. She might have wanted him to come under the influence of wine to put him in a good mood.

While Xerxes did not know at this point what Esther wanted, he would not think it strange to have Haman present. His position made it necessary for him to know all that was going on in the empire. Further, having Haman present would give Esther the advantage of surprising him with her charge. He would have no time to prepare a defense, v. 4.[108] Xerxes agreed to come to the "banquet" (*mišteh*) and sent for Haman to accompany him.[109]

The word *mišteh*, referring to banqueting, occurs more in Esther than in any other OT book (20x vs. 22x elsewhere; the word also occurs 4x in Daniel referring to "drink"). Several authors see a pattern of banquets and feasting in Esther, with the two banquets given by Xerxes (1:2–4, 5–8) parallel to the two banquets of Purim (9:17, 19; 9:18), Esther's coronation banquet (2:18) parallel to the celebration of Mordecai's promotion (8:17), and Esther's first banquet for the king and Haman (5:1–8) parallel to her second banquet for them (7:1–9).[110] To gain this parallelism, Vashti's feast for the women (1:9) and Mordecai's command to the Jews regarding Purim (9:20–22) must be ignored.

Another way of analyzing the banquets looks at their hosts. The first four banquets have Persian hosts (Xerxes, 1:3, 5; 2:18; or Vashti, 1:9). The next four references to banquets relate to Esther, either as she hosts the feasts (5:4–8; 6:14; 7:2–8) or as others

[108]Jewish commentators have suggested that she wanted to make Xerxes jealous of Haman. *Megillah* 15*b* gives the additional reason that the invitation to Haman would cause Israel to fear that Esther was catering to Haman. This in turn would lead them to repent and pray rather than trusting Esther to solve the problem with her connections in the king's palace. The Targum *Sheni* gives four reasons for Haman's presence: (1) Haman knew of the connection between Esther and Mordecai, and the invitation would appease him. (2) It would create good will in Haman toward her and her people. (3) It would create jealousy on the part of Xerxes toward Haman. (4) Knowing of Haman's presence at the banquet would cause Israel to pray for mercy from God (Grossfeld, pp. 164–65). While these are all possible reasons, we cannot be certain whether any of them are correct.

[109]Zlotowitz, p. 85, notes that the first letters of the words יָבוֹא הַמֶּלֶךְ וְהָמָן הַיּוֹם ("let the king and Haman come") are the Hebrew letters that spell God's name. Since the name is hidden in the text, God's name is not mentioned in *Megillah*, the section of the Talmud that deals with the book of Esther. See also the chart on p. 205.

[110]While their approaches vary slightly, Bechtel, pp. 5–6; Jobes, p. 155; and Levenson, pp. 5, 8, all see a parallelism in the banquets.

anticipate these feasts (5:12; 5:14). The final four references relate to the feasts of the Jews (8:17; 9:17, 19; 9:18; 9:22).[111]

Note that the banquet had already been prepared. There was no delay. In fact, Haman was told to "make haste" as he made his way to the meal. This small incident shows Esther's belief that God would prosper her plans. Rather than waiting to see how the king would respond to her uninvited presence, she took action assuming that he would come, v. 5.

2. The Second Invitation 5:6–8

Following the banquet, there was a "banquet [*mišteh*] of wine" in which the three relaxed while sipping wine. Xerxes asked Queen Esther again that she make her wishes known, v. 6. She postponed her answer once more, requesting—if she had the "favour" (*ḥen*) of the king—that he and Haman come to another "banquet" (*mišteh*). At that time she would make her request known. We do not know the reason behind Esther's delay. Her courage may have failed her.[112] She may have wanted the opportunity to influence the king through intimacy.[113] She may have sensed that he was not in the right mood to hear her request.[114] She may have wanted the king to be "under the influence of wine" so that he would be in a good mood and more willing to carry out her wishes.[115] She may have been feeling strain from the circumstances and felt she needed to think through her request after a night of sleep.[116] She may have

---

[111]Levenson, pp. 5–6, groups the banquets in five sets of two each. These include the first two banquets hosted by Xerxes (1:2–4; 1:5–8); the banquet of Xerxes and Haman (3:15) paired with the Jew's feast celebrating Mordecai's advancement and the counterdecree (8:17), the two banquets for Esther, Xerxes, and Haman (5:1–8; 7:1–9); the two feasts of Purim (9:17, 18); and the fifth and eighth banquets, celebrating the advancement of Esther and Mordecai (2:18; 8:17). Levenson, p. 5, includes 3:15 in his list of banquets even though this reference does not use the word *mišteh*, "banquet" or "feast." For good reason he does not explain how the third and sixth banquets are parallel.

[112]M'Crie, p. 146, supports this view.

[113]Naomi Harris Rosenblatt, "Portraits in Heroism: Esther and Samson," in *BR* 15, no. 1 (February 1999): 22, suggests this possibility.

[114]McIntire, p. 71, suggests this view.

[115]Levenson, p. 90, mentions this as a possibility.

[116]Kennedy, p. 104, argues for this view.

sought to heighten a feeling of suspense in Xerxes so he would respond quickly when she revealed her request.[117] She may have wanted to avoid pressuring the king into an immediate decision.[118] The delay may have been intended to heighten the king's curiosity as well as giving Esther time to recover from the fast.[119] We can only guess at Esther's reason for hesitating to tell the king her true desires.[120]

Whatever the reason for the delay, we must ultimately say that the Holy Spirit used the human cause to bring about God's will. The record given in 5:9–6:14 shows clearly the providential nature of the delay. This delay of one day let the king discover his failure to reward Mordecai (6:1–3) and put Haman in the position of having to give public honor to his bitterest enemy. It brought Mordecai to the king's mind as a loyal subject (6:6–11). After Haman's death the king promoted Mordecai, knowing that he was loyal (8:2). God's providence is clear, vv. 7–8.

C. The Plot of Haman 5:9–14

Haman left the banquet in a good frame of mind. Undoubtedly he was congratulating himself on being invited to both of the queen's banquets. As he left, he saw Mordecai seated in the king's gate, where he carried out his official responsibilities (cf. 2:19). Mordecai had in some way heard about Esther's favorable reception by the king and was no longer wearing sackcloth (cf. 4:1–2). Mordecai did not stand to do Haman honor nor was he "moved for him," i.e., he did not show fear or tremble in Haman's presence. The thought of a royal official not giving him honor caused Haman to be filled with "indignation" (*ḥemâ*, see 1:12), v. 9. After arriving home, Haman called for his "friends," seen in 6:13 to be

---

[117]Fox, p. 72, adopts this view.

[118]Henry, p. 1136, suggests that Esther knew that putting off her request "would be well taken as an expression of the great reverence she had for the king, and her unwillingness to be too pressing upon him."

[119]Kennedy, p. 103, makes this suggestion.

[120]Among others, Paton, p. 236, and Moore, *Esther* in *The Anchor Bible*, p. 57, suggest that the delay is purely literary in nature. The author requires time to develop the circumstances by which Mordecai will gain his ascendancy over Haman. This, however, is an inadequate explanation. The writer could simply have Esther hold her first banquet on the day after Mordecai had been exalted and Haman humiliated.

his advisors ("wise men"), and his wife Zeresh, v. 10. He bragged to them about his success—his wealth, his family, his exalted position above other "princes" (*śar*, see Ezra 7:28), the fact that he alone had been invited to accompany the king to the queen's "banquet" (*mišteh*) and that he would attend another banquet on the next day. The Targum *Rishon* says that Haman had 208 sons in addition to the ten who were generals over provinces and another who served the king as his scribe. Esther 9:10 more reasonably refers to only "ten sons of Haman," vv. 11–12.

Despite Haman's accomplishments and all that he possessed, he was still upset because Mordecai did not honor him, v. 13. Zeresh and Haman's friends suggested that he build a "gallows" (*ʿeṣ*, "tree," i.e., a wooden pole, treelike in standing erect) fifty cubits high, which would be about seventy-five feet. This would have included a raised platform or a nearby hill with the spike mounted on it. As with the two servants who had plotted against Xerxes (2:23), the plan was to impale Mordecai. After making these preparations, Haman could seek permission from the king to put Mordecai to death. After he taking that step, he would be able to attend the queen's "banquet" (*mišteh*) in a merry state of mind.

The Targum *Sheni* describes a process that eliminates other potential means of execution. Haman could not use a sword for fear that Mordecai might be a righteous man and the sword would fall on Haman. He could not use a stone since David used a stone to kill Goliath. He could not chain him since Manasseh broke a chain and escaped (2 Chron. 33:11). He could not throw him into the sea because Moses earlier extracted himself from it. He could not cast him into a fire since the three Hebrews escaped from Nebuchadnezzar's fire. He cannot throw him into a den of lions since Daniel escaped from the lions. He could not set dogs on him since the mouths of dogs were shut in Egypt (Exod. 11:7). He could not send him into the wilderness since the Jews had earlier multiplied in it. He could not put him in prison because Joseph came from prison to a royal office. He could not set a knife to his throat since the knife was once turned away from Isaac. He could not put out his eyes lest he kill others as Samson did the Philistines. Only impalement would succeed. As with most of the additions in the Targums, these comments are fanciful.

Haman agreed with the plan and ordered the structure built. Since this "gallows" was completed in a single day (5:14 cf. 7:9–10), it is likely that some existing structure served as support for the spike, v. 14.

ESTHER 6

Here begins the account of the series of events that resulted in Haman's death. Anticipating the execution of Mordecai, Haman found instead that he had to give public honor to him. Complaining about this to his friends and family, he received only a dire prediction of further failure. Without being given additional time to refine his plot, he was called to the second feast given by Esther. This led to the final moments of his life, described in c. 7.

D. The Humiliation of Haman 6:1–13

1. Xerxes' Sleeplessness 6:1–3

That night the king had difficulty sleeping. In desperation he asked that a servant read from "the book of records of the chronicles" (lit. "the book of remembrances, the words of the days"), mentioned earlier in 2:23, v. 1. It happened that the record of Mordecai's part in delivering the king from the plot of his servants (cf. 2:21–23) was read. The name of the servant Bigthana is written more fully here than in 2:21. It is the same person, however, v. 2. The king asked what had been done to honor Mordecai for his action. The servants replied that nothing had been done.[121] The providence of God is clear in bringing Mordecai to the notice of the king at this point in time, v. 3.

[121]Cumming, p. 76, suggests that Xerxes' preoccupation with the preparation for the war against the Greeks had caused the king to overlook a reward for Mordecai. The chronology of the book of Esther, however, places the failed war against Greece earlier, after c. 1 but before c. 2 (see introduction to c. 2).

2. Haman's Suggestion 6:4–9

Early the next morning the king asked if any nobles were in the court. Some authors place these events at night rather than in the morning.[122] It was now long past the king's bedtime, however, and unlikely that he would be up at that time. In addition, Haman's wife had suggested that he ask for Mordecai's life "to morrow" (5:14) rather than at that same night. Finally, Haman carried out the king's command to honor Mordecai before Esther's banquet on the following day (5:8). For these reasons, I prefer to place the events of this chapter early in the morning of the next day.

Haman had just arrived, intending to ask permission to put Mordecai to death. Perhaps because he knew the king's usual schedule, Haman had come early to speak with the king before he got caught up in his daily routine, v. 4. The king told his servants to admit Haman, v. 5. The king asked Haman what honor should be given to someone he wished to honor. Filled with pride, Haman assumed that the king was planning to honor him, v. 6. Since he himself needed no more wealth, he suggested a public display of honor—allowing the person the king wished to honor to wear royal garments (cf. Gen. 41:42), v. 7. This was a suitable way of giving honor in that era. Herodotus 3.84 describes the giving of raiment as a gift. Xenophon, *Cyropedia* 8.2.8, refers to "beautiful robes" given by Cyrus to his friends. First Maccabees 10:20, 62 describes the king's honoring of Jonathan, one of the Maccabean family, after his rise to leading his family. The king sent him "a purple robe and a gold crown."

Haman continued his suggestions. Let the honoree ride the king's horse through the "street" (or "open space," i.e., a plaza area, most likely one near the palace where crowds would be present during the day, *rᵉḥôb*, see Ezra 10:9) with a royal crown of some kind placed on the horse's head so that all would know whose it was. Both Persian and Assyrian art depict horses with royal crowns, v. 8.[123] Let one of the highly placed "princes" (*šar*,

[122]E.g., Berlin, p. 58, and Paton, p. 247.

[123]Baldwin, p. 90, and Rademacher and Allen, p. 327, consider the "crown" on the horse's head as a special plaiting of the forelock that formed a crown-like appearance. See AB, plate 4. On the other hand Luter and Davis, p. 271, and Mattoon, p. 82, adopt the view that the horse wore a royal crown. Since

see Ezra 7:28) place the robe on him and lead him through the "street" (or "open space") of the city. As they went, the noble was to proclaim, "Thus shall it be done to the man whom the king desires to honor," v. 9.

3. Mordecai's Honor 6:10–11

The Bible gives no greater illustration than this of Proverbs 16:18: "Pride goeth before destruction, and an haughty spirit before a fall." Haman's suggestions pleased the king. He ordered Haman to carry them out and then identified Mordecai as the one Haman was to honor, v. 10. Haman led the king's horse through the "street [*r*ᵉ*ḥôb*] of the city," apparently the same open area where Mordecai had earlier displayed his grief (4:6), v. 11.

4. Haman's Mourning 6:12–13

The roles of the two men were then reversed. Mordecai again sat in the king's gate. Possibly the humiliation of Haman had given Mordecai hope that God had begun His working to undo Haman's wicked plan. No longer self-confident of his honor, Haman now covered his head to show his grief. The Bible does not say how the head was covered to show grief. The OT mentions the custom only here and in 2 Samuel 15:30, Jeremiah 14:3–4, and Ezekiel 24:17, v. 12.[124] Haman later recounted to his wife and friends what had happened. The "friends" are called "wise men," apparently indicating that these men also held positions of responsibility under the king. Rather than giving counsel to Haman, they interpreted the events superstitiously. In view of his requirement to proclaim Mordecai's honor, they predict further failure in his plan against the Jews, v. 13. Verse 14 logically introduces the events of c. 7 and is discussed there.

---

archaeology supports both views, it is not possible to be dogmatic as to which view is correct.

[124]Armerding, p. 74, suggests that a veil served to indicate mourning. From the occurrence in Jeremiah 14:4, referring to workers in the fields, a veil is unlikely. Some cloth covering the head would be more readily available. We cannot, however, be certain of how the head was covered to indicate grief.

ESTHER 7

The time for Haman's doom had now arrived. His glorious ascent to position and power ended with a crashing fall into judgment that fulfilled the prediction of failure given by his wife and friends in the previous chapter (6:13). Haman arrived at Esther's second feast with every expectation of enjoying the unique privilege of dining alone with the king and his queen. He found out instead that his plans for vengeance on the Jews were a direct attack on the queen. Instead of enjoyment he received impalement since the king decreed his death.

E. The Second Banquet of Esther 6:14–7:10

1. The King's Request 6:14–7:4

In the midst of Haman's lament to his family, the king's "chamberlains" (or "eunuchs") arrived to take him to Esther's second "banquet" (*mišteh*, see 1:3). There is nothing unusual indicated in this. It was a mark of honor that an escort would conduct him to the banquet, v. 14. The king and Haman came to eat with Esther, v. 1. The phrase "on the second day at the banquet [*mišteh*] of wine" does not refer to a two-day banquet. This was the second day of banqueting, i.e., the second banquet.

Once again, after the feasting at the "banquet of wine" (cf. 5:6), the king asked Esther what she desired. Again, the phrase "unto the half of my kingdom" is idiomatic (cf. 5:3, 6), v. 2. On the basis of finding "favour" (*ḥen*, see Esther 2:15) from the king, she asked for her life and the life of her people. This revealed to Xerxes for the first time that she was Jewish, v. 3. She alluded to the agreement between the king and Haman with her statement "we are sold" (cf. 3:9). Had this been into slavery, she would not have troubled the king "although the enemy could not countervail the king's damage" (or "because the enemy [*ṣar*] could not equal the damage [*nezeq*] to the king"). This phrase suggests that canceling the sale of the Jews into slavery would not have merited causing the king the financial loss of the expected income from their sale.[125] The king would then have had to repay the money paid him by Haman. Haman's plan for destroying the Jews, however, was a matter grievous enough to cause Esther to speak. While she did not mention this, putting the Jewish people to death would have caused the king to suffer the loss of taxes and service from them throughout his kingdom. It may well be that the king now thought of this, something that had not been brought up in the earlier deal with Haman (3:9), v. 4.

2. The King's Decision 7:5–10

Xerxes asked who had planned this destruction and where he could be found. When Haman suggested the agreement, (3:8–10) he did not mentioned the Jews by name. We may fault the king for entering into the agreement without knowing the full scope of Haman's plan. At this time it seems Xerxes had forgotten the agreement altogether, v. 5. Esther identified Haman as the guilty party. Haman, hearing the queen accuse him, immediately "was afraid" (*ba*ᶜ*at*). The word *ba*ᶜ*ât* is strong and indicates that Haman was "terrified," v. 6.

The king, filled with "wrath" (*ḥemâ*, see 1:12), left the "banquet" (*mišteh*) to go into the palace garden, where he could think through the matter. He faced several difficult decisions. He himself had approved the decree. Did he want to act against Haman, an obviously talented individual who had risen to a position of importance to the empire? Could the king get around the unalterable law of the Medes and the Persians that stood behind his order to destory the Jews?

Whatever the reason that caused the king to leave the others, it was providential. The king's absence allowed him to return to

---

[125]The phrase is often interpreted as though the slavery of the Jews would not have been serious enough to "disturb" (*nezeq*) the king about (NASB, NET, NIV). Haupt, p. 51 understands the word *nezeq* as "annoyance." Although the word *nezeq* occurs only here in the OT, a variety of cognate words insure the meaning of "damage" rather than "annoyance." In Aramaic the word *n*ᵉ*zak* occurs in Ezra 4:13 ("endamage"), 4:15 ("hurtful"), 4:22 ("hurt"), and Daniel 6:2 ("damage"). The sense of "damage," i.e., financial harm, is appropriate here. In addition, the word *ṣar* is often understood as "trouble" or "distress," referring to slavery. This word, however, is overwhelmingly translated "enemy" or "adversary" in the OT. The word occurs again in 7:6, where it must have this meaning.

a scene that he interpreted as Haman's attempt to rape his wife. If there had been any hesitancy before on pronouncing judgment against Haman, it was now gone. He immediately declared his feelings in words that led one of the eunuchs to suggest the impalement of Haman.

During the king's absence Haman had pleaded with Esther for his life. He had seen "that there was evil determined against him by the king." Knowing the king, he had probably concluded that his fate was already sealed, v. 7. When the king returned to the room where the "banquet" (*mišteh*) was being held, he found Haman stretched out on Esther's "bed" (better "couch"), where he was pleading with the queen. The Targum *Rishon* explains this by stating that the angel Gabriel pushed Haman onto the couch. He apparently had taken hold of Esther as he pleaded with her.

Xerxes concluded that Haman was trying to molest the queen. It is possible that the king did not really think that the queen had been in danger of being raped with her husband still in the area but rather seized upon the situation as a way of getting rid of the troublemaker. Since he himself had approved Haman's plan and had likely already received the money offered by Haman, he was in a difficult position. Deliberately interpreting Haman's position as an attempt at rape gave him a different reason to decree his death. Herodotus 4.43 gives impalement as the punishment for rape.

The king's servants understood his angry words as a sentence of death. They "covered Haman's face," apparently a Persian custom preparatory to execution, v. 8. While we have no other example of covering the face as the first step in executing a death sentence, both the Greeks and Romans adopted this practice. Quintus Curtius refers to the head of Philotas "veiled in a worn-out cloak" as he is brought into his trial. Livy describes an expiatory rite in which a father makes his son pass under a beam "with covered head." Cicero refers to condemning a man, saying, "Veil his head, hang him to the tree of shame."[126]

---

[126]Quintus Curtius, *History of Alexander the Great of Macedon*, trans. John C. Rolfe (Cambridge, MA: Harvard University Press, 1956), 2.85; Livy, *From the Founding of the City*, trans. B. O. Foster (Cambridge, MA: Harvard

Harbonah, one of the king's "chamberlains" (or "eunuchs"), was aware of the "gallows" (ʿeṣ, as before, 5:14, "tree") built "fifty cubits high" (about seventy-five feet) by Haman to be used for Mordecai. It stood "in [or 'by'] the house of Haman," not in the house itself but on the grounds near it.[127] He told the king about this and also reminded him that Mordecai had "spoken good for the king." This caused the king to realize that Haman's plot was against the very man who had saved the king's life. The king responded, "Hang him thereon," v. 9. The servants led Haman away and impaled him immediately on the spike. While Xerxes would not have been involved in this, the knowledge that it was taking place calmed his spirit, pacifying his "wrath" (*ḥemâ*), v. 10.

ESTHER 8

The preceding chapters record the rise and fall of Haman. Despite this sudden reversal, nothing had at this point occurred to remove the danger that threatened the entire nation of captive Israel. The king's decree was still in place. This chapter records how the king unexpectedly elevated Mordecai to Haman's former position of authority. With the authority now vested in him by the king, Mordecai took steps that let Israel escape the threat posed them by Haman's plan to avenge Mordecai's failure to render honor to him.

F. The Promotion of Mordecai 8:1–17

1. Possession of Haman's House 8:1–2

The king now gave Haman's "house," i.e., his estate, to Esther. This may have been to compensate her for her trouble.

University Press, 1976), 1.26.13; Cicero, *Pro Rabirio*, trans. H. Grose Hodge (Cambridge, MA: Harvard University Press, 1979), 4.13.

[127]Rawlinson, p. 129, locates the gallows "within the walls of [Haman's] own house." It is unlikely that Haman's house had walls seventy-five feet high that would have allowed the gallows to be erected inside it.

It may also have been a reward for pointing out the economic loss that would have come if the Jews had been slain. Josephus, *Antiquities* 11.1.3, refers to the disposal of a condemned man's possessions. In quoting Cyrus's decree allowing the Jews to return and having made certain grants to assist them, he stated, "My will is, that those who disobey these injunctions, and make them void, shall be hung upon a cross [i.e., impaled], and their substance brought into the king's treasury."

Esther had revealed her relationship to Mordecai, the man who had already proved his loyalty to the king. Xerxes now called him to come before him, v. 1. Since Mordecai already held a position in the king's government, indicating his executive skills, and since he had earlier proved his loyalty by revealing the plot against the king, Xerxes now promoted him to the prime minister's position. He took the ring that Haman had formerly worn and gave it to Mordecai. In addition, Esther placed him over Haman's estate. This gave Mordecai the appearance appropriate to his new position with the king, v. 2.

2. Plea of the Queen 8:3–6

In an emotional scene some time later, Esther once more approached the king, v. 3.[128] Xerxes extended his scepter to her, indicating that she had found favor with him again, v. 4. On the basis of this "favour" (*ḥen*, see 2:15), she asked him to overturn Haman's decree to destroy the Jews throughout the empire. By referring to the decree as "the letters devised by Haman," Esther tactfully placed the blame on Haman rather than on the king v. 5. She said the destruction authorized in the decree would be more than she could bear, v. 6.

3. Decree by the King 8:7–14

Xerxes responded to Esther and to Mordecai. Although Mordecai had not been mentioned, his new position required

[128]Whitcomb, pp. 100–101, understands v. 3 as continuing the action described in vv. 1–2. If this were the case, there would be no need for the king to extend his scepter to Esther (v. 4). The events of c. 4–7 took place shortly after Haman's decree in "the first month" (3:7). The events in this chapter took place in the "third month" (8:9). This timing supports making Esther's plea at a later time rather than at the time of vv. 1–2.

that he be with the king to carry out his wishes. Xerxes noted that he had already given Haman's estate to Esther and that Haman had been executed because of his plot against her people, v. 7. He gave them permission concerning the Jews to write in his name and to seal the writing with his seal. He reminded them that the previous decree could not be set aside since the king's decrees could never be reversed (cf. 1:19; Dan. 6:8, 12, 15), v. 8.[129]

Mordecai used his newly given authority to issue a decree. It was written in the month "Sivan," mid-May to mid-June, a little more than two months after Haman's decree. We do not know the reason for the delay. Mordecai may have solicited advice from the Jews. He may have been too busy with the king's business to think the matter through. He may have waited until he had the king's express permission to reverse the intent of the earlier decree. He may simply have required time to learn the responsibilities of his new office.[130] We can speculate, but we will never be certain of the reason since Scripture is silent on this point.

Mordecai's decree went to the "lieutenants [or 'satraps,' *ʾaḥašdarpan*, see Ezra 8:36], the deputies [*peḥâ*, see Ezra 8:36] and rulers [*śar*, see Ezra 7:28]" in all 127 provinces of the empire (cf. 1:1), ranging "from India unto Ethiopia [or 'Cush']."[131] It was written in all of the languages of the empire, including Hebrew, so that the Jews would know about it, v. 9. After Mordecai sealed it to give it the king's authority, the decree went out to the empire. The phrase "posts [*raṣîm*, see 3:13] on horseback, and riders on mules, camels, and young dromedaries" is better translated

[129]Katz, p. 95, argues that the king's decree could not be recalled because "nearly the entire empire had received word of it," and this would have created an anti-Jewish feeling that could not be undone. This, however, is not what the verse says. The emphasis is on the impossibility of reversing the king's decree "which has been written in his name and sealed with his ring." The fact that he gave Mordecai permission to write shows his willingness to undo the harm.

[130]Zlotowitz, p. 111, gives the view of Yosef Lekach (see c. 2, note 6), that Mordecai waited for the return of Haman's couriers to Shushan. He felt that the same couriers should deliver his letters. While an interesting Jewish view, it also must remain uncertain since the text states no reason for the delay.

[131]The discussion at 1:1 takes up the phrase "from India unto Ethiopia."

"couriers on horses, riding on royal steeds bred from *special* mares" (cf. 1:22), v. 10.

In agreement with the king's direction (v. 8), the new decree did not revoke the earlier one given under Haman's influence. This document gives the Jews authority to defend themselves against any attack against "them." This makes clear the king's will without violating the Persian policy against reversing a formal order of the king.

The phrase "*both* little ones and women" is often linked to *them*, referring to multiple objects of the attackers, i.e., "that would assault them, *both* the little ones and women." The wording recalls Haman's decree that included "all Jews, both young and old, little children and women" (3:13). In addition they would have the right to take the property of their attackers.[132] While the previous decree could not be undone, this clearly showed that Xerxes had changed his mind, v. 11. Since Haman had scheduled his plot to be carried out on the thirteenth day of Adar, mid-February to mid-March, the new decree set that same date for the Jews to defend themselves, v. 12. The decree that gave the Jews the right to defend themselves went throughout the empire, v. 13. Once more, the "posts" (or "couriers," *raṣîm*) carried the message from Shushan on the royal animals (cf. v. 10), v. 14.

The unusual nature of the deliverance again shows God's providential care for His people. The timing of the king's sleeplessness, the willingness of Esther to approach Xerxes, her sense of the right way to accuse Haman, the king's willingness to hear a charge against his highly placed official, and Haman's response that triggered the king's rage all meshed together to bring about the king's decision. Haman was put to death,

---

[132]The rendering of the KJV unnecessarily adds *both*, making the verse seem to state that the Jews could kill the women and children of their attackers. Various translations and commentators disagree about the proper meaning of the Hebrew. The GNB, NIV, and NLT clarify the translation to include the women and children among those being attacked, while the CEV, GW, and NASB include the "little ones and women" among those of the enemies being killed. Among commentators, Baldwin, p. 75; and Bechtel, p. 97; and Robert Gordis, "Studies in the Esther Narrative, *JBL* 95 (March, 1976): 51–52, adopt the first position, while Jobes, Levenson, and Rawlinson accept the second position.

Mordecai was promoted, and Israel was delivered as God worked on behalf of His chosen nation.

4. Rejoicing of the Jews 8:15–17

Mordecai went out from the king wearing royal apparel and a "great" (or "large") golden "crown" (^{ca}*tarâ*) to indicate his new office. Clearly this was not the royal crown, but a lesser one designed to show his authority.[133] Upon hearing of the new decree, the Jews in the city of Shushan (see discussion at 3:15) rejoiced, v. 15. The connection of "light" with "gladness, and joy, and honour" suggests a figurative use. Elsewhere, "light" represents spiritual favor (Ps. 27:1; Isa. 5:20) and prosperity (Job 30:26; Ps. 97:11). We see the "honour" given to the Jews in the next verse, as others tried to become Jews, v. 16.

The Jews rejoiced throughout the empire, celebrating with "feast[s]" (*miṣteh*, see 1:3). Because of the obvious favor of the king toward the Jews, many of the heathen converted to Judaism for "fear" (*paḥad*, "terror, dread") of what the Jews might otherwise to do them. The word *paḥad* is appropriate here. It carries with it a strong emotional component, referring elsewhere to calamity, destruction, or distress of a serious nature (e.g., Deut. 11:25; 1 Chron. 14:17; Ps. 105:38). Recognizing the royal favor that had been shown to the Jews, others throughout the kingdom chose this way to attach themselves to the Jews. Some commentators see this as a pretense entered into by the people merely to save themselves from revenge for their past treatment of the Jews. Esther 9:27, however, indicates that others did indeed join the Jews in their religious festivities, v. 17.

---

[133]Omanson and Noss, p. 209, understand ^{ca}*tarâ* as a turban decorated with gold or gold stitching. The word ^{ca}*tarâ*, however, is translated "crown" all 23x it occurs in the KJV. While some of these are not crowns as we typically think of them (e.g., Prov. 12:4; Isa. 28:1), ^{ca}*tarâ* never clearly refers to a turban. When the OT uses the word metaphorically, the context makes this clear.

ESTHER 9

The time had now arrived for the deliverance of the Jews from Haman's plan. Mordecai's decree giving the Jews permission to defend themselves had gone forth throughout the Persian Empire. The Jews had identified their enemies and had prepared themselves to exact vengeance on them. Rather than the destruction of the Jews, we find instead the destruction of those who had opposed God's people by planning to attack them.

G. The Vengeance of Israel 9:1–16

1. Destruction of Israel's Enemies 9:1–11

When Haman issued the first decree from the king, there would have been some who taunted the Jews and who openly spoke of their plans to execute and take the possessions of Jews. The new decree now gave the Jews the right to defend themselves. Because of the taunts and threats made against them, the Jews knew who their enemies were. The king's decree gave them "rule" (or "dominion") over them, v. 1.

The Jews gathered together to better defend themselves and to "lay [their] hand on" their enemies. No one could stand against them. Instead, a great "fear" (*paḥad*, see 8:17) of them fell on the people, v. 2. Having a great "fear" (*paḥad*) of Mordecai because of his increased influence, many of the "rulers" (*śar*, see Ezra 7:28), "lieutenants" (or "satraps," *ᶜaḥašdarpan*, see Ezra 8:36), "deputies" (*peḥâ*, see Ezra 8:36), and "officers" of the empire helped the Jews. The record does not make clear the nature of this help. It may have been the provision of troops to protect them, the offering of money to allow them to hire protection, political rhetoric to make clear to the people that the Jews were now in favor, some other form of help, or a combination of these, v. 3. During the months he had held the office, Mordecai's power had become known throughout the Persian Empire, v. 4.

The Jews took advantage of the new circumstances to destroy "all their enemies," i.e., those who had indicated an attempt to carry out Haman's decree, v. 5. In Shushan alone they killed five hundred of their enemies. The number is clearly a round number, v. 6. These included the ten sons of Haman, named in

9:7–10. Although the sons have not been named as participating in Haman's plot against the Jews, their execution agrees with OT practice elsewhere where some association might be presumed (e.g., Deut. 11:6; Josh. 7:24–25), vv. 7–10.

In the celebration of Purim today, the Jews intentionally de-emphasize the names of Haman's sons. According to *Megillah* 16*b*, the reader must say all of the names in one breath "because all their souls departed together." This rapid recitation of the names shows contempt for them.

The listing of the names in the MT is unusually arranged in columns rather than a sequential list of the names.[134] Other than a poetic representation of the names, there does not seem to be any particular purpose in this.

וְאֵת	
וְאֵת	פַּרְשַׁנְדָּתָא
וְאֵת	דַּלְפוֹן
וְאֵת	אַסְפָּתָא׃
וְאֵת	פּוֹרָתָא
וְאֵת	אֲדַלְיָא
וְאֵת	אֲרִידָתָא
וְאֵת	פַּרְמַשְׁתָּא
וְאֵת	אֲרִיסַי
וְאֵת	אֲרִדַי
	וַיְזָתָא׃

Zlotowitz offers two explanations for the format of the list. (1) First, he cites the view of Yosef Lekach (cf. p. 225, n. 72) that names of important people are usually written prominently on a separate line. This prominence did not save them from death. This shows the greatness of God's triumph. This view faces the problem that some versions of the Hebrew Bible bracket two men on a line. Also, many great men in the Bible are not listed separately on a line (e.g., Mordecai elsewhere in the book,

[134]Similar lists of names occur elsewhere, e.g., Josh. 12:9–24; 1 Sam. 30:27–31. There does not appear to be any special significance to the form of the lists. Other lists of names in the OT have no special form attached to them.

Moses, David). (2) Second, Zlotowitz says the word *w*^{e}*ʾat* is an abbreviation representing five hundred men. Each of Haman's sons was thus equal in eminence to all the other five hundred enemies of the Jews in Shushan who were slain (9:6). This explanation is obviously contrived.

The Jews, however, did not take "spoil" (or "plunder," *bizzâ*), i.e., claim for themselves the possessions of Haman's family. The word *bizzâ* refers to goods seized from an enemy. Elsewhere God gives the people of Israel the right to take such spoil from their enemies (e.g., 2 Chron. 14:14; Jer. 30:16), and the king's decree had given them that same right here (8:11). While the text does not say what happened to the spoil, it would have been politically expedient for the Jews to give it to the king. The noun *bizzâ* occurs three times this chapter (9:10, 15, 16). In each case the Hebrew is identical: *babizzâ loʾ šalḥû ʾet-yadam* ("and on the plunder they did not send forth their hand"). The KJV's use of "prey" in vv. 15–16 obscures this repetition.

Xerxes received a report of the number that had been killed in the capital city, v. 11.

2. Death of Haman's Family 9:12–16

The king wanted to please Esther. He told her about the five hundred enemies of the Jews that were slain in Shushan and asked if there were anything further that he could do for her. His seemingly callous disregard for life is typical of the times, v. 12. She asked that an additional day be given to the Jews in the city of Shushan to continue killing their enemies. Five hundred was the number of those killed in the fortress part of Shushan. Esther now asked to eliminate the enemies of the Jews throughout the rest of the city. She also asked that Haman's sons be impaled. The presumption is that they held the same views as their father and therefore their corpses should also be displayed publicly as an object lesson to others. This public degradation of the sons would show to all that Haman's plans had come to nothing, v. 13.

The king turned Esther's request into a command, and Haman's sons were "hanged," i.e., impaled, so those living in the city could see for themselves the downfall of Haman and his family, v. 14. The Jews continued to avenge themselves on their enemies, killing three hundred more in the city area. Once again they did not take the plunder from their enemies, v. 15. Throughout the empire seventy-five thousand enemies of the Jews were killed.[135] As in v. 6, this is a round number. This gave the Jews "rest" (*nôaḥ*) from the threat posed by their enemies after Haman's decree.[136] In all of this, the Jews did not take the plunder from their enemies' estates. Again, it was undoubtedly left for the emperor to use, v. 16.

H. The Feast of Purim 9:17–10:3

1. The Jews' Celebration 9:17–19

The Jews made the next day a time of rest and celebration with "feasting" (*mišteh*, see 1:3) and great joy, v. 17. In the city of Shushan, they celebrated on the fifteenth, the day following their conquest of their enemies, also "feasting" (*mišteh*) and having great joy. They were the only ones who had two days to slaughter those who had opposed them, v. 18. Elsewhere, throughout the empire, Jews living in country areas in unwalled towns celebrated by "feasting" (*mišteh*) on the fourteenth day, v. 19.

2. Mordecai's and Esther's Instructions 9:20–32

Since a celebration of this nature would keep the Jews from work, Mordecai acted to give them authority for the celebration. He wrote to Jews living throughout the empire, v. 20. He commanded them to keep the fourteenth and fifteenth days of Adar in remembrance of their deliverance from their enemies.[137]

---

[135]Kennedy, p. 8, suggests that when the writer of Hebrews mentioned those who "escaped the edge of the sword" (11:34), he had the story of Esther in mind. While this is possible, it was probably not the purpose of the author of Hebrews. The record of Esther does not put much emphasis on faith, which was the author's focus in Hebrews 11. Israel's faith is more prominent in other accounts of deliverance in the OT (e.g., 2 Chron. 13:13–18; 14:9–12).

[136]Some versions translate *nôaḥ* to the effect that the Jews "rid" themselves of their enemies (e.g., GNB, NASB). Other versions emend *nôaḥ* to *niqqôm* and translate it something like "gained relief from their enemies" (e.g., ESV, NIV). The first interpretation requires an unusual meaning for *nôaḥ*. Since the word occurs again with the sense of "resting" in vv. 17–18, it is unlikely that it has a different meaning here. The proposed emendation is unnecessary and lacks textual support.

[137]M'Crie, p. 288, comments, "it is reasonable to conclude that the feast of Purim was not instituted without divine counsel and approbation." This is speculative. Since the OT give no command from God regarding the feast of Purim, we should not state dogmatically that it is a divinely ordained festival.

By ordering the keeping of both days, Mordecai brought the Jews throughout the empire into unity, v. 21. This was a celebration, a time for "feasting" (*mišteh*) and rejoicing, for expressing thankfulness by giving gifts to one another and especially by remembering the poor with gifts. The Talmud, *Megillah 7a*, says that gifts should be given to at least two poor persons, v. 22.[138]

The Jews throughout the empire obeyed Mordecai's instructions. They had earlier begun to celebrate (vv. 17–18). They now brought their celebrations into agreement with Mordecai's instructions, v. 23. In doing this they recalled Haman's plot, in which he had cast "Pur" (*pûr*, see 3:7), the lot, to determine the best day for annihilating the Jews, v. 24. When "Esther (better 'it' or 'the matter') came before the king," he authorized the Jews to defend themselves. Although the KJV reads "when *Esther* came before the king," this is interpretive of the feminine suffix on the verb. Since Esther has not been mentioned since v. 13, it is better to refer the suffix to the event discussed in v. 24.

Haman's plan had come to nothing, and he and his sons were "hanged" or impaled, v. 25. In remembrance of this, the Jews called the feast "Purim," the plural form of *Pur*. The Jews throughout the empire entered into the feast. This included "all such as joined themselves unto them," proselytes to Judaism. Second Maccabees 15:36 refers to the "day of Mordecai," showing that first-century BC Jews kept this feast.

[138]Those who reject the historicity of the book of Esther often see the feast developing from an existing heathen feast celebrated at this time. Julius Lewy, "The Feast of the 14th Day of Adar," *HUCA* 14 (1939): 149, calls it "a perpetuation of the Old Persian *Fervardigan* festival which, at the beginning of the Persian rule, was celebrated from Adar 11 to 15." Helmer Ringgren, "Esther and Purim," in Moore, *Studies in the Book of Esther*, pp. 185–86, says "it is probable that the festival was adopted by the Jews of the diaspora from the people among which they lived and that the festival legend has grown out of the need for an explanation of the cultic facts." After giving the book a late date, 191–113 BCE, Roger Herst, "The Purim Connection," also in Moore, p. 220, suggests that Purim "is an adaptation of the Day of Nicanor holiday which was proclaimed as an annual celebration by the followers of Judas Maccabeus in 161 B.C.E." Other origins have been suggested, but these are enough to show the possibilities mentioned by those who reject the historicity of the book. Further, the lack of agreement among them demonstrates that their theories have no foundation.

The Bible does not command the Jews to keep the Feast of "Purim."[139] The Jews, however, to this day consider it one of their most important feasts, vv. 26–27. The Jews in the Persian Empire agreed to teach future generations about these things so that the observance of the feast would continue, v. 28.

Esther joined Mordecai, lending her authority to another letter. This is the "second letter" relating to Purim in that it came after the letter of vv. 20–22, 26, which was the letter that followed the initial decree allowing the Jews to defend themselves, v. 29. This letter went out to Jews throughout the empire. As an encouragement to them, the document contained words of "peace and truth," v. 30, words that authorized the Jews to celebrate Purim each year.

In addition, the letter reminded the Jews that they had "decreed for themselves," in some nonbiblical source which no longer exists, that they would include fasting and lamentation in connection with Purim. This reminded the Jews of their fasting after hearing of Haman's decree and of Esther's fast in preparation for going in to the king (4:3, 16), v. 31. The words were written "in the book" (*seper*, better "scroll"), the historical chronicles kept by the Persians (cf. 2:23; 6:1; 10:2), v. 32.

Modern Jews still celebrate Purim. The day before is a fast, commemorating Esther 4:15–16. On the day of the fast, the Jews meet in their synagogues and read the book of Esther. Each time the name of Haman is spoken, the congregation stamps on the floor and says, "Let his name be blotted out," "Cursed be Haman," or something similar to show their disdain for Haman. Children often use noisemakers and rattles and stamp their feet to drown out Haman's name. The name of Haman may be written on the soles of the shoes so it is blotted out as it is trodden underfoot.[140]

---

[139]To this point, 3:7 and 9:24, the singular *Pur* has been used. The plural *Purim* is introduced without explanation. Berlin, p. 90, and Levenson, p. 128, suggest that the holiday and its name came into being apart from the book. The book is merely a means of reinterpreting the holiday to give it a Jewish background. The use of the plural, however, apparently refers to the casting of Pur several times (3:7). There is no conflict with its earlier mention in the book.

[140]Theodore Herzl Gaster, *Purim and Hanukkah in Custom and Tradition* (New York: Henry Schuman, Inc., 1950), p. 50; Aaron Judah Kligerman,

ESTHER 10

The establishment of the Feast of Purim, including the events leading up to it and the deliverance of the Jews, concludes the major part of the book. The author now moves on in this chapter to summarize the continuing career of Mordecai. His position of authority gave him the opportunity to help his people. In the few words of this brief chapter, we find Mordecai's contribution to the overall good of the nation.

3. Exaltation of Mordecai 10:1–3

Xerxes exacted tribute throughout his empire, including nations occupying both inland territory and "the isles [*ʾî*] of the sea." The word *ʾî* occurs widely in the OT, referring to the coastal areas around the Mediterranean. Although Persia had lost some of its territory in its disastrous defeat by the Greeks, it continued to control areas in the southern and eastern parts of the Mediterranean region, v. 1.

The king advanced Mordecai in power. While it may have been unusual for a foreigner to rise to power in the Persian court, it was not impossible. The rise of Haman earlier to the same position demonstrates the potential available to foreigners in the Persian Empire. In addition the name *Mordecai* indicates that he had been born in the empire. This let him grow up knowing well the Persian ways. The names *Marduka* or *Marduku* occur on tablets over thirty times, referring to at least four separate individuals.[141] The name *Marduka*, equivalent to *Mordecai*, an official in the court of either Darius in his final years or Xerxes during the early years of his rule, has been found on a tablet from Borsippa. While we cannot certainly identify one of

Feasts and Fasts of Israel (Baltimore: Emmanuel Neighborhood House, 1931).

[141]See note 72 at Esther 2:6.

these names as belonging to the biblical Mordecai, it is tempting to equate the two.

The rise and accomplishments of Mordecai were recorded in "the book of the chronicles of the kings of Media and Persia." This is the only time in Esther that the Medes are mentioned before the Persians, who at that time had greater authority in the alliance (cf. 1:3, 14, 18, 19). The document title likely refers to a journal that was begun under the Median leadership and not retitled after the ascension of the Persians, when Cyrus conquered Astyages, the Median king. We have no record of this book, but it is undoubtedly similar to other historical records mentioned in the OT that no longer exist (e.g., 1 Kings 14:19; 16:5; 1 Chron. 27:24), v. 2.

In his position Mordecai was second in authority to Xerxes. He worked to advance the cause of the Jews. He contributed to their "wealth" (better, "good"). He also spoke to establish the "peace" (better "welfare") among the Jews, v. 3.

For the first time in the book, the honor due Mordecai is openly declared. He was a loyal family man, rearing his cousin after the death of her parents, a highly placed Persian official who became the chief official under the king, and a faithful Jew who secured the deliverance of his people. His refusal to bow before Haman and his confidence that Esther had come to the kingdom "for such a time as this" shows his trust in God. While the book carries Esther's name, it is clear that Mordecai is also a major character in the record of one of the most serious crises faced by Israel in its history. He is truly worthy of the honor stated here.

SELECTED BIBLIOGRAPHY

Commentaries and Other Books on Ezra, Nehemiah, and Esther

Albright, William F. "The Lachish Cosmetic Burner and Esther 2:12." In *A Light Unto My Path: Old Testament Studies in Honor of Jacob M. Myers*. Edited by Howard N. Bream, Ralph D. Heim, and Carey A. Moore. Philadelphia: Temple University Press, 1974.

Anderson, Bernhard W. *The Book of Esther*. In *The Interpreter's Bible*. Vol. 3. Edited by George Arthur Buttrick. Nashville: Abingdon Press, 1954.

Armerding, Carl. *Esther: For Such a Time as This*. Chicago: Moody Press, 1955.

Baldwin, Joyce. *Esther: An Introduction and Commentary*. Downers Grove, IL: InterVarsity Press, 1984.

Barnes, Albert. *1 Samuel–Esther*. Edited by F. C. Cook. 1834. Reprint, Grand Rapids: Baker Book House, 1977.

Batten, Loring W. *The Books of Ezra and Nehemiah.* In *The International Critical Commentary*. 1913. Reprint, New York: Charles Scribner's Sons, 1972.

Bechtel, Carol M. *Esther* in *Interpretation: Bible Commentary for Teaching and Preaching*. Edited by James L. Mays and Patrick D. Miller. Louisville, KY: John Knox Press, 1989.

Berg, Sandra Beth. *The Book of Esther: Motifs, Themes and Structure*. Missoula, MT: Scholars Press, 1979.

Berlin, Adele. *Esther*. In *The JPS Bible Commentary*. Edited by Michael Fishbane. Philadelphia: The Jewish Publication Society, 2001.

Blenkinsopp, Joseph. *Ezra-Nehemiah*. Philadelphia: The Westminster Press, 1988.

Bowman, Raymond A. *The Book of Ezra and the Book of Nehemiah*. In *The Interpreter's Bible*. Vol. 3. Edited by George Arthur Buttrick. Nashville: Abingdon Press, 1954.

Breneman, Mervin. *Ezra, Nehemiah, Esther*. In *The New American Commentary*. Vol. 10. Edited by E. Ray Clendenen and Kenneth A. Matthews. Nashville: Broadman & Holman Publishers, 1993.

Brown, A. Philip, II. *Hope Amidst Ruin: A Literary and Theological Analysis of Ezra*. Greenville, SC: Bob Jones University Press, 2009.

Brown, Raymond. *The Message of Nehemiah*. In *The Bible Speaks Today*. Edited by J. A. Motyer. Downers Grove, IL: InterVarsity Press, 1998.

Browne, L. E. "Esther," *Peake's Commentary on the Bible*. Edited by Matthew Black and H. H. Rowley. 1919. Reprint, Camden, NJ: Thomas Nelson and Sons, 1967.

Butler, John G. *Nehemiah the Wall Builder*. Clinton, IA: LBC Publications, 1998.

Carson, Alexander. *God's Providence Unfolded in the Book of Esther*. Swengel, PA: Bible Truth Depot, 1962.

Clarke, Adam. *A Commentary and Critical Notes*. New York: T. Mason & G. Lane, 1840. Vol. 2.

Coggins, R. J. *The Books of Ezra and Nehemiah*. In *The Cambridge Bible Commentary*. Edited by P. R. Ackroyd, A. R. C. Leaney, and J. W. Packer. New York: Cambridge University Press, 1976.

Cumming, James Elder. *The Book of Esther: Its Spiritual Teaching*. London: The Religious Tract Society, n.d.

Fox, Michael V. *Character and Ideology in the Book of Esther*. Columbia: University of South Carolina Press, 1991.

Fensham, Charles. *The Books of Ezra and Nehemiah*. Grand Rapids: Wm. B. Eerdmans, 1982.

Gordis, Robert. *Megillat Esther*. New York: The Rabbinical Assembly, 1974.

Grossfeld, Bernard, trans. *The Two Targums of Esther*. In *The Aramaic Bible: The Targums*. Edited by Kevin Cathcart, Michael Maher, and Martin McNamara. Collegeville, MN: The Liturgical Press, 1991.

Haupt, Paul. *The Book of Esther: Critical Edition of the Hebrew with Notes*. Chicago: The University of Chicago Press, 1908.

Henry, Matthew. *Ezra*. Vol. 2 in *Commentary on the Whole Bible*. 1708. Reprint, New York: Fleming H. Revell Company, 1935.

Holmgren, Fredrick Carlson. *Israel Alive Again: A Commentary on the Books of Ezra and Nehemiah*. Grand Rapids: Wm. B. Eerdmans, 1987.

Ironside, H. A. *Notes on the Books of Ezra, Nehemiah and Esther.* Neptune, NJ: Loizeaux Brothers, Inc., 1976.

Keil, C. F. *Ezra*. In *Biblical Commentary on the Old Testament*. Translated by Sophia Taylor. 1875. Reprint, Grand Rapids: Wm. B. Eerdmans, 1978.

Kennedy, H. D. *Does God Care?* New York: Christian Alliance Publishing Co., 1920.

Kidner, Derek. *Ezra and Nehemiah: An Introduction and Commentary*. In *The Tyndale Old Testament Commentaries*. Edited by D. J. Wiseman. Madison, WI: InterVarsity Press, 1979.

Knight, George A. F. *Esther, Song of Songs, Lamentations*. In *Torch Bible Commentaries*. Edited by John Marsh, Alan Richardson, and R. Gregor Smith. London: SCM Press Ltd., 1955.

Laney, J. Carl. *Ezra/Nehemiah*. Chicago: Moody Press, 1982.

Larson, Knute, and Kathy Dahlen. *Ezra, Nehemiah, Esther*. In *Holman Old Testament Commentary*. Edited by Max Anders. Nashville: Broadman & Holman Publishers, 2005.

Levenson, Jon D. *Esther: A Commentary*. Louisville, KY: Westminster John Knox Press, 1997.

Levering, Matthew. *Ezra & Nehemiah*. Grand Rapids: Brazos Press, 2007.

Luck, G. Coleman. *Ezra and Nehemiah: A Commentary*. Chicago: Moody Press, 1961.

Luter, A. Boyd, and Barry C. Davis. *Ruth & Esther: God Behind the Seen*. Fearn, Ross-shire, Scotland: Christian Focus Publications, 2003.

M'Crie, Thomas. *Lectures on the Book of Esther*. New York: Robert Carter, 1875. Reprint, Birmingham, AL: Solid Ground Christian Books, 2006.

McGee, J. Vernon *Exposition on the Book of Esther*. Wheaton: Van Kampen Press, 1951.

Mattoon, Rod. *Treasures from Esther*. Springfield, IL: Lincoln Land Baptist Church, 2002.

Maxwell, Lawrence. *Another Chance*. Boise: Pacific Press Publishing Association, 1993.

Moore, Carey A. *Esther*. In *The Anchor Bible*. Edited by William Foxwell Albright and David Noel Freedman. Garden City, NY: Doubleday & Company, Inc., 1971.

———, ed. *Studies in the Book of Esther*. In *The Library of Biblical Studies*. Edited by Harry M. Orlinsky. New York: KTAV Publishing House, Inc., 1982.

Myers, Jacob M. *Ezra, Nehemiah*. In *The Anchor Bible*. Edited by William Foxwell Albright and David Noel Freedman. Garden City, NY: Doubleday & Company, Inc., 1965.

Noss, Philip A., and Kenneth J. Thomas. *A Handbook on Ezra and Nehemiah*. In *UBS Handbook Series*. Edited by Donald Slager. New York: United Bible Societies, 2005.

Omanson, Roger L. and Philip A. Noss. *A Handbook on the Book of Esther: The Hebrew and Greek Texts*. In the *UBS Handbook Series*. New York: United Bible Societies, 1997.

Parker, Joseph. *The People's Bible: Discourses upon Holy Scripture*. New York: Funk & Wagnalls, Publishers, 1889.

Paton, Lewis Bayles. *A Critical and Exegetical Commentary on the Book of Esther*. Edinburgh: T. & T. Clark, 1976.

Patrick, Symon. *The Book of Esther*. In *A Critical Commentary and Paraphrase on the Old and New Testament and the Apocrypha*. Philadelphia: Carey and Hart, 1859.

Pope, W. B. *The Book of the Prophet Ezra*. In the *Layman's Handy Commentary Series*. Edited by Charles John Ellicott. Grand Rapids: Zondervan Publishing House, 1961.

Rabinowitz, Yosef. *Ezra*. Brooklyn, NY: Mesorah Publications, 1984.

Rademacher, Earl, and Ron Allen, eds. *Compact Bible Commentary*. Nashville: Thomas Nelson Publishers, 2004.

Rawlinson, George. *Ezra, Nehemiah, Esther & Job*. In *The Pulpit Commentary*. Edited by H. D. M. Spence and Joseph S. Exell. 1887. Reprint, Peabody, MA: Hendrickson Publishers, 1975.

Reid, Debra. *Esther: An Introduction and Commentary*. Vol. 13 in *Tyndale Old Testament Commentaries*. Edited by David G. Firth and Tremper Longman III. Downers Grove, IL: InterVarsity Press, 2008.

Roop, Eugene. *Ruth, Jonah, Esther*. In *Believers Church Bible Commentary*. Edited by Elmer Martens. Scottdale, PA: Herald Press, 2002.

Ryle, Herbert Edward. *The Books of Ezra and Nehemiah*. In *The Cambridge Bible for Schools and Colleges*. Edited by A. F. Kirkpatrick. London: Cambridge University Press, 1923.

Slotki, Judah J. *Daniel·Ezra·Nehemiah*. London: The Soncino Press, 1970.

Streane, A. W. *The Book of Esther*. In *The Cambridge Bible for Schools and Colleges*. Edited by A. F. Kirkpatrick. Cambridge, England: University Press, 1907.

Throntveit, Mark A. *Ezra-Nehemiah*. Louisville, KY: John Knox Press, 1989.

Whitcomb, John C. *Esther: The Triumph of God's Sovereignty*. Chicago: Moody Press, 1979.

Wright, J. Stafford. *The Date of Ezra's Coming to Jerusalem*. 1947. Reprint, London: The Tyndale Press, 1958.

Zlotowitz, Meir. *The Megillah: The Book of Esther*. Brooklyn, NY: Mesorah Publications, Ltd., 1987.

Linguistic Aids

Girdlestone, Robert Baker. *Synonyms of the Old Testament*. Grand Rapids: Wm. B. Eerdmans Publishing Company, 1951.

Harris, R. Laird, ed. *Theological Wordbook of the Old Testament*. 2 vols. Chicago: Moody Press, 1980.

Unger, Merrill F. and William White, eds. *Nelson's Expository Dictionary of the Old Testament*. Nashville: Thomas Nelson Publishers, 1980.

General Works

Cicero. *Pro Rabirio*. Translated by H. Grose Hodge. Cambridge, MA: Harvard University Press, 1979.

Cross, Frank Moore, Jr. *The Ancient Library of Qumran and Modern Biblical Studies*. Garden City, NY: Doubleday & Company, Inc., 1958.

Curtius, Quintus. *History of Alexander the Great of Macedon*. Translated by John C. Rolfe. Cambridge, MA: Harvard University Press, 1956.

De Lange, N. R. M. *Origen and the Jews*. New York: Cambridge University Press, 1976.

Eusebius, *Ecclesiastical History*. Translated by Kirsopp Lake. Cambridge, MA: Harvard University Press, 1953.

Epstein, J., ed. *The Babylonian Talmud*. London: The Soncino Press, 1938.

Godley, A. D., trans. *Herodotus*. Cambridge, MA: Harvard University Press, 1963.

Gulick, Charles Burton, trans. Athenaeus, *The Deipnosophists*. Cambridge, MA: Harvard University Press, 1969.

Jones, Horace Leonard, trans. *The Geography of Strabo*. Cambridge, MA: Harvard University Press, 1966.

Livy. *From the Founding of the City*. Translated by B. O. Foster. Cambridge, MA: Harvard University Press, 1976.

Moore, George Foot. *Judaism in the First Centuries of the Christian Era: the Age of the Tannaim*. Cambridge, MA: Harvard University Press, 1927.

Perrin, Bernadotte, trans. *Plutarch's Lives*. Cambridge, MA: Harvard University Press, 1975.

Pfeiffer, Charles F., Howard F. Vos, and John Rea, eds. *Wycliffe Bible Encyclopedia*. Chicago: Moody Press, 1975.

Pfeiffer, Robert H. *Introduction to the Old Testament*. New York: Harper & Brothers Publishers, 1948.

Pritchard, James B., ed. *Ancient Near Eastern Texts Relating to the Old Testament*. Princeton, NJ: Princeton University Press, 1969.

Richardson, Cyril C., trans. and ed. *Early Christian Fathers*. Philadelphia: The Westminster Press, 1953.

Thucydides. *History of the Peloponnesian War*. Translated by Charles Forster Smith. Cambridge, MA: Harvard University Press, 1962.

Unger, Merrill F. *Unger's Bible Dictionary*. Chicago: Moody Press, 1967.

Welles, C. Bradford, trans. *Diodorus of Sicily*. Cambridge, MA: Harvard University Press, 1963.

Whiston, William, trans. *The Works of Josephus: New Updated Edition*. Peabody, MA: Hendrickson Publishers, 2000.

Xenophon, *Anabasis*. Trans. Carleton L. Brownson. Cambridge, MA: Harvard University Press, 1968.

———. *Cyropaedia*. Trans. Walter Miller. Cambridge, MA: Harvard University Press, 1968.

Yamauchi, Edwin M. *Persia and the Bible*. Grand Rapids: Baker Book House, 1990.

Periodicals Relating to Ezra, Nehemiah, and Esther

Aharoni, Y. "*Ramath Raḥel*," *IEJ* 6 (1956): 137–57.

Albright, W. F. "New Identifications of Ancient Towns," *BASOR* 9 (February 1923): 5–10.

Bailey, Nicholas Andrew. "Nehemiah 3:1–32: An Intersection of the Text and the Topography," *PEQ* 122 (January–June 1990): 34–40.

Boda, M. J. "The Use of *Tôdôt* in Nehemiah XII," *VT* 44, no. 3 (July 1994): 387–93.

Browne, Lawrence E. "A Jewish Sanctuary in Babylonia," *JTS* 17 (1916): 400–401.

Crawford, Sidnie White. "Has Every Book of the Bible Been Found Among the Dead Sea Scrolls?" *BR* 12, no. 5 (October 1996): 28–33, 56.

Cross, F. M., Jr. "Geshem the Arabian, Enemy of Nehemiah," *Biblical Archaeologist* 18, no. 2 (February 1955): 46–47.

Demsky, Aaron. "*Pelekh* in Nehemiah 3," *IEJ* 33, nos. 3–4 (1983): 242–44.

Emery, D. L. "Ezra 4—Is Josephus Right After All?" *JNWSL* 13 (1987): 33–44.

Friedberg, Albert D. "A New Clue in the Dating of the Composition of the Book of Esther," *VT* 50, no. 4 (2000): 561–65.

Gevaryahu, Haim M. L. "Esther Is a Story of Jewish Defense, Not a Story of Jewish Revenge," *JBQ* 21, no. 1 (January 1993): 3–12.

Gordis, Robert, "*Studies in the Esther Narrative*," *JBL* 95, no. 1 (March 1976): 43–58.

———. "Esther—a New Solution," *JBL* 100 (September 1981): 359–88.

Hallo, William W. "The First Purim," *Biblical Archaeologist* 46, no. 1 (Winter 1993): 19–26.

Haran, Menahim. "Explaining the Identical Lines at the End of Chronicles and the Beginning of Ezra," *BR* 11, no. 3 (Fall 1986): 18–20.

Heltzer, Michael. "The Book of Esther: Where Does Fiction Start and History End?" *BR* 8, no. 1 (February 1992): 25–30.

Hyman, Ronald T. "Esther 3:3: the Question with No Response," *JBQ* 22, no. 2 (April 1994): 103–9.

Jackowski, Karol. "Holy Disobedience in Esther," *Theology Today* 45, no. 4 (January 1989): 403–14.

Katz, Ben Zion. "Irrevocability of Persian Law in the Scroll of Esther," *JBQ* 31, no. 2 (April–June 2003): 94–96.

Lewy, Julius. "The Feast of the 14th Day of Adar," *HUCA* 14 (1939): 127–51.

McFall, Leslie. "Was Nehemiah Contemporary with Ezra in 458 BC?" *WTJ* 53 (Fall 1991): 263–93.

Maciariello, Joseph. "Lessons in Leadership and Management from Nehemiah," *Theology Today* 60, no. 3 (October 2003): 397–407.

Margalith, Othniel. "The Political Role of Ezra as Persian Governor," *ZAW* 98, no. 1 (1986): 110–12.

Moore, Carey A. "Eight Questions Most Frequently Asked About the Book of Esther," *BR* 8, no. 1 (Spring 1987): 16–31.

Rosenblatt, Naomi Harris. "Portraits in Heroism: Esther and Samson," *BR* 15, no. 1 (February 1999): 20–25, 47.

Sabua, Rachel B. K. "The Hidden Hand of God," *BR* 7, no. 1 (February 1992): 31–33.

Schiemann, Richard. "Covenanting with the Princes: Neh VI 2," *VT* 17, (1967): 367–69.

Shumate, David R. "The Theological and Practical Value of the Name Lists in Ezra 2 and 8," *BV* 38 (November 2003): 21–29.

Talshir, David, and Zipora Talshir. "The Double Month Naming in Late Biblical Books: A New Clue for Dating Esther?" *VT* 54, no. 4 (2004): 549–55.

Ungnad, A. "Keilinschriftliche Beitrage zum Buch Esra und Esther," *ZAW* 58 (1940–41): 240–44.

———. "Keilinschriftliche Beitrage zum Buch Esra und Esther," *ZAW* 59 (1942–43): 219.

Wiebe, John M. "Esther 4:14: 'Will Relief and Deliverance Arise for the Jews from Another Place?'" *CBQ* 53, no. 3 (July 1991): 409–15.

Williams, Gary R. "Contextual Influences in Readings of Nehemiah 5: A Case Study," *Tyndale Bulletin* 53, no. 1 (2002): 57–74.

Williamson, Hugh G. M. "Did the Author of Chronicles Also Write the Books of Ezra and Nehemiah?" *BR* 3, no. 1 (Spring 1987): 56–59.

———. "The Composition of Ezra I–VI," *JTS* 34 (April 1983): 1–30.

Wong, G. C. I. "A Note on 'Joy' in Nehemiah VIII 10," *VT* 45, no. 3 (July 1995): 383–85.

Yamauchi, Edwin M. "Was Nehemiah the Cupbearer a Eunuch?" *ZAW* 92, no. 1 (1980): 132–42.

———. "Mordecai, the Persepolis Tablets, and the Susa Excavations," *VT* 42, no. 2 (April 1992): 272–75.

Zadok, Ran. "A Note on sn'h," *VT* 38, no. 4 (October 1988): 483–85.

———. "Notes on Esther," *ZAW* 98, no. 1 (1986): 105–7.

HEBREW AND ARAMAIC WORDS